Asymmetric Warfare in South Asia

The 1999 conflict between India and Pakistan near the town of Kargil in contested Kashmir was the first military clash between two nuclear-armed powers since the 1969 Sino-Soviet war. Kargil was a landmark event not because of its duration or casualties, but because it contained a very real risk of nuclear escalation. Until the Kargil conflict, academic and policy debates over nuclear deterrence and proliferation occurred largely on the theoretical level. This deep analysis of the conflict offers scholars and policymakers a rare account of how nuclear-armed states interact during a military crisis. Written by analysts from India, Pakistan, and the United States, this unique book draws extensively on primary sources, including unprecedented access to Indian, Pakistani, and US government officials and military officers who were actively involved in the conflict. This is the first rigorous and objective account of the causes, conduct, and consequences of the Kargil conflict.

PETER R. LAVOY is the Deputy Director of National Intelligence for Analysis. Previously he served as Director of the Center for Contemporary Conflict at the Naval Postgraduate School and Director of Counterproliferation Policy in the Office of the Secretary of Defense.

Asymmetric Warfare in South Asia

The Causes and Consequences of the Kargil Conflict

Edited by

Peter R. Lavoy

CAMBRIDGE UNIVERSITY PRESS

CAMBRIDGE UNIVERSITY PRESS
Cambridge, New York, Melbourne, Madrid, Cape Town, Singapore,
São Paulo, Delhi, Dubai, Tokyo

Cambridge University Press
The Edinburgh Building, Cambridge CB2 8RU, UK

Published in the United States of America by Cambridge University Press,
New York

www.cambridge.org
Information on this title: www.cambridge.org/9780521767217

© Cambridge University Press 2009

First published 2009

Printed in the United Kingdom at the University Press, Cambridge

A catalogue record for this publication is available from the British Library

ISBN 978-0-521-76721-7 Hardback

Contents

Maps and tables

Maps

Tables

Contributors

PETER R. LAVOY is the Deputy Director of National Intelligence for Analysis. Previously he served as director of the Center for Contemporary Conflict at the Naval Postgraduate School and director of counterproliferation policy in the Office of the Secretary of Defense.

RAJESH M. BASRUR is an associate professor of S. Rajaratnam School of International Studies at Nanyang Technological University, Singapore. Previously he was the director of the Centre for Global Studies, Mumbai, India. He specializes in international security, the politics of nuclear weapons, and the theory of international relations.

M. ZAFAR IQBAL CHEEMA was Dean of the Faculty of Social Sciences and the Chairperson and a founding member of the Department of Defence and Strategic Studies at Quaid-i-Azam University, Islamabad, Pakistan.

CHRISTOPHER CLARY was Assistant Country Director for South Asia in the Office of the US Secretary of Defense and served as Research Associate with the Center for Contemporary Conflict at the Naval Postgraduate School during 2004 and 2005.

C. CHRISTINE FAIR is a senior political scientist at RAND, where she specializes in South Asian political and military affairs. Previously, she worked as Program Officer in the Research and Studies Program of the US Institute of Peace.

JOHN H. GILL is a professor at the National Defense University's Near East–South Asia Center for Strategic Studies. He retired from the US army as a Colonel, with over ten years of experience in regional affairs with intelligence and policy postings in the Joint Chiefs of Staff, the US Pacific Command Staff, and the Defense Intelligence Agency.

TIMOTHY D. HOYT is Associate Professor of Strategy at the US Naval War College. He works on projects assessing security in the developing world, technology and defense policy, US grand strategy in the war against terrorism, and Indo-Pakistani relations.

FEROZ HASSAN KHAN is Senior Lecturer with the Center for Contemporary Conflict and the National Security Affairs Department at the Naval Postgraduate School. He retired from the Pakistan army as Brigadier, last serving as Director, Arms Control and Disarmament in the Strategic Plans Division.

ROBERT JERVIS is Adlai E. Stevenson Professor of International Politics at Columbia University. He serves on numerous editorial boards, is a co-editor of the Cornell Studies in Security Affairs, and is a Fellow of the American Association for the Advancement of Science and the American Academy of Arts and Sciences.

RODNEY W. JONES is President of Policy Architects International and a consultant to the Defense Threat Reduction Agency. He has worked on India–Pakistan security issues and strategic nuclear arms control at Columbia University, the Center for Strategic and International Studies, and in the US State Department.

JOSEPH McMILLAN is a distinguished research fellow at the National Defense University's Institute of National Strategic Studies, focusing on issues affecting US strategy toward the Middle East and South Asia. Previously he served as Principal Director for Near East and South Asia in the Office of the Secretary of Defense.

SURINDER RANA is a Senior Instructor in the Emerging Languages Task Force of the US Army's Defense Language Institute. He served in the Indian army from 1978 to 2001, with operational assignments in almost all parts of India, including three tenures in Jammu and Kashmir. He fought in the Kargil conflict of 1999.

BRUCE RIEDEL is a Senior Fellow for the Saban Center for Middle East Policy at the Brookings. He is a former CIA officer and was senior advisor to three US presidents on Middle Eastern and South Asian affairs.

HASAN-ASKARI RIZVI is an independent political and defense analyst based in Pakistan. He contributes political commentaries to Pakistan's national dailies and has published several books on Pakistan's defense policy and civil–military relations.

SAEED SHAFQAT is a founding member and former chairman of the Department of Pakistan Studies at the Quaid-i-Azam University in Islamabad. Currently, he is a professor at Forman Christian College, Lahore, Pakistan.

PRAVEEN SWAMI is Deputy Editor and Chief of Bureau (New Delhi) with *Frontline Magazine*, a widely read Indian biweekly magazine, and has reported since 1993 on security-related issues, including the north Indian states of Jammu & Kashmir and Punjab. He is the author of *The Kargil War* (1999).

JAMES J. WIRTZ is Dean of the School of International Graduate Studies at the Naval Postgraduate School. Dr. Wirtz teaches courses and writes on nuclear strategy, international relations theory, and intelligence.

Preface

This volume took six years to research and compile. From the beginning, this study was a challenge. This crisis, in comparison to previous conflicts in the region, drew an unprecedented level of controversy, competing narratives, and implications for domestic politics specifically in Pakistan, but also in India and for the course of international relations in South Asia. For this reason alone, I owe a great deal of gratitude to those who contributed to this volume and many people who were forthcoming with their candor in formal interviews and private exchange of views with me and my colleagues over the past six years. This multi-authored volume is a testimony of the Clauswitzian proverb of "wading through the water" and an earnest attempt to provide the most objective and authenticated version and analysis of this conflict.

The project editor and authors interviewed dozens of policymakers, intelligence officials, and military officers in Pakistan, India, and the United States. They also received a formal presentation by the commander of the Pakistani formation that conducted the Kargil intrusion, Force Command Northern Areas (FCNA), and several other civilian and military officials associated with the operation. Project authors presented preliminary findings and received helpful feedback from other scholars and various governmental and military representatives at conferences in Monterey, California in June 2002, at the United Services Institute in New Delhi in September 2002, and at the Institute of Strategic Studies, Islamabad in January 2003. Subsequent research trips and interviews in South Asia were undertaken to provide as complete and balanced an account as possible.

I am especially indebted to former Pakistani President General Pervez Musharraf and General Ved Prakash Malik, who were the respective Chiefs of Army Staff at the time of the conflict, for giving their candid views during my several meetings with them. Special thanks are owed to Lieutenant General Mahmood Ahmed and Lieutenant General Javed Hassan, commanders of the Pakistan army's 10 Corps and FCNA respectively at the time of the Kargil operation, for their extensive interviews with this author, and to Lieutenant General Nadeem Ahmed, Commander of FCNA in 2003, for his detailed briefing and views in Gilgit at FCNA Headquarters. Without these insights, the Pakistani side of the story would have remained murky.

Finally, I owe a word of gratitude to the team of the Center for Contemporary Conflict (CCC), who in the past five years conducted extensive research, and kept pace with new events and narratives, just when they thought they had reached the final version. My special thanks go to Brigadier (retd.) Feroz Hassan Khan of the Pakistan army and Lieutenant Colonel (retd.) Surinder Rana of the Indian army, both senior researchers with CCC and having the experience of command in the area of operation, for their insights, inputs, edits, and comments. This research would have been incomplete without the relentless efforts of CCC researchers, Christopher Clary, Adam Radin, and Puja Verma. Lastly, a very special thanks to my wife Debra Lavoy and our two children for bearing the brunt of my distractions, midnight-oil burning, and their support. Debra never believed this would come to an end. Publication of this book is fulfillment of one promise among many that I vowed to her.

Abbreviations and acronyms

APP	Associated Press of Pakistan
BBC	British Broadcasting Company
BJP	Bharatiya Janata Party
BSF	Border Security Force
BSP	Bahujan Samaj Party
CCC	Center for Contemporary Conflict
CCS	Cabinet Committee on Security
CDS	Chief of Defence Staff
CENTCOM	United States Central Command
CFL	Cease-Fire Line
CGS	Chief of General Staff
CI	Counterinsurgency
CIA	Central Intelligence Agency
COAS	Chief of Army Staff
COMINT	Communications intelligence
CSDS	Centre for the Study of Developing Societies
CSP	Civil Service of Pakistan
CTBT	Comprehensive Test Ban Treaty
DCC	Defence Committee of the Cabinet
DGMI	Directorate General of Military Intelligence
DGMO	Director General of Military Operations
DIA	Defence Intelligence Agency
DMG	District Management Group
ELINT	Electronic intelligence
FCNA	Force Command Northern Areas
G-8	Group of Eight industrialized nations
GHQ	General Headquarters
GOC	General Office Commanding
GoM	Group of Ministers
HUMINT	Human intelligence
IAF	Indian air force
IAS	Indian Administrative Service

IB	Intelligence Bureau
IDSA	Institute for Defence Studies and Analyses
IMET	International Military Education and Training
IMINT	Imagery intelligence
INC	Indian National Congress
IPS	Indian Police Service
ISID	Inter-Services Intelligence Directorate
ISPR	Office of Inter-Services Public Relations
ITBP	Indo-Tibetan Border Police
JI	Jamaat-e-Islami
JIC	Joint Intelligence Committee
JUI-F	Jamiat-ul-Ulema-e-Islam (headed by Maulana Fazal-ur-Rehman)
JUI-S	Jamiat-ul-Ulema-e-Islam (headed by Maulana Sami-ul-Haq)
LoC	Line of Control
MAC	Multi-Agency Centre
MMA	Muttahida Majlis-e-Amal (six-party coalition of Pakistani religious parties)
MoD	Ministry of Defence
NBC	Nuclear, biological, and chemical warfare or weapons
NCP	Nationalist Congress Party
NH-1A	National Highway 1A
NLI	Northern Light Infantry
NPT	Nuclear Nonproliferation Treaty
NSA	US National Security Agency
NSAB	National Security Advisory Board
NSC	National Security Council
NSCS	National Security Council Secretariat
NTFO	National Technical Facilities Organisation
NWFP	North-West Frontier Province
OSD	Office of the Secretary of Defense
PAF	Pakistan Air Force
PML-N	Pakistan Muslim League (Nawaz Sharif)
PPP	Pakistan Peoples Party
PTV	Pakistan Television
RAW	Research and Analysis Wing
RSS	Rashtriya Swayamsevak Sangh
SAARC	South Asian Association for Regional Cooperation
SAD	Shiromani Akali Dal
SSG	Special Services Group

SSW	Sub-sector West
TES	Technology Experiment Satellite
UAVs	Unmanned aerial vehicles
UN	United Nations
UNCIP	United Nations Commission of India and Pakistan
UNMOGIP	United Nations Military Observer Group in India and Pakistan
UNSC	United Nations Security Council
VCDS	Vice Chief of Defence Staff
VHP	Vishwa Hindu Parishad (World Hindu Council)
VVFs	Village Volunteer Forces
WASO	Winter Air Surveillance Operations

1   Introduction: the importance of the Kargil conflict

Peter R. Lavoy

In the spring of 1999, Indian soldiers patrolling near the town of Kargil about 5 miles on their side of the Kashmir Line of Control (LoC) were ambushed by assailants firing from unseen positions high atop frozen peaks of the Great Himalayan mountain range. After several weeks of confusion, Indian officials realized the intruders were not Kashmiri militants, as they initially had thought, but well-trained troops from Pakistan's Northern Light Infantry (NLI), and that the infiltration was much larger and better organized than previously assessed. India then mounted a major military and diplomatic campaign to oust the intruders. After two months of intense fighting at altitudes ranging between 12,000 and 17,000 feet, during which both sides lost several hundred soldiers, Pakistan ordered its forces home, and the crisis ended.[1] Although no territory changed hands – as it had done in previous Indo-Pakistani wars – the Kargil conflict was a landmark event. Occurring less than a year after India and Pakistan openly tested nuclear weapons, Kargil dispelled the common notion that nuclear-armed states cannot fight one another. Like the only other direct military clash between nuclear powers – the Sino-Soviet conflict over Damanskii (*Zhenbao* to the Chinese) Island in the Ussuri (*Wusuli*) River starting in March 1969 – the Kargil conflict did not

---

[1] Some Indian and American analysts call Kargil the fourth Indo-Pakistani war. Certainly, for the soldiers fighting along the LoC, it was a war. But we prefer to call it a "conflict," or a "near war." The scale and intensity of the fighting exceeded even the high levels of peacetime violence along the Kashmir LoC, where fierce artillery duels and ten-person-a-day body counts have been all too common. However, the 1999 engagement was confined to a small section of mountainous terrain in Indian-held Kashmir; only a small fraction of each side's soldiers and weapons was used; and both tried to reduce the risk of escalation by pursuing limited political and military objectives. Moreover, because probably about 750 to 950 soldiers died in the heights near Kargil, this conflict did not meet the classical definition of war as an armed conflict with at least 1,000 battlefield deaths, as per J. David Singer and Melvin Small, *The Wages of War, 1816–1965: A Statistical Handbook* (New York: John Wiley and Sons, 1972). John H. Gill provides details on Kargil casualty assessments in chapter 4 of this book.

come close to causing a nuclear war.[2] However, we now know that Indian troops were within days of opening another front across the LoC and possibly the international border, an act that could have triggered a large-scale conventional military engagement, which in turn might have escalated to an exchange of recently tested Indian and Pakistani nuclear weapons.

Why this study matters

Until now, the debate between those who are optimistic about the operation of nuclear deterrence and those who are pessimistic about the effects of nuclear proliferation was waged largely on theoretical terrain.[3] Observers made assumptions about how new nuclear weapons states should behave, but were unable to provide much empirical evidence to support or falsify competing claims.[4] The Kargil conflict offers scholars and policymakers a rare opportunity to investigate how a pair of countries equipped with nuclear weapons entered into, interacted during, and then concluded an armed conflict. Written by analysts and practitioners from India, Pakistan, and the United States, *Asymmetric Warfare in South Asia: The Causes and Consequences of the Kargil Conflict* draws extensively upon primary sources, including interviews with Indian, Pakistani, and US government officials and military officers who were actively involved in the fighting and management of the conflict. The level of cooperation from the Indian and the Pakistan governments was unprecedented. In particular, the Pakistani military, which previously had not even acknowledged its role in the conflict, was instrumental in helping us create a detailed account of what happened on the Kargil heights and in the capitals of the concerned powers.

---

[2] However, it is now known that the risk of an escalatory Sino-Soviet war was a real possibility. The US Central Intelligence Agency (CIA) assessed after the March 1969 border fighting caused several hundred deaths, that "the potential for a war exists," and that even if Moscow did not launch a conventional attack against Chinese nuclear and missile facilities, as it then was contemplating, "escalation of the conflict will be a continuing possibility." CIA, "The USSR and China," declassified National Intelligence Estimate, 11/13-69, 12 August 1969, pp. 6, 9, available on the CIA-Freedom of Information Act (FOIA) website, www.foia.cia.gov/default.asp. For background on the crisis, see Lyle J. Goldstein, "Do Nascent WMD Arsenals Deter? The Sino-Soviet Crisis of 1969," *Political Science Quarterly* 118, no. 1 (Spring 2003): 53–79.

[3] Scott Sagan and Kenneth Waltz offer the most recent articulation of this debate, in Scott D. Sagan and Kenneth N. Waltz, *The Spread of Nuclear Weapons: A Debate Renewed* (New York: Norton, 2003). Earlier rounds of the debate are discussed in Peter R. Lavoy, "Strategic Consequences of Nuclear Proliferation," *Security Studies* 4, no. 4 (Summer 1995): 695–753.

[4] Lavoy, "Strategic Consequences of Nuclear Proliferation."

Asymmetric Warfare in South Asia is the first rigorous, comprehensive, and objective case study of the causes, conduct, and consequences of the Kargil conflict. It differs significantly from the existing literature on the conflict, in which the most widely cited study, *From Surprise to Reckoning: The Kargil Review Committee Report*, is the product of an independent Kargil Review Committee, appointed by the Indian government and chaired by the respected Indian defense analyst, K. Subrahmanyam. Drawing extensively on Indian intelligence and military sources, this committee sought to establish why India failed to detect the massive infiltration across the LoC. When it tried to discern the motivations, assumptions, and objectives of Pakistani planners, however, it resorted to "enemy images" that obscured the true strategic objectives, perspectives, and behavior of the adversary.[5]

Other Indian narratives on the conduct of the Kargil conflict offer important insights but share this bias because they rely almost exclusively on reports from Indian officials and troops.[6] Breaking with the tradition of past Indian service chiefs who generally have refused to write about the military campaigns in which they were involved, former army chief General V. P. Malik has produced the most recent and by far the most controversial Indian book on the Kargil conflict. Labeling the event a "strategic and tactical intelligence failure," Malik has come down hard on the shortcomings of the intelligence agencies, provoking strong responses from Indian intelligence officials and journalists.[7]

The Pakistani literature on Kargil is even more one-sided. For a long time, there had been no official Pakistani governmental or military account of what took place on the Kargil heights – in part because the story of how Pakistani troops occupied and then withdrew from this territory quickly became intertwined with the civil–military dispute between former Prime Minister Nawaz Sharif and former President Pervez Musharraf, who during the Kargil affair was Sharif's army chief. The

---

[5] Kargil Review Committee, *From Surprise to Reckoning: The Kargil Review Committee Report* (New Delhi: Sage, 2000).

[6] Prominent examples include Y. M. Bammi, *Kargil 1999: The Impregnable Conquered* (Noida, India: Gorkha Publishers, 2002); Amarinder Singh, *A Ridge Too Far: War in the Kargil Heights 1999* (Patiala: Motibagh Palace, 2001); Ashok Mehta and P. R. Chari, eds., *Kargil: The Tables Turned* (New Delhi: Manohar, 2001); Praveen Swami, *The Kargil War* (New Delhi: LeftWord, 2000); Harinder Baweja, *A Soldier's Diary. Kargil: The Inside Story* (New Delhi: Books Today, 2000); and Jasjit Singh, ed., *Kargil 1999: Pakistan's Fourth War for Kashmir* (New Delhi: Institute for Defence Studies and Analyses, 1999).

[7] General V. P. Malik, *Kargil: From Surprise to Victory* (New Delhi: HarperCollins, 2006), 77–112; B. Raman, "Gen. Malik on Gen. Malik," *South Asia Analysis Group*, no. 1788, 5 May 2006, www.saag.org/papers18/paper1788.html. Also see Praveen Swami, "Resolving the Kargil Conundrum," *The Hindu*, 6 May 2006, www.hinduonnet.com/thehindu/thscrip/print.pl?file=2006050604971100.htm&date=2006/05/06/&prd=th&.

few detailed articles and media analyses that have been published in Pakistan are fundamentally flawed in their assumptions about the depth of infiltration and the number of irregular militants involved in the occupying force.[8] Pakistani defense analyst Shireen Mazari has published a quasi-official account of the Kargil operation, but its value is uneven because of her attempt to reconcile recently available information about the Kargil operation with self-serving statements by Pakistani authorities.[9]

The publication of former President Musharraf's autobiography in 2006 has clarified several contentious issues, such as Pakistani concerns about the Indian military buildup in Kashmir in 1998, the scale of the cross-border intrusion (over 500 square miles) into Indian-held Kashmir, and the timing and location of the Pakistan army's six briefings to the prime minister on the operation between January and June 1999.[10] However, this book actually has deepened several other controversies, such as the likelihood of an Indian offensive in early 1999 (Musharraf claims that a "planned offensive" was "preempted" by Pakistan's Kargil operation), the identity of the occupying forces (called *mujahideen*, or freedom fighters by Musharraf), and, at the time of Nawaz Sharif's 4 July 1999 agreement to an unconditional withdrawal, the military situation on the ground (deemed "favorable" and "strategically advantageous" to Pakistan).[11]

Treatments of the conflict by American scholars and former US policy-makers generally overemphasize the strategic roles and risks of nuclear weapons in South Asia.[12] Lurking around every corner of this Indo-Pakistani crisis, American commentators saw the risk of nuclear use and validation of their arguments about nuclear instability in South Asia and, more generally, the perils of nuclear proliferation.[13] These concerns, while certainly understandable, contribute to a selective reading of the

---

[8] One notable exception is Shaukat Qadir, "An Analysis of the Kargil Conflict 1999," *Journal of the Royal United Services Institution*, 147, no. 2 (April 2002), 24–30.

[9] Shireen M. Mazari, *The Kargil Conflict 1999: Separating Fact from Fiction* (Islamabad: Ferozsons, 2003).

[10] Pervez Musharraf, *In the Line of Fire: A Memoir* (New York: Simon and Schuster, 2006), 87–98.

[11] *Ibid.*

[12] See chapter 5 in this book by Bruce Riedel; as well as Strobe Talbott, *Engaging India: Diplomacy, Democracy, and the Bomb* (Washington, DC: Brookings Institution Press, 2004); and Ashley J. Tellis, C. Christine Fair, and Jamison Jo Medby, *Limited Conflict under the Nuclear Umbrella: Indian and Pakistani Lessons from the Kargil Crisis* (Santa Monica, Calif.: RAND, 2001).

[13] A partial exception is Sumit Ganguly and Devin T. Hagerty, *Fearful Symmetry: India–Pakistan Crises in the Shadow of Nuclear Weapons* (Seattle: University of Washington Press, 2005), which appropriately downplays the risk of nuclear war during the Kargil episode and in five other recent Indo-Pakistani crises, but greatly exaggerates the impact of nuclear weapons on Pakistan's calculations to undertake the Kargil operation.

initiation and termination of the Kargil conflict, which exaggerates warning signs and generally ignores evidence of caution and restraint. Moreover, these accounts fail to bring to light the motivations, political assumptions, and detailed military planning behind Pakistan's daring Kargil incursion – subjects this book elucidates in print for the first time.

One claim in the American literature on Kargil is that the intrusion was a "limited probe" strategy to challenge India's conventional deterrence.[14] In reality, the Kargil campaign was a very different kind of military operation, which is best described as a *"fait accompli"* strategy. Alexander George and Richard Smoke discuss each of these strategies in their classic *Deterrence in American Foreign Policy: Theory and Practice*. A limited probe occurs "when the initiator creates a controlled crisis in order to clarify the defender's commitments."[15] In the spring of 1999, the Pakistani leadership had no doubt about India's commitment to defend its territory along the LoC, and it certainly did not want to create a major crisis. Rather, it tried a "quick, decisive" military operation to take key mountain peaks across the LoC before the Indians could organize an effective defense or counterattack.[16]

As Feroz Hassan Khan, Peter R. Lavoy, and Christopher Clary point out in chapter 3 of this book, the planners of Kargil believed that a military *fait accompli* across the LoC could not be reversed because of the unique high-altitude terrain in the Northern Areas of Kashmir. They further judged, as George and Smoke would expect, that this strategy was the least risky under the circumstances. James J. Wirtz and Surinder Rana show in chapter 8 of this book that the Kargil operation was launched when the weaker party played down the extreme risks inherent in the effort to benefit from surprise because of the prospect of achieving gains that otherwise were beyond its grasp. Although the Kargil operation turned into a major military crisis, this was not the intent of its planners. Moreover, the fact that they were so poorly prepared to deal with a major military crisis provides further evidence that they did not intend to create a crisis to test India's deterrence commitments.

Controversies clarified

Because the Indian, Pakistani, and American authors of this book conducted extensive fieldwork and graciously subjected their analyses to

[14] Ganguly and Hagerty, *Fearful Symmetry*, 152.
[15] Alexander George and Richard Smoke, *Deterrence in American Foreign Policy: Theory and Practice* (New York: Columbia University Press, 1974), 540.
[16] *Ibid.* 536–537.

multiple rounds of review and refinement, they were able to identify and overcome implausible stories, gaps in evidence, and contradictory interpretations. There are at least five important, controversial issues on which this book brings forth major, original findings.

Mujahideen *cover*

First, prior to our research, it was widely believed that *mujahideen*, or civilian "freedom fighters" involved in a Muslim war or struggle, played a significant part in the Kargil intrusion – a falsehood caused by the initial confusion of India's civilian and military intelligence services, a carefully planned Pakistani denial and deception campaign, and opportunistic Islamic militant groups. The Indian Kargil Review Committee, which was highly dubious about the role of militants in the conflict, still concluded that "the regular/irregular ratio may well have been in the range of 70:30, if the overall numbers are taken into account."[17] Our interviews with Pakistani and Indian ground commanders revealed that local civilians played only minimal reconnaissance and logistical roles in the operation. In fact, numerous Pakistani officers and soldiers told us they did not encounter a single civilian combatant during the conflict.

Eight years after the event, Pakistan still officially maintains that freedom fighters and not the Northern Light Infantry conducted the cross-LoC intrusion. Former President Musharraf states in his 2006 memoir that the "freedom fighting mujahideen occupied the Kargil Heights that the Indian army had vacated for the winter."[18] Three reasons can be offered to explain why Pakistan concocted the *mujahideen* cover and why it maintains this façade even today. First, until the Kargil operation, the Pakistan army did not consider the Northern Light Infantry at par with regular troops. Being locals of the area, most NLI soldiers came from villages near the LoC, which even today do not have the legal status as being a full part of the Pakistan nation-state. Therefore, it was easy for

---

[17] Kargil Review Committee, *From Surprise to Reckoning*, 97. V. P. Malik has written that well into the conflict, the heads of the Intelligence Bureau (IB), the Research and Analysis Wing (RAW), and National Security Council Secretariat (NSCS) believed that the composition of enemy forces was 70% *jehadi* militants (*mujahideen*) and 30% Pakistan regulars. After Malik challenged this assessment, the NSCS secretary reversed the estimate to 70% Pakistani regulars and 30% militants. See Malik, *Kargil: From Surprise to Victory*, 111; and the detailed treatment of this issue by C. Christine Fair in chapter 9 of this book.

[18] However, he creates some ambiguity by admitting that he had ordered "FCNA to improve our defensive position in coordination with the freedom fighters to deny access to the watershed by India," and that "five battalions [were involved] in support of freedom fighter groups." Musharraf, *In the Line of Fire*, 87, 91.

government officials to refer to these soldiers as freedom fighters as opposed to regular army troops.

A second explanation, as the FCNA commander told CCC researchers in 2003, was that the army never intended to turn the *mujahideen* ruse into a cover story. NLI troops, who are often deployed to isolated posts for months at a time, prefer to wear tracksuits and light, athletic outer garments (usually clothing left over by Western climbers and then resold in local markets) instead of Pakistani army jackets that feel heavy and unwieldy to them. FCNA says the Indians first claimed that the occupiers were Kashmiri *mujahideen*. The Pakistan army intended for Indian intelligence initially to believe that these soldiers were civilian combatants – for this would create confusion and delay India's eventual military response, perhaps until well into the summer, after which there would be little time for India to mount a suitable counterattack before the fall snows stopped the fighting. But when the Indians persisted in believing that the intruders were *mujahideen*, Pakistan simply continued the deception because it compounded Indian confusion and took on a whole life of its own in the Pakistani media. As the FCNA Commander told us, "We are not obliged to clarify to the enemy."[19]

This still begs the question as to why Pakistan maintained the façade after NLI soldiers had been captured and proof of their involvement was abundant. As strange as it may seem, the reason rests largely in the legality of the position. The Pakistan government concluded that it could not have admitted occupation by Pakistani troops across the LoC because the area was demarcated under the 1972 Simla Accord and covered under the 1949 Karachi Agreement, and Pakistan's admittance of the cross-LoC operation was judged in Islamabad to be tantamount to admitting aggression. The legal context differed significantly from that of India's 1984 Siachen military occupation, which India had been able to justify because Siachen was a contested area that was not demarcated with the rest of the LoC. To the Pakistanis, however, Siachen violated the Simla Accord, as pointed out in chapter 2 by Zafar Iqbal Cheema. Although Siachen was still a major Pakistani grievance, Pakistan's Foreign Office believed that an admission of regular troops crossing the defined LoC would be difficult to justify internationally. In its assessment, continuation of the *mujahideen* story, along with a narrative that defensive positions were improved, would preserve some degree of plausible deniability.[20]

---

[19] Maj. Gen. Nadeem Ahmed briefing, 12 January 2003.
[20] Interviews with Pakistani officials knowledgeable about various Defence Committee of the Cabinet (DCC) deliberations in May and June 1999.

Pakistan's perpetuation of the *mujahideen* deception may have provided a thin veneer of legal deniability and a face-saving formula, but in the end it severely damaged Pakistan's credibility both inside and outside South Asia, as C. Christine Fair discusses in chapter 9. It also altered the standing of Kashmir insurgency. Instead of being regarded internationally as a "freedom struggle," the Kashmir insurgency came to be seen after Kargil (and especially after the 9/11 terrorist attacks against the United States) as "terrorist" activity. If Pakistan had hoped the Kargil operation would stimulate international focus on the Kashmir issue, this was not the intended result.

Asymmetric warfare

The second controversy we clarify relates to the provocative title of the book, *Asymmetric Warfare in South Asia*. Many Pakistanis will take issue with the assertion that the LoC operation was an asymmetric military strategy, claiming instead that "nibbling of the posts" is a time-honored practice of conventional forces not only in Kashmir, but also at many other times and places where armies meet. This contention is true in part: the Kargil intrusion was only the most recent in a long series of military maneuvers in the Northern Areas that began in 1947, escalated in 1965, and saw Indian troops cross the LoC and establish military posts in the Chorbat La sector in 1972, the Siachen Glacier area in 1984, and the Qamar sector in 1988.[21] However, the Kargil operation was quite different too. In terms of the scope, scale, and objectives of the plan, it dwarfed other attempts to alter the territorial disposition of forces in the Northern Areas. But more significantly, it embodied the three features that have come to define asymmetric conflicts.

First, the Kargil conflict was a classic case of asymmetric warfare because the relative balance of power of the forces involved differed so vastly. The fact that India had a two-to-one advantage in soldiers over Pakistan (1 million to 500,000) had little bearing on the planning or conduct of the Kargil gambit. In fact, Musharraf boasts in his autobiography of Pakistan's ability to tie down disproportionately large numbers of Indian forces on the Kargil heights: "Considered purely in military terms, the Kargil operations were a landmark in the history of the Pakistan army. As few as five battalions in support of the freedom fighter groups were able to compel the Indians to employ more than four divisions," deplete artillery sources from strike formations, and force them to "mobilize

---

[21] Information provided in a Pakistan Defence Attaché briefing document, dated 14 August 1999, Washington, DC.

their entire national resources, including their air force."[22] Even though Musharraf concedes that India recaptured several posts, he takes pride in the fact that such a small number of Pakistani troops forced India to expend vast military and economic resources, which in itself was seen as a victory. As Rizvi points out in chapter 13, this David and Goliath dynamic has been a persistent theme in Pakistani strategic culture. In a full-scale war the strategy of tying down large numbers of forces makes sense as it would deplete troops from other sectors, which Pakistan could exploit; however, this strategy invited disaster in 1999, for India had abundant resources to escalate the conflict vertically and even horizontally.

Second, the Kargil operation could only succeed through the use of asymmetric strategy and tactics, but this ultimately caused its undoing. Weak states sometimes can prolong and ultimately win wars against stronger states if they employ asymmetric strategies to deflect or mediate the stronger state's use of its material advantages in resources,[23] but time is generally not on their side. As Wirtz and Rana explain in chapter 8, Kargil was a classic case of a weak opponent perceiving great incentives to surprise its stronger opponent using military means (concealment, cunning, deception) that the stronger opponent would not expect. The Kargil planners believed that a combination of surprise, military *fait accompli* on superior terrain, and a well-considered denial and deception strategy would inhibit India from dislodging the occupying troops before the onset of winter, which would freeze the forces in place, thus enabling Pakistan to restock its forward posts and lock in its territorial gains across the LoC. What the army leadership did not foresee was India's will and capacity to "conventionalize" the unconventional conflict. Gill explains in chapter 4 that because Pakistan was unable to sustain its asymmetric strategy, India was able to apply its vast military resources to force key posts to fall. Initially Pakistan beat back Indian assaults, forcing India to bring in more troops and firepower, but relentless attacks on the outposts were too much for the NLI troops. The capture of Tololing broke the myth that ground once lost on such heights could not be regained and entirely changed the battle scenario. If Pakistan's strategy in Kashmir during the 1990s "succeeded" in using militants to tie down Indian forces in a costly counterinsurgency campaign, Kargil ultimately tested India on its strong suit: its conventional military superiority.

[22] Musharraf, *In the Line of Fire*, 93.
[23] Ivan Arreguin-Toft, *How the Weak Win Wars: A Theory of Asymmetric Conflict* (Cambridge University Press, 2005).

Third, Kargil can be seen as an asymmetric conflict because Pakistan was willing to sacrifice such a great deal – the lives of its NLI soldiers, tactical military advantages that could have been exploited in a major war,[24] and its international reputation – in order to achieve the smallest of victories in the contest for Kashmir and its perceived struggle for existence with India. Much like suicide bombers today forfeit their lives in the interest of a supposed greater cause, Pakistan historically has been willing to sacrifice virtually every resource at its disposal in order to sustain the Kashmir dispute. Musharraf is quite categorical about the value of Kargil in upholding this cause: "I would like to state emphatically that whatever movement has taken place so far in the direction of finding a solution to Kashmir is due considerably to the Kargil conflict."[25] This episode should be a lesson to India and the international community that Pakistan would be willing to sacrifice even more than it did in 1999 to defend its stake in Kashmir and more generally protect its national sovereignty and territorial integrity.

The role of nuclear weapons

The impact of nuclear arms on the Kargil crisis is another big controversy. The debate revolves around three competing narratives. First, US officials assert that Pakistan made some nuclear preparations at the later stage of the conflict and generally tried to manipulate the fear of nuclear war to alter the territorial status quo in Kashmir. As Bruce Riedel writes in this book and former Deputy Secretary of State Strobe Talbott states elsewhere,[26] President Clinton received credible, unambiguous intelligence of Pakistani nuclear preparations shortly before meeting with Nawaz Sharif in Washington on 4 July 1999. As a result, Clinton demanded the immediate withdrawal of all Pakistani troops from across the LoC and refused to allow Sharif to leave the negotiations with a victory that might validate nuclear brinksmanship in the post-Cold War era. Second, Pakistani authorities flatly deny readying their nuclear arsenal for use,[27]

---

[24] In our numerous discussions with Pakistan army officers not directly associated with the Kargil operation, the strongest criticism was that Pakistan squandered its ability to conquer large portions of militarily significant territory in the Northern Areas, which military intelligence had shown to be one of its greatest wartime opportunities. Not only did Pakistan gain precious little, but India recognized its weaknesses in the area, redoubled its defenses, and turned the northern LoC into yet another area where it now had the military advantage.

[25] Musharraf, *In the Line of Fire*, 98.

[26] Talbott, *Engaging India*, 161–162.

[27] Musharraf called the claim "preposterous." See *In the Line of Fire*, 98.

suggesting that US intelligence might have confused conventional military movements at the Sargodha Ammunition Depot for nuclear-force preparations.[28] Third, knowledgeable Indians state that neither side prepared for nuclear war, but claim that Pakistan's goal was to wage low-intensity warfare in Kashmir under the nuclear umbrella. Then Indian army chief General V. P. Malik asserts: "There was a strong belief that Pakistan's demonstrated nuclear weapons, in May 1998, were sufficient to prevent the escalation of the situation in Kargil to a full-scale conventional war. The military high-command, headed by Pervez Musharraf, was confident about Pakistan's 'nuclear shield.'"[29] Until now, no evidence has emerged to settle this debate.

Our research illuminates five major points about the role of nuclear weapons before, during, and after the Kargil conflict. First, Pakistani planners were not motivated by a calculation that the risk of nuclear escalation would deter India from counterattacking. As explained by Cheema in chapter 2 and Khan, Lavoy, and Clary in chapter 3, other considerations – the local terrain, the military balance in Kashmir, and domestic civil–military relations – shaped the decision to advance across the LoC. Second, neither Pakistan nor India readied its nuclear arms for employment. If some preparation occurred in Pakistan, as US officials insist, the nature and purpose of that action is unclear. Our research confirms Musharraf's claim that "in 1999, our nuclear capability was not yet operational."[30] The push to operationalize Pakistan's deterrent for the most part took place *after* Kargil. Third, although some Pakistani officials issued veiled statements that could have been interpreted as nuclear threats,[31] neither side tried to raise the risk of nuclear escalation to win the crisis. The statements that were made were *ad hoc* individual initiatives – not part

---

[28] Lt. Gen. Khalid Kidwai, Director General of Strategic Plans Division (SPD), made this observation in discussions with the author in Rawalpindi, Pakistan on 20 December 2005 and 14 June 2007. The ammunition depot, located in the Kirana Hills near Sargodha, has been in focus for several reasons. This was the suspected location of the Chinese M-11 missiles supplied to Pakistan in the early 1990s. Also, both the Khan Research Laboratories (KRL) and Pakistan Atomic Energy Commission (PAEC) conducted nuclear cold tests in the Kirana Hills in the 1980s.

[29] Malik, *Kargil: From Surprise to Victory*, 272.

[30] As Musharraf explains, "Merely exploding a bomb does not mean that you are operationally capable of deploying nuclear force in the field and delivering a bomb across the border over a selected target." *In the Line of Fire*, 98.

[31] Most importantly, Pakistan Foreign Secretary Shamshad Ahmad said in an interview on 30 May that while Pakistan desired peace, "we will not hesitate to use any weapon in our arsenal to defend our territorial integrity." Then on 30 June Pakistan's Senate leader, Raja Muhammad Zafarul Haq, stated that Pakistan would not hesitate to use nuclear weapons if required: "The purpose of developing weapons becomes meaningless if they are not used when they are needed to be used."

of a coordinated Pakistani signaling campaign to deter Indian military escalation.[32] Fourth, as indicated by the author in chapter 7 and Rodney W. Jones and Joseph McMillan in chapter 14, the fear of nuclear war did drive the international community to end the crisis as quickly as possible and prevent Pakistan from claiming a victory that could validate a defense strategy based on nuclear threats and military aggression. Fifth, as argued by Basrur in chapter 12 and Rizvi in chapter 13, some nuclear learning took place after Kargil, but the lessons India and Pakistan drew from the crisis did not significantly lessen the likelihood of another military crisis or the prospect of it escalating out of control – as the world witnessed all too clearly during the 2001–2002 military standoff. In this case, India and Pakistan displayed better nuclear discipline than during the Kargil crisis, but came much closer to fighting a major conventional war, which had a greater risk of going nuclear.

The potential for military escalation

A fourth controversy this book helps to clarify is the issue of how close Pakistan and India came to turning the Kargil conflict into a major conventional war. Indian army chief V. P. Malik has written that India came very close to enlarging the Kargil fighting in the middle of June 1999. It is well known that Prime Minister Vajpayee had ordered Malik to restrict military operations to India's side of the LoC and the international border. But with intense fighting in all sectors and not a single battle won by India, and a growing number of senior defense officials now urging the government to allow Indian forces to cross "the border/LoC," Malik ordered his senior commanders on 18 June to "be prepared for escalation – sudden or gradual – along the LoC or the international border and be prepared to go to (declared) war at short notice."[33] When two days later Pakistan Prime Minister Nawaz Sharif threatened that "many more Kargil-like issues can crop up" if the Kashmir dispute was not resolved,[34] India's senior-most defense decision-making body, the Cabinet Committee on Security (CCS), concluded that "we had to be prepared for an escalation."[35] Based on interviews with senior Indian officials involved with this decision, it appears that India would have opened up other military fronts, thus turning the Kargil clash into a major war, had

---

[32] Information based on multiple interviews with senior Pakistani civilian and military officials, 2003–2005. These statements were made at the height of the conventional conflict.

[33] Malik, *Kargil: From Surprise to Victory*, 146–147.

[34] "Sharif Warns of More Kargil-like Situations," *Times of India*, 21 June 1999.

[35] Malik, *Kargil: From Surprise to Victory*, 148.

Indian soldiers not recaptured later that very day the vital Tololing-Point 5140 mountain complex in the Dras sector, from which Pakistani troops had been able to interdict India's military buildup and troop movements with impunity.[36] Had India's 56 Mountain Brigade not won the five-day, hand-to-hand contest for Tololing – which turned the tide of the battle because Indian forces were now able to operate inside of Pakistan's defense perimeter and recapture several other military posts – India's leadership would have been forced either to acquiesce to Pakistan's control of territory across the LoC or to escalate the conflict and run a real risk of nuclear war and international opprobrium.

Viewed from Pakistan, however, the prospect of a wider war seemed very different. The army leadership assessed that India was in no position to launch an all-out offensive on land, air, or sea; that India's major formations were bottled up inside Kashmir, leaving no capability to attack elsewhere, and, more seriously, leaving the field open for a counteroffensive which could choke the Kashmir Valley; and that the NLI troops could not be dislodged from their mountain positions.[37] Meanwhile, Pakistan's 19 Infantry Division was repositioned from its Mangla encampment for either a counterattack or a defensive stand against possible Indian incursions across the LoC. The reinforcement and redeployment of troops along the LoC were clear indications of preparations for possible military escalation.[38]

This stark contrast of strategic thinking in India and Pakistan – and the consequent movement of military forces – indicates that each side had great difficulty in assessing the other side's intentions and capabilities. This factor in itself is a potential cause for military escalation. Ironically, India's tactical successes, beginning with the capture of Tololing, halted its plan to escalate elsewhere along the LoC or perhaps across the international border. Had India not achieved these victories (and had the international community been less involved), the conflict probably would have slipped out of control, thus marking the first Indo-Pak crisis to escalate to a major war with the eventual risk of a nuclear exchange.

Implications for the 2002 military crisis

The way in which the Kargil conflict ended and the military lessons that were learned (or not learned) by India and Pakistan in 1999 sowed the seeds for another major military confrontation just three years later. A fifth

---

[36] Interviews with senior Indian defense officials, New Delhi, May 2005; and *ibid.* 148–149.
[37] Musharraf, *In the Line of Fire*, 93, 96.
[38] Interviews with Pakistani military officials, 2003.

contribution of this book thus is to show how the learning process from Kargil reinforced India's planning for limited war and Pakistan's resolve to deter this through aggressive conventional-force deployments, and, if required, the employment of conventional and possibly even nuclear weapons. Interviews conducted by the CCC research team with civilian and military officials in India and Pakistan show beyond a doubt that each side came away from the Kargil conflict believing that it had an escalation advantage in 1999 and that this advantage would carry over into a future military engagement. In other words, each side had learned the wrong lesson from the Kargil crisis.

Kargil did not dampen the intense rivalry between India and Pakistan. In the aftermath of the crisis, new nuclear and conventional war-fighting doctrines were initiated. India announced a draft nuclear doctrine in August 1999. And on 25 January 2000, the Indian defence minister and army chief each announced a new "limited-war doctrine," which paved the way for India to devise new military measures in response to future crises in Kashmir. Further, Indian officials began to speak more openly about punitive actions in the form of preemptive strikes against alleged Pakistani training camps in Kashmir.

Almost as soon as normalcy returned to the Kargil mountain peaks, therefore, Indian and Pakistani troops began preparing to fight the next war. While insurgencies continued unabated in the region, after 1999 any terrorist event became a potential trigger for a serious military crisis. For example, a 13 December 2001 terrorist attack on the Indian parliament became the catalyst event for a nine-month military standoff, bringing South Asia once again to the brink of major war. The 2001–2002 military mobilization provided India with a real chance to test its limited-war doctrine conceived in the aftermath of Kargil. After this tense military standoff, the Indian army added a new strategic component – called Cold Start – to its limited-war doctrine. Because India's military mobilization in 2001–2002 was so slow that Pakistan had plenty of time to counter-mobilize and allow international diplomacy to intervene, the Cold Start concept was devised to enable India to strike promptly and decisively in response to a triggering event without waiting for a larger mobilization and or diplomatic intervention.

The Kargil conflict in context

This introduction and the following fourteen chapters explain how and why Pakistan and India started, fought, and terminated the 1999 Kargil conflict; the impact this event has had on the political, social, and military life of each country; the influence of outside powers, especially the

United States; and the lessons learned, or – more ominously – not learned, by key groups within the Indian and Pakistani governments, armed forces, and societies. More generally, our "anatomy" of the Kargil conflict provides unique insights into the evolving nature of South Asia's enduring political–military rivalry and the effects and limitations of the nuclear revolution in the post-Cold War world. Our findings in these two areas, which will enable readers to rethink and refine many conventional arguments, are described more fully in the remainder of this chapter – after this section in which the Kargil conflict is put into the historical context of the longstanding India–Pakistan strategic competition.

Historical roots of warfare

The Kargil operation was another in a series of failed attempts to resolve Indo-Pakistani disputes through force or diplomacy. Prior to 1984, neither country placed much emphasis on military action along the northern portions of the Kashmir Line of Control. The rugged terrain and harsh climate of Ladakh (the northern section of the erstwhile princely state of Jammu and Kashmir, which is divided into two districts: Kargil and Leh) significantly complicated military operations, which not only raised the costs and limited the size of any military offensive, but also dramatically diminished the strategic utility of the remote region. William Moorcroft, the first European to cross the Himalayan mountains in 1819, described this area – which at the time was contested not by India and Pakistan but by Russia, China, and Britain – as a series of narrow valleys "of extreme sterility and barrenness," generating commerce "of no great value or interest," and situated between gigantic mountains "ordinarily towering to a height which surpasses that of the pinnacles of the Alps."[39] This situation has not changed much. In addition to the cold weather, heavy snows, and rugged terrain, the thin air of the Northern Areas produces a wide range of physiological effects and illnesses, which severely complicate military operations and make Ladakh a most unlikely battlefield.[40]

---

[39] William Moorcroft and George Trebeck, *Travels in the Himalayan Provinces of Hindustan and the Panjab from 1819 to 1825*, 2 vols. (1841; reprint, Oxford University Press, 1979), 259, 266, 346.

[40] All of the soldiers interviewed by the author who operated along the northern LoC before, during, or after the Kargil conflict commented on the intense physical stresses caused by the harsh climate and terrain and the phenomenon of thin air (produced by low barometric pressure), and generally remarked that the latter was the most dangerous and disorienting condition they had to confront during their high-altitude warfare operations. On the unique challenges of high-altitude battlefields, see Marcus P. Acosta, "High Altitude Warfare: The Kargil Conflict and the Future," Master's thesis, Monterey,

But it did become a battlefield of major political and military significance on several occasions in the past sixty years. The first armed conflict in the Northern Areas took place shortly after the partition of British colonial India into independent India and Pakistan in August 1947. In what is now called the First Kashmir War, Indian forces fought a combination of Pakistani troops and Pathan tribesmen for control of the Kashmir Valley and the Northern Areas. After a year of intense fighting, Pakistan secured the territory to the east and north of the Kashmir Valley (from Mirpur up to Muzaffarabad, Chilas, and Gilgit, and across to Skardu and Khapalu), and India gained possession of the valley and the mountainous territory to the west through the towns of Dras, Kargil, and Leh.[41] Prior to the Kargil operation, the most recent conflict in this area occurred in 1984 when Indian military forces successfully occupied the disputed Siachen Glacier in the northernmost area of Kashmir.[42] The loss of well over 100 square miles of territory – even in this desolate, barren, and practically uninhabitable region – was a deep scar for the Pakistani military, and in particular for the Force Command Northern Areas (FCNA), which was responsible for the defense of this sector. Map 1.1 shows the entire area of the previous princely state of Jammu and Kashmir.[43]

After the Siachen operation, any perceived vulnerability along enemy lines was to be surveyed, probed, and, if possible, attacked. From the late 1980s onward, both the Indian and Pakistan armies launched daring operations to seize opposing posts – and tried to retrieve those they had lost to the enemy. Nonetheless, certain vestiges of tacit restrain remained. Opposing troops often coordinated access to common drinking water and occasionally exchanged symbolic gifts on major holidays. More significantly, both sides continued to engage in a partial winter retreat, vacating forward posts which were too difficult and dangerous to maintain during the harsh winter months. When the snow would melt in the spring and the

---

Calif.: US Naval Postgraduate School, June 2003, 11–26. The odd optical conditions of this environment were described in a nineteenth-century British travelogue: "In this thin, dry air, far-away objects appear quite near; mountains sixty miles away might be heaps of stones forty yards off, and *vice versa*. There is no atmospheric effect to give any idea of distance." E. F. Knight, *Where Three Empires Meet: A Narrative of Recent Travel in Kashmir, Western Tibet, Gilgit, and the Adjoining Countries* (1893; reprint, Karachi: Indus Publications, 1980), 43.

[41] See Sudhir S. Bloeria, *The Battles of Zojila, 1948* (New Delhi: Har-Ananad, 1997).
[42] India claims that its occupation of Siachen was a preemptive measure, executed only after India received intelligence of a Pakistani plan to seize the glacier. Most Pakistanis deny that any such plan was contemplated. For background, see Lt. Gen. V. R. Raghavan, *Siachen: Conflict Without End* (New Delhi: Penguin, 2002).
[43] Kashmir Study Group, *A Way Forward* (February 2005), www.kashmirstudygroup.net/awayforward05/p4_jamukashmir.html.

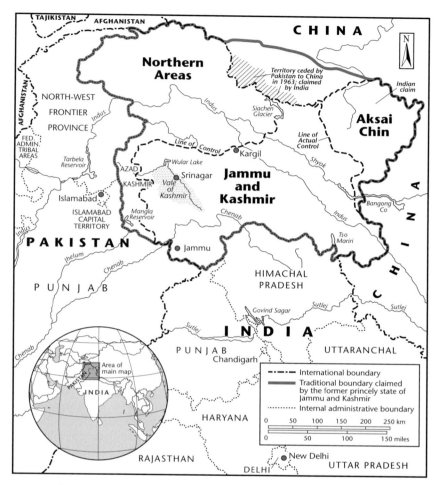

Map 1.1 Jammu and Kashmir

strategic mountain passes again would become usable, opposing troops would reclaim and restock their mountain posts, and another season of artillery shelling and counter-post operations would resume.

As military tensions and low-scale conflict simmered along the northern stretches of the LoC, the rest of Kashmir erupted in violence in 1989. Decades of Indian mismanagement of the Jammu and Kashmir state – including rigged elections in 1987 – spawned a mostly indigenous insurgency, which Pakistan's security apparatus gradually exploited for its own ends.[44] The dispute over the political and territorial status of Kashmir, which had occupied a back burner in bilateral relations since 1965, reemerged as the core source of Indo-Pakistani tension. India initially was forced to deploy an estimated 150,000 army and paramilitary troops in operations to counter the insurgency and prevent militants from infiltrating across the LoC, with that number more than doubling by the end of the decade.[45]

The dangerous decade

From the mid-1990s, opposing forces along the northern parts of the LoC increasingly mounted artillery attacks to convey pointed messages to the other side. Such exchanges resulted in extensive civilian casualties and the disruption of normal life on both sides. Pakistan was especially affected in the Neelum Valley. Shelling and small-arms fire from India's dominant positions on the eastern bank of the Neelum River blocked civilian and military resupply to Pakistani positions. Pakistan's 10 Corps, which has operational control over most of the LoC, sought to mitigate the interdiction of the Neelum Valley by returning the favor in areas where Indian lines of communication were vulnerable – most notably, along the Srinagar–Leh highway (NH-1A) near the towns of Kargil and Dras.

The Kashmir conflict entered a dangerous new phase when India conducted a series of nuclear explosive tests on 11 and 13 May 1998 in the western state of Rajasthan. Indian officials insisted that the tests were not intended to apply a new form of military pressure on Pakistan, but authorities in Islamabad were not comforted, and, by the end of May, Pakistan had conducted its own nuclear tests. Under intense pressure from the international community, India and Pakistan began broadranging bilateral consultations in October 1998, culminating in a historic bus ride by Indian prime minister Atal Behari Vajpayee to Lahore on 20 February 1999. In a widely celebrated Lahore Declaration, Vajpayee and Pakistani prime minister Nawaz Sharif agreed to "intensify their efforts to resolve all issues, including the issue of Jammu and Kashmir" and pledged to "refrain from intervention and interference in each other's internal affairs."[46] As Timothy Hoyt explains in chapter 6 of this book, the

---

[44] For background, see Praveen Swami, *India, Pakistan, and the Secret Jihad: The Covert War in Kashmir, 1947–2004* (New Delhi: Routledge, 2006), 163–171; and Victoria Schofield, *Kashmir in Conflict: India, Pakistan and the Unending War* (London: I. B. Tauris, 2003), 143–160.

[45] Tim McGirk, *The Independent*, 17 September 1991, cited in Schofield, *Kashmir in Conflict*, 157; Malik, *Kargil: From Surprise to Victory*, 68–70.

[46] Lahore Declaration, 21 February 1999, available at www.indianembassy.org/South_Asia/Pakistan/lahoredeclaration.html.

Lahore process led many observers – and many in the Indian government – to conclude that nuclear weapons had fundamentally transformed the India–Pakistan relationship.

It was in this tense environment – after Siachen, after a decade of the Kashmiri insurgency, after the nuclear tests, and concurrent with bilateral political talks – that the Kargil operation was planned and executed. Sometime after late November 1998, a handful of officers at the highest level of the Pakistan army decided to retake the tactical initiative along the Line of Control. The main actors in the planning of the Kargil operation were the Chief of Army Staff (COAS) General Pervez Musharraf, Chief of General Staff (CGS) Lieutenant General Muhammad Aziz Khan, 10 Corps Commander Lieutenant General Mahmud Ahmed, and General Office Commanding (GOC) of the Force Command Northern Areas Major General Javed Hassan.[47]

Indian forces in the Kargil sector regularly vacated their posts during the winter. The planners of the Kargil operation decided to seize these posts in March and April 1999 – well before they could be reoccupied by Indian troops. This infiltrating force of over a thousand Pakistani troops, none of whom were *jehadi* militants, executed an elaborate denial and deception campaign, completely avoiding detection by Indian patrols. The intruding forces were almost entirely drawn from the local area – NLI combat battalions logistically supported by Chitral and Bajaur Scouts – thus eliminating a large troop buildup, which would alert Indian military intelligence. To maintain secrecy, the intruding force operated mainly at night and during adverse weather conditions, used effective camouflage and concealment, restricted radio transmissions to the minimum, and operated in small groups. Civilian clothing and radio transmissions in Balti and Pashtu languages were a deliberate part of a larger Pakistani strategy to create the impression that the intruding forces were *jehadi* militants, thus enabling the Pakistan army to retain surprise and secrecy for as long as possible. Troops in mufti also provided an element of deniability when surprise was lost, allowing Pakistani officials to disown the operation even after the militants withdrew back across the LoC. Pakistan's military planners maintained strict secrecy about the Kargil plan, and excluded other parts of the government, including the navy, air force, and the Inter-Services Intelligence Directorate (ISID), from the decision-making loop. A compulsion for secrecy, initial exclusion of key national security institutions, and the *jehadi* deception, all of which were deemed necessary for the plan to succeed, significantly limited

---

[47] Qadir, "An Analysis of the Kargil Conflict 1999."

Pakistan's options when it was forced to respond to India's counterattack and international political pressure.

The 1999 crisis

In many respects, the Kargil gambit was a victim of its own success. By the end of April 1999, the intruding force had occupied approximately 130 posts in the Dras, Mushkoh, Kaksar, Batalik, and Chorbat La sectors of Kargil, covering an approximate area of 65 miles in depth and 5 to 6 miles in width. Some of the captured positions directly overlooked National Highway 1A, which ran between Srinagar and Leh, and were in a position to interdict the road with artillery and long-range small-arms fire. This far exceeded the original plan to seize 25 to 30 posts in a much smaller swathe of territory closer to the LoC. As Major General Nadeem Ahmed, who took command of FCNA after the Kargil conflict, told us, "mission creep" was a major problem. There was a "compulsion" to push patrols forward, and thus "we got a little overstretched." "In the mountains, you cannot do anything more than is planned," Major General Nadeem remarked.[48]

The Indian army first learned about the intrusions through unofficial sources on 3 May 1999 and four days later confirmed that some intrusion had taken place.[49] The Indian army's initial attempts to retrieve the heights, which they initially believed were held by Kashmiri militants, were rebuffed. As information moved up to senior command levels, Indian officials soon began to realize that things were more serious than they initially had estimated. Local commanders maneuvered their forces to detect and engage the intruders and launched patrols to determine

---

[48] Briefing by FCNA Commander Maj. Gen. Nadeem Ahmed to CCC research team, 12 January 2003.

[49] Like nearly all aspects of the Kargil conflict, the actual start of hostilities is controversial. V. P. Malik, India's army chief in 1999, has written that because Indian field units were slow to report enemy engagements to command elements, and because Indian intelligence agencies believed the enemy to be militant *jehadis* rather than Pakistani soldiers, senior Indian civilian and military authorities did not have a clear understanding of events until the third week of May. Malik, *Kargil: From Surprise to Victory*, 105–112. In its quasi-official report on the conflict, the Kargil Review Committee stated that two local shepherds first observed the enemy in the Jubar Hill area of the Batalik sector on 3 May and that 3 Punjab battalion confirmed the intrusion on 7 May. The first recorded combat was on 6 May, when a 12 Jat patrol was ambushed in the Turtok sector. Kargil Review Committee, *From Surprise to Reckoning*, 98–99. Pakistani officers indicate that the first hostile encounter actually occurred on 30 April. Nadeem briefing, 12 January 2003. In interviews with the CCC research team, Indian military sources confirmed that this indeed was the first military contact, but explained that it went unreported in India because of a battalion command decision.

the extent of the Pakistani intrusion. Due to poor intelligence, non-acclimatized troops, a shortage of high-altitude equipment, and coordination difficulties, Indian troops suffered heavy casualties during this initial stage of the conflict.

The Indian army launched a major counteroffensive during the third week of May 1999, codenamed Operation *Vijay* (Victory). On 26 May, the Indian air force commenced air strikes in support of ground troops, vertically escalating the conflict. To intensify strategic pressure on Pakistan, Indian troops began mobilizing to war locations in other parts of the country, which included the deployment of troops along the India–Pakistan international border. The Indian navy was deployed against an unprepared Pakistan navy, and also positioned itself for a blockade around Karachi, an event that could have been disastrous especially because its energy reserves were then dangerously low.[50] In the mountains, Pakistani planners had assumed that the Zojila Pass, India's main access route from the Kashmir Valley to the northern LoC in Ladakh, would remain blocked with snow from mid-November to early June, as it normally does. However, in 1999 the Zojila Pass opened in early May, thus facilitating the Indian army's early induction of troops, supporting units, and logistics necessary for the counteroffensive (including 19,000 tons of ammunition).

After several failed attempts to dislodge Pakistani forces from the mountain heights, India achieved its first military success during the third week of June when it captured a pair of posts along the Tololing Ridge in the Dras sector. The Tololing complex was Pakistan's deepest penetration in the Dras sector and strategically the most significant. From high atop their mountain posts Pakistani soldiers could interdict India's buildup along Highway 1A, severely restricting the movement of Indian soldiers to other posts along the LoC. After nearly a week of intense hand-to-hand fighting, India's 56 Mountain Brigade captured point 4590 on 17 June and then point 5140 on 20 June, thereby taking control of the entire Tololing Ridge. This achievement was a turning point for the counteroffensive, because now that Indian troops had a foothold inside Pakistan's linear defenses, they could more deliberately clear out the other lightly defended and poorly positioned outposts scattered along the ridgelines. Ultimately, Pakistan's tactically weak defense plan combined with inadequate manpower, equipment, and logistical support made sustaining

---

[50] Briefing by Commander P. K. Ghosh, Indian navy, to CCC research team, Institute for Defence and Strategic Analyses, New Delhi, India, 30 September 2002. See also Anil Bhat, "Full Steam Ahead," *Rashtriya Sahara English Monthly* (Delhi), December 1999, 54–57.

the intrusion practically impossible against sustained Indian attacks.[51] Several more posts were captured in the Dras, Batalik, and Mushkoh sectors before combat operations concluded and Pakistani forces began their withdrawal on 12 July.

As the Indian military reclaimed more territory, Pakistani prime minister Nawaz Sharif found himself under increasing international pressure to pull back all Pakistani forces from the Indian side of the Line of Control. After a rushed and uninvited visit to Washington, DC on 4 July, Sharif signed the Washington Declaration with President Clinton and agreed to vacate the captured territory. On 11 July, the Directors General of Military Operations (DGMOs) of the Indian and Pakistan armies met at the Attari border checkpoint, where the Pakistani DGMO agreed to commence a sector-by-sector withdrawal the following day and complete it by 16 July, a date that later was extended by a day at Pakistan's request. Pakistanis insist that this ceasefire was not implemented in good faith, and that their forces along the LoC suffered casualties throughout July. Indians counter that the use of force was only authorized to counter resistance or to attack positions where Pakistani troops remained deployed across the LoC after the ceasefire had expired. All remaining pockets were cleared on 25 July, and, on the following day, the Indian DGMO declared at a press conference that all Pakistani intrusions had been vacated in the Kargil sector, thereby marking an official end to the conflict.

The Kargil conflict is significant not only for what happened, but also for what did not occur in 1999 and in subsequent years. Rather than moving toward mutual deterrence secured through arms control, as the United States and the Soviet Union did after the Cuban missile crisis, India and Pakistan suspended all dialogue after Kargil, ramped up their production of nuclear weapons and missile delivery systems, and accelerated preparations for conventional war, which nearly occurred in January 2002 and again in May 2002.[52] The behavior of India and Pakistan during and after the Kargil conflict, therefore, offers important new insights about the political–military behavior of competing states equipped with nuclear weapons and engaged in an enduring rivalry. Kargil also illuminates new realities about the conflict-management strategies of international actors when confronted with the risk of a regional

---

[51] For critical analyses of Pakistan's operational tactics at Kargil, see Acosta, "High Altitude Warfare," 35–41; and chapters 2 and 3 of this book.

[52] The near war of 2002 is the subject of another CCC book project: "Crisis and Escalation in South Asia: The 2002 India–Pakistan Military Standoff" (book manuscript in preparation).

Neither the military balance nor the prospect of nuclear war had much effect on strategic calculations in 1999, although they played very significant roles during the subsequent military crisis in 2001–2002.[77]

Arms control

The sixth expectation of the theory of the nuclear revolution – that nuclear rivals will pursue arms control to stabilize their strategic competition – has not yet been realized in the aftermath of the Kargil crisis. Chapters 12 and 13, written by Basrur and Rizvi, respectively, explain how the Kargil episode taught key constituencies in India and Pakistan important lessons about needed improvements in their military force structure, planning, training, and equipment, as well as about intelligence deficiencies and other strategic issues, such as the role the United States, China, and other concerned parties are likely to play in future crises. These lessons had a powerful influence on the behavior of each country during their 2001–2002 military standoff. And they still shape the way India and Pakistan conduct their strategic rivalry at present. But very low, if anywhere, among these lessons is the recognition that arms control ought to be pursued to reduce the costs, dangers, and risks of strategic rivalry.[78]

True enough, New Delhi and Islamabad have come together in recent years to discuss nuclear risk-reduction measures and even to sign in October 2005 an agreement to notify each other in advance of ballistic missile flight tests. But these moves have largely been at the behest of the international community, and do not yet reflect a transformation of security thinking along the lines that occurred (eventually) between the United States and the Soviet Union after the Cuban missile crisis. In February 2004, India and Pakistan agreed to resume their composite dialogue on normalization of bilateral relations, which had been agreed in the February 1999 Lahore Declaration, but which had been suspended since the Kargil conflict. As part of this dialogue, dozens of senior-level and working group meetings have been held, but none has of yet produced

---

[77] Malik explains the various considerations that led India's civilian leadership to insist on military restraint throughout the Kargil crisis, and observes: "The nuclear factor too must have been weighing on the minds of the prime minister and his CCS colleagues, though this aspect was never mentioned or discussed in the meetings." Malik, *Kargil: From Surprise to Victory*, 126.

[78] For background on impediments to arms control between India and Pakistan, see Peter R. Lavoy, "South Asia," in *Arms Control: Cooperative Security in a Changing Environment*, ed. Jeffrey A. Larsen (Boulder, Colo.: Lynne Rienner, 2002), 241–252; and Zafar Nawaz Jaspal, "Arms Control: Risk Reduction Measures between India and Pakistan," *SASSU Research Paper* no. 1, University of Bradford, June 2005, www.brad.ac.uk/acad/sassu/publications/ZJ_research_paper_no1.pdf.

Table 1.1 *The Kargil conflict's implications for nuclear-deterrence theory*

Expectation	Outcome	Comment
1. No war between nuclear powers	Mixed	Armed conflict occurred, but remained limited.
2. No nuclear threats to gain territory	Positive	Neither side seriously threatened nuclear use; the nuclear stability–instability paradox did not motivate the Kargil operation.
3. No initiation or escalation of crises	Mixed	A crisis and limited conflict occurred, but escalation was controlled.
4. Durability of status quo	Very positive	The territorial status quo was soundly preserved.
5. Irrelevance of balance of power	Mixed	The conventional military imbalance did not cause Pakistan's withdrawal, but neither did the prospect of nuclear war.
6. Initiation of arms control	Negative	Real arms control remains elusive, even long after Kargil.

major breakthroughs. However, if India and Pakistan do move toward a more formal strategic restraint regime, it is likely to take place through the auspices of the composite dialogue.

This book thus presents important findings for the theory of the nuclear revolution, but many of them are nuanced, apparently contradictory, and cannot be expressed in simple statements. At the risk of glossing over important complexities and fine distinctions, Table 1.1 summarizes six of the book's key findings for this theory. Beyond this theoretical stocktaking exercise, however, readers are encouraged to consider a perspective that all of our authors have had to entertain, and that Robert Jervis examines head on in chapter 15: deterrence optimists and proliferation pessimists are each right and each wrong in various respects.

Deterrence theory does explain much of Indian and Pakistani strategic behavior both during and after the Kargil conflict, but mainly in a dialectical manner. That is, a nuclear revolution is taking place, but only gradually through risky moves, dangerous crises, and limited conflicts, all of which modify prevailing strategic structures and beliefs. Unlike the US–Soviet strategic rivalry, which was a twin born with nuclear weapons, the India–Pakistan rivalry preceded the introduction of nuclear weapons, and thus the impact of the nuclear revolution has been slow and uneven. Proliferation pessimists can point to a series of military crises in the late 1980s and 1990s, including the Kargil conflict, to indicate the dangers of the India–Pakistan nuclear rivalry and slowness of these nations to engage in fundamental nuclear learning. On the other hand, deterrence optimists can rightly point to considerable expressions of caution and restraint during difficult times and real improvements in the safety, security, and nonuse of the region's nuclear forces to bolster their understanding of South Asia's strategic stability.

In true dialectical fashion, each of these interpretations – thesis and antithesis – have merit. The key to the matter is the fact that India and Pakistan generally fought the Kargil conflict as if were just another in the long line of their bilateral conventional military crises, whereas the rest of the world viewed the dangerous developments of the summer of 1999 as a nuclear crisis. Remarkably, Kargil was just the beginning of true nuclear learning in India and Pakistan. After Pakistani forces withdrew back to their side of the Line of Control and the crisis subsided, both countries, but particularly India, began the process of developing integrated deterrence strategies and started to think more seriously about nuclear weapons, strategy, command and control, and actual nuclear operations. Most crucially, however, is the nature of the synthesis, the eventual culminating condition of the enduring strategic competition between India and Pakistan. Will the dialectical struggle end in nuclear war or a fundamental realization of the implications of the nuclear revolution? Of course, this question can be answered only with the passage of time.

Part 1

Causes and conduct of the conflict

2   The strategic context of the Kargil conflict: a Pakistani perspective

Zafar Iqbal Cheema

Introduction

Pakistan's motivation for conducting the Kargil operation has long been a matter of controversy, especially for most outside observers. Why would the Pakistan government and army jeopardize the peace process with India that came alive in February 1999 after many decades of failed starts and unsatisfactory conclusions? Why would Islamabad risk a major war with India – one that could have escalated to the exchange of nuclear weapons – for a relatively small reorientation of the Kashmir Line of Control? And finally, why was the Pakistan government never able to convince the international community with a compelling rationale for its military action? The list of unanswered questions remains long, even today, despite the publication of competing narratives by Pakistani, Indian, and American authors. In retrospect, the risks of the Kargil intrusion and the costs of the military clash with India would seem to far outweigh any potential gains that the Kargil planners could have imagined. So why did they do it? This chapter argues that the conditions that compelled Pakistani military officers to mount the Kargil operation were symptomatic of the conflict over Kashmir enmeshed into broader strategic rivalry of an enduring security struggle between India and Pakistan, and thus can only be understood through the prism of the broad historical, geographical, and strategic compulsions of the conflict over Kashmir.

The Kargil operation was one of many military crises occurring between India and Pakistan since the two nations signed a peace accord at Simla in 1972. It can be seen as a consequence of the non-resolution of the Kashmir conflict between dyadic rivals in the international subsystem. Essentially this operation was launched by Pakistan to gain an advantageous position vis-à-vis India in the northern areas along the Line of Control (LoC), which separates Indian-administered Kashmir from Pakistani-administered Kashmir. Although geographically confined to the northern region of the Kashmir LoC, the crisis rapidly deepened with the induction of greater troops and air support by India. The crisis

41

had the potential to escalate into a total war with the possibility of a nuclear exchange. Pakistan was isolated in the international community, which did not view this crisis in a narrow military sense. Rather, it was concerned about the prospect of a nuclear catastrophe in a volatile and important region of the world. Indian and Pakistani crises were not unfamiliar to the international community, but the timing of the crisis in the wake of the nuclear tests presented an entirely new dimension that distinguished the Kargil crisis from previous crises.

This chapter is confined to analyzing the strategic context of the Kargil conflict and describes the framework in which the Kargil intrusion occurred. It examines the experiences and beliefs that led Kargil's planners to conclude that an aggressive "preemptive defense" strategy was desirable. It places the military operation in the larger context of the Kashmir dispute and specifically examines the troubled Indo-Pakistani confrontation in the Northern Areas. The first three sections of this chapter place the Kashmir conflict in historical perspective, define the establishment of the ceasefire line, and explain the outcome of the wars between India and Pakistan that established the Line of Control. The following section describes the geographical and operational environment of the Northern Areas, within which the Pakistani 10 Corps, Force Command Northern Areas (FCNA), and the Indian 15 Corps operate. It then elucidates the Siachen Glacier operations of 1984, which the Pakistan armed forces have viewed as the basis of ongoing conflict in the rugged northern areas of Kashmir. The next section discusses the dynamics of the LoC in the context of renewed Kashmiri uprisings in the 1990s and a series of Indian attacks across the LoC on the Neelum Valley. Finally, the chapter presents the Government of Pakistan's officially stated reason for mounting the operations and then critically analyzes the basis and timing of the operation.

The historical rationale

In a broader historical and political sense, the Kargil conflict was an outgrowth of the Indo-Pakistani dispute over Kashmir – a dispute that has remained on the UN agenda for over fifty years, a *casus belli* for wars in 1948 and 1965, and a serious military crisis in 1990. Despite sixty years of independence, the Kashmir dispute is still hotly debated and contested. Kashmir was a princely state contiguous to Pakistan with a dominant Muslim majority but whose maharajah acceded to India under the pressures of war in 1947 without taking into account the wishes of its people. Pakistan has long believed it has moral, political, historical, and strategic reasons to stake a claim to Kashmir, which was taken by India through conspiracy and deception during the 1947 division of the Indian subcontinent. Pakistan states that the Hindu maharajah was coerced to accede to India to justify its veritable invasion and continued occupation.[1] Pakistan accuses India of not honoring United Nations resolutions to hold a plebiscite for ascertaining the wishes of the people of Kashmir or bilateral pledges to resolve the Kashmir dispute.

Kashmir is a strategically important area. It borders China's two most volatile western provinces – Tibet and Xingjian. Kashmir's geographical location is critical to Pakistan because India maintains upstream control of all rivers flowing into Pakistan. More importantly, control over Kashmir is central to the national ideologies of both India and Pakistan. For Pakistan, because Kashmir was a Muslim-majority princely state, it should naturally have opted for accession to it, based on the principle that was the basis for the division of British India into two countries, India (Bharat) and Pakistan. Kashmir has taken on such enormous political and psychological proportions that it is hard to imagine any Pakistani leader agreeing to give up this cause. On the other hand, India sees Kashmir's inclusion in the Indian state as secular credentials of its national myth. If Kashmir were to become part of Pakistan or even gain independence, Indian officials believe that they would be hard pressed to resist other religious or ethnic minorities from seeking their own exclusion from the Indian state, through either enhanced autonomy or outright secession.

The Kashmir dispute and ceasefire line

Kashmir, one of the many princely states of British India, was asked by the departing British colonial government to accede to either India or Pakistan at the time of the subcontinent's independence in 1947. When the princely states of Junagadh and Hyderabad resisted joining India, the new Indian government used military force to take control, justifying this extreme move on the grounds that the majority of people in those states were Hindus and wanted to accede to India against the wishes of their "autocratic" Muslim rulers. India applied different criteria in regard to the political disposition of the state of Jammu and Kashmir, arguing that the "autocratic" Maharajah of Kashmir, who was a Hindu, had the legitimate authority to accede to India, without regard to the wishes of the vast majority of the people, who were Muslims.[2]

[1] India's claim that the maharajah signed an instrument of accession has never been substantiated and no such document has been made public.
[2] See Victoria Schofield's *Kashmir in Conflict: India, Pakistan and the Unfinished War* (London: I. B. Tauris, 2000), and *Afghan Frontier: Feuding and Fighting in Central Asia* (New York: Palgrave Macmillan, 2003), 243–247.

Failure to resolve the Kashmir issue led to the first war between India and Pakistan in 1948. This conflict produced a military stalemate, but when the ground situation appeared to be going against India, Indian prime minister Jawaharlal Nehru approached the United Nations Security Council in an attempt to resolve the political and territorial dispute over Kashmir.[3] The Security Council decided that the accession of Kashmir to India or Pakistan must be decided by the Kashmiri people through a plebiscite.[4] Nehru and subsequent Indian leaders gradually reneged from their promise of a plebiscite (although, to be sure, other UNSC terms also remained unfulfilled), but continued to accept the disputed nature of Kashmir.[5]

The stalemate of the 1948 war led to a suspension of hostilities and the establishment of the Cease-Fire Line (CFL) that took effect on 1 January 1949. The CFL was delimited in general terms in the Karachi Agreement, formally signed on 27 July 1949 by military representatives under the auspices of the Truce Sub-Committee of the United Nations Commission of India and Pakistan (UNICIP), which was mutually verified on the ground with the aid of UN military observers and completed on 3 November 1949. As Robert Wirsing observes, "The CFL possessed very few of the attributes of a permanent boundary. It was wholly military in conception; and, drawn on the basis of positions held by the combatants at the time fighting between them ended, it was clearly designed for temporary use. Over most of its length, it followed no natural geographic barrier or traditional political boundary; and it was viewed officially by both countries as a temporary line, limited in function and, in principle, subject at some future date to a more rational and permanent division."[6]

---

[3] UNSC Resolution 47 of 21 April 1948, accepted by India, states that the Security Council, "Noting with satisfaction that both India and Pakistan desire the question of the accession of Jammu and Kashmir to India or Pakistan should be decided through the democratic method of a free and impartial plebiscite ... Recommends to the Governments of India and Pakistan the following measures as those which in the opinion of the Council are appropriate to bring about a cessation of the fighting and create proper conditions for a free and impartial plebiscite to decide whether the State of Jammu and Kashmir is to accede to India or Pakistan ..." See Official Records of the UN Security Council, Third Year, 286th meeting, 21 April 1948 (Document S/726).

[4] India initially accepted the principle of a plebiscite. Prime Minister Nehru stated in 1952, "We have taken the issue to the United Nations and given our word of honor for a peaceful solution. As a great nation, we cannot go back on that. We have left the question for final solution to the people of Kashmir and we are determined to abide by their decision." *Amrita Bazar Patrika* (Calcutta), 2 January 1952.

[5] The resolution continues by laying out specific steps that the governments of Pakistan and India should take in preparation for a free and impartial plebiscite. Official Records of the UN Security Council, Third Year, 286th meeting, 21 April 1948 (Document S/726).

[6] Robert G. Wirsing, *India, Pakistan, and the Kashmir Dispute* (New York: St. Martins, 1994), 62.

The CFL extended from a point west of the Chenab near Chamb in Jammu in a rough arc of about 500 miles north and then northeastward to a point (map coordinate NJ 9842) approximately 12 miles north of the Shyok River in the Saltaro Range of the Karakoram mountains.[7] To its south, the boundary stretches about 124 miles to what was the pre-independence boundary between Kashmir and Punjab (now Pakistan). This stretch now lies between the CFL and the international border and is commonly referred to in Pakistan as the "working boundary." Overall, there were three distinct types of boundary situations to contend with in Kashmir: no demarcation in the extreme north (40 miles); ceasefire line (500 miles); and working boundary (124 miles).[8] The Karachi Agreement also defined the rules of engagement along the CFL. During peacetime, both Indian and Pakistani militaries made Standing Operating Procedures, recognized each other's positions, and followed the agreement in letter and spirit. From January 1949 onwards, the UN deployed an observer group, the United Nations Military Observer Group in India and Pakistan (UNMOGIP), to monitor the ceasefire between India and Pakistan.[9]

The Second Kashmir War

India and Pakistan fought their second war over Kashmir in 1965, the outcome of which was another stalemate. The path toward this war was set when India and Pakistan failed to resolve the dispute in the early 1960s. The administration of US president John F. Kennedy tried to broker a settlement of the Kashmir dispute but failed. The US delegation leader Averil Harriman concluded, "the trouble was that the terms for a settlement acceptable to Pakistan were unacceptable to India ... [and] the chances of successful Kashmir negotiations [were] quite remote."[10] The perception in Pakistan is that the US did not exert enough pressure on India, which allowed it successfully to cope with the difficult environment in the aftermath of the 1962 conflict with China.

Two developments at this time had major consequences for Kashmir. India's defeat at the hands of China in 1962 was followed by Pakistan's

---

[7] The CFL was not demarcated beyond NJ 9842 and stopped well short of the international border with China that lies 40 miles to the north, if measured against the boundary agreed in the Border Agreement of 1963 between China and Pakistan. *Ibid.* 75.

[8] *Ibid.* 76.

[9] Department of Public Information, United Nations, "United Nations Military Observers Group India and Pakistan," www.un.org/Depts/dpko/missions/unmogip/.

[10] Dennis Kux, *The United States and Pakistan 1947–2000: Disenchanted Allies* (Washington, DC: Woodrow Wilson Center Press, 2001), 135.

rapprochement and border agreement with China leading to a long-term Sino-Pakistan friendship. After successive failures for a political resolution of the Kashmir dispute, General Ayub Khan's government decided to use military force to break the resultant impasse. India's retreat in the Rann of Kutch area in the spring of 1965 presented what Pakistani defense planners took as a golden opportunity to apply military force.[11] Feroz Hassan Khan, Peter R. Lavoy, and Christopher Clary point out in chapter 3 of this book that after initial reluctance, Ayub Khan allowed the establishment of the newly created, secret Kashmir cell, headed by Mr. Aziz Ahmad, a career diplomat and friend of Foreign Minister Zulfiqar Ali Bhutto, to devise a plan for cropping insurgency in the Indian-held Kashmir. In the summer of 1965, four individuals – Ayub Khan, Zulfiqar Ali Bhutto, Aziz Ahmad, and army commander Akhtar Hussein Malik of the 12 Infantry Division – met in the hill station of Murree to approve *Operation Gibraltar*, an operation to infiltrate troops across the ceasefire line to foment uprisings in Kashmir and engage in protracted guerrilla warfare.[12] This was to be followed by another operation, code-named *Grand Slam*, which was intended to capture Akhnur in order to sever the only road link between India and Kashmir. The infiltration began during the night on 5–6 August 1965. Two days later, on 7 August, Pakistan infiltrators raided the Kargil area with the intention of cutting Indian road links between Srinagar and Ladakh. This was a diversionary attack meant to force India to react and thereby divert resources, which would affect its operations in southern Kashmir.[13]

Pakistan's operational planning in 1965 was confined to a handful of individuals. This is analogous to the situation that prevailed in Pakistan prior to the initiation of the Kargil cross-border operation in early 1999. Another similarity was that the 1965 and 1999 operations were planned to succeed at the local level, without much residual thought to the strategic repercussions. Pakistan completely miscalculated India's reaction. In both cases, New Delhi perceived Pakistan's actions as a threat to its national integrity. In the first instance, the Indian army attacked across the international border toward Lahore on 6 September 1965. Pakistani planners' inability to foresee a possible Indian attack across the international border was a major miscalculation, which adversely affected the outcome of the war from its perspective. Like Kargil, it also did not adequately assess the likely reactions of its Western allies, most notably

---

[11] Brian Cloughley, *A History of the Pakistan Army: Wars and Insurrections* (Oxford University Press, 1999), 61.

[12] For details of the 1965 war and *Operation Gibraltar*, see *ibid.* 50–123.   [13] *Ibid.* 69.

the United States, and subsequently found itself isolated. The United States not only failed to support Pakistan, but also placed an arms embargo. Pakistan underestimated India's reaction to its operations and its dependence on its Western allies. Pakistan also failed to learn from the mistakes it made in 1965 and repeated them in 1999. Pakistan did not anticipate India's vertical escalation of the Kargil conflict by inducting major arms, especially Bofors guns, and the air force.

The 1972 Simla Agreement and the Line of Control

After a third war in 1971 over East Pakistan (now Bangladesh), both countries signed a new agreement in Simla on 2 July 1972. India insists that the Simla Agreement is the main point of reference for resolving Indo-Pakistani disputes, a contention that the United States and most Western governments accept but Pakistan rejects. Nevertheless, Article 6 of the accord reaffirms the disputed status of Kashmir, in terms of a larger list of outstanding issues:

Both Governments agree that their respective Heads will meet again at a mutually convenient time in the future and that, in the meanwhile, the representatives of the two sides will meet to discuss further modalities and arrangements for the establishment of durable peace and normalization of relations, including the questions of repatriation of prisoners of war and civilian internees, a final settlement of the Jammu and Kashmir and resumption of diplomatic relations.[14]

New Delhi and Islamabad started to disagree on the interpretation of the Simla Agreement before its ink could dry. India asserts that its relations with Pakistan are governed through a bilateral framework envisioned in the Simla Agreement. As a result, Pakistan has lost the right to raise the Kashmir dispute in the United Nations or any other multilateral forum. This argument is derived from Article 1 (ii) of the Simla Agreement, which states:

That the two countries are resolved to settle their differences by peaceful means through bilateral negotiations or any other peaceful means mutually agreed upon between them. Pending the final settlement of any of the problems between the two countries, they shall not unilaterally alter the situation and both shall prevent the organization, assistance or encouragement of any acts detrimental to the maintenance of peaceful and harmonious relations.[15]

---

[14] Text of the Agreement on Bilateral Relations between the Government of India and Government of Pakistan, signed by Prime Minister Indira Gandhi and President Zulfiqar Ali Bhutto in Simla on 2 July 1972, available at www.stimson.org/southasia/?sn=sa20020114291.

[15] *Ibid.* Article 1 (ii).

Pakistan, however, points to Article 1(i) of the Simla Agreement, which states, "That the principles and purposes of the Charter of the United Nations shall govern the relations between the two countries."[16] As a consequence, Pakistan claims that Article 1(ii) does not annul the relevant UN Security Council resolutions pertaining to Kashmir. Thus, for Islamabad, the political status of Kashmir remains a very live issue. If India refused to permit an international negotiation process to settle the issue to the satisfaction of all concerned parties, then Pakistan must find innovative ways to bring India to the negotiating table. The Kargil conflict can be seen as part of a broader problem of managing and securing a contested "boundary," with both parties searching for political and military advantages wherever possible.[17]

The Simla Agreement renamed and realigned the 1948 positions, and henceforth, the CFL was renamed the Line of Control (LoC). This was done under Article 4(ii) of the Simla Agreement. It states: "In Jammu and Kashmir, the line of control (LoC) resulting from the ceasefire of December 19, 1971 shall be respected by both sides without prejudice to the recognized position of either side."[18] Much like the former CFL, the LoC has three distinct parts. The first part, approximately 128 miles long, delineates the boundary between Indian-administered Kashmir and Pakistan, and is referred to as the Working Boundary by Pakistan. It runs from Border Pillar 1 at the Sialkot border to the Chamb sector north of the Marala headworks.[19] The second segment, about 500 miles long, meanders northeastward to Pt. NJ 9842 due east of the Shyok River in the north. This segment gains height as it proceeds northward. The third portion, about 40 miles long, linking NJ 9842 to its culmination on the Chinese border, was left undemarcated due to the inaccessibility of the area.[20]

After the Simla Agreement, India unilaterally terminated the supervision of the LoC by UNMOGIP, although Pakistan continues to cooperate with the UN observers on its side of the LoC. The Simla Agreement makes no mention of the role of UNMOGIP; however, Simla did not explicitly disestablish UNMOGIP nor repudiate the UN resolutions. As a

---

[16] *Ibid.* Article 1(i).
[17] Words matter in this dispute. Boundary connotes a settlement with some permanence, the "ceasefire line" implied the position of forces with a potential for negotiated settlement, while the "line of control" reflects only the ground reality of where forces were stationed at the end of the 1971 war.
[18] Agreement on Bilateral Relations, Article 4(ii).
[19] After 1972, India ceased to refer to this portion as the working boundary.
[20] Uerinder Grover and Ranjana Arora, eds., *Events and Documents of Indo-Pak Relations* (New Delhi: Deep & Deep, 1999), 511.

result, both sides walked away from the Simla negotiations with different reinterpretations of the role of the UN resolutions and UNMOGIP in regard to Kashmir and the LoC.[21] From a Pakistani perspective, UNMOGIP could play no role when India occupied the Siachen Glacier in 1984. Similarly, this body failed to play any constructive role during the Kargil crisis. However, Pakistan has not effectively and persuasively raised the issue of India's termination of the supervision of the UNMOGIP at the United Nations despite a strong case in its favor.

From India's point of view, the Simla pact removed the role of third parties in the dispute and instead confined the issue as a bilateral disagreement between India and Pakistan. Further, Simla committed both parties to refrain from using force to resolve that dispute. For Pakistan, however, India almost immediately violated the "sanctity" of the LoC. As Shireen Mazari points out, "India seriously undermined – I would contend *de facto* destroyed – the Simla Agreement almost immediately after it was signed, when, in 1972, the Indian military crossed the LoC in the Chorbat La sector and established three to four posts, about 1 mile into the Pakistan side (around 4 square miles)."[22] India was able to seize this territory because Pakistani forces were thinned out around Chorbat La, and were unable to secure all approaches. India seized four Pakistani posts in the Qamar sector across the LoC in 1988. India again captured the "Anzbari feature" near Kanzalwan in 1992, returned it after hotline talks between the Directors General of Military Operations, but then recaptured it again after the Kargil conflict.[23] (See Map 2.1 showing Indian ingress before the Kargil conflict and Pakistan intrusion afterwards.)

FCNA and the Northern Areas

The Kargil sector is divided into Batalik, Dras, Kaksar, and Mushkoh sub-sectors and extends over a frontage of 104 miles along the LoC from Kaobal Gali to Chorbat La. The Batalik sub-sector, consisting of Chorbat La, the Jubar Ridge, Eastern sub-sector, and Central sub-sector, lies on the Ladakh Range between the Indus and Shyok rivers about 30 miles north of Leh. It dominates the Indus Valley and the old trade route from Gilgit to Ladakh, and the Shyok Valley, which leads to Siachen from Pakistan-held Kashmir. It is the second highest battlefield in the world after the Siachen, with altitudes between 16,000 to 18,000 feet. The main

[21] Wirsing, *India, Pakistan, and the Kashmir Dispute*, 68–75.
[22] Shireen M. Mazari, *The Kargil Conflict 1999: Separating Fact from Fiction* (Islamabad: Ferozsons, 2003), 24.
[23] *Ibid.*

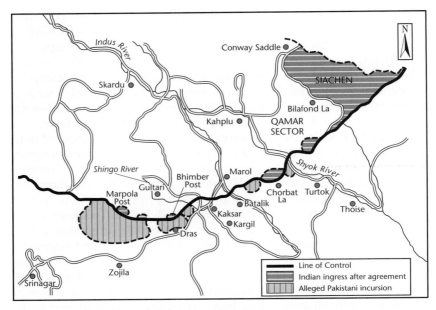

Map 2.1 Indian ingress after 1972 and alleged Pakistani incursion

Pakistani logistic bases are at Olingathang and Mian Lungpa. The main features on the Indian side of the LoC are the Jubar Ridge, Turtok, Chorbat La, and Yaldor.[24] The Jubar Ridge consists of Tharu and the Jubar heights, a dominating feature that extends about 4 miles. The area was occupied by India during the 1971 war. Chorbat La sits along the northernmost stretches of the Line of Control in the Ladakh region of Indian-administered Kashmir.

The Indian state of Jammu and Kashmir consists of two other provinces in addition to Ladakh: the Kashmir Valley and Jammu. The valley and Jammu each consist of six districts and each has a population of around 4 million. They are spread over an area of 6,156 and 10,150 square miles respectively. In contrast, Ladakh consists of two districts (Leh and Kargil), with a sparse population of only 17,000, and covers an area of 37,327 square miles.[25] To the west of Chorbat La lies the Indian town of Kargil. The Kargil heights are very militarily significant, as they overlook Indian National Highway 1A, the only strategic connector

---

[24] *Indian Defense Yearbook 2000* (New Delhi: Natraj Publishers, 2000).

[25] Kargil Review Committee, *From Surprise to Reckoning: The Kargil Review Committee Report* (New Delhi: Sage, 2000), 35–36. Also see *Friday Times*, 5 August 1999.

between the Ladakh province and the valley. The terrain along the LoC in this area is mostly high altitude, glaciated, mountainous, avalanched, desolate, and uninhabited desert. It is the weather that largely rules these wastelands.

On the Pakistani side of the Line of Control, the FCNA is tasked with the defense of a 109-mile stretch from the Conway Saddle to Anzbari and to deny India success in prospective "hot pursuit" and commando operations. The four main approaches in the FCNA area are the Siachen Glacier, Shyok Valley, Indus Valley, and Kaksar-Shaqma-Gultari-Burzil Pass (Shaqma is a village in the valley northwest of Kaksar, between Kaksar and Buniyal).[26]

The FCNA area of responsibility is divided into four sectors: (1) the Baltoro sector, which is northwest of the Siachen Glacier and controls K2 and other high peaks; (2) the Dansum-Shyok sector, which abuts the Siachen Glacier; (3) the Skardu sector, from where Batalik and Kargil are visible from some Pakistani positions; and (4) the Minimarg sector, which can be reinforced only through the Burzil Pass. Portions of Indian NH-1A are visible from several Pakistani positions throughout FCNA. From Shaqma, Pakistan is able to interdict the highway.[27]

From Gilgit to Skardu, roads running along the Indus River and its tributaries (Shingo and Shyok) provide the two axes of Gultari-Shaqma via the Burzil Pass (which closes during the winter) and Olingathang via Kharmang, respectively. A lateral road skirting Shaqma connects these two axes. For the denial of approaches through the Indus and Shingo valleys, Indians claim to have allotted an infantry battalion in each of the sub-sectors near Kargil from 121 Brigade (having four infantry battalions and one Border Security Force battalion) before the Kargil conflict.[28] However, the Indians left the unmanned gaps on the belief that it would not be viable for Pakistan to carry out any meaningful and sustained military incursion in such difficult terrain. These unmanned gaps were at the Mushkoh Valley (22 miles wide), Marpola to Bimbat (6 miles), Bimbat to Kaksar (5.6 miles), and Yaldor (15.5 miles from Batalik to Chorbat La).[29]

Since 1993, out of declared concerns over infiltration in the Mushkoh, Dras, and Batalik sub-sectors, India reinforced its military positions, bringing in additional forces to augment 121 Brigade and seal these areas during the summer months.[30] Dras is a small town located at an

---

[26] Briefing by FCNA Commander to the CCC research team, Gilgit, Pakistan, 13 January 2003.
[27] Ibid.   [28] Kargil Review Committee, *From Surprise to Reckoning*, 47–48.
[29] Ibid. 85–86.   [30] Ibid.

altitude of 10,800 feet on the Srinagar–Leh road (NH-1A), 40 miles west of Kargil. It is the second coldest inhabited place in the world, where the temperature drops to minus 60 degrees Celsius. In this area, the incursion took place at Pt. 4875, Tiger Hill, Pt. 4590, Black Rock, Tololing Top, Pt. 4051, and Pt. 5140. As Indian forces sought to vacate the intrusion, the Dras sector was a priority, because Pakistani troops were able to bring down accurate artillery fire around Kargil and Dras and along NH-1A.[31] The Tololing Top was one of the deepest penetrations in the Dras sector, and it directly dominated 2.5 miles of NH-1A.

The Kaksar sector lies between the Dras and Batalik sectors, and extends from Mushkoh to the Indus River. The main feature in this sector is the Bajrang Post at Pt. 5299. The Mushkoh Valley, like Kaksar, was militarily less important, since it did not dominate the Srinagar–Leh road.

Large-scale operations are not feasible in the Northern Areas. They require extensive logistical and troops buildup, which is impossible to achieve secretly. An operation has to be limited to one to two divisions, at most. Self-sufficiency of the forces is critical. Secrecy is of vital importance in any operation since with warning the defender could easily block any intrusion. Maintenance of logistics is critical for an offensive because at least three to four months of preparation are required to mount an offensive. Four to six weeks are required just to acclimatize troops.

The unique geography, climate, and terrain of the Northern Areas provide the backdrop for the Kargil operation. The region's uniquely rugged, extremely high-altitude terrain allows for an operation to occur in secret, whereas such preparations would be quickly noticed anywhere else along the Line of Control. Further, as the next section makes clear, those Pakistani troops entrusted with protecting the Northern Areas were struggling to find answers to difficult tactical and strategic quandaries as they jockeyed with India for position along the northern stretches of the LoC.

Contemporary rationale: the Siachen Glacier

The most blatant violation of the Simla Agreement by India was the occupation of two-thirds of the Siachen Glacier in 1984. As mentioned above, the Simla Agreement forbids the use of military force to occupy territory even if it is disputed or contentious. The controversy over the Siachen Glacier ensued because of the "imprecise" wording of the 1949

---

[31] See General V. P. Malik, *Kargil: From Surprise to Victory* (New Delhi: HarperCollins, 2006).

Karachi Agreement. The area was left undemarcated beyond point NJ 9842: "From Delunang onwards the cease-fire line (CFL) will follow the general line point 15495, Ishmam, Manus, Gangam Gunderman, point 13620, Junkar (Point 17628), Marmak, Natsara, Shungruti (Point 17531), Chorbat La (Point 16700), Chalunka (on the Shyok river), Khor, thence north to the glaciers."[32] The distance from point NJ 9842 up to the Chinese border is 40 miles.[33]

Both India and Pakistan interpret the statement "thence north to the glaciers" differently.[34] India maintains that the *de facto* border for the Siachen Glacier would extend northwesterly along the high crests separating watersheds.[35] According to this interpretation, the delineation would be along the Saltaro ridgeline up to the Chinese border in the vicinity of K2. The Saltaro Range is west of the great Karakoram Range, which begins at Sia Kangri and terminates at Shyok and Nubra Valley.[36] On the other hand, Pakistan argues that the LoC would extend beyond point NJ 9842 following immediately its previous course of direction. This northeasterly line places the Siachen Glacier within Pakistani-controlled territory, with the LoC terminating at the Karakoram Pass.[37] In this way, Pakistan considers the Siachen Glacier as the eastern extremity of Baltistan, while India takes it as a western boundary of the Nubra subdivision of the Ladakh district of Jammu and Kashmir.[38]

The Pakistani claim over the Siachen Glacier is supported by the fact that the majority of foreign mountaineering expeditions sought Pakistani permission to enter the area between 1974 and 1981.[39] Moreover, Pakistan points to the publication of successive editions of atlases and maps as evidence for its claim. Among others, the National Geographic Society, *Atlas of the World*, the *Times Atlas of the World*, and the *Historical Atlas of South Asia* depicted the LoC to extend from point NJ 9842 to the

---

[32] "Agreement between Military Representatives of India and Pakistan Regarding the Establishment of a Cease-Fire Line in the State of Jammu and Kashmir," 27 July 1949, available at http://kashmir-information.com/LegalDocs/KashmirCeasefire.html.

[33] Robert G. Wirsing, "The Siachen Glacier Dispute: Can Diplomacy Untangle It?" *Indian Defence Review* (July 1991): 95.

[34] Robert G. Wirsing, *Pakistan's Security under Zia, 1977–1988: The Policy Imperatives of a Peripheral Asian State* (New York: St. Martin's, 1991), 156.

[35] Maj. Gen. (retd.) Tariq Mahmud, "Siachen Dispute and Status of Northern Areas," *Defence Journal* 19, nos. 5–6 (1993): 21.

[36] Jasjit Singh, "Siachen Glacier: Facts and Fiction," *Strategic Studies* 12, no. 7 (1987): 667.

[37] Lt. Gen. (retd.) M. I. Chibber, "Siachen: The Untold Story (A Personal Account)," *Indian Defence Review* (July 1989): 146.

[38] Raspal S. Khosa, "The Siachen Glacier Dispute: Imbroglio on the Roof of the World," *Contemporary South Asia* 8, no. 2 (July 1999), 194.

[39] Wirsing, *Pakistan's Security under Zia*, 154.

Karakoram Pass. Perhaps more significantly, maps·produced by the US Defense Mapping Agency also used this delineation.[40]

In the 1971 war, a Pakistani position along the CFL in the northern areas was lost to the Indian army when the latter captured the area along the Shyok River, up to Turtok located just south of NJ 9842. In the early 1980s, the Pakistan army had observed frequent Indian intrusions into the Siachen Glacier area. In 1983, the Pakistan army dispatched a team from the Special Services Group (SSG) to confirm the reports. The team confirmed Indian intrusions and warned about the possibility of India occupying the glacier. Top-secret discussions began as to how to block potential Indian invasion. Pakistan would have preempted the Indian occupation, but the Operation Commander in the Force Command Northern Areas opposed the actions because of the harshness of the terrain.[41]

Pakistani planning for military operations in the Siachen area was deficient and was confined to only classified discussions in the General Headquarters (GHQ). One such meeting was held in December 1983, chaired by General Zia ul-Haq and attended by the then Corps Commander Lt. Gen. Jahan Dad Khan (Commander of Pakistan's 10 Corps from 15 March 1980 to 31 March 1984). This meeting discussed the ongoing developments in the Siachen Glacier area and contemplated various operational possibilities to deal with the situation. The meeting concluded that only limited operations were feasible in that area, and even these could not be conducted before May 1984.[42]

The Indians had however planned an operation to seize the glacier. The Indian army began the operation in April 1984 by deploying troops via helicopters. The first such troops landed on 13 April 1984, and India continued to build up forces in a systematic fashion over the subsequent months.[43] By the time the Pakistani side had estimated the scale, scope, and purpose of India's military operation and had readied itself for a military reaction, Indian forces had already occupied major passes on the Saltaro Range. The Pakistan army in general and the FCNA in

---

[40] Even the Kargil Review Committee noted that this "cartographic encroachment" had been "to India's detriment." *From Surprise to Reckoning*, 48–49.

[41] Pervez Musharraf, *In the Line of Fire: A Memoir* (New York: Simon and Schuster, 2006), 69.

[42] Lt. Gen. (retd.) Jahan Dad Khan, *Pakistan: Leadership Challenges* (Oxford University Press, 1999), cited in Lt. Gen. V. R. Raghavan, *Siachen: Conflict Without End* (New Delhi: Penguin Books, 2002), 51–52. Musharraf reinforces this timeline of Pakistani operational consideration, though he does not cite names. The 10 Corps Commander at the time was Lt. Gen. Jahan Dad Khan and the FCNA Commander was Maj. Gen. Pir Dad Khan; see Musharraf, *In the Line of Fire*, 69.

[43] Raghavan, *Siachen*, 53–54.

particular were deeply embarrassed by the loss of the Siachen Glacier to Indian forces. And this loss reinforced the central lesson to the Pakistani armed forces that vulnerable areas, even of questionable strategic value, must be defended at all costs.

Because the Indian army had occupied its military positions on the glacier with aerial operations, it became extremely difficult to sustain the logistics for these positions over time. In fact, India's challenge was far more difficult than Pakistan's, for Pakistani positions in the vicinity of the glacier were sustained by ground transportation and communications. Indian forces suffered far more casualties from environmental conditions than from hostile fire, since it took them three to seven days' travel over the Siachen Glacier before they could finally reach and maintain the passes. The Pakistanis, though late in arriving and having lost militarily important ground, had an advantage because of the shorter distance from their staging positions and the availability of a gravel road which reaches very close to Pakistani positions on the Saltaro Range – making sustenance of their posts relatively easy.[44]

Pakistan's "loss" of Siachen had immediate domestic political repercussions. The military government of Zia ul-Haq was facing domestic criticism at the time and the loss provided political ammunition for the young opposition leader, Benazir Bhutto.[45] Notwithstanding Pakistani domestic politics, the Zia government went to great lengths to highlight that the undemarcated area was by all counts a no man's land and India's annexation went against the Simla Agreement.

Since 1984, a series of military operations were conducted by both sides in the Northern Areas – in the *de jure* demarcated LoC and undemarcated area that includes Bilafond La, Sia La, and Saltaro Ridge, commonly referred to as the Siachen area. The Kashmir uprising in 1989–1990 compounded the LoC competition. In the Northern Areas a new military culture for dominance along the LoC took shape. All throughout the Northern Areas the militaries of India and Pakistan jockeyed for better tactical positions and operational advantages.

The Kashmir uprising: the Line of Control and the Neelum Valley

After India's 1984 operation to seize the glacier, both parties scrambled to ensure that any remaining large-scale tactical vulnerabilities were eliminated. The occupation of Siachen, combined with troubles in Punjab in

---

[44] *Ibid.* 69.   [45] *Ibid.* 37–38.

India and Sindh in Pakistan, began a dramatic deterioration in the political relations between the two countries, punctuated by the 1990 Kashmir crisis.

Beginning in the early 1990s, Indian shelling of the Muzaffarabad–Kel road as it ran through the Neelum Valley vexed Pakistani commanders, causing great logistical difficulties for 10 Corps and dislocating civilians in the Neelum Valley area.[46] These grievances were significant for Pakistan's military planners, particularly those within 10 Corps, but they were poorly presented and understood, and little discussed by Pakistan's official spokesmen and the Pakistani media. For over two decades, the 10 Corps was subjected to what it viewed as constant encroachment by Indian forces. When it attempted to return the favor at Kargil, however, Pakistan was unable to explain its historical grievances and present a strong case for military action in the Northern Areas. This section examines Pakistan's compulsions for taking the Kargil decision.

India's difficulty in managing the Kashmir insurgency immediately heated up the entire Line of Control.[47] The Pakistan army faced a serious challenge in the Neelum Valley, which roughly runs from Kel to Nosari (Tithwal on the Indian side). Here, Indian-controlled heights dominated the road along the river, which supplied Pakistani positions in the Nauseri-Jura, Athmuqam-Kiran, and Kel sectors. As a result, from 1992 onward, this road was subject to artillery and small-arms interdiction from tactically located Indian military positions, which ultimately forced the road's closure in 1994. In fact, both parties sought to exploit vulnerabilities as they presented themselves along the LoC. India shelled the Neelum Valley in order to coerce Pakistan to stop infiltration in the Kashmir Valley, and Pakistan sought to exploit Indian vulnerabilities to stop the Neelum shelling. One area where Pakistani positions could interdict the important Srinagar–Leh road was in the Kargil sector. The Kargil heights dominate the Srinagar–Leh road, which also serves as the lifeline for Indian troops deployed around the Siachen Glacier. The LoC runs almost parallel to NH-1A in the area around Kargil, at distances varying from 6 to 12 miles as the crow flies. Indian positions around the Zojila Pass, Dras, and Kargil are vulnerable to shelling by Pakistani artillery.

---

[46] Neelum Valley refers to the river called Kishanganga (Indian maps) and renamed Neelum as it flows into Pakistani-administered Kashmir where it subsequently joins the River Jhelum near Muzaffarabad. In most parts, the LoC runs along the River Neelum. The Indian side located on the higher grounds across the river is in a position to interdict with direct fire upon the road that serves the Neelum Valley.

[47] For an Indian account of the difficulties encountered see Malik, *Kargil: From Surprise to Victory*, 25–101.

This linkage with Siachen and the Neelum Valley was not adequately conveyed to the outside world during the Kargil crisis. As a consequence, Pakistan could not project an internationally acceptable rationale for its military intervention across the LoC. This linkage would have been evident immediately to Kargil's planners, because the operation was coordinated by the FCNA, the command operationally responsible for the Siachen Glacier, and by 10 Corps, which had responsibility for the Neelum Valley.[48] As the official version presented to the CCC research team by the FCNA Commander makes clear, the Kargil campaign was in large part motivated to preempt future Indian actions. Pakistani planners knew that their ability to retaliate for the Neelum Valley shelling was contingent upon holding key positions astride the Kargil–Dras highway. They feared that these positions were becoming increasingly vulnerable to potential Indian attack, and pointed to numerous cases of India demonstrating that it was likely to take offensive action to secure its interests. The FCNA version focused on this vulnerability and Pakistan's desperate attempt to secure it.

Pakistan's official version

The first publicly available official account of the Kargil operation by the Government of Pakistan was offered in the briefing by FCNA on 12 January 2003. This was followed by a published account by Pakistani defense analyst Shireen Mazari.[49] Since then, several additional accounts have been published, most notably former President Pervez Musharraf's memoir. In the briefings to the CCC team, FCNA did not view the Kargil conflict as an "asymmetric" operation. It portrayed the Kargil operation as an exercise in "preemptive defense" against India's likely "military ingress" in the Siachen–Kargil sectors, which was anticipated on the basis of the movement and concentration of troops, interception and assessment of intelligence information, and historical precedents of such military ingress since the Simla Agreement of 1972.[50] FCNA believes it has faced "India's

---

[48] Shaukat Qadir, "An Analysis of the Kargil Conflict," *RUSI Journal* 147, no. 2 (April 2002): 24–30.

[49] See Mazari, *The Kargil Conflict 1999*. The political dimension of this version obviously represents the viewpoint of the Musharraf government, since Nawaz Sharif was not only out of power, but also out of Pakistan. He has commented on the crisis as well. See Raj Chengappa, "Nawaz Sharif Speaks Out," *India Today* (26 July 2004), 6–12. The Pakistan army Director General of Military Intelligence, then Maj. Gen. Ehsan ul-Haq, did brief foreign military attachés in late May, but this information was not available to the media or the Pakistani public.

[50] FCNA briefing, 13 January 2003.

creeping forward policy" since 1971, especially along the northern sectors of the LoC. India occupied important areas in 1965 and 1971, which previously had been held by Pakistan. As noted above, even after the Simla Agreement, India mounted a mile-deep incursion across the LoC near Chorbat La in 1972 and seized four posts in the Qamar sector across the LoC in 1988. The Indians captured the "Anzbari feature" near Kanzalwan in 1992, returned it after hotline talks between the Directors General of Military Operations, but then recaptured it again after the Kargil conflict.[51]

Pakistan also claims to have intercepts of Indian communications that point to an offensive operation. One of them is apparently from the 15 Corps Commander to the General Officer Commanding of 3 Division, telling him to be more aggressive along the LoC, including carrying out raids and taking posts. Another one of these communications is from the Indian army chief, criticizing the 15 Corps on this matter. The FCNA briefing also presented Indian media reports of seventeen attacks by Pakistan in the Siachen sector in this timeframe, when "none actually had occurred." Pakistani military leaders viewed these reports as intentional Indian government misinformation to the media designed to build the case for an attack in the Northern Areas.[52] Pakistan also believed that India's 70 and 114 Brigades were retained opposite the FCNA area of responsibility during the winter of 1998–1999, rather than returning to the Kashmir Valley as usual. They claimed that 70 Brigade had two battalions in the Dras area and 114 Brigade had five battalions. All of these indicators raised the prospect to FCNA of a possible and imminent Indian offensive.

Specifically, the briefing provided a narrative of possible Indian actions that concerned Pakistani commanders. As noted above, India's interdiction of traffic to the Neelum Valley on the Muzaffarabad–Kel road since 1992 caused great difficulties for the Pakistan army and local populace, ultimately leading to the road's eventual closure in 1994.[53] Pakistan retaliated by interdicting the Srinagar–Leh road. FCNA began the interdiction of NH-1A as early as 1996 in response to the Indian firing in the Neelum Valley. According to the FCNA briefing, Pakistan army commanders believed that the Indian army contemplated an offensive operation in the summer of 1999 to address the vulnerability of the NH-1A.[54] Pakistan speculated that India would take the offensive in 1999 at the Siari feature, opposite the Turtok sector (to capture the ridge that gave

---

[51] *Ibid.*   [52] *Ibid.*   [53] Mazari, *The Kargil Conflict 1999*, 7.
[54] FCNA briefing, 13 January 2003.

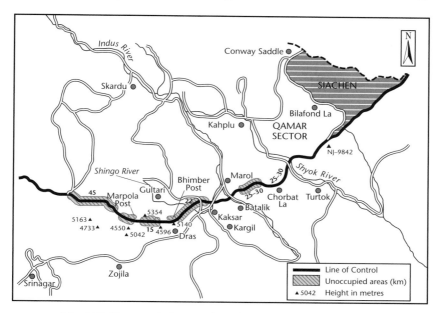

Map 2.2 Unoccupied areas along the LoC

Pakistan observation of the Turtok–Chalunka road), and at Shaqma to reduce visibility on NH-1A. Pakistan expected a brigade-sized offensive.

The FCNA briefing asserted that the "preemptive defense" strategy of the FCNA Commander in 1999 was entirely within his responsibility to address the possibility of an anticipated Indian offensive, an assessment based upon the intercepted communications and intelligence of a possible Indian attack. However, the briefing claimed that Pakistani forces became "incrementally sucked into an action–reaction syndrome." The Pakistan army believes that India overreacted to what was a "limited tactical operation" to take over the unoccupied areas along the LoC.[55] (See Map 2.2, which shows the unoccupied areas along the LoC.)

The involvement of the Pakistan army was acknowledged in these briefings, something privately accepted but adamantly denied to the public in the past. The NLI units were supported by paramilitary forces, including the Chitral and Bajaur Scouts.[56] An interesting revelation that came out of these briefings is that the personnel whom the Indians initially

[55] *Ibid.*   [56] *Ibid.*

alleged were "Taliban" fighting along the Pakistani side were in fact soldiers of the Chitral Scouts who all spoke Pashtu and invariably had beards. The Indians mistook them for Taliban because of their language and physique – an interpretation that the Pakistan government believed was in its interest, as Christine Fair points out in chapter 9 of this book. A large number of local civilians were also employed, mostly as *razakars*, or porters, who also might have been taken as *mujahideen* by the Indians. While FCNA denied any operational, logistical, and administrative collaboration with the *mujahideen*, it did not rule out the possibility of their presence in the vicinity of the areas of military operations on the Indian side of the LoC.

In his memoir, Musharraf notes that the FCNA plan was a "defensive maneuver" designed to plug the gaps – ranging from 9 to 28 miles. The plan was approved in mid-January 1999.[57] Further, he does not refer to the incursions by the NLI, instead calling them "freedom fighters," and makes a special mention that the NLI, composed of locals from the area, were to occupy forward positions and given special instructions not to cross the watershed along the LoC.[58] According to Musharraf, around the end of April, 100 new posts, each comprising ten to twenty people, were established in the unoccupied gaps along 75 miles of the LoC. The Chief of Army Staff was consistently informed on the move of "freedom fighters" until May 1999 when the first two encounters with Indian troops occurred on 2 May and 7 May respectively. By 15 May, fighting had erupted along the incursion areas when the Chief of Army Staff ordered the FCNA to "deny access to the watershed by India."[59]

Pakistan, however, did not anticipate Indian vertical escalation through the introduction of air forces and state-of-the-art artillery to the Kargil sector. Pakistan could not retaliate to the high-altitude and precision-guided strikes by the Indian air force nor to accurate and heavy shelling from the Bofors guns at the peaks occupied by the NLI soldiers, which not only contributed to the capture of some of the posts but also resulted in many casualties on the Pakistani side. Pakistan had few options to neutralize these threats. It could not stop the Bofors or the Indian air force (IAF) without the Pakistan air force (PAF) crossing the LoC. India, on the other hand, was able to maintain aerial and artillery bombardment while remaining on its side of the LoC.[60] If the PAF had crossed the LoC, it might have enlarged the conflict, placing the PAF in a deleterious war of attrition.

---

[57] *Ibid.*   [58] Musharraf, *In the Line of Fire*, 90.   [59] *Ibid.* 91.

[60] Indian air force (IAF) aircraft appear to have crossed the LoC during some sorties, though this appears to have been inadvertent. Pakistani forces on their side of the LoC recovered the wreckage of two IAF airplanes after Pakistani forces shot them down on 27 May.

Apparently, the Pakistani military did not anticipate what it calls the Indian "overreaction" of inducting additional forces, helicopters, and fixed-wing aircraft, which started "an unending chain of action and reaction" on both sides. Even with this escalation, according to the Pakistani military, India retook only 10 to 15 percent of the posts occupied by Pakistani forces prior to their withdrawal.[61]

Finally, there may have been a calculation that nuclear weapons acted as a backstop for potential escalation. India's mobilization in 1999 was obvious – the army canceled leave, and moved elements of mechanized units to the borders of Gujarat, Rajasthan, and Punjab – but its reluctance to consider horizontal escalation strongly suggests that it was deterred.

Potential objectives of the Kargil conflict

As the above narrative indicates, the Pakistani military believed there were multiple strategic and tactical rationales for Pakistan to launch the Kargil operation. At least three strategic objectives and four tactical objectives can be readily discerned.[62] At the strategic level, Pakistan may have been attempting to secure a better bargaining position as it negotiated with India over the Siachen Glacier.[63] It may have sought to induce international support for the resolution of the Kashmir dispute through third-party intervention, or at least win a time-bound Indian commitment in this regard.[64] Third, by "stirring up" events along the Line of Control, it may have sought to prevent the formation of a consensus to divide Kashmir permanently along the LoC, in the process underscoring the continued disputed nature of the present dispensation.

At the tactical level, the Pakistani military sought to intercept the Srinagar–Leh road to disrupt vital supplies and reinforcements to the Indian troops stationed at the Siachen Glacier.[65] It desired to outflank India's defenses from the south in the Turtok and Chalunka sectors

---

[61] There is considerable debate between Indian and Pakistani experts as to the percentage of posts that India had been able to recapture by the 4 July ceasefire.

[62] See Shahbaz Hussain Khokhar, "Management of the Kargil Crisis: A Systemic Approach," M.Sc. Dissertation, Department of Defence and Strategic Studies, Islamabad: Quaid-i-Azam University, Pakistan, 2001.

[63] Altaf Gauhar, "Four Wars, One Assumption," *The Nation*, 5 September 1999, reproduced at http://pakistanlink.com/Opinion/99/Sept/10/01.html.

[64] Nawaz Sharif's address to the nation on 12 July 1999. Also see Pakistan Foreign Secretary Shamshad Ahmad's statement, cited in *The News*, 31 May 1999; Lt. Gen. (retd.) Asad Durrani, *The News*, 28 July 1999; and Air Marshal (retd.) M. Asghar Khan, *The Nation*, 29 July 1999.

[65] General (retd.) Mirza Aslam Beg, "Kargil Conflict and Beyond," *The Nation*, 30 May 1999. Also see Lt. Gen. Javed Nasir, "Kargil: A Flashpoint," *The News*, 26 June 1999.

through unheld areas, thus rendering Indian defenses untenable in Turtok and Siachen. Kargil may have been a feint to weaken the Indian counterinsurgency (CI) operations in Kashmir by drawing away troops from the valley to Kargil. This maneuver would also give a boost to the morale of the Kashmiri freedom fighters in the valley.[66] Finally, the Kargil operation may have been an attempt to increase the cost of Indian occupation in the Northern Areas along the LoC (Khan, Lavoy, and Clary consider these potential motivations in depth in the following chapter of this book.)

Conclusion

The Kargil operation did not emerge in a strategic vacuum. Given the long history of Indo-Pakistani conflict over Kashmir, the Kargil conflict represents a continuation and a reaction by Pakistan to the Indian forward military policy in Kashmir, which culminated in the occupation of the Siachen Glacier in 1984. Since 1947, Pakistan has seen a gradual erosion in its position vis-à-vis India. In the Northern Areas, in particular, Pakistan has suffered from continual losses since the 1971 war. Such Indian nibbling at Pakistani posts was not arrested by the Simla Agreement, which Pakistan believes was violated numerous times by Indian forces, most blatantly during the occupation of the Siachen Glacier. The military planners in Pakistan thought that the occupation of "unheld" and "undemarcated" areas of Kargil along the LoC would enable its forces to interdict the Srinagar–Leh road, vital for the supplies and reinforcements to the Indian troops stationed in the Siachen Glacier. In this way, the Siachen dispute spilled into a new territorial dimension in 1999 – control over the Kargil heights.

The Kargil operation, however, appears to have suffered from fatal mission creep. Initially designed to protect Pakistani positions that overlooked NH-1A, the operation appears to have expanded to include capturing new positions that could directly interdict the Srinagar–Leh highway. Apparently designed to maintain a *quid pro quo* in this area, the operation became more ambitious. Pakistan sought a better bargaining position in competitive negotiations with India on the Neelum Valley and the Siachen Glacier, in particular, and the Kashmir dispute, in general.

The operation was launched at a time that did not favor Pakistan. The international community, which had expressed its opprobrium over the May 1998 tests, gradually became hopeful in the progress of the Lahore

---

[66] Lt. Gen. (retd.) Durrani, *The News*, 28 July 1999; and *Friday Times*, 5 August 1999.

process. This jarring return to conflict caused intense international pressure on Pakistan to withdraw. Further, while Pakistani planners had made many correct calculations about India's ability to escalate, the Pakistani military was never able to silence the Bofors guns and stop the aerial bombardment by the Indian air force. And despite the extensive rationale for the operation, as narrated above, the Pakistan government was unable to explain its viewpoint and motivations to a skeptical world community.

3   Pakistan's motivations and calculations for the Kargil conflict

Feroz Hassan Khan, Peter R. Lavoy, and Christopher Clary

The Kargil operation was an audacious attempt to seize an opportunity of historic proportions.[1] Indian troops predictably vacated posts along the Line of Control (LoC) as they retreated to winter positions – a normal measure taken by both Indian and Pakistani forces to reduce the strains on forces during the harsh winter months.[2] Pakistani planners aimed to seize this unprotected territory to the maximum feasible limit, with an eye on interdicting National Highway 1A, the strategically important Indian road that runs between Srinagar and Leh. But the plan's boldness also made it dangerous and ultimately untenable. Its success would require hundreds of troops to infiltrate across the LoC and maintain their positions for weeks without being detected. After their inevitable discovery, they would have to hold off Indian counterattacks until the onset of winter, which would close the passes, halt military operations, and allow Pakistani infiltrators to harden their positions. This military *fait accompli* would enable Pakistan to redraw the LoC.

---

[1] This chapter is based on an official briefing provided by Maj. Gen. Nadeem Ahmed, Commander of the Force Command Northern Areas (FCNA) in January 2003, and interviews by Peter Lavoy with Lt. Gen. (retd.) Mahmud Ahmed, 10 Corps Commander during Kargil, and Lt. Gen. (retd.) Javed Hassan, FCNA Commander during Kargil. Another author, Brig. (retd.) Feroz Hassan Khan, has operational experience in this region, having commanded from 1991 to 1993 the 5th Northern Light Infantry battalion, which later took part in the Kargil operation. The authors extend special thanks to Zafar Iqbal Cheema, who presented a paper at the Monterey conference in June 2002 on this topic and has an accompanying chapter in this volume.

[2] At remote posts in higher altitudes, both Indian and Pakistani forces would retreat to lower heights during the winter to reduce the intense logistical and weather hazards incumbent in deploying troops during such conditions. After the establishment of the Cease-Fire Line (and subsequently the Line of Control), both India and Pakistan tacitly allowed such winter retreats to occur without attempts to take advantage of them, a norm consistent with the letter and spirit of the Karachi Agreement of 1949. Following the seizure of the Siachen Glacier by Indian troops in 1984, both sides dramatically reduced the number of forward posts they would vacate during the harsh winter months. For a study of the harsh terrain for military operations in the Northern Areas, see Lt. Gen. V. R. Raghavan, *Siachen: Conflict Without End* (New Delhi: Penguin Books, 2002), 58–85.

The operation's planners seemed convinced that India would not expand the conflict elsewhere along the LoC or the international border, and that the international community would view the Kargil incursion as part of the normal pattern of military activity along the LoC, similar to India's occupation of the contested Siachen Glacier fifteen years before. While some of the calculations of Pakistani planners were borne out by events, the faulty assumptions they made, when combined with tactical missteps on the ground, doomed the Kargil operation to failure. Perhaps most crucially, Kargil's planners failed to recognize the significance of the nuclear revolution. The international community could not endorse any effort to redraw boundaries, even if they were disputed, and in particular would not permit what looked like the manipulation of nuclear escalation, even though that almost certainly was not what Kargil's planners had in mind.

This chapter examines the calculations made by Pakistani decision-makers in the months leading up to the Kargil operation. Until now, public explanations of the planning for this gambit have been too parsimonious, too biased, or both. Indian commentators typically view Kargil as the outgrowth of a revisionist Pakistani state seeking to alter the political and territorial status quo.[3] An extension of this line of thought can be found in the Kargil Review Committee report, which portrays the operation as an example of the relentless probing of an aggressive Pakistani military looking for chinks in Indian defenses.[4] Other Indian commentators and some liberal Pakistani authors have asserted that Kargil exemplifies the frustration of the Pakistani military leadership as it struggled to reassert primacy over a civilian government that was pursuing a peace process that endangered the corporate interests of the Pakistani armed forces.[5] Quasi-official Pakistani accounts, most notably the 2004 book by Pakistani defense analyst Shireen Mazari, present Kargil as the natural outgrowth of historical grievances and a continuation of tit-for-tat military

---

[3] See, for instance, Jasjit Singh, "The Fourth War," in *Kargil 1999: Pakistan's Fourth War for Kashmir*, ed. Jasjit Singh (New Delhi: Knowledge World, 1999), 120–121; Lt. Gen. (retd.) Y. M. Bammi, *Kargil 1999: The Impregnable Conquered* (New Delhi: Gorkha, 2002), 83, 89–90.

[4] See "Pak Modus Operandi and India's Response in the Past," in *From Surprise to Reckoning: The Kargil Review Committee Report* (New Delhi: Sage, 2000), 49–52.

[5] Bammi, *Kargil 1999*, 110; Gurmeet Kanwal, "Nawaz Sharif's Damning Disclosures," *The Pioneer*, 16 August 2000. For Pakistani critics of the military, see Babar Sattar, "Pakistan: Return to Praetorianism," in *Coercion and Governance: The Declining Role of the Military in Asia*, ed. Muthiah Alagappa (Stanford University Press, 2001), 385–412; and Samina Ahmed, "Pakistan: Professionalism of an Interventionist Military," in *Military Professionalism in Asia*, ed. Muthiah Alagappa (Honolulu: East-West Center, 2001), 151–161. Sattar and Ahmed argue that the military has justified its unique role in Pakistani politics by playing up the Indian threat. Implicitly, the disappearance of that threat would

practices common since the establishment of the LoC.[6] Shaukat Qadir has argued that Kargil was the product of a unique confluence of individuals in the Pakistani chain of command, all of whom had something to prove.[7] And publications and statements by US policy-makers have tended to emphasize the role of nuclear weapons, high-lighting how a nuclear deterrent can provide an umbrella under which limited conflicts can be fought.[8] In 2006, the Indian and Pakistani army chiefs during the Kargil conflict wrote books under-scoring the differing narratives of the conflict. While both publica-tions provided added detail on the thoughts of senior Indian and Pakistani officials, they continued to misread the motivations and actions of adversary decision-makers across the border.[9]

All of these accounts tell some portion of the story – but they do not capture the whole story, even when taken together. In particular, no existing explanation adequately explores the crucial driver of the conflict: the unique strategic culture of the Pakistan army, in general, and the 10 Corps and Force Command Northern Areas (FCNA), in particular.[10] Pakistan repeatedly has resorted to asymmetric military means to resolve the Kashmir dispute with India on the belief that India would refuse to negotiate a just solution for the Kashmiris. The Pakistan army assumed that India would not respond to such maneuvers with military escalation,

---

mean the disappearance of that unique role. This perspective is in line with much earlier Indian analyses of Pakistani military behavior. See, for instance, Aswini Ray, *Domestic Compulsions and Foreign Policy* (New Delhi: Manas Publications, 1975).

[6] Shireen M. Mazari, *The Kargil Conflict 1999: Separating Fact from Fiction* (Islamabad: Ferozsons, 2003).

[7] Shaukat Qadir, "An Analysis of the Kargil Conflict," *RUSI Journal* (April 2002): 24–30.

[8] Strobe Talbott compares Kargil to the Cuban missile crisis and quotes President William J. Clinton referring to it as "nuclear blackmail." *Engaging India: Diplomacy, Democracy, and the Bomb* (Washington, DC: Brookings Institution Press, 2004), 161, 165, and 167. Bruce Reidel also discusses Clinton's worry that "if the United States appeared to be acting under the gun of a nuclear threat its ability to restrain others from threatening use of their nuclear forces would be forever undermined." See chapter 5 of this book, 138–139. Sumit Ganguly's invocation of the "stability–instability" paradox is typical of academic analysts. See *Conflict Unending: India–Pakistan Tensions since 1947* (New York: Columbia University Press, 2001), 122, 127. Also see Sumit Ganguly and Devin Hagerty, *Fearful Symmetry: India–Pakistan Crises in the Shadow of Nuclear Weapons* (Seattle: University of Washington Press, 2005), 143–166.

[9] Pervez Musharraf, *In the Line of Fire: A Memoir* (New York: Simon and Schuster, 2006); and V. P. Malik, *Kargil: From Surprise to Victory* (New Delhi: HarperCollins, 2006).

[10] For background on Pakistan's strategic culture, see Peter R. Lavoy, "Pakistan's Strategic Culture: A Theoretical Excursion," *Strategic Insights* 4, no. 10 (October 2005), www.ccc.nps.navy.mil/si/2005/Oct/lavoyOct05.asp; Feroz Hassan Khan, "Comparative Strategic Culture: The Case of Pakistan," *Strategic Insights* 4, no. 10 (October 2005), www.ccc.nps.navy.mil/si/2005/Oct/khan2Oct05.asp; and Hasan-Askari Rizvi, "Pakistan's Strategic Culture," in *South Asia in 2020: Future Strategic Balances and Alliances*, ed. Michael R. Chambers (Carlisle, Pa.: Strategic Studies Institute, 2002), 305–328.

and if it did, Pakistani troops (and pressure from allies) would be able to neutralize any Indian riposte. The Pakistan army also feels deeply wronged by an India that exploited an internal crisis in eastern Pakistan, captured the Siachen Glacier despite the 1972 Simla Agreement, planned a preemptive attack on Pakistan's nuclear facilities in the garb of the 1987 Brasstacks exercise, and suppressed the Kashmiri people for decades.[11] Pakistanis always have had great difficulty in comprehending why the international community allowed India to get away with these perceived injustices.

The 10 Corps and FCNA were particularly embarrassed by the loss of the Siachen Glacier, which was undemarcated and unoccupied until 1984 when India launched Operation *Meghdoot* to capture it. The 10 Corps has the most demanding operational responsibility in the army, constantly defending Pakistani positions on the LoC. Since the Cease-Fire Line (CFL) was negotiated in 1948, India has held more tactically advantageous positions on the higher ground. As a consequence, the 10 Corps historically has strived to neutralize these advantages. FCNA, in particular, is focused on tactical concerns in an extremely difficult terrain – where vulnerabilities can be secured only by daring and dangerous high-altitude operations. Regardless of the actual circumstances, FCNA was held responsible for the loss of Siachen and other significant Indian incursions on the Pakistani side of the LoC, such as in the Qamar and Chorbat La sectors.[12] Officers posted to FCNA are quickly socialized to remember the past and at all cost defend their area of responsibility. They would rather be reprimanded for over-aggressiveness, than leave a perceived vulnerability unprotected.[13] This tendency was given more latitude in an area where the terrain does not allow for the clear demarcation of boundaries. Finally, the FCNA had an institutional memory of success in the Kargil area. Kargil had been a pivotal battlefield in past Indo-Pakistani conflicts. The grandfathers of current Northern Light Infantry (NLI) forces had taken part in successful operations to capture Kargil, Dras, and the Zojila Pass.[14] Although those forces subsequently lost this

---

[11] For a comprehensive elaboration of these views by one of the Kargil planners, see Javed Hassan, *India: A Study in Profile* (Rawalpindi: Army Education Press, GHQ, 1990). See also Stephen Philip Cohen, *The Idea of Pakistan* (Washington, DC: Brookings Institution Press, 2004), 102–110.

[12] See Mazari, *The Kargil Conflict 1999*, 23–25.

[13] This sense was quite clear in the interviews with Lt. Gen. (retd.) Mahmud Ahmed, Lt. Gen. (retd.) Javed Hassan, and other officers who have commanded in this area.

[14] FCNA units trace their heritage to the Gilgit Scouts, created in 1913, and the Karakoram Scouts, created in the 1960s. Both were merged in 1975 to form the paramilitary NLI. After Kargil in 1999, NLI was inducted as the fifth Infantry Regiment in the Pakistan army (the other four being Punjab, Baluch, Frontier Force, and Sindh Regiments).

territory to India, the memory of their forefathers' heroics had become legendary.

This chapter begins with an explanation of why the Kargil occupation was attractive to Pakistani military leaders. We analyze this issue on several levels. First, we show how Pakistan's sense of historical grievance – fueled especially by the 1971 Bangladesh war, India's 1984 occupation of the Siachen Glacier, and a series of subsequent incursions and skirmishes along the northern LoC – induced Kargil's planners to undertake such a risky gambit. We explain how the distinct military problems of the Pakistan army's 10 Corps, along with the peculiar strategic culture of FCNA, made the Kargil region a likely venue for such an operation. Next, we examine the impact of the unique constellation of military leaders, from the army chief to the ground commander, who decided to carry out such a bold move. We then examine how Pakistan's unhealthy civil–military relations indirectly contributed to the Kargil decision and directly damaged Pakistan's subsequent handling of the crisis. Finally, we conclude with an assessment of the Kargil planners' assumptions – and how reality differed from pre-conflict expectations. Because of these miscalculations, the Kargil operation failed to achieve its apparent objectives and impaired, rather than strengthened, Pakistan's security.

A history of grievance

Pakistanis generally believe that the status quo in Kashmir is illegitimate. The outcome of the partition of British India, in their view, was neither fair nor just. The border drawn by the Radcliffe commission was controversial, the division of civil and military assets inequitable, and, most importantly, the accession of princely states was improper. The most glaring injustice was created by the accession into India of the state of Jammu and Kashmir – a Muslim-majority state under a Hindu ruler, or maharajah.[15]

Pakistanis believe that Hindu leaders have long oppressed the Muslim population of Jammu and Kashmir, and the questionable accession into the Indian Union has denied the populace their right to self-determination. They emphasize the UN Security Council's demand for a "free and impartial plebiscite," but overlook the other UN demands in the same resolution which include, *inter alia*, a cessation of fighting; withdrawal of forces, "tribesmen," and "Pakistani nationals not normally

---

[15] Cohen, *The Idea of Pakistan*, 46–47.

resident in Jammu and Kashmir"; prevention of "any aid to intruders"; and the creation of "proper conditions" for such a vote to take place.[16]

India's heavy-handed policies over the Kashmiri populace are taken as proof that only through extensive oppression can the Indian state suppress the desire for Kashmiri self-determination. Indian abuses are amplified in the Pakistani press – and are even louder in the vernacular press than in the calmer English dailies. Pakistanis, on the streets and in uniform, look across the LoC and see a long history of vote rigging, arbitrary arrest, torture, and rape by an occupying Indian force.

This popular perception is both a product and a cause of Pakistani government policies. There is a reality of hardship for the Kashmiri people – caused in significant part by heavy-handed Indian policies – and it is hard to imagine any government in Pakistan completely abandoning a decades-long policy to provide political, moral, and at times military support to the Kashmiri people. At the same time, this emphasis on the plight of the Kashmiris for both domestic and international audiences pushes the leadership toward policies that require the use of force to correct this injustice. This in turn restricts the Pakistan government's ability to maneuver. The Kargil operation must be seen as an extension of Pakistan's decades-long quest to make headway on the Kashmir issue.

Pakistan always has faced a larger, more populous, wealthier, and militarily more powerful neighbor in India. Pakistani security planners have had great difficulty finding ways to compensate for these profound structural asymmetries. The sense of political and strategic necessity, when wedded to a strong belief of moral righteousness, has justified the use of almost any means both for the sake of Kashmir and to resist Indian primacy in the subcontinent. Pakistan repeatedly has attempted daring and unconventional methods to wrest Kashmir militarily from India and liberate the Kashmiri Muslims from Indian rule – and has repeatedly been stymied in those efforts. The Kargil operation was the latest failed attempt to take the advantage in this perennial competition.

In late 1947, Maharajah Hari Singh delayed acceding to either India or Pakistan, ignoring the hastily crafted rules of partition drafted by the British viceroy, Lord Louis Mountbatten. Hari Singh's dreams of an independent Jammu and Kashmir were interrupted by a tribal rebellion near Poonch. With the assistance of Pakistan army officers, tribal *lashkars* (forces) from Pakistan's North-West Frontier Province streamed into Kashmir seeking religious glory and temporal loot. India and Pakistan

---

[16] Official Records of the UN Security Council, Third Year, 286th Meeting, 21 April 1948 (document S/726), www.un.org/Depts/dpa/repertoire/46-51_08.pdf.

found themselves engaged in their first war within months of their independence.[17]

Kargil was a pivotal battleground during the First Kashmir War. In October 1947, Gilgit Scouts, assisted by Muslim soldiers in the Kashmir state army, mounted a successful coup d'état in the Northern Areas. The so-called Azad (Free) Forces set up headquarters in the valley town of Astore. The rebels then recruited additional volunteers in the Gilgit and Baltistan regions and moved along the valleys and Indus River while pushing back the Kashmir state army.[18] In February 1948, the "Azad Forces" besieged the garrison in Skardu where non-Muslim civilian and military personnel had taken refuge. In response, the Kashmir state army aided by Indian troops twice crossed the Kargil heights in failed attempts to liberate the Skardu garrison.[19] In April 1948, the Azad army extended its control southward to the Gurais Valley, Kishangana Valley, and Tragbal Pass, and then successfully captured the strategically important Zojila Pass and with it the surrounding towns of Kargil and Dras in May 1948.[20] Maj. Gen. D. K. Palit, who was then serving in a nearby Indian unit at Poonch, noted India's concern: "As a result of the fall of Skardu and Kargil, the Valley of Kashmir was threatened from the north as well as the east; what is more, the only line of communication between Srinagar and Leh, over the Zojila and through Kargil, was disrupted. Failing rapid reinforcements, it would be only a matter of months before the enemy could walk into Leh."[21] India then counterattacked with a brigade-size force from Srinagar and Leh. Pitched fighting took place throughout the Northern Areas from June to December 1948, ultimately leaving the Indian army in control of Dras, Kargil, and the Zojila Pass.

---

[17] The legality and timing of the accession of Jammu and Kashmir remain matters of controversy. For background, see Owen Bennett Jones, *Pakistan: The Eye of the Storm* (New Haven, Conn.: Yale University Press, 2002), 64–68. For background on the 1948 war, see Maj. Gen. Shaukat Riza, *The Pakistan Army 1947–1949* (Lahore: Services Book Club, 1989), 263–297; Maj. Gen. Akbar Khan, *Raiders in Kashmir* (Karachi: Pak Publishers, 1970); Ganguly, *Conflict Unending*, 15–29; and Pervez Iqbal Cheema, *Pakistan's Defence Policy, 1947–1958* (New York: St. Martin's Press, 1990), 38–45.

[18] Manzoom Ali, *The Northern Area of Pakistan: Physical and Human Geography Map/Atlas-1*, rev. edn (Lahore: Department of Geography, University of the Punjab, 2004).

[19] M. Ilyas Khan, "Kargil: A Strategic History," *The Herald* (July 2000): 28.

[20] The Zojila Pass is the only strategic pass that links Srinagar with the Northern Areas and Leh on the Indian side of the LoC. See Bammi, *Kargil 1999*, 93–101. It is analogous to the Burzil Pass on the Pakistani side that feeds from the Skardu and Gilgit areas into Pakistan's portion of the Deosai plains and the Shaqma sector. Mazari explains the significance of the Burzil Pass, *The Kargil Conflict 1999*, 36–39.

[21] Maj. Gen. D. K. Palit, *Jammu and Kashmir Arms: History of the J&K Rifles* (Dehra Dun: Palit & Dutt, 1972), 241. Also see Bammi, *Kargil 1999*, 56–57; Riza, *Pakistan Army 1947–1949*, 290–294; and C. Dasgupta, *War and Diplomacy in Kashmir: 1947–48* (New Delhi: Sage, 2002), 172–173.

This episode is significant for at least two reasons. First, the Gilgit Scouts were eventually incorporated into the NLI as part of the FCNA. These units remembered, through stories from previous generations and evidence retained in their archives, that they had captured the Kargil heights with a small, determined force.[22] Second, India demonstrated that it was unwilling to accept such an outcome and would retaliate forcefully to vacate any intrusion in this strategically important area. In the end, the fighting proved inconclusive, and Pakistani and Indian forces reached a military stalemate in Kashmir. The negotiated Cease-Fire Line was codified in the Karachi Agreement of 1949.

Kargil also figured in the Second Kashmir War, the origins of which lie in late 1964, when Pakistani president Ayub Khan established a secret planning cell, composed of Foreign Office, army, and intelligence representatives to find ways to regain momentum in the Kashmir dispute. Their ambitious plan entailed launching a low-scale guerrilla operation to foment a Kashmiri uprising, followed by a limited incursion into Indian-held Kashmir, which, they calculated, would prompt the international community to force negotiations on the issue. When the plan was first presented in February, President Ayub rejected the proposal.[23] But subsequently, in May 1965, emboldened by India's poor showing in the Rann of Kutch that summer,[24] Ayub ordered the army to execute the plan.

In August 1965, a mixture of Pakistani commandos and local *mujahideen* were sent across the ceasefire line to foment an indigenous uprising in Indian-administered Kashmir, in an operation code-named *Gibraltar*. As part of this operation, on 7 August, Pakistani irregular forces conducted a raid on the Kargil area with an aim of severing the Indian road link between Ladakh and Srinagar – echoing the 1948 attempt and foreshadowing the 1999 operation.[25] The infiltrators failed to incite a local uprising, with most being captured by Indian forces with the assistance of the local population. The initial proposal had assumed that a successful insurgency would prompt overbearing Indian oppression, hence justifying Pakistani intervention. Despite the fact that none of the plan's assumptions were borne out – because the commandos were not successful, no

---

[22] The 1947–1948 conflict is remembered as "The Liberation War of 1947–48" in the Northern Areas of Pakistan. See Ali, *The Northern Area of Pakistan.*

[23] Dennis Kux, *The United States and Pakistan, 1947–2000: Disenchanted Allies* (Baltimore, Md.: Johns Hopkins University Press, 2001), 155–165.

[24] The Rann of Kutch is a tidal mud flat off of the Arabian Sea claimed by both parties. The one-week mini-war ended with the withdrawal of Indian forces on 18 April 1965. See Brian Cloughley, *A History of the Pakistan Army: Wars and Insurrections* (Oxford University Press, 1999), 61–62; and Maj. Gen. Shaukat Riza, *The Pakistan Army: War 1965* (Lahore: Services Book Club, 1984), 77–98.

[25] Cloughley, *A History of the Pakistan Army*, 68–77; and Riza, *The Pakistan Army*, 103–111.

uprising occurred, and no subsequent suppression of the Kashmiri populace ensued – Ayub still continued with the plan's next step, Operation
Grand Slam, a limited incursion to take Akhnur, the location of India's only
road link with Kashmir. In a 29 August letter to the chief of the Pakistan
army, Ayub ordered General Mohammad Musa to "take such action as will
defreeze [the] Kashmir problem, weaken India's resolve and bring her to a
conference table without provoking a general war."[26]

Ayub recognized that India might expand the dispute into a general war
and ordered preparations for such a contingency. Brian Cloughley, the
former Australian defense attaché to Islamabad, points out the contradictions inherent in the Pakistani plan:

> The extraordinary thing is that the person giving the direction was himself a soldier
> who should have known that India would react violently to assaults on what she
> regarded as her territory. And the president should have been aware that "our
> action should be such that [it] can be sustained over a long period" is tantamount
> to advocating a policy of attrition, and that his acknowledgement that India had
> "larger forces" is a direct negation of attrition as a political tool.[27]

Pakistani planners refused to grapple with a possibly untenable war of
attrition, and decided to initiate Operation *Grand Slam*, which was almost
guaranteed to provoke India to escalate. India did retaliate by expanding
to a full-scale war along the international border, which caught Pakistan
unprepared. Pakistani leaders incorrectly had assumed that their close ties
with the United States would discourage Indian escalation, and, if India
did expand the conflict, the US alliance would provide some political and
military cover for Pakistan.[28] These basic lessons of 1965 appear not to
have been considered by Kargil's planners in 1999. When its territory was
threatened, the Indian military reacted forcefully and was willing to escalate the conflict to remove that threat. In both 1965 and 1999, the Indian
reaction far exceeded the expectation of Pakistani planners. Also in both
cases, a core group of Pakistani leaders operating in secrecy did not bring
the other state institutions, including important components of the armed
forces, into synchronization with their plans, and as a result were unprepared for Indian "overreaction." Any increase in Kashmiri discontent was
woefully insufficient to inhibit this counterattack, and the international
community was both unable and unwilling to halt Indian escalation.[29]

---

[26] Cloughley, *A History of the Pakistan Army*, 70.   [27] *Ibid.* 71.
[28] Kux, *United States and Pakistan*, 159–160.
[29] The analogy does have its limitations. Unlike 1965, if India had horizontally escalated the
Kargil conflict, it would have drawn forces away from the Kargil front, and dissipated the
strength of the attack. However, India did escalate vertically through the introduction of
artillery and air power.

with battalion-size forces at three to four separate locations along the ridgeline.

The new plan was presented at GHQ before the president and Chief of Army Staff Zia ul-Haq, the prime minister, and the key ministers of the cabinet.[42] During the discussion, Foreign Minister Sahibzada Yaqub Khan opposed any major operation in view of the broader political and diplomatic repercussions. Yaqub Khan's advice was pertinent as earlier in spring of 1987 India and Pakistan had just demobilized after nearly six months of military standoff resulting from India's aggressive military exercise "Brasstacks." The leadership decided to scale down the operational plan, approving a limited attack on one location in the vicinity of the Bilafond La sector. That operation, involving the army's SSG, was launched at night in September 1987 under the direct leadership of Lt. Gen. Imranullah Khan, Commander 10 Corps.[43] This operation nearly succeeded, but ultimately failed to dislodge the Indian troops, as daylight broke the attackers' momentum forcing them to withdraw after heavy losses.[44] After the failure to retake the Quaid-Bana post, it became clear that only large-scale operations, supported by tremendous firepower, would be capable of dislodging Indian positions along the Saltaro ridgeline. This added further to the frustration of 10 Corps and FCNA.

A second account, written in 2004, places the timing of the plan's genesis after Zia's death in 1989–1990.[45] According to Lt. Gen. (retd.) Javed Nasir, former Director General of the Inter-Services Intelligence Directorate (ISID), army chief Gen. Aslam Beg ordered Lt. Gen. Shamim Alam, the Chief of General Staff (CGS), and then-Maj. Gen. Jehangir Karamat, the DGMO, to make a plan to respond to the occupation of Siachen. They presented an operation to seize posts left vacant during the winter retreat in Kafir Pahar, Damgal, and Turtok-Challunka in the Kargil sector, which would allow Pakistani forces to "overlook" and "dominate" the road running along the Shyok River. This would so

---

[42] It is not clear if this meeting was under the newly structured Defence Committee of the Cabinet (DCC) or if it was an extraordinary session. But President Zia was insistent that the plan be presented to the prime minister and key cabinet officials before a final decision was taken.

[43] Some Indian accounts have asserted that the SSG was then commanded by then-Brig. Pervez Musharraf. B. Raman, "General Pervez Musharraf: His Past and Present," corde@vsnl.com, 1 July 1999, as cited by Raghavan, *Siachen*, 93. This is incorrect. Although Musharraf had served in the SSG, at the time he was posted in another military assignment in command of an infantry brigade in Bahawalpur and later as Deputy Military Secretary in General Headquarters.

[44] Raghavan, *Siachen*, 86–94; and interviews with Pakistani officers who have served in the Northern Areas.

[45] Javed Nasir, "Kargil: The Bitter Hard Facts," *The Nation*, 30 August 2004.

complicate India's ability to maintain logistical support to the glacier that it would make the Indian force presence untenable.

According to Nasir, when the operation was brought before Prime Minister Benazir Bhutto and President Ghulam Ishaq Khan, ISID, led by Lt. Gen. (retd.) S. R. Kallue, and the army disagreed about the strategic risks of the operation. The GHQ felt that India was not in a position to escalate because it was bogged down in Sri Lanka, internationally weakened because of the ensuing collapse of its traditional ally, the Soviet Union, and mired in its own economic problems at home. The Benazir Bhutto government also retained Foreign Minister Yakub Khan, who reportedly had dissuaded Zia in 1987. Whether he played a similar role during these deliberations is unclear, but according to Nasir, Bhutto agreed with the ISID analysis that India maintained "undisputed nuclear, qualitative and quantitative overwhelming superiority" and that the Kashmiri freedom struggle "was not ripe." India would be inclined to escalate the conflict, which Pakistan, given its economic and relative military position, "would not be able to endure."[46] Based on our interviews, including with individuals who supposedly were involved in this meeting, we cannot confirm Nasir's account. It does not appear that any "Kargil-like" plan was ever presented to Benazir Bhutto in 1989, although it is plausible that the military was continuing to make operational plans on the LoC. There are analogies between the regional situation in 1989 and the situation ten years later. Before the Kashmir uprising in 1989, the Benazir Bhutto government was attempting a rapprochement with the Rajiv Gandhi government. Therefore, had a plan been formally presented, it is highly unlikely that the government would have approved. Bilateral talks on the Siachen dispute also were undertaken in the summer of 1989. A summit between the two prime ministers took place on 16–17 July. Although Bhutto and Gandhi failed to reach agreements on other matters, they did agree to push for a resolution on Siachen.[47]

A third account comes from former Prime Minister Benazir Bhutto. In 2003, she claimed that Kargil-type plans were presented to her as prime minister – though she has stated it was while Gen. Musharraf was Director General of Military Operations (DGMO), implying that such a briefing transpired during her second term, from 1993 to 1997.[48] Then-army chief Gen. Karamat, for his part, has consistently denied presenting such a plan to the Bhutto government, suggesting instead that Benazir Bhutto was referring to a plan to respond to the interdiction of a key road in the

---

[46] *Ibid.*   [47] Raghavan, *Siachen*, 138–152.
[48] See Muralidhar Reddy, "PPP for Panel to Discuss Kargil," *The Hindu*, 4 September 2003, www.thehindu.com/2003/09/04/stories/2003090404011100.htm.

Neelum Valley, which runs along the LoC.[49] Again, our research and interviews provide no corroborating evidence to Bhutto's claim.

Meanwhile, as planning may or may not have been occurring at higher levels, tactical operations continued along the Siachen Glacier area. Two years after the failed operation in the Bilafond La sector, in May 1989, Pakistan launched a second tactical operation to seize a position adjacent to the Chumuk Glacier. The daring feat, which successfully captured a post at the height of 22,700 feet, was widely lauded in the FCNA annals and merited mention in *Time* magazine.[50] The post was subsequently named after Capt. Naveed, who led the operation. A third tactical operation launched in 1992 in the Chulung sector ended with heavy casualties – including the loss of the brigade commander, Brig. Masood Anwari, when Indian forces shot down his helicopter. This failure stimulated several official inquiries and resulted in several FCNA officers – including FCNA Commander Maj. Gen. Zahir-ul-Islam Abbasi – being sacked from their posts.[51]

Two major lessons come out of the military culture of FCNA. First, successful tenure in FCNA implied gaining something, even of minimal importance, rather than losing ground. The name of a successful leader would be remembered, perhaps by renaming the post in his honor, as happened at the Bana post for India and the Naveed post for Pakistan.[52] An FCNA commander would much rather take a risky tactical initiative and seize a post than lose it to his Indian counterpart through complacency.[53] Second, a belief grew that given the difficulty of the terrain and

---

[49] Gen. Karamat, as quoted in Mazari, *The Kargil Conflict 1999*, 17.

[50] Edward W. Desmond, "War at the Top of the World," *Time*, 31 July 1989, 26. Also see Mazari, *The Kargil Conflict 1999*, 11–12, fn. 27. For an Indian perspective on the Chumuk Glacier operations, see Raghavan, *Siachen*, 94–97. Raghavan correctly observes that one of the posts in the Chumuk Glacier section was demilitarized, but he fails to indicate India's maintenance of the Sher post at lower altitudes nearby.

[51] Zahir-ul-Abassi later gained infamy by planning a military coup in 1995. He subsequently was court-martialed. Lt. Gen. Ghulam Muhammad then commanded the Corps. Both of these officers were reputed for their Islamist leanings.

[52] After the Kargil operation, the Turtok sector was renamed the Hanif sector for a soldier who died in action.

[53] This impulse is identical on the Indian side of the LoC, and the impulse appears to remain even after Kargil. In the summer of 2002, an operation was launched to capture a position on the Anzbari feature, which Pakistan claims was on its side of the LoC and India claims is *on* the LoC. Pakistani forces retaliated by capturing another vacant post along the Indian side of the LoC. India's operation to recapture the post received national press coverage because of its use of the Indian air force to reclaim the position. It is important to note that the Indian colonel was sacked for his initial failure to defend the position and the Pakistani brigade commander was not promoted. See Josy Joseph, "CO Removed for Allowing Pak Troops to Occupy LoC Position," Rediff.com, 15 August 2002, www.rediff.com/news/2002/aug/15josy.htm; and Praveen Swami, "When Pakistan Took Loonda Post," *Frontline*, 31 August 2002, www.frontlineonnet.com/fl1918/19180220.htm.

harsh weather conditions, ground once lost cannot be regained without a major offensive. The terrain allowed military ventures to occur in the north that would have merited incredibly forceful responses in other sections of the LoC.[54] Because of this legacy, the FCNA has an entirely different approach to dealing with the LoC than other commands.

The above narrative brings two issues to light that provide the context of the Kargil operation for Pakistan. First, 10 Corps had a serious problem of operational management around the LoC and Siachen, which goes well beyond a sense of grievance and pride, and this problem had intensified after the April 1984 loss of Siachen and the failed talks in 1989 to settle the Siachen dispute. This was a serious military problem that was not well understood outside army ranks. Second, throughout the 1990s, successive Pakistani governments tried to keep the Kashmir insurgency alive and simultaneously sought rapprochement with India for geopolitical reasons. This political strategy was largely disconnected from the deteriorating military situation on the ground around the LoC, Siachen, and the Saltaro Ridge.

By late 1998, the historical setting for the Kargil decision was in place. The status of Kashmir remained in dispute. After Siachen, the practice of seizing adversary posts was limited only by the successful defense of those positions. The 10 Corps and FCNA had a legacy of embarrassment from Siachen and were looking to reclaim lost honor. In addition, 10 Corps was growing more determined to alleviate the frustrating fire along the Neelum Valley road, and FCNA was increasingly concerned about the vulnerability of its defensive positions. From an army perspective, a Kargil-like operation was only a matter of time and boldness of command. When Pakistan learned that Indian posts in the Kargil sector were being vacated in large numbers during the winter retreat, and a new chain of command took over the army, the temptation to seize the initiative became too strong to resist.

The immediate cause of Kargil

The 12 Division, also under command of 10 Corps, is responsible for defense of the territory just south of the FCNA area of responsibility. Since 1992 it faced interdiction from Indian forces on the Muzaffarabad–Kel road along the Neelum Valley. Indian positions on the heights across

---

[54] The incredible difficulty of maneuvering in this terrain is explained by Marcus P. Acosta, "High Altitude Warfare: The Kargil Conflict and the Future," Master's thesis, Monterey, Calif.: US Naval Postgraduate School, June 2003, 11–26; and Raghavan, *Siachen*, 58–71.

from the LoC dominated the road, which runs alongside the Neelum River, and were able to interdict it in three sectors: Titwal, Athmukam, and Kel. The interdiction successfully prevented Pakistani military and civilian resupply, despite bypasses constructed by Pakistan at Kirin and Laswa to avoid Indian small-arms fire.[55] This daily harassment was irresolvable through the hotline between Indian and Pakistan Directors General of Military Operations. India treated the interdiction as an acceptable response to Pakistani-sponsored infiltration in the Kashmir Valley. However, Pakistan's 10 Corps was intent on finding an operational way to resolve the Neelum Valley problem. One way was to interdict vulnerable Indian lines of communication, which Pakistan did along the Dras–Kargil road with direct and indirect fire starting in 1996 and 1997.[56]

Pakistani military planners also had grown increasingly concerned about India's military buildup in Kashmir. In 1990 the Indian army's 8 Division and 39 Division moved from the Eastern Command to become permanent parts of the Northern Command. There were growing concerns over Pakistan's own vulnerabilities in this sector, especially in light of the Siachen experience and lost posts on the LoC at Turtok, Marpola, and Chorbat La.[57] There remained wide gaps between Pakistani defensive positions, as well as similarly large gaps on the Indian side.[58] Interviews with Pakistani planners and official briefings all told a similar story: the past experience of Indian incursions, combined with a continuous, gradual increase in Indian forces in the region, along with the wide gaps between Pakistani defensive positions caused concern for all responsible in the military chain of command. In the winter of 1998, when India's 70 and 114 Brigades did not return to their original positions in the Kashmir Valley, Pakistani planners became particularly troubled. In their minds, their failure to move toward a "forward defense posture across the LoC" would leave Pakistani positions dangerously vulnerable when Pakistani intelligence reportedly indicated an increase in Indian forces in the area.[59] These vulnerable positions were precisely those locations necessary to

---

[55] These bypasses are still subject to Indian artillery interdiction. Later, the Pakistan army found a different route, which is not vulnerable to Indian interdiction, to maintain the supply of Neelum Valley positions.

[56] Maj. Gen. Nadeem Ahmed used the 1996 date, while then-army chief Karamat used the 1997 date. Maj. Gen. Nadeem Ahmed, FCNA Commander, briefing at FCNA Headquarters, Gilgit, Pakistan, 12 January 2003. See also Karamat, as cited in Mazari, *The Kargil Conflict 1999*, 17.

[57] Interviews with senior Pakistani officers involved in the Kargil operation, January 2003.

[58] *Ibid.*

[59] *Ibid.*; and Nadeem briefing, 12 January 2003. Mazari also has argued that Pakistani planners were worried about an Indian operation against Pakistani positions in the Shaqma sector. Mazari, *The Kargil Conflict 1999*, 28–32.

sustain the indirect interdiction of the Srinagar–Leh highway.[60] So instead of retreating to their normal winter positions, Pakistani forces moved forward into previously unoccupied gaps and positions left vacant by Indian forces during the winter months.

The FCNA is not an offensive formation designed to capture and sustain new positions. As a result, it suffered from great problems of logistics and equipment. It was not until after the Kargil operation that NLI paramilitary troops, though commanded by Pakistan army officers and organized similar to an infantry battalion, were trained in offensive operations. Previously, they were not considered on par with regular infantry units. Plans for Kargil-type operations likely envisioned the use of regular units rather than the paramilitary. However, the perceived need for a "forward defense posture" taken in the utmost secrecy likely compelled the Kargil planners to use only the forces that they had readily available. If they had inducted fresh troops, India would have suspected an offensive operation, and Pakistan would have lost surprise. As the Kargil operation unfolded, NLI troops moved forward and became the victims of their own success. They were able to secure much more territory than they initially had planned or could have logistically sustained in the long run, much less defend against deliberate and sustained Indian counterattacks. The FCNA compulsion to push forward led to dangerous "mission creep," whereby a limited defensive operation mutated into a much more ambitious offensive action, which would end up with control over parts of India's strategic artery, National Highway 1A.[61] Lt. Gen. (retd.) V. R. Raghavan has summarized a similar impulse on the Indian side during the Siachen operation:

The Indian deployment on the Saltaro quickly extended to the whole mountain range. Militaries the world over are particular about securing the next height and the Indian army is no exception to that visceral military compulsion. The belief that if one does not take the next higher ground, the enemy will, creates that unending urge. It leads to the occupation of ground, which would otherwise have been left unoccupied.[62]

Pakistani planners at Kargil pushed the same defensive forces to occupy vacant Indian positions and gaps. Ground commanders clearly felt the urge to creep forward so as to occupy the best tactically feasible ground, though it is unclear whether the higher commands at FCNA and 10 Corps authorized the push forward. In either case, it remains the responsibility of the formation commanders to ensure that the troops are not overextended

---

[60] See Zafar Iqbal Cheema's treatment of this issue in chapter 2 of this book.
[61] Nadeem briefing, 12 January 2003.   [62] Raghavan, *Siachen*, 41–44.

and are logistically capable and operationally coherent to maintain the integrity of defense and sustain counterattacks. It is unclear what the calculations of the formation commanders were about the sustainability of the extended troops. The only conclusion that can be drawn here is that the operational commanders either overestimated the strength of the terrain or underestimated the intensity of counterattacks by India.

A new chain of command

After the death of the former President Zia ul-Haq in an air crash in October 1988, political power in Pakistan was split between three institutions: the president, the prime minister, and the army chief. Throughout the 1990s, these three institutions jockeyed for influence and authority. Successive governments under Benazir Bhutto and Nawaz Sharif sought to consolidate the hold of their party, weakening the other civilian institutions of the bureaucracy, presidency, and the judiciary. Civilian institutions seeking protection asked the military to play an extra-constitutional role in protecting them from prime ministerial machinations, even when the army chief wanted to steer away from active involvement in civil affairs. In 1997, this issue reached a peak when Prime Minister Nawaz Sharif successfully weakened the presidency and the judiciary at the same time.[63] In October of the next year, in an ostensible display of civilian authority over the military, Sharif precipitated the resignation of the army chief, General Jehangir Karamat, over the latter's suggestion to depersonalize governance and institutionalize national decisions in a body that would have a formal army role, the National Security Council (NSC).[64] Karamat had been due to retire on the completion of his tenure in January 1999. The army viewed his sacking three months early as an unnecessarily punitive attempt to assert prime ministerial power and a deliberate move to undermine the confidence and strength of the armed forces.

In Karamat's place, Sharif appointed General Pervez Musharraf as army chief on 8 October 1998. Musharraf took control of an institution that had been demoralized by the manner of his predecessor's departure. Among Musharraf's immediate concerns were to restore the morale of the armed forces, reshuffle commands, and fill vacant posts. Musharraf noted, "There was even greater resentment in the army than I had

---

[63] Both the president and the Supreme Court chief justice asked for the intervention of the Pakistan army on their behalf in their dispute with the Sharif government.

[64] After Benazir Bhutto was removed in November 1996, the interim arrangement made by President Farooq Leghari operated under the Council for Defence and National Security, which was dissolved upon the election of Nawaz Sharif's government.

imagined over General Jehangir Karamat's forced resignation."[65] Musharraf promoted and then appointed Lt. Gen. Muhammad Aziz Khan into the vacant Chief of General Staff position. Second, he replaced the Rawalpindi corps commander with Lt. Gen. Mahmud Ahmed. Third, he approved the posting of Lt. Gen. Ziauddin as Director General of ISID, a powerful position with significant domestic and international influence.

Like most army chiefs before him, Musharraf was vehemently opposed to civilian interference in his military command. This became apparent by the early fall of 1998, when friction began as a result of Prime Minister Sharif providing direct access to the ISID chief, Lt. Gen. Ziauddin. Ziauddin, who like the prime minister was ethnically Kashmiri and was often observed fraternizing with Sharif's family.[66]

The attempt by the Sharif administration to woo senior military leaders for rewards and appointment had a severe bearing on the Kargil campaign. The handling of the Kargil plan was also a major cause of friction between the civilian leadership and the armed forces because Sharif's attempt to create fissures within the military affected coordination within military institutions. Most severely, it affected the relationship between GHQ and ISID – two key institutions now suspicious of each other. This had severe repercussions on the planned operations in FCNA. On the one hand, the new leadership in the army was planning a serious military operation with 10 Corps and FCNA to redress the LoC problem; while on the other hand a cat and mouse game was on between Islamabad (the location of the prime minister's office and ISID) and Rawalpindi (army headquarters).

---

[65] Musharraf, *In the Line of Fire*, 85.

[66] Musharraf's predecessor, Jehangir Karamat, also had observed Ziauddin, then Adjutant General on the army staff, fraternizing with the Sharif family in Lahore, and he warned him politely hoping he would get the message that senior leadership movements were monitored. Apparently Ziauddin did not register the point. As Director General of ISID, he had direct access to the prime minister, which Musharraf saw as bypassing appropriate chains of command. Musharraf made his concerns known to Ziauddin. As a result, friction and suspicion grew between GHQ and ISID just as the initial Kargil planners were approaching the COAS with their plan. In another incident, though after the Kargil conflict in the summer of 1999, the Quetta Corps Commander Lt. Gen. Tariq Pervez was found meeting with the prime minister and other civilian leaders without clearance from the army chief. Though Tariq Pervez's first cousin, Raja Nadir Pervez, was a federal minister in the Nawaz Sharif cabinet, Musharraf came down heavily on him. Within a day, the corps commander was retired with immediate effect. The intent of this sacking was to serve as a deterrent to other senior military leaders and to protect the army's institutional discipline, especially in the wake of a spate of backroom deals being conducted by the Sharif government with members of the bureaucracy, judiciary, and other state institutions in the preceding years.

To complicate matters further, Nawaz Sharif's personalized role, which had been the source of Jehangir Karamat's dispute, continued to sideline institutional inputs from the national security bureaucracy and the military, and particularly those of the army. Simultaneously, India and Pakistan, both under international sanctions as a result of their May 1998 nuclear explosive tests, were being pushed by the United States into a peace process.

Under these circumstances, Musharraf was presented with a risky plan to regain the initiative in Kashmir and demonstrate that Pakistan's new military leadership was capable of taking decisive action. A core group at the highest levels of the Pakistan army coordinated this plan: the COAS, the CGS, the 10 Corps Commander, and the General Office Commanding (GOC), FCNA.[67] This plan would require the utmost secrecy from all involved, and would require stealth and deception if it were to be executed successfully. The appointments of Mahmud and Aziz were not in place until late October and they would not have been oriented in their new positions before early November. Even if the decision to undertake the operation was made at the very outset of Musharraf's tenure, it still would have required a couple of months to orient and update the operational plan, even if contingency plans had existed earlier. The plan could not have been presented to the new army chief – and the decision could not have been made – before late November or mid-December. Lt. Gen. Mahmud recalls that he briefed the CGS and the army chief in mid-January.[68] In any case the ongoing suspicions between ISID and GHQ made it even more difficult to have proper interagency coordination.

Prime Minister Nawaz Sharif visited the town of Skardu in the Northern Areas on 29 January 1999. Sharif's visit seems to indicate that he had been briefed earlier, prompting his decision to go to the FCNA area.[69] According to Lt. Gen. Mahmud, he personally briefed Sharif during his visit to Skardu. He explained the vulnerabilities and what he suspected the Indians were planning. Sharif replied with a characteristic economy of words, simply telling Mahmud to "fix it." A week later, Prime Minister Sharif again visited 10 Corps area on 5 February 1999. This time he visited the LoC in the 12 Division area at Kel in the Neelum Valley, also

[67] This conclusion is consistent with Qadir, "An Analysis of the Kargil Conflict," 26.
[68] Interview with Lt. Gen. Mahmud Ahmed, 13 January 2004.
[69] *Ibid.* During the prime minister's address at Skardu, Sharif rewarded the army by raising its pay scale. A discussion of Sharif's visits and briefings can be found in Mazari, *The Kargil Conflict 1999*, 57.

located in the Northern Areas of Pakistan. Lt. Gen. Mahmud again briefed the prime minister on developments along the LoC and in particular explained the Neelum Valley problems.[70] It is significant to note that at this very time, the first reports of Indian prime minister Atal Behari Vajpayee's impending Lahore bus visit began to appear in the press.[71] By mid-February, the Pakistani government, under Nawaz Sharif, found itself on two contradictory tracks with India. Permission to launch a sizable stealth operation to capture the Kargil heights had been given only weeks before the dramatic Lahore visit by Vajpayee. Even after the Lahore process was underway, Sharif did not reverse the military operation that was then well in motion.

Assumptions and miscalculations

The Pakistan army perceived the Kargil incursion as a tactical operation to create a local advantage that also might have broader benefits, such as improving the morale of the army, enhancing the military's position in domestic politics, and increasing bargaining power for negotiations with India. Pakistani planners made a number of critical assumptions. The first was that the Indian army, involved in counterinsurgency in the Kashmir Valley, would be unable to undertake the massive operation necessary to dislodge Pakistani troops in such a difficult terrain, and therefore their counterattacks would be limited, which would end in a stalemate, leaving the Pakistani military in a position of advantage. The critical Zojila Pass, necessary for Indian troops to reach the seized territory, would most likely be inaccessible until June, which, in their calculus, would hamper India's buildup for a counteroffensive.

Second, Pakistani officials involved in planning the Kargil operation assumed that the infiltration would not be discovered at least until the end of May or early June, meaning that no Indian counteroffensive could be planned, built up, and executed in time to recapture the posts before the onset of the next winter's snows. Until that time, Pakistani positions could have held off whatever feeble counterattacks India could hastily muster. They calculated that the major Indian reaction likely would start with a force buildup in late June or early July, by which time either the Pakistan army would reinforce its new positions or Kashmiri militants in the valley

---

[70] Interview with Lt. Gen. Mahmud Ahmed, 13 January 2004. February 5 is a national holiday in Pakistan marking solidarity with the Kashmiris.

[71] See K. K. Katyal, "PM to Take Bus to Lahore," *The Hindu*, 4 February 1999; and Malina Parthasarathy, "US Sees Potential in Indo-Pak 'Bus Diplomacy,'" *The Hindu*, 6 February 1999.

would be in a position to jeopardize Indian plans.[72] In addition, the monsoon rains, which came from July through September, probably would hamper India from expanding its military operations elsewhere along the lower heights of the LoC, in the Kashmir Valleys, and along the green belt of the Himalayas. Typically the monsoons do not reach the high heights where Kargil is located and the incursions were planned. If Pakistani troops were able to sustain the momentum until October (and the onset of winter), Indian operations would be stalled, thus enabling the Pakistan military to further consolidate and restock its defenses.

Third, in addition to these operational considerations, Pakistani planners assumed that the risk of escalation to general war was minimal because the presence of nuclear weapons might deter India, but in any case would also ensure the involvement of the international community to pressure India against turning a limited high-altitude adjustment of the LoC into a full-fledged war. Even without nuclear weapons, however, Pakistani planners may have assumed that India would not be willing to risk general war in response to an incursion along the LoC, just as Pakistan ultimately had accepted India's Siachen operation as an unfortunate but unalterable *fait accompli*.[73]

The planners made several serious miscalculations. First, the NLI troops were discovered a month earlier than planned, giving India an additional month to organize a response without the harassment of insurgency in the Kashmir Valley. Second, unseasonable weather permitted the Zojila Pass to open unusually early that year, becoming passable by early May, allowing India to bring in heavy weapons, most significantly the Bofors artillery, which proved to be deadly against Pakistani positions in the Kargil-Dras sector. Additionally, Pakistani reinforcements reached the FCNA during June, too late to affect the outcome of the battle. Third, the deception that these were *mujahideen* rather than Pakistani troops was dispelled shortly after battle was joined. This left Pakistan in an untenable political position, having publicly stated that the fighting forces were independent *mujahideen*.[74] Fourth, Pakistani planners did not anticipate

---

[72] FCNA did receive reinforcements during June, including the 28 Brigade of 19 Division, one commando battalion (minus two companies), and one wing of the Bajaur Scouts. Such reinforcements arrived too late, however, to decisively affect the battle. Nadeem briefing, 12 January 2003. Lt. Gen. Mahmud also discussed contingency plans: "We expected the posts to be held at least through the summer ... We started out with prevention. What would happen after would be determined by what happened over the summer." Interview with Lt. Gen. Mahmud Ahmed, 10 May 2003.

[73] These assumptions roughly conform to those presented by the Kargil Review Committee Report. See *From Surprise to Reckoning*, 20.

[74] Based on our interviews with senior Pakistani officials, it appears that the Foreign Office, which was not involved in the initial planning of the incursion, lobbied to keep the

India's coordinated and relentless counterattack, particularly in the face of the heavy casualties suffered by Indian troops (which would have been anticipated); and they did not expect vertical escalation involving Indian artillery and air force attacks.

Fifth, and perhaps most importantly, the Kargil planners did not realize that such an operation was being carried out in a very different international environment. The motivations for the primary external actors – the United States and China – had changed over the years. Even when Pakistan had close ties with Washington and Beijing, neither capital intervened to help militarily in 1965 and 1971. Pakistan's ties with both countries were even weaker in 1999, while conversely both American and Chinese leaders had sought to improve relations with New Delhi.[75] Even more significantly, the international community, especially the United States, was increasingly concerned by the idea of even limited conflicts occurring between two nuclear-armed neighbors.[76]

While Kargil's planners may have assumed that nuclear weapons would prevent India from initiating a general war, the true effect was that nuclear weapons did not prevent a vigorous Indian response in the local area, while simultaneously making Pakistani military actions even less acceptable to the international community. Any analogy with Siachen fell flat in this nuclearized environment – an analogy even more difficult to make with the incoherent cover story about *mujahideen*. The Lahore peace process, occurring side by side with Pakistani military maneuvers and deceptions, made the Kargil operation even more jarring, and allowed India to secure the widespread backing of the international community as it forcefully responded to the incursions.

The gaps between competing bureaucratic and political entities also significantly complicated the handling of the Kargil crisis. As Maleeha Lodhi has noted, "The Kargil affair has exposed systematic flaws in a decision-making process that is impulsive, chaotic, erratic, and overly secretive. The elimination of internal checks and balances ... yielded a personalized system of governance which delivers hasty decisions, whose consequences are not thought through, and which are predicated on lack of consultation and scrutiny even within the establishment, much less

mujahideen story alive, arguing that international legal problems would arise if the Government of Pakistan admitted that the army was complicit in the infiltration. More information on the *mujahideen* cover story is provided in chapter 7 of this book.

[75] For background, see Feroz Hassan Khan and Christopher Clary, "Dissuasion and Regional Allies: The Case of Pakistan," *Strategic Insights* 3, no. 10 (October 2004), www.ccc.nps.navy.mil/si/2004/oct/khanOct04.asp.

[76] Talbott, *Engaging India*, 165; and Riedel, chapter 5 of this book.

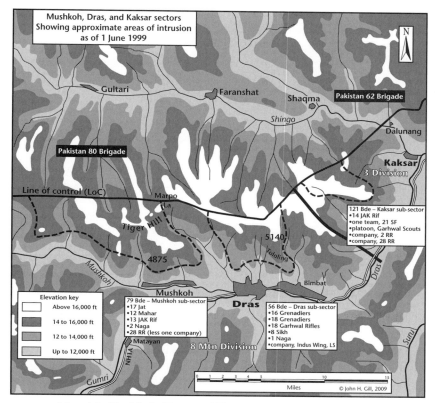

Map 4.1 Mushkoh, Dras, and Kaksar sectors

logistical challenges became. In addition to increasing the time required to transport supplies, tracks and trails could not be improved for fear of alerting the Indians.[21] Occasional helicopter deliveries eased the burden on man and beast but could not replace either. By the time hostilities began, the infiltrators had built more than 130 positions up to 5 miles deep on the Indian side of the LoC and equipped them with machine guns, antipersonnel land mines, man-portable air defense missiles, mortars, and, in some cases, light artillery pieces. The bulk of the force's artillery

---

[21] Retired Lieutenant General Imtiaz Waraich is one of several Pakistanis who claim that logistical preparations for the Kargil incursion were completely inadequate (interview by A. H. Amin in *Defence Journal*, October 2001); also Abbas, *Pakistan's Drift into Extremism*, 173. Rikhye highlights the problems imposed by the need for stealth in "Northern Light Infantry."

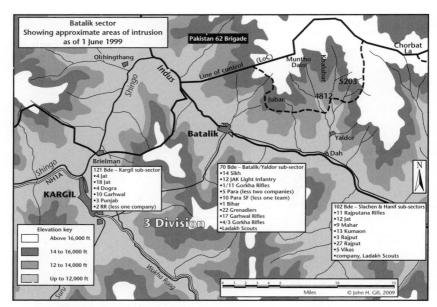

Map 4.2 Batalik sector

support, however, could only come from Pakistani guns emplaced in and around the Shingo river valley on the northern side of the LoC. Additionally, the intruders had to cope with the weakness of any static defense. Despite their best efforts to establish mutually supporting positions with interlocking fields of fire, a determined and imaginative attacker would eventually be able to dismantle the defense, however painfully, unless the defending troops could be resupplied and reinforced on a regular and tactically significant basis. Furthermore, as James Wirtz and Surinder Rana point out in chapter 8 of this book, the absolute requirement for surprise precluded a large buildup of troops in the Kargil sector. This in turn meant that Pakistan would not have a ready force of acclimatized men to insert into the battle if necessary, while the tension of crisis to be expected once hostilities opened would prevent Pakistan from transferring significant reinforcements from other areas of the LoC. The intruders, therefore, would be in a precarious situation if India decided to act decisively against them.

On the other side of the LoC, the Indian army found itself surprised in the Kargil sector when fighting broke out in early May. Kargil had been a historically quiet area. Artillery exchanges had blossomed since 1997, and the Indian army had plans to increase troops levels during the summer

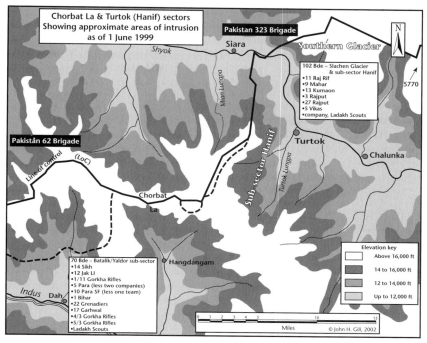

Map 4.3 Chorbat La and Turtok (Hanif) sectors

starting in 1999 as a precaution against militant infiltration. But a major intrusion of any sort, let alone one conducted by Pakistani regulars and NLI, seemed extremely unlikely. Winter was considered a particularly inauspicious time to mount a serious operation. Indian forces in the sector were therefore slender and the "mindset" was defensive.[22] With only five battalions (at most 3,000 to 4,000 infantrymen), 121 Infantry Brigade of 3 Infantry Division, 15 Corps had to cover some 90 miles of the LoC opposite parts of three Pakistani brigades. Given an insufficient number of troops to watch the entire sector, the brigade traditionally blocked the key approach routes from the LoC, principally the *nullahs* (ravines), and left the higher elevations mostly unoccupied. The result was a series of long gaps in the brigade's front, as much as almost 25 miles from its left flank battalion to the next nearest brigade to the west, and from 6 to 16 miles between 121 Brigade's own battalions. Likewise, other than a lone

---

[22] Saikat Datta, "War Against Error," *Outlook*, 28 February 2005; Malik, *Kargil: From Surprise to Victory*, 143; Praveen Swami, "Ghosts of Kargil," *Frontline*, 6–19 May 2006.

Border Security Force (BSF) platoon at Chorbat La, the eastern extension of the boundary, another 16 miles from Chorbat La to the 102 Infantry Brigade sector just west of Turtok, was not defended at all.[23]

In previous years, Indian commanders had withdrawn their men from the higher altitude posts on the LoC (eight in the Kargil sector) during the winter months. For the winter of 1998/1999, however, 15 Corps had ordered continued occupation of all posts in view of the increased activity along the LoC during 1997 and 1998 (one post, "Bajrang" near Kaksar, was evacuated in March 1999 on the decision of local commanders).[24] The brigade was to screen the desolate, snow-covered heights with periodic foot and helicopter patrols. As related by Wirtz and Rana in chapter 8 of this volume, neither these limited traditional measures nor India's other intelligence capabilities proved adequate to detect the well-planned and conducted infiltration scheme carried out during the first months of 1999. The first indication that an intrusion had occurred reportedly was on 30 April 1999 in the Turtok sector (at that time also known as sub-sector West or SSW), but the Indians apparently saw this exchange as nothing more than another routine local affray on the LoC.[25] The first major intrusion was detected only on 3 May when local shepherds informed 3 Punjab of 121 Brigade that they had spotted suspicious interlopers southwest of Jubar in the Batalik sector. Over the next eleven days, as 121 and 102 Brigades sought to gather information about this initial sighting of intruders, patrols in other parts of the 3 Infantry Division front reported activity near Turtok (6 May), Dras (12 May), Mushkoh and Kaksar (both 14 May).[26]

Fortunately for India, two factors worked in its favor. In the first place, the Zoji La (or Zoji Pass), through which NH-1A passes to connect the Dras-Kargil valley with Srinagar, was declared open on 22 April, more

---

[23] The figures should not be taken as precise measurements. They are compiled from *KRC Report*, 83, and Singh, *A Ridge Too Far*, 29.

[24] Malik, *Kargil: From Surprise to Victory*, 90–91.

[25] In this brief skirmish, which was the first reported by the Indian army, an Indian patrol came under fire and apparently lost a few casualties. However, our interviews with Indian and Pakistani military officers reveal that the first firing on Indian troops took place several days earlier, but that engagement was not reported by Indian military commanders owing to their assessment that the incident was not especially serious and their concern about complications that might arise from such a report. Similarly, two men believed to be Pakistani artillery observers were reportedly killed well on the Indian side of the LoC during the spring; it is not clear where this occurred (Jason Burke, "India Walks into Kashmir Trap," *Observer*, 30 May 1999).

[26] Some Indians suggest that the intrusions may have been deliberately revealed by the Pakistanis in a sequence from north to south as a ploy to draw in the available reserves within the Ladakh sector and thus lessen the Indian reaction against the intrusions further to the west. Interview, 2005.

than a month earlier than usual. Repairs would delay complete use of the road until 6 May, but the early opening of this crucial pass meant that troops and munitions could flow with relative ease almost as soon as the intrusions were reported. Second, another brigade headquarters was already setting up in Dras. Owing to the increases in artillery exchanges since 1997, the Indian army had decided to boost its troop presence in the Dras-Kargil area during the summer season to counter the danger of possible infiltration. This new brigade headquarters was intended to command two additional battalions scheduled for induction into the area. Although it did not yet have any assigned combat troops, the head-quarters of 70 Brigade thus arrived in Dras on 3 May in accordance with the Indian army plan for a new standard routine for the summer months.[27] The availability of this command staff under Brigadier Devinder Singh and its familiarity with high-altitude warfare helped speed the Indian response to the crisis.

Much in the Indian army's initial reaction to the disturbing but impre-cise reports from the LoC during the first two weeks of May suggested overconfidence in its own strength and underestimation of the oppo-nent.[28] During at least the first three weeks of May, many in senior command positions assumed that the intruders were poorly trained and equipped militants who could be evicted with relative ease. This persistent confusion notwithstanding, shortly after receipt of the 3 May report from the shepherds near Batalik, orders were issued for four infantry battalions and a company of the locally raised Ladakh Scouts to move to the Kargil area.[29] This prompt action contributed to containing the incursions and helped set the stage for counterattacks later in the conflict. Equally important, two of these four battalions were in the process of de-induction after having just completed tours of duty on the Siachen Glacier. Though at half strength in numbers and equipment after their strenuous stints on the glacier, they were already acclimatized and thoroughly experienced in operations under the extraordinary conditions prevailing in Ladakh.

In the meantime, 121 Brigade had launched several patrols to probe the intruders' positions in the Batalik sector. These reconnaissance efforts

---

[27] *KRC Report*, 85–86; Singh, *A Ridge Too Far*, 30, 54; interviews in India, September 2002. It is possible that Pakistani intelligence misinterpreted the establishment of the 70 Brigade headquarters in Dras as a potential offensive threat.

[28] See, for example, Praveen Swami, "A Bloodbath Foretold," *Frontline*, 17–30 July 2004. The Indian army's internal review of Kargil highlighted the prevalence of a "defensive mindset" and delay in recognizing the seriousness of the intrusions (Datta, "War Against Error").

[29] These were: 14 Sikh (at least part), 12 Jammu and Kashmir Light Infantry, 2 Naga and 1/11 Gorkha Rifles. From Singh, *A Ridge Too Far*.

gathered some information, but at fairly high cost. The results in the Dras sector were similar. Hobbled by terrain, weather, and lack of acclimatized troops, almost two weeks passed before the Indian army began to achieve "a good degree of clarity" regarding the strength, composition, and extent of the incursions. The challenge of evicting them remained unclear, however, and even a month later reports at corps level were often still overoptimistic.[30] When Pakistani artillery destroyed a major ammunition dump near Kargil on the night of 9/10 May, for instance, the Indian army's Northern Command concluded that the strike had been a "chance hit."[31] Indeed, General Malik has observed that "the fog of war remained thick until the end of May."[32] Even as the realities of the situation were in the process of emerging, the 121 Brigade Commander erroneously continued to believe (as did his higher headquarters) that his men were facing nothing more than a limited number of ill-equipped insurgents. On 16 May, therefore, he gave the now infamous "briefing" directing 8 Sikh to capture Tiger Hill northwest of Dras: "There are a few mujahideen on the top, go and throw them off."[33] The men of 8 Sikh had left the sweltering foothills in the Punjab only ten days previously. Now they were suddenly expected to attack an entrenched enemy at altitudes upwards of 14,000 feet in what defense sources told the press was to be the "final, decisive action" to eliminate the intruders.[34] They were not acclimatized and lacked cold-weather clothing, mountain equipment, and decent maps; but senior leaders confidently expected the infiltrators to be "flushed out within 48 hours."[35] Their advance, despite tremendous sacrifice, predictably stalled after four days of painful effort, and they settled in to what would become a month-long siege of Tiger Hill. Similarly, troops on the ground in the Batalik sector held a fairly realistic appreciation of the situation, but differences of assessment with higher headquarters led to some equally hasty and equally abortive attempts to drive out the intruders during the initial stages in the crisis.[36]

---

[30] In a postwar interview, the 15 Corps Commander, Lieutenant General Krishan Pal, said that he had "a good degree of clarity" by 17 May. See *Frontline*, 14–27 August 1999; and Somnath Batabyal, "Withering Heights," *The Week*, 21 May 2000. However, Pal's 19 May press briefing still characterized the fighting as "a local situation to be dealt with locally," *Daily Excelsior*, 20 May 1999. This early optimism has been severely criticized by some commentators, for example, Lt. Col. Thakur Kuldip S. Ludra, "Operations in Kargil," in *Musharraf's War*, ed. Maj. Gen. Rajenrda Nath (New Delhi: Lancer, 2003), 126–129.

[31] Malik, *Kargil: From Surprise to Victory*, 106.   [32] *Ibid.* 340.

[33] Quoted in Singh, *A Ridge Too Far*, 108.   [34] *Daily Excelsior*, 17 May 1999.

[35] *Ibid.*, quoting Defence Minister George Fernandes.

[36] Singh, *A Ridge Too Far*, 107–111. See also 56 Mountain Brigade after-action report cited in Harinder Baweja, *A Soldier's Diary. Kargil: The Inside Story* (New Delhi: Books Today, 2000), 42, 166. For insightful narratives of the early problems at several points, see Bammi, *Kargil 1999*, 356–360, 529–534.

Buildup: local and national

Absorbing these initial setbacks and indisputable evidence concerning the extent of the incursion, India settled down to prepare for a methodical, set-piece campaign aimed at gaining the initiative and evicting the infiltrators. Indian army chief General Malik outlined tactical priorities and political limitations for what was now termed *Operation Vijay* (Victory). He accorded top priority to the clearance of the Tololing and Tiger Hill complexes as these posed the most direct threat to NH-1A. Next in importance in the initial assessment was Turtok sector, which could afford an attacker access to the Shyok river valley and the base areas supporting Indian troops on the Siachen Glacier. Being smaller and less tactically significant, the Kaksar and Mushkoh penetrations were slated to be cleared next. Batalik sector, remote and formidable, was to be tackled last. These priorities were later reshuffled and Batalik was upgraded second after Dras. The key political limitation imposed on local commanders was the restriction not to cross the LoC. Developed through close consultation between the civilian and military elements of the Indian government, this constraint generated considerable controversy at the time and in subsequent analysis, with many commentators arguing that cross-LoC action was imperative to hasten the conclusion of the offensive and to save the lives of Indian soldiers.

Despite these calls to violate the LoC and some Pakistani claims that Indian troops and aircraft indeed did so, it appears that India's ground and air forces largely abided by this restriction. Certainly there is no evidence to indicate that there were major intentional violations during the course of the war. However, the Indian military and political leadership was careful to keep the option of cross-LoC operations open and used public statements by senior officials to highlight the latent threat of escalation. Nor was this a hollow threat. While very shallow incursions at the local level on the Kargil front were the most likely retaliatory option, the introduction of additional forces into Kashmir (such as 6 and 27 Mountain Divisions) made attacks elsewhere along the LoC a possibility. Moreover, India also had the capability to act along the recognized border in Punjab or Rajasthan. The key offensive formations intended for the international border, the three "strike corps," were "untouched" by Kargil deployments and thus available if the political decision had been made to employ them.[37] The induction of additional medium artillery regiments in the

---

[37] See General V. P. Malik's forward to Singh, *A Ridge Too Far*, xii; also his "Lessons from Kargil," *Indian Defence Review* 16, no. 5 (2002). Prime Minister Vajpayee, Home Minister Advani, Defence Minister Fernandes, and General Malik all made public statements

Kargil sector meant that some units in Punjab and Rajasthan may not have had their full complement of Bofors artillery pieces, but they certainly retained all of their other combat elements and could have taken the offensive in Kashmir or along the actual international border.[38] Likewise, the Indian air force (IAF) was "ready for a full-scale war" by 26 May when it initiated air operations over Kargil and was not "unbalanced" or over-committed despite its important role at Kargil.[39]

While observing the limitations imposed by the LoC, India's national leadership decided to change the battlefield equation significantly by introducing air power, especially fixed-wing aircraft, for the first time since the 1971 war.[40] This decision, however, did not come without more than a week of debate and interservice friction. In mid-May, when the extent of the incursion was still unclear, the army had requested air force assistance in the form of attack helicopters (the Indian air force had responsibility for most rotary wing aircraft). The army contended that this was a tactical step that the two services could take without securing specific political approval from the cabinet. Air Chief Marshal Anil Yashwant Tipnis, on the other hand, adamantly opposed the use of helicopters alone and "insisted that fighters will go in *ab initio*."[41] Futhermore, convinced that the use of air power represented a significant escalation, Tipnis would not commit his service without government sanction or before he felt fully prepared to cope with the possible broad-ening of the war. When the question was raised in the 18 May meeting of the Cabinet Committee on Security (CCS), Minister of External Affairs

---

concerning the possibility of crossing the LoC. For 27 Mountain Division, see Vinod Anand, "India's Military Response to the Kargil Aggression," *Strategic Analysis* 23, no. 7 (October 1999).

[38] Three additional medium regiments were inducted to the Kargil sector from units in Punjab and Rajasthan.

[39] Air Marshal Vinod Patney, Commander of Western Air Command, quoted in Josy Joseph, "Commander Sums Up Indian Air Operations in Kargil," *Asian Age*, 13 July 1999. See also the extensive excerpts from a briefing given by Air Marshal Patney on 12 July 1999 in "Op. Safed Sagar: Western Air Command Operations in Kargil," *Vayu Aerospace Review 2000*, V/1999.

[40] A controversy erupted in 2004 over the supposed "delay" in employing air power during early May 1999 (*Deccan Chronicle*, 14 June 2004). However, the new Congress-led government in New Delhi denied that its Bharatiya Janata Party (BJP) predecessor had erred in waiting till 26 May to launch air strikes (*Deccan Herald*, 10 June 2004). Gen. Malik outlined the timeline of decision-making on this issue in a June 2004 statement (newkerala.com, 15 June 2004), but echoes of the debate persist (for example, see Saikat Datta's interview with Patney in *Outlook*, 7 March 2005). The army–air force controversy reemerged in the autumn of 2006 (see below).

[41] Raj Chengappa and Rohit Saran, "This Isn't the End of the Story," *India Today*, 26 July 1999 (interview with ACM Tipnis).

Jaswant Singh also expressed reluctance to authorize employment of air force assets owing to concerns about escalation. These objections and the erroneous belief that the enemy consisted of nothing more than militants temporarily blocked use of the IAF, but the issue remained a topic of intense, and sometimes heated, discussion among the service chiefs. Malik, Tipnis, and their navy counterpart, Admiral Sushil Kumar, however, eventually settled upon a joint strategy that Malik, in his role as Chairman of the Chiefs of Staff Committee, presented at a 24 May CCS meeting along with a fairly grim assessment of the situation on the ground. Vajpayee and other senior civilian leaders faced an increasingly gloomy operational picture, and with a unified recommendation from the military readily approved the use of air and naval forces.[42]

The air campaign, appropriately entitled *Safed Sagar* (White Sea), began on 26 May, but had little direct physical impact at first as the IAF was neither trained nor equipped to conduct precision attacks against small targets at high altitude. The LoC restriction was also a major hindrance, but intelligence took time to develop, procedures for army–air force cooperation had to be refined, and some equipment had to be modified locally to suit the mountainous environment.[43] Nonetheless, the unprecedented use of the IAF in a situation short of all-out war had dramatic shock value. There were two audiences. First, at the tactical level, Indian analysts believe that the close air-support missions degraded the morale of the infiltrators on the ground, adding a psychological blow to complement whatever physical damage was inflicted.[44] At the very least, the NLI soldiers would have to ask: "where is our own air force?" The appearance of friendly aircraft overhead also gave a boost to the morale of the Indian soldiers who had thus far been facing a discouraging situation. A similar effect was evident among India's domestic civilian population: the IAF involvement created "an upsurge in country-wide

---

[42] Malik, *Kargil: From Surprise to Victory*, 116–126, 244–245; A. Y. Tipnis, "My Story: The Chief of Air Staff on Operation Safed Sagar," *Force*, October 2006; "Army was Reluctant to Tell Govt about Kargil: Tipnis," *Times of India*, 7 October 2006; "Army Was Caught Off Guard in Kargil: Tipnis," *The Hindu*, 10 October 2006; "More Fodder for Kargil Quibble," *Telegraph*, 10 October 2006. The issue of helicopters is complicated by the longstanding dispute between the army and air force over which service should control rotary wing aircraft.

[43] Philip Camp, "The Mirage-2000 at Kargil," www.bharat-rakshak.com; "Army Disputes Effectiveness of Indian Airstrikes in Kargil," *Asian Age*, 21 July 1999; Lt. Gen. Sardar F. S. Lodi, "Indian Air Force in Kargil Operations," *Defence Journal*, January 2000; Rahul Bedi, "Paying to Keep the High Ground," *Jane's Intelligence Review*, 1 October 1999; "Divided by Space," *Force*, July 2005.

[44] Tufail, "Kargil Conflict and Pakistan Air Force"; interview with General Malik, 26 July 2001, www.rediff.com.

awareness" at the village level that bolstered the morale of troops at the front.[45] Second, by adding the IAF to the tactical picture in a highly publicized fashion, New Delhi sent an unmistakable signal of its serious-ness to international audiences, especially to decision-makers in Rawalpindi and Islamabad.[46] The employment of combat aircraft, of course, had the additional domestic benefit of giving the IAF a direct role in a major national crisis, not unimportant for future bureaucratic struggles.

The loss of two fighters and a helicopter during the first two days of air operations vitiated the psychological effect somewhat and handed the Pakistanis a useful morale boost of their own.[47] However, this demon-stration of the intruders' air-defense capability and the unique local con-ditions forced a reassessment of IAF tactics that resulted in more effective utilization of air power for the remainder of the campaign. First, helicop-ters, slow and vulnerable under the prevailing terrain and flying condi-tions, were removed from the combat role (although they continued to play a vital part in support missions, particularly in medical evacuations). Second, strikes by fixed-wing aircraft shifted focus away from defensive positions to command posts and logistic support bases. These attacks, especially those carried out by Mirage-2000s with innovative tactics and a small number of laser-guided munitions, seem to have enjoyed consid-erable success, reducing the ability of the intruders to resist by cutting off their supplies and disrupting their command and control structure. The most important strikes were those carried out against the infiltrators' logistic base at Muntho Dalo and those in support of the assault on Tiger Hill. From the Indian perspective, the destruction caused at Muntho Dalo in mid-June was especially significant as it drastically reduced the supply of food, water, and ammunition available to the intruders at a critical point in the struggle for the Batalik sector.[48] Few if any of these attacks would have been possible without detailed air

---

[45] Author's discussion with Maj. Gen. Ashok Kalyan Verma, New Delhi, September 2002.
[46] *KRC Report*, 105; *Frontline*, 5–18 June 1999.
[47] Indians maintain that one MiG-21 and one Mi-17 helicopter were lost to SAMs and that a MiG-27 suffered a mechanical failure that forced the pilot to eject. Pakistan claims to have shot down all three. Additionally, an Indian Canberra reconnaissance aircraft was dam-aged on 21 May but returned safely to base.
[48] D. N. Ganesh, "Indian Air Force in Action," in Singh, ed., *Kargil 1999*, 178–188; Ashok Mehta, "The Kargil War," in *Kargil: The Tables Turned*, ed. Ashok Mehta and P. R. Chari (New Delhi: Manohar, 2001), 105–106, 132–135; R. K. Jasbir Singh, *Indian Defence Yearbook 2000* (Dehra Dun: Natraj, 2000), 95–97; "Indian Army and Air Force Operations in Kargil: Summer of 1999," *Vayu Aerospace Review 2000*, IV/1999, 30; Patney, "Op. Safed Sagar," *Vayu*, V/1999; Indian Air Force, "Understanding Air Operations in Kargil," http://indianairforce.nic.in/. For more skeptical views of the IAF

reconnaissance carried out by the IAF to prepare target information and assess damage after strikes had been conducted.[49] Furthermore, the IAF had to consider the possibility that the Pakistan air force would enter the battle. Indian air operations thus were consciously designed to foreclose any opportunity for Pakistani air attack against Indian aircraft or ground troops. The Pakistan air force took similar precautions.[50]

The employment of the IAF in the Kargil area had ramifications elsewhere along the entire India–Pakistan border. To be postured to counter any Pakistani reaction, Tipnis and the Commander of Western Air Command, Air Marshal Vinod Patney, had insisted that the air commands elsewhere in India be activated before committing the IAF to Kargil.[51] The army implemented similar measures to demonstrate readiness outside of the Kargil theater.[52] These steps included moving some formations to forward positions along the international border, pushing ammunition to wartime deployment areas, stocking fuel, commandeering civilian rail assets for military use, and placing all armed forces on high alert.[53] In Kashmir, 15 and 16 Corps were relieved of counterinsurgency duties so that they could both concentrate for possible conventional conflict with Pakistan.[54] In addition to increasing levels of preparedness in this fashion, at least one division (27 Mountain) was deployed to Kashmir from the Indian army's Eastern Command on the China border.[55] This transfer was in addition to 6 Mountain Division, which moved from its garrison in north-central India to serve as a general reserve for *Operation Vijay* (ordered on 20 May).[56] The transfer of these two

role, see Praveen Swami, *The Kargil War* (New Delhi: LeftWord, 2000), 12; Bammi, *Kargil 1999*, 443–455; and Brijesh Jayal, "Air Power and the Land Battle," *Vayu Aerospace Review 2000*, V/1999.

[49] Ambarish K. Diwanji, "The Invisible Heroes," www.bharat-rakshak.com/IAF/History/Kargil.

[50] Tufail, "Kargil Conflict and Pakistan Air Force." For a comprehensive review of the Indian air force's role in a historical context, see Wing Commander R. Sukumaran, "The 1962 India–China War and Kargil 1999: Restrictions on the Use of Air Power," *Strategic Analysis* 27, no. 3 (July–September 2003).

[51] Mehta, "The Kargil War," 105.

[52] Bhalachandra Jani, "War-Like Situation Along the Kutch Border," *Gujarat Samachar*, 13 June 1999; *Times of India*, 14 and 15 June 1999; Prasun K. Sengupta, "Mountain Warfare and Tri-Service Operations," *Asian Defence Journal*, 11/99; Pravin Sawhney, "Pulling Along," *Pioneer*, 23 October 2002.

[53] Raj Chengappa, Rohit Saran, and Harinder Baweja, "Will the War Spread?" *India Today*, 5 July 1999; Raj Chengappa, Zahid Hussain, and Sujatha Shenoy, "Face-Saving Retreat," *India Today*, 19 July 1999; Bhavdeep Kang, "Vigil on the West," *Outlook*, 5 July 1999.

[54] Malik, *Kargil: From Surprise to Victory*, 128.

[55] Anand, "India's Military Response to the Kargil Aggression"; S. S. Chandel, "The Indian Army: A Paper Tiger?" IPCS article no. 445, 30 December 2000, www.ipcs.org; and Dinesh Kumar, "Army to Raise 30 More Paramilitary Battalions," *Times of India*, 12 February 2001.

[56] Datta, "War Against Error."

divisions provided India's leadership with benefits on two levels. From an operational perspective, their arrival increased the number of divisions in Kashmir by approximately 20 percent and thereby enhanced overall Indian readiness and expanded the range of military options available to regional commanders. These two formations could have been employed on the Kargil front itself if necessary or they could have been committed to other parts of the LoC if India had decided to expand the conflict. Equally important was their value from the diplomatic perspective. In the past, such redeployments of large formations to Kashmir from elsewhere in India had quickly come to Islamabad's notice, and India could expect that these moves would communicate its determination to Pakistan and thus to other international audiences. Furthermore, Pakistani intelligence was also likely to notice the transfer of several other divisions from the peace-time garrisons in eastern India to wartime locations near the Pakistan border.[57]

The Indian navy also changed its training and deployment patterns in response to the crisis. Although its lone aircraft carrier was undergoing refit, the navy moved major elements of its Eastern Fleet from the Bay of Bengal to the Arabian Sea. Furthermore, the navy opened "Summerex," one of its premier large-scale training exercises, during the first week of June, but shifted the area of operations from the planned east-coast venue to the west in a deliberate effort to engage in what it called "naval deterrence." The Indian navy's actions, named *Operation Talwar* (Sword), included expanded maritime surveillance and intelligence-gathering operations as well as public statements by senior navy officers designed to signal Indian readiness and resolve.[58] Of equal importance was the transfer of India's lone amphibious brigade from the Andaman and Nicobar Islands to India's west coast where it represented a visible threat to Pakistan's long littoral flank.[59] These naval moves, carried out in what one analyst called a "calibrated manner," did not go unnoticed at the time and may have had some influence on Pakistani policy beyond the 1999 crisis.[60]

[57] Malik, *Kargil: From Surprise to Victory*, 130.

[58] Mehta, "The Kargil War," 135–157; Chowdhury, *Despatches from Kargil*, 172–181; Jasbir Singh, *Yearbook*, 81.

[59] Gaurav C. Sawant, *Dateline Kargil* (New Delhi: Macmillan, 2000), 273; "Navy 'Was Poised to Hit' Karachi," *Asian Age*, 27 July 1999.

[60] Gurmeet Kanwal, "Pakistan's Military Defeat," in Singh, ed., *Kargil 1999*, 158–159. See also "Army, Navy to Remain on Full State of Alert," *Daily Excelsior*, 14 July 1999; Malik Ayaz Hussain Tiwana, "Pakistan's Security Concerns and the Navy," *Defence Journal*, April 2002; Bammi, *Kargil 1999*, 435–440; Malik, *Kargil: From Surprise to Victory*, 131, 150.

Pakistan, surprised by the strength and determination of the Indian reaction at Kargil and elsewhere, took similar steps during May and June to improve the preparedness of its land, air, air defense, and sea forces.[61] Its senior military leaders also issued public statements of resolve and complete faith in their ability to "give a befitting reply" to any aggressive action by the other side. It is significant, however, that neither side seems to have initiated the more drastic and difficult-to-reverse measures, such as massive movement of mechanized units, issuance of war-reserve ammunition, and the emplacement of land mines that both sides regard as key intelligence indicators.[62] Both thus seemed intent on taking prudent military precautions and using these steps as warnings to the other side, but both also evidently wanted to avoid measures that could ignite unpredictable escalatory reactions by those across the border.[63] Furthermore, the two sides were careful to remain in contact throughout the crisis via several channels: phone calls between the prime ministers, interaction with their respective high commissioners, exchange of special envoys, and the hotline between the respective Directors General of Military Operations (DGMO). The DGMO link later provided the key means of implementing the political decision to de-escalate as the two sides used it to facilitate the face-to-face DGMO meeting on 11 July where they developed the modalities under which the Pakistani troops would be withdrawn.

On the other hand, there are persistent reports that both sides moved ballistic missiles and possibly initiated nuclear weapons readiness measures during the crisis. It is not clear whether the alleged activities were merely intended to protect scarce and valuable assets by dispersal, or if they were undertaken as intentional signals of readiness and resolve designed to warn the other side. Nor is the sequence of supposed action and reaction clear. Some Indian commentators claim that activity at a Pakistani missile test site and alarming public statements by the Pakistani

---

[61] Some examples: Mahamud Hamdani, "Pakistan CDO Volunteers Ready to Meet Any Threat," *Pakistan Observer*, 16 June 1999; *Al Akhbar*, 21 June 1999; *The Nation*, 22 June 1999; R. Prasannan, "Know Your Enemy," *The Week*, 11 July 1999.

[62] Pakistan's army spokesman noted that the Indian moves were not overly worrisome: reported in *The Nation*, 20 June 1999. See studies of the 1990 confrontation for examples of measures both taken and avoided: Michael Krepon and Mishi Faruqee, eds., *Conflict Prevention and Confidence-Building Measures in South Asia: The 1990 Crisis*, Occasional Paper No. 17 (Washington, DC: The Henry L. Stimson Center, 1994); and Stephen P. Cohen, P. R. Chari, and Pervaiz Iqbal Cheema, *The Compound Crisis of 1990: Perception, Politics, and Insecurity*, Institute for Arms Control and Disarmament Research Report (Champaign-Urbana: University of Illinois, 2000).

[63] "Infiltrators Abandon Two Key Positions in Kargil," *Daily Excelsior*, 1 June 1999; Chengappa, Saran, and Baweja, "Will the War Spread?" *India Today*, 5 July 1999.

foreign secretary and other officials during May and June were seen in New Delhi as a "not so veiled" threat.[64] In response, India may have readied as many as four Prithvi short-range ballistic missiles and one Agni medium-range missile according to some accounts.[65] A first-person narrative by a senior American official supports the view that Pakistan took some steps to prepare its missile and nuclear assets (possibly without the knowledge of the prime minister), but makes no mention of any Indian actions. These reports remain unconfirmed and may be partly or largely false, but they highlight both the miscalculation danger inherent in the India–Pakistan dynamic and the potential role of nuclear and missile forces as constraints on the behavior of both states.[66]

As these moves were being taken outside of Kashmir, India was developing the local battlefield situation and slowly assembling the strength it believed necessary to retake the heights around Kargil. The buildup was retarded by the need to allow troops to acclimatize and by logistic constraints, especially the heavy reliance on NH-1A and the lack of a major airfield capable of accepting large transport aircraft. Nonetheless, by early

---

[64] Raj Chengappa, *Weapons of Peace* (New Delhi: HarperCollins, 2000), 437; Raj Chengappa interview with General Sundarajan Padmanabhan, "Pakistan Threatened India with Nuclear Attack during Kargil War: Army Chief," *The News Today*, 12 January 2001, www.newspapertoday.com; Raj Chengappa, "The Nuclear Shadow," *India Today Web Exclusive*, 24 January 2001, www.india-today.com. General Padmanabhan did not state which Pakistani missile test site had been "activated." According to Kamran Khan in *The News*, 24 June 1999: "the prime minister has also been told that deployment of short and long range missiles with 'extremely effective warheads' has been completed." Foreign Secretary Shamshad Ahmed was quoted as saying that "We will not hesitate to use any weapon in our arsenal to defend our territorial integrity" (*The News*, 31 May 1999); a spokesman later claimed that the foreign secretary had been quoted out of context (Radio Pakistan, 1 June 1999). Other examples of provocative statements include an unnamed Pakistani official highlighting progress in missile development and "sophisticated weapons systems" ("Pakistan Developing Advanced Versions of Ghauri, Shaheen," *The Nation*, 25 June 1999), as well as praise for Pakistan's nuclear and missile capabilities by prominent scientist Samar Mubarakmand ("Pakistani Nuclear Scientist Says Agni-II Test Failed," *Jang*, 29 June 1999). Dr. A. Q. Khan may have made similar statements: see Mohammed Ahmedullah, "During Kashmir Crisis, India, Pakistan Cocked Nuclear Trigger," *Space & Missile Defense Report*, 3 August 2000; and *Amn*, 18 and 19 June 1999.

[65] M. Ahmedullah, "Kashmir Crisis," *Space & Missile Defense Report*, 3 August 2000; Malik, *Kargil: From Surprise to Victory*, 260.

[66] Bruce Riedel, chapter 5 of this book; and "Musharraf Moved Nuclear Weapons in Kargil War," *The Nation*, 6 July 2006. Note that then-Brigadier Feroz Hassan Khan, an expert in Pakistani nuclear affairs, explicitly denied that Pakistan had prepared its nuclear arsenal ("Absolutely not! No such mobilization had taken place during the Kargil crisis") in an interview with Aziz Haniffa published in *India Abroad*, 14 June 2002. For another dismissal of Riedel's piece, see "Crying Nuclear Wolf: Nothing New in Riedel's Revelations," *Times of India*, 20 May 2002.

June, a new divisional headquarters was in place at Dras with three complete brigades under its command and more troops were on the way. In combat units alone, the Indians were able to move nineteen infantry battalions and six artillery regiments to the Kargil front in approximately three weeks, a remarkable achievement.[67] To control this growing force, 15 Corps crafted an organizational arrangement placing the newly arrived 8 Mountain Division, drawn from the Kashmir Valley, in charge of operations against the Mushkoh and Dras incursions with 56 and 79 Mountain Brigades in the front line and 50 Para Brigade in reserve. To the east, 3 Infantry Division continued to control the Kaksar sector with 121 Brigade and had injected 70 Brigade to take over Batalik sector as far as Chorbat La; but it also retained responsibility for the Turtok area (sub-sector West) and the Siachen Glacier (both 102 Brigade) as well as the frontier with China (114 Brigade).[68] The other major change in command structure was the departure of Brigadier Surinder Singh, Commander of 121 Infantry Brigade (which had been holding the bulk of the operational area less Turtok sector), relieved for unsatisfactory performance on 9 June, and replaced by Brigadier O. P. Nandrajog.[69]

Of critical importance for the conduct of the coming battle on the Indian side was the decision to induct large numbers of guns, along with the new infantry battalions and Special Forces units. To cope with the challenge of negotiating extraordinarily difficult high-altitude terrain and evicting an entrenched enemy under conditions where use of air power was severely restricted, Indian commanders relied heavily on artillery. Between 8 May and 12 July, more than 280 guns, mortars, and rocket launchers were added to the sixty or so available to 121 Brigade when the war began.[70] Operational priority and terrain considerations ensured that the bulk of additional artillery was deployed to support Dras and Mushkoh sectors with lesser numbers in Batalik and other areas. The army's Bofors FH-77B 155 mm howitzers, acquired under the shadow of bribery scandals during the 1980s, were especially significant. Offering greater range, accuracy, and destructive power than any other Indian gun, they earned the admiration of soldiers at all levels and fully justified their presence in the army's inventory. Many of the Bofors howitzers were

---

[67] Indian and Pakistani artillery regiments are equivalent to US battalions.
[68] Jagjit Singh, *With Honour and Glory* (New Delhi: Lancer, 2001), 168.
[69] Singh, *A Ridge Too Far*, 62. Brig. Surinder Singh's relief led to considerable controversy. Some observers and journalists argued that he had been denied needed resources before the incursions and was then sacrificed as a scapegoat after the conflict in order to spare senior officers. For a review of this continuing debate, see Praveen Swami, "General Suspects," *Frontline*, 21 June–4 July 2003.
[70] Singh, *A Ridge Too Far*, 73.

drawn from other sectors of Kashmir or the India–Pakistan border; some even turned up in desert camouflage paint.[71] Using both indirect and direct fire, the Bofors howitzers and an array of other artillery pieces played the crucial role in paving the way for the infantry assaults that began to gain momentum in early June.

Indian counteroffensive

With its strength accumulating, the Indian army began the slow process of retaking the heights, starting with those in the Dras sector in accordance with General Malik's strategic guidance. Moreover, thanks to constant and aggressive patrolling, the Indian commanders now had a relatively complete picture of the various incursions and felt much greater confidence in their intelligence appraisals. The first major objective was the Tololing ridge complex in the Dras sector as it posed the greatest immediate danger to NH-1A. Although initial attempts against this dominant feature by 8 Mountain Division were repulsed on 3 June after a nine-day struggle, a second offensive culminated in success, and by 13 June, India could announce the capture of Tololing proper, the first significant Pakistani outpost to fall. Another week was required, however, to complete the conquest by taking point 5140, less than 2 miles straight-line distance from Tololing Top. At approximately the same time, a parallel success was achieved in the comparatively lower-priority Batalik sector where 70 Brigade announced the capture of point 5203. The seizure of these objectives illustrated the nature of the combat under the prevailing conditions, particularly the difficulty in closing on an entrenched enemy in extremely rugged terrain almost devoid of cover, and the enormous logistical challenge of supplying the assaulting teams over narrow dirt paths many miles from the nearest road.

The Indian army overcame the tactical problem through aggressive small-unit leadership, massive application of artillery firepower, interdiction of Pakistani logistics, and resort to night attacks as a matter of routine. Detailed, on-the-spot reconnaissance by senior commanders and comprehensive rehearsals were also essential. The local logistical difficulties required a heavy investment in manpower, between four and sixteen persons being dedicated to supplying every one soldier in the lead assault elements. In retrospect, the conquest of Tololing, combined with the near-simultaneous fall of point 5203 in the Batalik sector, was probably the turning point in the war. Their capture demonstrated that the Indian

---

[71] Sawant, *Dateline Kargil*, 21.

army's combination of careful planning, determination, firepower, and tactical maneuver would slowly but surely overcome the defenders, barring significant reinforcement from north of the LoC or gross bungling on the part of the Indians. Moreover, the capture of Tololing and point 5203 set the context for the visit of American envoy General Anthony Zinni to Islamabad on 25 June, doubtlessly increasing the pressure on the Pakistani government to find a way to arrange a withdrawal.

These opening battles also highlighted the difficulty of communicating information about the combat to domestic and international audiences. Because many of the individual terrain features were so extensive and ill defined, it was often possible to capture part or most of a hill complex days or weeks before the entire feature was cleared. As a result, press reporting from the Indian side sometimes seemed confused (reporting the fall of Tololing multiple times, for example) and was frequently contradicted by statements from the other side. In many cases, owing to the tortured nature of the terrain, both could be correct: as at Tololing, Indian troops could occupy part of a feature, while Pakistanis continued to hold out on other parts of the same complex. Additionally, the relative accessibility of the Dras Valley as compared to Batalik skewed press focus toward the former and often meant that operationally significant events in Batalik did not receive apposite attention and analysis until after the conflict.

The success at Tololing allowed 8 Division to shift resources, especially artillery, for the assault on the 16,700 feet high Tiger Hill by the recently inducted 192 Mountain Brigade. The brigade carefully applied the lessons learned at Tololing: thorough reconnaissance and training were conducted, and the attacking infantry was assisted by elite mountaineering experts, engineers, army mule transport units, and civilian porters. Indicative of the importance of artillery support, the fire plan included more than 120 guns and heavy mortars. At one point in the preparation for the assault, approximately 1,200 rounds fell on Tiger Hill in five minutes, and a total of 9,000 artillery shells were fired at this key objective during the course of one day, supplemented by repeated air strikes. Assisted by this heavy concentration of fire, 192 Brigade attacked on the night of 3–4 July (as Nawaz Sharif was arriving in Washington to meet with President Clinton). The brigade had gained a foothold by morning, but another four days and a costly attack by a detachment from 8 Sikh (thirty-nine of fifty-two men dead or wounded) were required to secure Tiger Hill top completely.[72]

---

[72] Singh, *A Ridge Too Far*, 86–93, 113–117, 125–130. Gurmeet Kanwal, *Kargil 1999: Blood, Guts and Firepower* (New Delhi: Lancer, 2000), 31, 65.

While the fight for the more visible Tiger Hill was in progress, the Indians were also making significant advances in other areas, especially 70 Brigade's sector around Batalik. The Indian commander in this area, Brigadier Devinder Singh, faced not only the same challenges of terrain, climate, and weather as his colleagues further west, but at Batalik these exigencies were compounded by the compartmentalized nature of terrain, the near inaccessibility of this sector, and its comparatively low priority in allocation of resources. The one poor road serving Batalik was even less robust than NH-1A in the Dras Valley, and the remoteness of the front meant that reinforcements and supplies required a two- or three-day foot march to reach the forward positions. Assault troops often faced approach marches of fourteen hours or more just to reach their starting positions.[73] The lack of roads and the broken nature of the landscape also imposed severe handicaps on Singh's ability to build up strength, to control his scattered battalions (at one point, he commanded ten infantry battalions, the equivalent of a full division), or to transfer troops or other resources from one area of his sector to another. Nonetheless, by carefully coordinating and sequencing his actions with the limited resources initially available, Singh created opportunities wherein "assailable flanks" were painstakingly secured to slowly but steadily pick apart the enemy defense and set the stage for a concerted eviction operation.[74] For example, the capture of point 5203 on 21 June exposed the flank of Khalubar Ridge to the west, allowing 70 Brigade to launch a series of multiple and widespread attacks in late June that resulted in the seizure of point 4812 on 3 July and the clearance of the rest of Khalubar over the next several days. During the same period, other elements of 70 Brigade succeeded in taking the key features of Jubar Ridge and nearby heights. By the time the Pakistani DGMO contacted his Indian counterpart on 9 July, therefore, the Batalik sector was almost entirely in Indian hands.[75] Unlike operations in the Dras sector, where the relatively flat terrain of the river valley allowed the Indian army to employ massive firepower in concert with infantry assaults, Singh relied primarily on skillful maneuver at the brigade level to clear his area of responsibility.[76]

---

[73] Col. Lalit Rai, "Undiluted Heroism," www.bharat-rakshak.com.

[74] Gurmeet Kanwal, *Heroes of Kargil* (New Delhi: Army Headquarters, 2002), 62.

[75] Best accounts are Bammi, *Kargil 1999*, 293–360; Ashok Kalyan Verma, *Kargil: Blood on the Snow* (New Delhi: Manohar, 2002), 114–120; and Kanwal, *Heroes of Kargil*, 49–86. Information from interviews in New Delhi, 2002, also used in this analysis.

[76] A number of Indian participants and observers note that the remoteness of the Batalik sector meant less media attention to 70 Brigade's achievements, but also less public pressure to produce immediate results. Commanders in the Dras Valley (Maj. Gen.

leave the shelter of their prepared positions and were thus exposed to Indian fire. Second, the defensive line occupied during the withdrawal phase was poorly chosen. Where the initial positions were carefully sited and mutually supporting, the new line, apparently derived from a map reconnaissance rather than actual knowledge of the terrain, left the intruders poorly disposed to counter the accelerating Indian offensive. Third, two battalions of fresh troops (19 and 33 Frontier Force), unprepared for the rigors of high-altitude warfare, were brought in at the last minute. The rationale behind this decision is unclear. Perhaps the intention was to have the two new battalions hold several small enclaves just across the LoC in an effort to salvage something from the situation. In any case, the two battalions were moved from the plains of Punjab to the Kargil heights sometime in July, and apparently had no time to train, equip, familiarize, or acclimatize themselves before being rushed into combat.[91] If this account is correct, it is hardly surprising that these units suffered heavy losses in the closing days of the conflict. As mentioned earlier, some Pakistanis contend that Indian violations of the *de facto* ceasefire caused many of the casualties.

The official accounts of the post-4 July events suggest that both sides had agreed on a sector-wise cessation of ground and air operations to facilitate disengagement between opposing forces in the agreement signed between Indian and Pakistani DGMOs during their 11 July meeting at Attari. India had set 16 July as a deadline for vacation of intrusions, which later was extended to 17 July. The Indian DGMO, Lieutenant General Nirmal Vij, was quoted to have communicated to his Pakistani counterpart during the talks that any intruder found on the Indian side of the LoC after the prescribed deadline of 16 July "would be treated as hostile and dealt with accordingly."[92] According to an Indian Ministry of Defence (MoD) spokesman, India reiterated its determination to physically evict every intruder, but pledged that it would not fire upon any enemy force retreating according to the terms of the agreement.[93]

Casualties are a constant source of controversy in contemporary military history, and the Kargil conflict is no exception. The Indian

---

[91] Interview. The identity of the two regular battalions is consistent with Indian assessments.

[92] A Ministry of External Affairs brief in New Delhi reported as "Deadline set for withdrawal, IAF strikes suspended," *The Hindu*, 13 July 1999.

[93] C. Raja Mohan, "Pak Begins Pullout," *The Hindu*, 12 July 1999. Brigadier Qureshi during an interview with the Japanese newspaper *Nikki* in Rawalpindi is quoted to have said, "Indian DGMO wanted disengagement by July 16, however, the deadline was extended to July 17 or 18. There has been no firing in the area. The disengagement continues and there was no problem." The interview was reported by Pakistan media as, "Army Never Crossed LoC, says Brig. Qureshi," *The News*, 19 July 1999.

government's official figures are 471 dead (including 25 officers), 1,060 wounded (including 62 officers), and 2 missing and presumed dead. Five of those killed were from the Indian air force. The remainder of the dead and all of the wounded and missing were from the army. These figures are probably close to the mark, but there are persistent rumors that they are far below actual losses and it is possible that they only include combat casualties, not those killed or injured as a result of accident or illness.[94]

Pakistani losses are much harder to divine. Indian sources generally place the number of dead at more than 700 (including 40 to 70 officers), plus some 1,000 wounded, and 8 prisoners. In part, the Indians justify this estimate by claiming to have recovered and buried or returned the bodies of some 250 to 270 infiltrators. Pakistan's Inter-Services Public Relations (ISPR) Director, then-Brigadier Rashid Qureshi, stated in August 1999 that Pakistani casualties included 97 men killed, 200 wounded, and 24 missing during the Kargil conflict (all, he said, on the Pakistani side of the LoC). Qureshi simultaneously claimed that India's casualty toll was 1,717 dead and some 2,000 wounded.[95] The foreign minister, Sartaj Aziz, however, reportedly told the Pakistani Senate that the number killed was 200, and a Pakistani press estimate has placed the figure between 400 and 500.[96] The latter figures are consistent with other sources and seem the most probable.[97] If the Indian estimate for Pakistani casualties seems far too high and the acknowledged Pakistani figure rather low, they nonetheless set boundaries on the likely losses during this three-month war. Of particular note are the high losses among junior officers occasioned by the nature of combat and the tremendous demands on small-unit leadership under the most trying conditions. Furthermore, Indian analysts estimate that as much as 70 to 80 percent of the losses on both sides were due to

---

[94] Singh, *A Ridge Too Far*, 101–102; "Pranab Clears the Air on Kargil," *The Hindu*, 19 June 2004; Malik, *Kargil: From Surprise to Victory*, 342. Note that former Defence Minister George Fernandes gave slightly higher figures to the Indian legislature's upper house in late 1999: "Present Pak Rulers Likely to Intensify Proxy War: George," *Daily Excelsior*, 23 December 1999. Praveen Swami avers that large-scale falsification of casualty reports "is just not possible in India" ("Musharraf and the Truth about Kargil").

[95] Qureshi quoted in *Ausaf*, 9 August 1999. Numbers for "officers" do not include Junior Commissioned Officers (JCOs). Nawaz Sharif's claim that Pakistan lost 2,700 killed seems far too high ("Kargil Controversy," *The Nation*, 15 July 2006).

[96] Reuters report on Sartaj Aziz briefing to the Senate, Andrew Hill, "Pakistan Says N-Deterrent Prevented Indo-Pak War," 13 August 1999; M. Ilyas Khan, "Life After Kargil," *The Herald*, July 2000.

[97] Interviews with Pakistani and retired Indian officers. Two of the prisoners captured in the Batalik sector (from 33 Frontier Force) confirmed widespread casualties to their battalion, hastily inducted from 111 Brigade in Rawalpindi and deployed across the LoC in the culminating stages.

artillery fire – a clear indication of the key role this arm played in the fighting.[98]

Observations

A number of significant points emerge in reviewing the military narrative of the Kargil war as one manifestation of an asymmetric strategy. The following list, by no means exhaustive, offers several key observations that have relevance to the manner in which each side has interpreted the war. These observations are also useful in assessing any future application of military power in Kashmir regardless of whether that application is asymmetric or more conventional in character.

In the first place, the conflict reaffirmed the verities of combat in Kashmir. A combination of weather, terrain, and logistical hindrances (that is, poor infrastructure compounded by the first two factors) makes swift, deep penetrations unlikely if not impossible in the face of even minor resistance. Keeping in mind the variations in terrain within Kashmir, this statement applies to the more southerly reaches of the region as well as to Kargil, even though the landscape and climate further south are in no way as daunting as the battlefields of 1999. Analysis of previous fighting in Kashmir supports this conclusion. In high-altitude areas such as Kargil, these difficulties are magnified by the time consumed in acclimatizing soldiers and the technical challenges associated with adapting artillery and aircraft weapons to the unique environment.

Second, deciding whether the Kargil episode was "the fourth India–Pakistan war" or merely an expanded border skirmish is less important than recognizing that it was well beyond the norm of fighting in Kashmir. The length, intensity, level of forces involved, intentions of the combatants, and inherent ramifications (including possible escalation to full-scale war and perhaps eventually even nuclear use), place the Kargil conflict in a category which is at once completely different from and much more dangerous than the tragically "routine" artillery exchanges and cross-LoC firefights that have characterized India–Pakistan relations in Kashmir all too often.

Third, the tide of the war was beginning to turn in late June and early July before Prime Minister Nawaz Sharif boarded his plane for Washington, DC. By signing the joint statement with President Clinton, Sharif acknowledged the increasingly visible trend: that Pakistani positions on the Indian side of the LoC would likely be eliminated by autumn,

---

[98] Singh, *Honour and Glory*, 179; Harwant Singh, "Support Elements as Fighting Arms," *The Tribune*, 19 June 2001.

barring massive reinforcement and resupply for the infiltrators, or colossal Indian bungling. The Indians would have required more time and blood to accomplish their goal of restoring the LoC, but they were well on their way to doing so even before the Clinton–Sharif communiqué in Washington.[99]

Fourth, restraint by *both* sides was key to keeping the conflict contained. Both governments initiated prudent military measures to ensure that their armed forces were available and ready should a broader war eventuate, but each seemed to send clear signals that it had no desire to escalate "horizontally" (that is to other parts of Kashmir or the actual border) or "vertically" (by introducing more destructive weapons or targeting the opponent's "strategic assets"). India did use its air force and navy to pressure Pakistan and to emphasize its own resolve, but it limited its preparatory steps. Pakistan behaved in a similarly cautious but restrained fashion. Continuous contact between the two governments, both formal (the DGMO hotline) and back channel, doubtlessly played a key role in this restraint. As Lavoy points out in the Introduction, these decisions in both capitals allow for a fairly optimistic assessment. However, three aspects of this superficially reassuring situation deserve to be highlighted in support of a more pessimistic interpretation. First, although this tacit cooperation between the adversaries was a central feature of the Kargil war, it is not inherently obvious that it was then or is now sufficiently robust and flexible to withstand any additional stress. Preparation or repositioning of nuclear and missile assets, as may have been the case for both countries (at least according to some accounts), could have sparked unpredictable and potentially escalatory reactions by the other side. These reactions would have been difficult to manage, especially in an atmosphere of mistrust, tension, and domestic pressure. Second, the need for the adversary's cooperation is an important point to keep in mind when assessing the validity of concepts such as "limited war." For the

---

[99] Some Pakistani military officers and security commentators disagree with this contention, saying that up until 4 July 1999, the Indian military was able to evict only a small percentage of intrusions, and had Nawaz not signed the Washington Declaration, the Pakistan army would have been able to prevail in Kargil. According to Pakistan's Director ISPR Brig. Qureshi, "The Mujahideen kept Indian might at bay for two and half months. They had vacated just a single post in Mushkoh across the LoC, retained their position in Kaksar and retained fifty percent of the area in Batalik," Associated Press of Pakistan (APP), "Pakistan to Man LoC Peaks says ISPR," *Nation*, 29 July 1999. For a comprehensive review of the Pakistani view, see Mazari, *The Kargil Conflict 1999*; and Musharraf, *In the Line of Fire*, 95–97. On the other side of the border, Indian experts claim that they had regained control of 65 percent of the captured territory (85 percent in terms of strategic importance) by the time of the *de facto* ceasefire, "Deadline Set for Withdrawal, IAF Strikes Suspended," *Times of India*, 12 July 1999.

foreseeable future, it seems unlikely that either side will be able to control a confrontation unilaterally. It will require at least a minimum of cooperation with its foe or risk moving into dangerously unpredictable territory. Third, if Pakistani commentators are correct in ascribing some of the deeper advances to "local commanders" or "junior officers" (probably brigade or battalion level and below), then the ability of either side to keep a conflict "limited" could easily be in jeopardy. This would seem particularly dangerous in the heat of combat or in cases where the definition of "limited" is not shared by the two sides. The prospect thus arises that relatively junior military commanders could undermine a carefully crafted national strategy of restraint through what would otherwise be local or tactical actions.

A fifth general observation is that an understanding of the Kargil conflict helps explain subsequent political–military developments in both countries. On the Pakistani side, intimate details concerning the planning and approval of the Kargil operation, its execution, and the decision to withdraw remain highly controversial and may never be known with any reliability. It is clear, however, that Kargil was a contributing factor (some say that it was *key* factor) in the friction between military and civilian leaders that led to the October 1999 coup. It continues to feature prominently as Pakistanis evaluate their national policies, and the various Pakistani interpretations of the conflict are worthy of further study.[100]

Sixth, on the political–military front in India, the Kargil conflict has served as a catalyst for potentially significant changes in the structure of the nation's defense organization, a point that is discussed at length by Rajesh Basrur in chapter 12 of this book. Many schemes for defense reform had been under consideration for years without achieving much progress. For example, in the wake of Kargil, a nascent joint staff (the Integrated Defence Staff) and a joint service Defence Intelligence Agency (DIA) have been established even though the longstanding proposal to create a Chief of Defence Staff nominally senior to the three service chiefs remains stalled. Other measures to improve interservice coordination and to smooth links between the uniformed services and the Ministry of Defence are also under review. Most significant in the long run may be the apparent elevation of the military in national decision-making circles. Traditionally excluded from policy discussions, the uniformed military in

[100] For example: Khaled Ahmed, "What is Our Strategic Thinking?" *Friday Times*, 2 March 2001; Ayaz Amir, "The Ghost that Won't Go Away," *Dawn*, 23 July 2004; Sarmad Bashir, "Let the Truth Prevail," *The Nation*, 19 July 2006; "Ali Kuli Khan issues rejoinder to 'In the Line of Fire'," *The News*, 4 October 2006; Husain Haqqani, *Pakistan: Between Mosque and Military* (Washington, DC: Carnegie, 2005), 253–254; Abdul Sattar, *Pakistan's Foreign Policy* (Oxford University Press, 2007), 230–235; Nawaz, *Crossed Swords*, 508

India seems to have acquired a larger voice in New Delhi, at least in matters of national security. The military's new status likely includes more intimate involvement with nuclear weapons matters, as evidenced by the formation of a Strategic Nuclear Command in early 2002.[101] After almost daily meetings with the top levels of the government during Kargil, this is hardly surprising. Even though the level of uniformed influence remains small compared to some other countries, this topic would benefit from further study, particularly if security issues continue to remain prominent on the Indian national agenda as currently seems likely.

Seventh, the other major change on the Indian side of the LoC occurred at the operational and tactical levels. Kargil not only demonstrated the need for a larger troop presence along the northern stretches of the LoC, it also highlighted an imbalance in India's operational focus and the inadequacy of the command and control structure in the northern half of Indian Kashmir. India met the troop requirement by leaving 8 Mountain Division at Kargil after the war to cover the LoC from Mushkoh to Batalik; 3 Infantry Division retained its responsibility for Siachen and the frontier with China. The conflict had also shown, however, that the prewar span of control for 15 Corps in Srinagar had been too extensive. Prior to 1999, 15 Corps had managed the defense of Kashmir from Baramula to Siachen and Tibet, while simultaneously shouldering the onerous burden of the grinding counterinsurgency operations in the valley. India addressed these problems by instituting a major reorganization in late 1999. The army created a new corps headquarters (14 Corps) to oversee 3 and 8 Divisions along the northern leg of the LoC and established a new counterinsurgency command (Kilo Force) under 15 Corps in the valley.[102] The war thus left New Delhi with the cost of deploying thousands of additional men along the LoC year-round under conditions nearly as grim as those on the Siachen Glacier, but it also brought a much more efficient and agile command and control structure for the northern half of Kashmir.

Finally, it is important not to forget the escalatory potential inherent in the situation. Despite the commitment of troops in the Kargil sector, India retained the capability to conduct large-scale offensive operations

---

[101] Vishal Thapar, "India's Nuclear Command to be in Place by June," *Hindustan Times*, 25 April 2002.

[102] Interview with Lieutenant General (retd.) Arjun Ray, 13 June 2002; Rahul Bedi, "New Indian Corps for Kashmir Duty," *Jane's Defence Weekly*, 8 September 1999; Rahul Bedi, "Clashes in Kashmir Stretch Indian CI Ops," *Jane's Intelligence Review*, 1 August 1999; B. Bhattacharya, "The Rashtriya Rifles," *Bharat Rakshak Monitor*, September–October 2000; Kanwar Sandhu, "Security Forces Skate on J-K's Thin Ice," *Indian Express*, 7 December 1999. An additional counterinsurgency headquarters, Romeo Force, was also raised farther south at Rajouri. Ashok K. Mehta offers a counter-argument in "The Method Followed at Siachen Is Irrelevant in Kargil," 18 August 1999, www.rediff.com/news/1999/aug.

Table 4.1 *Indian and Pakistani forces in the Kargil conflict*

1. Indian forces in Kargil area on 5 May under 3 Infantry Division (Maj. Gen. V. S. Budhwar), 15 Corps[a]

    121 Infantry Brigade (Brig. Surinder Singh, HQ in Kargil)

       3 Punjab

       16 Grenadiers

       4 Jat

       10 Garhwal Rifles

       8 Border Security Force

    70 Infantry Brigade (HQ in Dras)

       (Brigade headquarters arrived on 3 May with no troops yet assigned)

2. Pakistani forces in the Kargil area at the beginning of May under FCNA, 10 Corps[b]

    80 Brigade

    Defending:

    18 Punjab

    5 Baloch

    24 Sindh

    11 Northern Light Infantry (NLI)

    two "Wings" (battalions) Khyber Rifles[c]

    Intruding:

    12 Northern Light Infantry, two companies

    Special Services Group (SSG), two companies

    28 Brigade (from 19 Division)[d]

    Defending:

    13 Azad Kashmir

    13 Northern Light Infantry

    Intruding:

    4 Northern Light Infantry

    6 Northern Light Infantry

    Special Services Group (SSG), one company

    62 Brigade

    Defending:

    32 Punjab

    69 Baloch

    3 Northern Light Infantry

    7 Northern Light Infantry

    8 Northern Light Infantry

    10 Northern Light Infantry

    Intruding:

    5 Northern Light Infantry with

    elements of 3 and 8 Northern Light Infantry – into Batalik sector

    elements of 7 Northern Light Infantry – into Chorbat La sub-sector

3. Indian forces in Kargil area in early July[e]

    Under 3 Infantry Division (Maj. Gen. V. S. Budhwar)

        6 Guards (elements)

        102 Infantry Brigade (Brig. Katoch, Siachen Glacier)

            12 Jat

            11 Rajputana Rifles

            3 Rajput

            27 Rajput

            13 Kumaon

            9 Mahar

            5 Vikas

            Missile teams from 5 and 19 Guards

        70 Infantry Brigade (Brig. Devinder Singh, HQ in Batalik)

            5 Para

            10 Para (Special Forces), including one company of 5 Para

            22 Grenadiers

            14 Sikh

            17 Garhwal Rifles

            1 Bihar

            12 Jammu and Kashmir Light Infantry

            4/3 Gorkha Rifles

            1/11 Gorkha Rifles

            Ladakh Scouts

        121 Infantry Brigade (Brig. Nandrajog, HQ in Kargil)

            21 Para (Special Forces) (one team)

            3 Punjab

            4 Jat

            18 Jat

            4 Dogra

            10 Garhwal Rifles

            14 Jammu and Kashmir Rifles

            2 Rashtriya Rifles

        (114 Infantry Brigade on the Line of Actual Control with China)

    Under 8 Mountain Division (Maj. Gen. Mohinder Puri)

        56 Mountain Brigade (Brig. Aul, HQ in Dras)

            16 Grenadiers

            2 Rajputana Rifles

            18 Garhwal Rifles

            1 Naga

            (1/3 Gorkha Rifles inducted in late July)

        192 Mountain Brigade (Brig. Bajwa, HQ in Dras)

            elements of 9 Para (Special Forces)

            18 Grenadiers

            8 Sikh

            3/3 Gorkha Rifles

        79 Mountain Brigade (Brig. Kakkar, HQ in Mushkoh)

            17 Jat

            12 Mahar

            13 Jammu and Kashmir Rifles

            2 Naga

            28 Rashtriya Rifles

50 Independent Para Brigade (Brig. Bhardwaj, HQ in Gumri)
1 Para (Special Forces)
6 Para
7 Para

Also: 6 Mountain Division (Maj. Gen. A. K. Hakku) in reserve as of 11 June.

Elements of the following Indian air force squadrons took part in *Operation Safed Sagar*:
1, 7, 9, 14, 17, 25, 27, 28, 48, 51, 102, 106, 108, 221, 223, 228, and 229.

Helicopter Units: 129, 130, 152, 153.[f]

[a] Singh, *A Ridge Too Far*, 29.
[b] *Ibid*. 43.
[c] There were two "wings" (battalions) of Pakistani Frontier Corps troops in the area, but they were apparently one wing each of Chitral Scouts and Bajaur Scouts, not Khyber Rifles as identified by Amarinder Singh.
[d] Pakistani sources state that 28 Brigade only arrived in the area in June. At least two other regular battalions (19 and 33 Frontier Force) were committed to the operation during June/July.
[e] Singh, *A Ridge Too Far*, 69–70; and Bammi, *Kargil 1999*, 302, 361.
[f] "IAF Order of Battle in the Kargil Conflict," www.bharat-rakshak.com/IAF/History/Kargil/Orbat90.html.

almost anywhere along the frontier with Pakistan. New Delhi could have launched local punitive attacks along the LoC to divert Pakistani resources from Kargil and to gain territory for subsequent exchange. Alternatively, India could have opted for all-out war by opening a massive assault across the international border. Most of the Indian army was deployed outside Kashmir, readily available for such a strike after a relatively brief period for concentration and other preparatory actions. The outcome of a major offensive would have been subject to all of the frictions of warfare, but the Indian capability and the imminent escalatory danger are beyond doubt.[103]

The Kargil war deserves continuing attention. It was in many ways a watershed for India–Pakistan relations and US interaction with both. It will doubtlessly inform the decisions of civilian and military leaders in New Delhi and Islamabad for years to come. Although Americans often exhibit a penchant for focusing on the immediate present, we would benefit enormously from the insights and regional texture afforded by a closer examination of the history and subsequent interpretations of this conflict. (See Table 4.1 for the forces involved in the Kargil conflict.)

[103] As explained earlier in the chapter, India had committed only two additional divisions to Kashmir during the Kargil conflict: 6 Mountain Division for a contingency role in *Operation Vijay*, and 27 Mountain Division from its northeastern border. Neither of these two divisions was critical to potential operations in Punjab or Rajasthan. The key strike components of the Indian army remained intact, thereby retaining a significant offensive capability. For a broad overview of escalatory potential, see P. R. Chari, Pervaiz Iqbal Cheema, and Stephen P. Cohen, *Four Crises and a Peace Process* (Washington, DC: Brookings, 2007), 127–142.

5   American diplomacy and the 1999 Kargil Summit at Blair House

Bruce Riedel

Prologue

From the day the Center for the Advanced Study of India published this essay on the Kargil crisis and President's Clinton meeting with Prime Minister Sharif at Blair House it received a lot of attention. The *Washington Post* and *The Times* (London) both featured the essay on their front page. Since then dozens of Indians and Pakistanis have looked me up to discuss the piece and give their own opinions or memories of the crisis. Several Pakistanis involved in the Blair House meeting have thanked me privately for getting out an in-depth account of what happened that day. President Clinton wrote me a handwritten note later in 2002 expressing his appreciation for putting together the account.

In the years since 2002 other participants on the American side have provided their own accounts of that day. The president briefly refers to it in his memoirs, *My Life*, highlighting his deep concerns about Osama bin Laden and the lack of Pakistani cooperation in bringing him to justice before he could attack America.[1] Deputy Secretary of State Strobe Talbott relates the events of 4 July 1999 in considerable detail in the context of his effort to persuade India and Pakistan to control their nuclear arms race after their twin tests in 1998.[2] Strobe's version of events is entirely consistent with mine including with regard to the disturbing reports we received about Pakistan's nuclear activity.

Pakistan's General Musharraf, who was not at Blair House, has provided his own version of the Kargil war and the Blair House meeting as well. His antagonism for Sharif, whom he refers to as a "fascist," and his

We thank the Center for the Advanced Study of India at the University of Pennsylvania for permission to reprint the article which originally appeared in CASI's Policy Paper Series in 2002.
[1] Bill Clinton, *My Life* (New York: Alfred A. Knopf, 2004), 863–865.
[2] Strobe Talbott, *Engaging India: Diplomacy, Democracy and the Bomb* (Washington, DC: Brookings Institution Press, 2004), 154–169.

anger at Sharif's "capitulation" in Washington, pervade his memoir.[3] He claims there was no danger of a nuclear exchange because Pakistan had no "operational" nuclear weapons in 1999! Musharraf argues that the military situation entirely favored Pakistan on 4 July and that India had made little or no progress in recovering the heights. He reports that he told this to Sharif on 2 July before the prime minister left for Washington.

Then Indian foreign minister Jaswant Singh has provided a not surprisingly different version of the situation and the Blair House Summit. In Singh's memoirs the Indian army had already achieved the decisive progress in recovering the Kargil heights when Sharif came to Washington but Singh credits President Clinton with taking a firm line with Sharif that led to Pakistan's final and complete withdrawal behind the line of control. Singh also indicates that India detected evidence of Pakistan "operationalizing its nuclear missiles" but is adamant that the conflict was not a nuclear one.[4] Finally, he credits the American position on Kargil as tested in Blair House as the key to the broader transformation of Indian–American relations.

In retrospect that is one of the most enduring impacts of the meeting on 4 July 1999, its transformative effect on the relationship between New Delhi and Washington. Before Blair House the United States and India were estranged especially over the proliferation issue; after Blair House they began to see their relationship in a new light. Presidents Clinton and Bush have wisely seized on this new opportunity to build a new partnership between the world's two largest democracies.

The other transformation was in the American posture toward nuclear weapons in South Asia. From 1974 to 1999 the American focus was primarily on preventing the development of nuclear weapons arsenals in India and Pakistan. Even after the 1998 tests the primary American objective was to cap the development of the two programs and restrain further expansion of their nascent nuclear arsenals. After Kargil the American objective turned to preventing the use of these arsenals and avoiding a nuclear exchange in the subcontinent. Again this would prove to be a bipartisan change of mission. Clinton faced his nuclear moment at Blair House; Bush would face his in 2002 when India and Pakistan again went to the brink of war.

The lost opportunity of Blair House was on Kashmir. As I relate in the article reprinted below, President Clinton was sincere when he told Sharif he would try to help and was eager for Sharif to send someone to Washington to explore how. The politics of post-Kargil Pakistan made that impossible. When Nawaz's brother finally came it was clear his focus

---

[3] Pervez Musharraf, *In the Line of Fire: A Memoir* (New York: Free Press, 2007), 58, 163.
[4] Jaswant Singh, *A Call to Honour: In Service of Emergent India* (New Delhi: Rupa, 2006), 227, 320.

was on Musharraf. When the coup came the door closed. We will never know what might have happened. The tragic losers were the Kashmiri people.

Introduction

July 4th, 1999 was probably the most unusual July 4th in American diplomatic history, certainly among the most eventful. President Clinton engaged in one of the most sensitive diplomatic high wire acts of any administration, successfully persuading Pakistani Prime Minister Nawaz Sharif to pull back Pakistani backed fighters from a confrontation with India that could threaten to escalate into a nuclear war between the world's two newest nuclear powers. The events of that 4th accelerated the road to a fundamental reconciliation between the world's two largest democracies, India and the United States, but also set the scene for another in the series of military coups that have marred Pakistani democracy. As the President's Special Assistant for Near Eastern and South Asia Affairs at the National Security Council I had the honor of a unique seat at the table and the privilege of being a key adviser for the day's events.

Kargil and Kashmir

For fifty years Pakistan and India have quarreled over the fate of Kashmir. The dispute is not a cold confrontation like that between the two super-powers over Germany in the Cold War. Rather it is a hot confrontation, which has been punctuated by three wars. Since the early 1990s it has been particularly violent with almost daily firefights along the Line of Control (LoC) that divides the state and within the valley between the Indian security forces and the Muslim insurgency. Both India and Pakistan deploy hundreds of thousands of troops in the area.

In the spring of 1999 the Pakistanis sought to gain a strategic advantage in the northern front of the LoC in a remote part of the Himalayas called Kargil. Traditionally the Indian and Pakistani armies had withdrawn each fall from their most advanced positions in the mountains to avoid the difficulties of manning them during the winter and then returned to them in the spring. The two armies respected each other's deployment pattern and did not try to take advantage of this seasonal change.

In the winter of 1999, however, Pakistani backed Kashmir militants and regular army units moved early into evacuated positions of the Indians, cheating on the tradition. The Pakistani backed forces thus gained a significant tactical advantage over the only ground supply route Indian forces can use to bring in supplies to the most remote eastern third of Kashmir. By advancing onto these mountaintops overlooking the Kargil highway, Pakistan was threatening to weaken Indian control over a significant (yet barren) part of the contested province.

What was all the more alarming for Prime Minister Atal Behari Vajpayee's hard-line Bharatiya Janata Party (BJP) government was that the Pakistani military incursion came after the Prime Minister had made a bold effort in early 1999 at reconciliation with Pakistan by traveling by bus to the Pakistani city of Lahore for a summit with Sharif. The spirit of Lahore was intended to be the mechanism for breaking the two giants of South Asia out of their half century of violence and fear and moving the subcontinent to a better future. Instead, the Indians felt betrayed, deceived and misled by Sharif and were determined to recover their lost territory.

By late May and early June 1999 a serious military conflict was underway along a hundred fifty kilometer front in the mountains above Kargil (some of which rise to a height of 17,000 feet above sea level), including furious artillery clashes, air battles and costly infantry assaults by Indian troops against well dug in Pakistani forces. Pakistan denied its troops were involved, claiming that only Kashmiri militants were doing the fighting – a claim not taken seriously anywhere.

The situation was further clouded because it was not altogether clear who was calling the shots in Islamabad. Prime Minister Sharif had seemed genuinely interested in pursuing the Lahore process when he met with Vajpayee and he had argued eloquently with a series of American guests, including US UN Ambassador Bill Richardson, that he wanted an end to the fifty-year-old quarrel with India. His military chief, General Pervez Musharraf, seemed to be in a different mold. Musharraf was a refugee from New Delhi, one of the millions sent into exile in the 1947 catastrophe that split British India and the subcontinent. He was said to be a hardliner on Kashmir, a man some feared was determined to humble India once and for all.

We will probably never know for sure the exact calculus of decision-making in Islamabad. Each of the players has his own reasons for selling a particular version of the process. Musharraf and Sharif have already put out different versions of who said what to whom. Others like former Pakistani Prime Minister Benazir Bhutto have also given their views. What is clear is that the civil-military dynamic between Sharif in Islamabad and Musharraf in Rawalpindi was confused and tense.

The United States was alarmed from the beginning of the conflict because of its potential for escalation. We could all too easily imagine the two parties beginning to mobilize for war, seeking third party support (Pakistan from China and the Arabs, India from Russia and Israel) and a deadly descent into full-scale conflict all along the border with a danger of nuclear cataclysm.

The nuclear scenario was obviously very much on our minds. Since the surprise Indian tests in May 1998 the danger of a nuclear exchange had dominated American nightmares about South Asia. Clinton had spent days trying to argue Sharif out of testing in response and had offered him everything from a State dinner to billions in new US assistance. Deputy Secretary of State Strobe Talbott, Central Command chief General Tony Zinni, Assistant Secretary for South Asia Rick Inderfurth and I had traveled to Islamabad to try to persuade him, but all to no avail.

After a few weeks of agonizing, Sharif had gone forward with his own tests citing as a flimsy excuse an alleged Israel plot to destroy Pakistan's nuclear facilities in collusion with India. (I had the Israeli Chief of Staff deny categorically to the Pakistani Ambassador in Washington any such plan the night before the tests but that fact mattered little to Islamabad.) In the new post-May era we confronted the reality of two nuclear tested states whose missiles could be fired with flight times of three to five minutes from launch to impact. One well-informed assessment concluded that a Pakistani strike on just one Indian city, Bombay, with a small bomb would kill between 150,000 and 850,000 alone.

Given these consequences for escalation, the United States was quick to make known our view that Pakistan should withdraw its forces back behind the Line of Control immediately. At first, Rick Inderfurth and Undersecretary Thomas Pickering conveyed this view privately to the Pakistani and Indian ambassadors in Washington in late May. Secretary Albright then called Sharif two days later and General Tony Zinni, who had a very close relationship with his Pakistani counterparts, also called Chief of Army Staff General Musharraf. These messages did not work. So we went public and called upon Pakistan to respect the LoC. I laid out our position in an on the record interview at the Foreign Press Center in Washington. The President then called both leaders in mid-June and sent letters to each pressing for a Pakistani withdrawal and Indian restraint.

The Pakistanis and Indians were both surprised by the US position: Pakistan because Islamabad assumed the United States would always back them against India and India because they could not believe the United States would judge the crisis on its merits, rather than side automatically with its long time Pakistani ally. Both protagonists were rooted in the history of their half-century conflict and astounded that the United States was not bound by the past.

For the previous fifty years, with a few exceptions, the United States had been tied to Pakistan, while India had been aligned with the Soviet Union

nuclear threat its ability to restrain others from threatening use of their nuclear forces would be forever undermined. Sharif must act today.

The room was tense and Sharif visibly worried. The President told the Pakistani team that he had just read John Keegan's new book on the First World War. The Kargil crisis seemed to be eerily like 1914, armies mobilizing and disaster looming. The President had sent Strobe and his team to South Asia a half dozen times in the last year to try to halt the proliferation of weapons of mass destruction, ease Indo-Pakistani tensions and build confidence on both sides. Pakistan was threatening to undo all of that and plunge the world into its first nuclear exchange.

Sharif handed the President a document which he said was a non-paper provided to him early in the crisis by Vajpayee in which the two would agree to restore the sanctity of the LoC (a formula for Pakistani with-drawal) and resume the Lahore process. Sharif said at first India had agreed to this non-paper but then changed its mind. Sharif then asked that the meeting continue just with the two leaders.

Everyone left the room except Sharif, Clinton and myself. The President insisted he wanted a record of the event. Sharif asked again to be left alone; the President refused. The Prime Minister then briefed the President on his frantic efforts in the last month to engage Vajpayee and get a deal that would allow Pakistan to withdraw with some saving of face. He had flown to China to try to get their help to press India to agree to a fixed timetable for talks to resolve Kashmir. Sharif's brief was confused and vague on many details but he seemed a man possessed with fear of war.

The Prime Minister told Clinton that he wanted desperately to find a solution that would allow Pakistan to withdraw with some cover. Without something to point to, Sharif warned ominously, the fundamentalists in Pakistan would move against him and this meeting would be his last with Clinton.

Clinton asked Sharif if he knew how advanced the threat of nuclear war really was? Did Sharif know his military was preparing their nuclear tipped missiles? Sharif seemed taken aback and said only that India was probably doing the same. The President reminded Sharif how close the US and Soviet Union had come to nuclear war in 1962 over Cuba. Did Sharif realize that if even one bomb was dropped … Sharif finished his sentence and said it would be a catastrophe.

Sharif asked again to have me leave the room. The President dismissed this with a wave of his hand and then told Sharif that he warned him on the second not to come to Washington unless he was ready to withdraw without any precondition or quid pro quo. Sharif had been warned by others as well. The President said he had a draft statement ready to issue that would pin all the blame for the Kargil crisis on Pakistan tonight.

The President was getting angry. He told Sharif that he had asked repeatedly for Pakistani help to bring Osama bin Ladin to justice from Afghanistan. Sharif had promised often to do so but had done nothing. Instead the ISID worked with bin Ladin and the Taliban to foment terrorism. His draft statement would also mention Pakistan's role in supporting terrorists in Afghanistan and India. Was that what Sharif wanted, Clinton asked? Did Sharif order the Pakistani nuclear missile force to prepare for action? Did he realize how crazy that was? You've put me in the middle today, set the US up to fail and I won't let it happen. Pakistan is messing with nuclear war.

Sharif was getting exhausted. He denied that he had ordered the preparation of their missile force, said he was against that but he was worried for his life now back in Pakistan. The President suggested a break to allow each leader to meet with his team and consider next steps. He would also call Prime Minister Vajpayee to brief him on the discussions. After ninety minutes of intense discussion the meeting broke up.

The President and I briefed the others in our room in Blair House while Sharif huddled with his team in another room. The President put through a short call to New Delhi just to tell Vajpayee that he was holding firm on demanding the withdrawal to the LoC. Vajpayee had little to say, even asking the President "what do you want me to say?" There was no give in New Delhi and none was asked for. After the intensity of the first round, the President lay down on a sofa to rest his eyes for a few minutes. We all were consumed by the tension of the moment and drama of the day.

After an hour break the President, Sharif and I returned to the discussion. The President put on the table a short statement to be issued to the press drawing from the non-paper Sharif had given us and the statement we had drafted before the meeting to announce agreement on withdrawal to the LoC. The key sentence read, "the Prime Minister has agreed to take concrete and immediate steps for the restoration of the LoC." Strobe, Sandy, Rick and I had drafted this key sentence during the break. The statement also called for a ceasefire once the withdrawal was completed and restoration of the Lahore process. Finally, the statement included a reaffirmation of the President's long-standing plans to visit South Asia.

The President was clear and firm. Sharif had a choice, withdraw behind the LoC and the moral compass would tilt back toward Pakistan or stay and fight a wider and dangerous war with India without American sympathy. Sharif read the statement several times quietly. He asked to talk with his team and we adjourned again.

military, tools, and assumed that they would stabilize their longstanding competition.[1] Leaders of each country made assumptions about the impact nuclear arsenals would have on the other side's behavior, but these assumptions were mutually contradictory, and ultimately failed to account for the attitudes and responses of the other side. As a result, nuclear weapons did not deter war. They did not cause the conflict, but they emboldened Pakistan to launch the Kargil operation and they significantly heightened the alarm with which India, the United States, and other countries viewed Pakistan's intrusion.

This chapter broadly assesses the nuclear dimension of the Kargil conflict beginning with the nuclear tests of 1998 and ending with the current nuclear competition. One section examines how Indian elites thought about the relationship between nuclear weapons and national security after the nuclear tests of May 1998. A second section examines how these tests changed the strategic beliefs of Pakistani elites. The third section assesses the nuclear gestures, signals, and threats during the conflict itself. The fourth and final section analyzes the evolution of Indian and Pakistani national security policies after 1999, and shows how instrumental the Kargil conflict was in shaping the nuclear competition in South Asia.

Indian doctrinal development, including the "limited-war doctrine," and Pakistan's efforts to redefine nuclear "red lines" both during Kargil and more recently during the 2001–2002 crisis, indicate that the subcontinent is entering a low-level arms race. The evolution of nuclear-deterrent postures since the 1998 tests roughly follows the pattern of emerging nuclear thinking in the United States in the 1950s: the hope that nuclear deterrence alone would provide for stability and peace; the recognition that at low levels of violence, strategic nuclear weapons do not deter; and the quest for more effective weapons, flexible targeting options, higher states of operational readiness, and sophisticated command and control – as well as the search for superior conventional capabilities to assure escalation dominance. These changes enhance military options, as well as providing for more secure deterrence. Whether India and Pakistan will achieve nuclear peace or find themselves involved in conventional war – this time one that could go nuclear – remains an open issue.[2]

---

[1] See Devin T. Hagerty, *The Consequences of Nuclear Proliferation: Lessons from South Asia* (Cambridge, Mass.: MIT Press, 1998); and Ashley Tellis, *India's Emerging Nuclear Posture: Between Recessed Deterrent and Ready Arsenal* (Santa Monica, Calif.: RAND, 2001).

[2] The case that nuclear weapons will create peace in South Asia and elsewhere is made most forcefully by Kenneth Waltz. Scott Sagan counters that nuclear war is more likely. See Scott D. Sagan and Kenneth N. Waltz, *The Spread of Nuclear Weapons: A Debate* (New York: W.W. Norton, 2003).

Prelude to Kargil: the May 1998 tests

The May 1998 nuclear tests did not directly cause the Kargil conflict, but the new nuclear environment did affect Pakistani calculations, Indian responses, and the diplomatic reaction of the United States. India entered the nuclear era in May 1974, when the Indira Gandhi government ordered the detonation of a "peaceful nuclear explosive." Pakistan accelerated its own nuclear weapons program in response, and as early as 1983 had developed a crude weapons capability.[3] In the late 1980s, regional crises were affected by the belief that nuclear weapons might be available to one or both combatants. In 1984, Pakistan feared an Indian preventive air strike against its Kahuta nuclear facility. In 1986–1987 and 1990, large-scale military exercises by India and Pakistan, respectively, led to widespread concerns of conventional war. These crises, however, occurred under conditions of nuclear opacity. Both states were strongly suspected of possessing nuclear weapons, and of having some means (probably airborne) of delivering those weapons in combat.[4] Kargil was fundamentally different, because both sides possessed tested and validated nuclear weapons, and this influenced the attitudes of all parties to the conflict.[5]

On 11 May 1998, India simultaneously detonated three separate nuclear devices: one reportedly a thermonuclear device, one a roughly Hiroshima-sized fission device, and the third a miniaturized, sub-kiloton device.[6] Two days later, India tested two more sub-kiloton devices. One reportedly used a reactor-grade, rather than the purer weapons-grade, mix of plutonium.[7] The nuclear tests met with nearly universal approval in

---

[3] George Perkovich, *India's Nuclear Bomb* (Berkeley: University of California Press, 1999), 252–255, 263–265.

[4] Hagerty, *The Consequences of Nuclear Proliferation*; and Waheguru Pal Singh Sidhu, "India's Nuclear Use Doctrine," and Zafar Iqbal Cheema, "Pakistan's Nuclear Use Doctrine and Command and Control," both in *Planning the Unthinkable: How New Powers Will Use Nuclear, Biological, and Chemical Weapons*, ed. Peter R. Lavoy, Scott D. Sagan, and James J. Wirtz (Ithaca: Cornell University Press, 2000), 125–157, 158–181.

[5] Office of the Secretary of Defense (OSD), *Proliferation: Threat and Response* (Washington, DC: GPO, January 2001), 21–30.

[6] See "The Prime Minister's Announcement of India's three underground nuclear tests on May 11, 1998," www.fas.org/news/india/1998/05/vajpayee1198.htm; and "Press Conference (Dr. R. Chidambaram, Chairman, AEC & Secretary, DAE; Dr. A. P. J. Abdul Kalam, Scientific Adviser to Raksha Mantri and Secretary, Department of Defence Research and Development; Dr. Anil Kakodkar, Director, BARC; Dr. K. Santhanam, Chief Advisor, DRDO) May 17, 1998," www.fas.org/news/india/1998/05/980500-conf.htm; and "Press Release on India's Nuclear Tests, May 11 and 13, 1998," at www.fas.org/news/india/1998/05/prmay1198.htm.

[7] Reactor-grade plutonium is typically 65–70 percent Pu-239, and has other isotopes that lower the explosive yield of the nuclear reaction. Weapons using reactor-grade plutonium

India, where polls suggested over 90 percent of the public supported the tests, and significant disapproval in the international community, which condemned the tests and imposed economic sanctions on India.

On 28 May 1998, after over two weeks of intense diplomatic activity, Pakistan also conducted nuclear explosive tests. The number of tests is still contested – Pakistani authorities claimed five, but other analysts were unconvinced.[8] Two days later, Pakistan tested another device.[9] The yields of both Indian and Pakistani tests remain disputed, but seismic evidence unquestionably confirms that both states detonated several nuclear weapons.[10]

The Pakistani public wildly supported its government's response to what was perceived as Indian provocation.[11] Pakistan joined India as the target of international sanctions, although world opinion generally sympathized with Pakistan's action, viewing it as a necessary response to India's tests, rather than as a destabilizing attack on the global nonproliferation regime.

In 1998 and early 1999, India and Pakistan also tested improved missile systems, capable of covering a broad range of targets throughout the subcontinent. By early 1999, therefore, both Pakistan and India had operational nuclear forces with tested, deliverable warheads.[12] The existence of these arsenals fundamentally changed the policies and assumptions of both adversaries and of concerned foreign powers.

A new nuclear environment: the Indian perspective

India began its pursuit of nuclear technology even before independence, at the urging of Jawaharlal Nehru's close friend and scientist Homi Bhabha. Although Nehru preferred to pursue policies that would lead to

---

were successfully tested by the United States, and George Perkovich believes one of India's "low-yield" tests used non-weapons-grade plutonium. Perkovich, *India's Nuclear Bomb*, 428–429.

[8] "Foreign Secretary Mr. Shamshad Ahmed's statement at the Press Conference in Islamabad on 30 May 1998," www.fas.org/news/pakistan/1998/05/980530-gop.htm.

[9] There is some confusion about this second set of tests. Foreign Minister Gohar Ayub Khan announced that Pakistan had detonated two devices at approximately 1:00 pm. At 6:00 pm, however, official Pakistani spokesmen corrected this statement and announced that only one detonation had occurred. Owen Bennett Jones, *Pakistan: Eye of the Storm* (New Haven, Conn.: Yale University Press, 2002), 189–190.

[10] See Hilary Synnott, *The Causes and Consequences of South Asia's Nuclear Tests*, Adelphi Paper 332 (London: International Institute for Strategic Studies, 1999), 54–56, and Tellis, *India's Emerging Nuclear Posture*, 519–522.

[11] There are now monuments to the nuclear test in most Pakistani cities and towns. Mary Anne Weaver, *Pakistan: In the Shadow of Jihad and Afghanistan* (New York: Farrar, Straus and Giroux, 2002), 9.

[12] OSD, *Proliferation: Threat and Response*, 21–30.

a more just and peaceful international system, the colonial experience left him wary of Indian vulnerabilities. Nuclear energy represented the highest echelon of science and technology in the 1940s and 1950s, and also offered dual-use capabilities: the same establishment that pursued nuclear energy could also, if necessary, create nuclear weapons.[13] By the mid-1960s, after the deaths of Nehru and Bhabha, India was in a position to respond to China's October 1964 nuclear tests within a reasonable interval. Efforts to find a foreign nuclear guarantee were unsuccessful, and the drafting of the Nuclear Nonproliferation Treaty (NPT) threatened to foreclose India's nuclear option. India tested its first nuclear device in May 1974.

India announced its first test as a peaceful nuclear experiment – an effort to take advantage of a loophole in the NPT.[14] Attacked for violation of a treaty it had not formally signed, India argued that it would not be denied access to the most technologically advanced weapons in the international system.[15] The 1974 nuclear test took place during a period of domestic political strain, and was intended for domestic appeal and as a symbol of international strength. However, no further tests were ordered and no weaponization took place. In later years, Indian prime ministers authorized and then canceled a nuclear test in 1982, ordered work on a series of land-based missiles delivery systems in 1983, and permitted the development of more advanced weapons designs.[16]

By 1994, India possessed an "opaque" nuclear deterrent. The emergence of growing support for an indefinite extension of the NPT and the possibility of additional sanctions under the entry into force provisions of the Comprehensive Test Ban Treaty (CTBT) caused a gradual shift from satisfaction with the symbolic nature of an opaque force to increased pressure among elites for tests to confirm Indian weapons designs. Tests were authorized and canceled in 1995 after US detection, considered strongly under the brief Vajpayee government of 1996, and finally took place shortly after the new Bharatiya Janata Party (BJP)-led coalition took power in 1998.

The new government reacted jubilantly to the successful tests. Prime Minister Vajpayee and others made considerable efforts to explain the tests as a response to increasing security threats. In a letter to President

---

[13] See Peter R. Lavoy, "Learning to Live with the Bomb: India, the United States, and the Myths of Nuclear Security," unpublished manuscript, 2004.

[14] Raj Chengappa, *Weapons of Peace* (New Delhi: HarperCollins India, 2000), 201.

[15] Jaswant Singh, "Against Nuclear Apartheid," *Foreign Affairs* 77, no. 5 (September–October 1998): 41–52.

[16] Perkovich, *India's Nuclear Bomb*, 242–249, 270–292; and Chengappa, *Weapons of Peace*, 253–261, 276–280, 303–305, 327, and 359–360.

Clinton, and in documents tabled before the Lok Sabha, the government explained the tests in terms of an emerging threat from China, Chinese nuclear cooperation with Pakistan, the increasing pressure of the non-proliferation regime, and the right to self-determination and security.[17] Other observers noted, perhaps cynically, the haste with which the new government retracted Defence Minister George Fernandes' statement that China was India's primary threat.

The Vajpayee government believed the nuclear tests fundamentally changed India's policy options, both within the region and internationally. L. K. Advani, India's hard-line home minister, insisted that India's tests would make Islamabad "realize the change in the geostrategic situation in the region" and "roll back its anti-India policy, especially with regard to Kashmir."[18] He suggested that India's demonstrated nuclear power would allow it to intervene forcefully across the Line of Control (LoC) in response to future attacks in Kashmir.[19] Pakistani elites regarded these statements with alarm. Pakistan prime minister Nawaz Sharif stated, "Can anyone forget the crass Indian bid to establish its overlordship over this region after detonating nuclear bombs on 11 and 13 May 1998? Highly provocative statements were issued and it was said that Pakistan would have to come to terms with its reduced status."[20]

The official explanations of the Indian nuclear tests emphasized extra-regional or international factors, only mentioning Pakistan in the context of Chinese missile and nuclear proliferation to Islamabad. Prime Minister Vajpayee observed that the military implications of the nuclear tests were not especially important: "India has never considered military might as the ultimate measure of national strength. It is a necessary component of overall national strength. I would, therefore, say that the greatest meaning of the tests is that they have given India *shakti*, they have given India strength, they have given India self-confidence."[21]

India's elites focused primarily on the symbolic, international ramifications of the tests, and not the potential regional security impact. This emphasis on symbols rather than hard security concerns is characteristic of much of India's post-independence foreign and national security

---

[17] "India's Letter to Clinton on Nuclear Testing," *New York Times*, 13 May 1998, www.nytimes.com.

[18] "India Ratchets Up Rhetoric against Pakistan and China," *Agence France Presse*, New Delhi, 18 May 1998, cited in Perkovich, *India's Nuclear Bomb*, 423, n. 102.

[19] "Advani Wants Troops to Strike Across LoC to Quell Proxy War in Kashmir," *Rediff*, 25 May 1998, www.rediff.com/news/1998/may/25geo.htm.

[20] See Pakistan prime minister Nawaz Sharif's Address to the Nation, 12 July 1999, www.geocities.com/siafdu/address.html.

[21] Vajpayee, interviewed in *India Today*, 25 May 1998, www.india-today.com/itoday/25051998/vajint.html.

policy.[22] It also played a crucial role in Indian nuclear developments, including the tight centralization of decision-making and the deliberate exclusion of military input for most of the program's history.

It is not surprising, then, that Indian elites viewed overt nuclearization as a relatively benign event – one that would confirm Indian regional dominance. Immediately after the Indian tests, some BJP leaders ratcheted up provocative and hostile rhetoric toward China and Pakistan. However, following the Pakistani tests in late May, New Delhi toned down its rhetoric, engaged in extensive discussions with the United States on a wide range of issues, and publicly considered adhering to the CTBT. Further indications of the Vajpayee government's fundamental reassessment of its security environment were the dramatic initiative to enter into the Lahore peace process and the subsequent decision of Vajpayee to travel to Pakistan.[23]

The Lahore process – a combination of composite dialogue, confidence-building measures, and positive-sounding declaratory statements – raised the possibility that the Indo-Pakistani conflict could be resolved peacefully. India believed the new nuclear-deterrent relationship with Pakistan would stabilize their military rivalry and lead to the normalization of relations between the two states. As Prime Minister Vajpayee put it, "Now both India and Pakistan are in possession of nuclear weapons. There is no alternative but to live in mutual harmony. The nuclear weapon is not an offensive weapon. It is a weapon of self-defense. It is the kind of weapon that helps in preserving the peace. If in the days of the Cold War there was no use of force, it was because of the balance of terror."[24] Indian elites concluded that Pakistan's Kashmir strategy was untenable in an overt nuclear environment. This was not, however, Pakistan's perspective. Islamabad believed its nuclear response, which effectively negated India's conventional advantage, indicated that the game was far from over in Kashmir – and sought to take advantage of the new nuclear environment.

A new nuclear environment: the Pakistani perspective

The driving factor behind Pakistan's nuclear capability is the perceived existential threat from India.[25] A peaceful nuclear research program was

---

[22] C. Raja Mohan, *Crossing the Rubicon: The Shaping of India's New Foreign Policy* (New York: Viking, 2003).

[23] Kargil Review Committee, *From Surprise to Reckoning: The Kargil Review Committee Report* (New Delhi: Sage, 2000), 68–69.

[24] Prime Minister A. B. Vajpayee, statement of 15 March 1999, cited in Prakash Karat, "Kargil and Beyond," *Frontline*, www.frontlineonnet.com/fl1614/16140150.htm.

[25] Timothy D. Hoyt, "Pakistani Nuclear Doctrine and the Dangers of Strategic Myopia," *Asian Survey* 41, no. 6 (November–December 2001), 956–977; and Cheema, "Pakistan's Nuclear Use Doctrine and Command and Control."

initiated in the 1950s, but the nuclear program really became a national issue during the 1960s and 1970s due to the persistent efforts of Zulfikar Ali Bhutto, later foreign minister and then president and prime minister of Pakistan. Bhutto saw nuclear weapons as a substitute for an unreliable alliance with the United States, as a counterweight to India's much larger and more advanced nuclear program, and as a means of undercutting the domestic political power of the Pakistan army.[26]

The nuclear weapons program began in earnest after the disastrous 1971 war with India, and accelerated sharply after India's nuclear test in 1974.[27] When General Zia ul-Haq deposed Bhutto in July 1977, the nuclear program was placed under military control. Pakistani nuclear capability quickly became an important factor in both regional and international politics. US economic and military assistance to Pakistan was tied to the 1985 Pressler Amendment of the Foreign Assistance Act of 1961. It required the US president to certify that Pakistan did not possess a nuclear weapon in order for foreign aid to be distributed. President Reagan so certified during each of his years in office, but with the waning of the Soviet war in Afghanistan and the increased evidence of Pakistan's nuclear weaponization, President Bush was unable to certify Pakistan in 1990 and US economic and military assistance was suspended.

Regional nuclear crises in 1984, 1986–1987, and 1990 brought troubling aspects of South Asia's new nuclear dimension to the attention of international observers.[28] A crisis in 1984 almost occurred as a result of poor intelligence capabilities, when Indian Jaguar attack aircraft capable of conventional preemptive strikes on Pakistan's Kahuta reactor disappeared from their air bases. It was later learned that the aircraft in question had simply been camouflaged as part of a tactical deception exercise.[29]

The 1986–1987 Brasstacks exercise and the associated *Operation Trident* raised fears that India might seek to utilize its conventional superiority to wage a preventive war.[30] These massive exercises, including virtually all of India's armored and mechanized forces, prompted

---

[26] Peter R. Lavoy, "Pakistan's Nuclear Doctrine," in *Prospects for Peace in South Asia*, ed. Rafiq Dossani and Henry Rowen (Stanford University Press, 2005).

[27] Chengappa, *Weapons of Peace*, 205.

[28] See Hagerty, *The Consequences of Nuclear Proliferation*; Sumit Ganguly and Devin T. Hagerty, *Fearful Symmetry: Indo-Pakistan Crises in the Shadow of Nuclear Weapons* (Oxford University Press, 2005).

[29] Perkovich, *India's Nuclear Bomb*, 252–259.

[30] Kanti P. Bajpai, P. R. Chari, Pervaiz Iqbal Cheema, Stephen P. Cohen, and Sumit Ganguly, *Brasstacks and Beyond: Perceptions and Management of Crisis in South Asia* (Urbana-Champaign, Ill.: Program in Arms Control, Disarmament and International Security, June 1995); and Ravi Rikhye, *The War That Never Was: The Story of India's Strategic Failures* (New Delhi: Chanakya Publications, 1988).

Pakistan to reposition its own armored reserves for a possible counter-strike. *Operation Trident*, a planned attack into the Pakistani-held portions of Kashmir and the Northern Areas, was only called off at the last minute, according to Indian reports.[31]

Finally, overlapping military exercises and Indian internal crises in Kashmir and Punjab sparked a near-nuclear crisis in 1990.[32] In addition to partial conventional mobilization along the border, some assembly of Pakistani nuclear assets and preparations of Pakistani aircraft point to a nuclear dimension of the crisis.[33] Interviews with regional sources indicate that the Pakistani military may have assembled a nuclear device. According to the US ambassadors in New Delhi and Islamabad at the time, however, the US government was unaware of any nuclear deployment, or even of the removal of nuclear materials from Kahuta.[34] Each of these crises raised international concern, and by the early 1990s most observers strongly suspected that both India and Pakistan had the capability to employ nuclear weapons.

Throughout this period, Pakistani nuclear doctrine and policy remained opaque. Leaders spoke openly of Pakistan's nuclear capability when in opposition – Benazir Bhutto, prime minister during the 1990 crisis, reported later that she had no control over Pakistan's nuclear forces during that period – but never when in power.[35] Officials implied that Pakistan possessed the capacity to make nuclear weapons, but continued to deny the existence of actual weapons.[36] The most authoritative study of Pakistani nuclear doctrine emphasizes that no serious effort was made to develop either a nuclear-use doctrine or a secure command and control system until *after* the nuclear tests – even though Pakistan had a nuclear capability for a decade.[37] Like India, therefore, Pakistan also followed a *laissez-faire* nuclear doctrine until the tests forced more

---

[31] Rikhye, *The War That Never Was*, 195; Chengappa, *Weapons of Peace*, 322–323; and P. N. Hoon, *Unmasking the Secrets of Turbulence* (New Delhi: Manas Publications, 2000), 102.

[32] A detailed account is P. R. Chari, Pervaiz Iqbal Cheema, and Stephen Philip Cohen, *Perception, Politics and Security in South Asia: The Compound Crisis of 1990* (London: RoutledgeCurzon, 2003).

[33] The nuclear deployment report comes from Seymour Hersh, "On the Nuclear Edge," *New Yorker*, 29 March 1993, 55–73, and is repeated in William E. Burrows and Robert Windrem, *Critical Mass* (New York: Simon and Schuster, 1994), 60–90.

[34] See Michael Krepon and Mishi Faruqee, eds., *Conflict Prevention and Confidence-Building Measures in South Asia: The 1990 Crisis*, Occasional Paper No. 17 (Washington, DC: The Henry L. Stimson Center, 1994).

[35] Hersh, "On the Nuclear Edge," 68–73.

[36] "Pakistan Can Build One Nuclear Device, Official Says," *Washington Post*, 7 February 1992.

[37] Cheema, "Pakistan's Nuclear Use Doctrine and Command and Control," 159; see also Pervez Musharraf, *In the Line of Fire: A Memoir* (New York: Free Press, 2006), 288–291.

serious reconsideration. Pakistani leaders deliberately maintained sufficient conventional force to successfully defend the country for short
periods, which raised the threshold for nuclear use and made their opaque nuclear deterrent credible for defensive purposes.

The new nuclear environment, significant turnover in top military leadership, and Pakistan's traditionally inadequate institutional framework
and dysfunctional civil–military relations all contributed to the decision
to stage the Kargil operation. When the planners of Kargil considered
the probable reactions to the operation, they most likely calculated that
India would be slower to respond, in part, because of its perception of
the effects of nuclear weapons on the military rivalry. They expected that
US officials would rush to freeze the status quo once the intrusion was
discovered, lest war break out. Pakistani planners, however, never seriously believed the conflict would escalate to full-scale conventional war,
let alone a nuclear exchange. In this sense, the "stability–instability paradox" – whereby stability at the central, strategic level allows for instability
at lower levels of conflict – was implicit in Pakistani thinking, reinforcing
key Pakistani assumptions. It was not, however, central to Pakistan's military
calculations.[38]

During Kargil, Pakistan used Northern Light Infantry (NLI) troops to
occupy disputed territory under Indian control. This was a substantial
shift from previous actions: Pakistan had not countered India's occupation of Siachen Glacier with a conventional riposte, when its strategic
focus was dominated by the anti-Soviet war in Afghanistan. While
Pakistan had been providing sanctuary, training, and support for militants
in both Punjab and Kashmir in the 1980s and 1990s, it never infiltrated
troops or soldiers formally affiliated with the Pakistani government.

Moving NLI forces across the LoC – and moving them in great numbers, over an extended front with little logistic backup – constituted a
major shift in Pakistani policy, and a major risk of a massive Indian
conventional response. Pakistani planners discounted full-scale escalation. Just as Pakistan had not responded to the Siachen occupation or the
Neelum Valley harassment with escalation – reasoning that provocation
was not worth the blood and treasure it would require – Pakistani planners
believed India might have to accept the intrusion near Kargil. Any Indian
move to escalate the conflict would bring intense pressure from a US
administration fearful of regional nuclear war.

---

[38] On the stability–instability paradox, see Glenn Snyder, "The Balance of Power and the
Balance of Terror," in *The Balance of Power*, ed. Paul Seabury (San Francisco: Chandler,
1964), 184–201; and Robert Jervis, *The Meaning of the Nuclear Revolution* (Ithaca: Cornell
University Press, 1989), 19–22.

The value of nuclear weapons as "cover" for the pursuit of Pakistani ambitions at lower levels of intensity was both recognized and publicly addressed. Shortly before the intrusion was discovered, Pakistan's Chief of Army Staff (CoAS) General Pervez Musharraf announced that while nuclear weapons had dramatically changed the nature of war, "this, however, does not mean that conventional war has become obsolete. In fact conventional war will still remain the mode of conflict in any future conflagration with our traditional enemy."[39] India's *military* leadership recognized this possibility, as did some intelligence analyses of Pakistani intentions. According to the Indian Kargil Review Committee report, as early as 1991 the Joint Intelligence Committee (JIC) anticipated that Pakistan would use its nuclear capability to limit Indian conventional retaliation in the event of low-intensity conflict.[40] On 10 February 1999, Indian CoAS General V. P. Malik said, "Having crossed the nuclear threshold does not mean that a conventional war is out."[41] While political elites were ruling out conventional war, within two months of each other both army chiefs were ruling conventional war back in.

The Lahore Declaration

The Lahore process was a natural consequence of the nuclear tests. Many on both sides believed nuclearization precluded conventional conflict in the region, and with neither party able to alter the status quo by force, only a negotiated settlement was possible. This faith was evident in the Lahore Declaration: "the nuclear dimension of the security environment of the two countries adds to their responsibility for avoidance of conflict between the two countries." It further states that both countries are "convinced of the importance of mutually agreed confidence building measures for improving the security environment" and that their respective governments "shall refrain from intervention and interference in each other's internal affairs." The Declaration further committed both governments to "take immediate steps for reducing the risk of accidental or unauthorized use of nuclear weapons and discuss concepts and doctrines with a view to elaborating measures for confidence building in the nuclear and conventional fields, aimed at prevention of conflict."[42]

---

[39] Statement by General Musharraf, 12 April 1999, cited in Kargil Review Committee, *From Surprise to Reckoning*, 242. See also his remarks to the Pakistan Military Academy in "Pak Defence Strong, Says Army Chief," *The Independent*, 19 April 1999.

[40] Kargil Review Committee, *From Surprise to Reckoning*, 197–199.

[41] Cited in John Cherian, "The Political and Diplomatic Background," *Frontline*, 5 June 1999, www.flonnet.com/fl1612/16120080.htm.

[42] The Lahore Declaration, 21 February 1999, www.indianembassy.org/South_Asia/Pakistan/lahoredeclaration.html.

In the Memorandum of Understanding signed by the Indian and Pakistani foreign secretaries, both sides further agreed to engage in "bilateral consultations on security concepts, and nuclear doctrines, with a view to developing measures for confidence building in the nuclear and conventional fields, aimed at avoidance of conflict." In addition, the two sides agreed to provide each other with advance notification of ballistic missile tests, reduce the risks of accidental or unauthorized use of nuclear weapons, and establish appropriate communications systems to provide prompt notification to the other side of any incident that might adversely affect either side or raise the risk of war. Finally, they both agreed to a continuing moratorium on nuclear tests and bilateral consultations on security, disarmament and, nonproliferation.[43]

Pakistani military leaders, however, doubted that the Lahore process would produce concrete results. They were satisfied with the tempo and tenor of parallel discussions with their Indian military counterparts. They were, however, concerned that Sharif – not known for his mental acuity – might naively agree to measures ultimately harmful to Pakistan's security. Discussions at Lahore quickly moved from a formal bureaucratic process to a much less structured and controllable dialogue between Sharif and Vajpayee. This high-level dialogue prevented the usual slow consensus building among Pakistani elites that is intended to ensure and preserve both organizational and national interests.

Sharif was not able to see the contradiction between pursuing the Lahore process and permitting the Kargil intrusion. The military had little use for the rosy language of the dialogue, and worried about the ramifications for Pakistani security. As the momentum grew for the Kargil intrusion, no institution or advisor existed to point out the obvious strategic flaws in a policy of simultaneous political bridge-building and military invasion. As a consequence, even as the Lahore Agreement was being signed, it was actively being undermined. In February, Pakistani forces already were infiltrating across the LoC. This remarkable inconsistency in Pakistani policy demonstrates significant institutional disconnects in thinking about the nature of India–Pakistan relations in the nuclear era.

Kargil as a nuclear crisis

The nuclear capabilities of India and Pakistan had important indirect effects on the Kargil conflict. Pakistan undertook the infiltration believing that international intervention, spurred by the fears of nuclear escalation,

---

[43] Memorandum of Understanding, 21 February 1999, www.stimson.org/southasia/?sn=sa20020109215#doc2.

would freeze the conflict before India could retake the captured areas, and would prevent India from escalating elsewhere on the LoC. On the other hand, India did not suspect such Pakistani adventurism, was slow to respond, and, when it did, was more dedicated to reclaiming the heights than Pakistan had expected. The international community, worried about escalation, was equally concerned about nuclear blackmail, and placed intense pressure on Pakistan to withdraw. Most importantly, both sides appear to have made serious efforts to learn from the nuclear aspects of the crisis.

A nuclear crisis can be distinguished from other crises by the simple presence, on one or more sides, of nuclear weapons. Four increasingly serious indicators determine the severity of the crisis: (1) demonstrated nuclear capability; (2) covert or public threats of nuclear use by officials of either side; (3) heightened readiness or deployment of nuclear weapons; and (4) actual nuclear use.

Kargil constituted an exceptional crisis in the Indo-Pakistani rivalry, because neither the adversaries nor the international community could deny the possession of nuclear weapons on both sides (step one). These demonstrated capabilities raised the risk of escalation, the potential for foreign intervention, and created strong but contradictory expectations in the minds of policymakers on both sides.

Veiled and direct threats from a range of official and unofficial sources permeated diplomatic interaction during the crisis, and not surprisingly added to general confusion, raising the fears of escalation through mis-perception (step two). While leaders on both sides engaged in nuclear rhetoric, neither side ever threatened nuclear weapons use and neither side feared the use of nuclear weapons by the other. However, observers in the United States and elsewhere were alarmed by the possibility that the limited conflict might escalate into a conventional war and then to nuclear use.

In late May, Pakistani foreign secretary Shamshad Ahmed made the most prominent nuclear statement of the conflict when he warned India that Pakistan could use "any weapon" to defend its territorial integrity.[44] This statement is significant, as Pakistani statements on nuclear doctrine usually focus on nuclear use as a "last resort" when the survival of the state is at stake. It also took place quite early in the crisis – shortly after India had escalated the military situation by authorizing use of the Indian air force for precision strikes against Pakistani positions on the Indian side of the LoC. This suggests that Pakistan was manipulating the nuclear threat,

---

[44] "Pakistan Warns It May Use Any Weapon in Defence," *Financial Times Information, Global News Wire*, 31 May 1999.

publicly setting a deliberately lowered nuclear threshold in an effort to spur international intervention and, as a consequence, to limit India's conventional response. As Zafar Iqbal Cheema indicates in chapter 2 of this book, Pakistani planners assumed that foreign intervention would freeze hostilities at an early stage of the crisis, leaving Pakistan in possession of at least some of its gains across the LoC and thereby enabling it to bargain over Kashmir from a stronger position.

The Kargil Review Committee notes that unlike Pakistan, India issued no nuclear threats. This statement is not entirely correct. India made nuclear threats in response to Pakistani statements. Indian leaders also issued several statements in June apparently intended for domestic audiences. Indian naval chief Admiral Sushil Kumar stated that the Indian navy could both survive a nuclear attack and launch one in retaliation.[45] Since the Indian navy had not taken custody of any nuclear weapons, this statement was probably intended to draw attention to the movement of elements of India's Eastern and Western fleets to strategic positions in the North Arabian Sea, and also to position the Indian navy more favorably for future budget debates.

On 20 June, an editorial in the newspaper of the BJP-affiliated, extremist Rashtriya Swayamsevak Sangh (RSS) urged Prime Minister Vajpayee to launch a nuclear strike on Pakistan.[46] Given the close ideological and political links between the RSS and the more militant members of the BJP coalition, Pakistani leaders could have interpreted this as an official statement. While it did not reflect Vajpayee's views, these provocative statements by figures outside the actual decision-making loop complicated crisis management.

The same was true for Pakistan, particularly at the height of the crisis. As Prime Minister Sharif prepared to travel to China and the United States to obtain support for Pakistan's position, Religious Affairs Minister Raja Zafarul Haq publicly warned that Pakistan could resort to the nuclear option to preserve Pakistani territory, sovereignty, or security.[47] Minister Haq was not involved in Pakistan's nuclear command and control apparatus. This statement was uttered for domestic, or perhaps even personal, political reasons.

The remark was received with some alarm by the international community, and also prompted a series of Indian responses. Prime Minister

---

[45] Cited in "The Warning from Kargil," *The Hindu*, 1 July 1999.
[46] Reported in "Warring Nations – India and Pakistan," *The Straits Times Press* (Singapore), 5 July 1999.
[47] "Pakistan Minister Says Use of Nuclear Weapons Justifiable if National Security Jeopardized," *Press Trust of India*, 2 July 1999.

Vajpayee stated that India was prepared for all eventualities.[48] According to *The Hindu*, "The Union Defence Minister, Mr. George Fernandes, said here today that Pakistan's threat of a full-fledged nuclear war should not be taken frivolously and that the country was prepared for any eventuality."[49] National Security Advisor Brajesh Mishra stated that India would not use nuclear weapons first and that India was prepared in case "some lunatic tries to do something against us."[50] In this case, an apparently unofficial remark prompted a series of retaliatory statements by Indian officials at the highest level.

Asked about the possibility that Pakistan might agree to a "no-first-use" declaration, Pakistan's minister of information, Mushahid Hussain, replied "Well, what do they say, 'Que sera, sera,' what will be will be. We hope it will not come to the nuclear thing."[51] This was an appallingly flippant expression of policy, and revealed a surprising lack of sophistication in nuclear diplomacy. Public statements in South Asia frequently are high on rhetoric and short on substance. In contrast to the US and Soviet experiences, India and Pakistan have no history, organizational apparatus, or guidelines in sending nuclear signals. What occurred during the Kargil crisis, and even during 2001–2002, was *ad hoc*, uncoordinated, and somewhat confused nuclear rhetoric. As a result, both sides took steps to tighten control over nuclear rhetoric in future crises.

In addition to the *ad hoc* nuclear posturing, it has been reported that both sides increased nuclear readiness and may have made nuclear weapons available for use (stage three). According to a report by an Indian journalist, nuclear warheads were readied, and delivery systems including Mirage-2000 aircraft, short-range Prithvi missiles, and medium-range Agni missiles were prepared for possible use. Nuclear weapons, according to this report, were placed at "Readiness State 3" – ready to be mated with delivery systems at short notice.[52] However, no US officials at the time mentioned it in any of their interviews or statements.

The most interesting recent testimony is that of Bruce Riedel, then-Special Assistant for Near East and South Asian Affairs at the US National Security Council. According to the monograph originally published in 2002 and reprinted in this book, on 3 July 1999 US intelligence detected "disturbing evidence that the Pakistanis were preparing their nuclear

---

[48] "India Not Daunted by Pak Nuke Threat: PM," *Times of India*, 1 July 1999.
[49] "India Ready for any Eventuality," *The Hindu*, 1 July 1999.
[50] "India Prepared for Pakistan Nuclear Attack," *Financial Times Information*, Global News Wire, 4 July 1999.
[51] Cited in "Kashmir Thwarts India–Pakistan Attempt at Trust," *New York Times*, 4 July 1999.
[52] Chengappa, *Weapons of Peace*, 437.

arsenals for possible deployment."[53] In a personal meeting with Prime Minister Sharif, President Clinton asked, "Did Sharif know his military was preparing their nuclear-tipped missiles?" Reportedly, Sharif responded only by saying "India was probably doing the same."[54] At a conference held in Monterey, California at the beginning of this project, many Indian and Pakistani participants rejected the Riedel assertion. Interestingly, however, this report apparently was confirmed by then Indian CoAS General Sundarajan Padmanabhan in early 2001, when he stated that Pakistan "activated one of its nuclear missile bases and had threatened India with a nuclear attack."[55] Pakistani authorities have denied moving missiles or preparing for a nuclear attack.

Although well-informed sources made the claims about Indian and Pakistani nuclear deployments, they have not been corroborated by other evidence. Moreover, they fly in the face of other, more official claims that no nuclear deployments took place. What probably occurred was that Pakistan dispersed its nuclear-capable missiles out of storage sites for *defensive* purposes – a development that could have been misinterpreted by intelligence agencies as an operational deployment. Similarly, accounts that India heightened the readiness of its nuclear forces have not been verified by others. In interviews with senior US officials after Kargil, there was no discussion of such deployment. However, it follows that any serious military crisis between India and Pakistan (or any other pair of nuclear states) probably will be accompanied by a great deal of confusion, controversy, and alarm over possible operational deployments – a condition that could have been predicted after the still-debated 1990 reports.

At Kargil, the combatants reached two of the four possible stages of a nuclear crisis. Forces were available, threats were issued and responded to in pursuit of political objectives, but nuclear weapons were not deployed. Simply because of the timing of the Kargil conflict – the first military crisis between India and Pakistan after the May 1998 nuclear explosive tests – nuclear weapons played a more overt and significant role in 1999 than in previous crises, when both countries kept their deterrents opaque. As noted above, there also were more references to nuclear weapons, some veiled and some blatant, by government and quasi-government officials than in previous Indo-Pakistani crises.

Another indicator of the role of nuclear weapons in this crisis was India's restrained military response. As early as 1949, India began planning to respond to Pakistani attacks in Kashmir with escalation across the

[53] See chapter 5 of this book, p. 136.   [54] *Ibid.* p. 139.
[55] Raj Chengappa, "The Nuclear Shadow," *India Today*, 24 January 2001, www.indiatoday.com/webexclusive/columns/chengappa/20010124.html.

ceasefire line and, if necessary, the international border.[56] In 1965, Indian troops crossed the ceasefire line in response to *Operation Gibraltar* – a major Pakistani infiltration of hundreds of irregular forces into Kashmir. Pakistan escalated to conventional war, launching an armored thrust (*Operation Grand Slam*) through the Chenab corridor, which threatened to sever the main highway leading to the Kashmir Valley. India retaliated in early September by launching major conventional offensives across the international border, aimed at the key cities of Lahore and Sialkot. India's response to Pakistani conventional or irregular attacks in Kashmir, therefore, relied on expanding the war in both intensity and in geographic scope – playing to India's quantitative advantages and greater military and economic resources.

Throughout the 1980s, under the prompting of General K. Sundarji, India had flirted with the concept of conventional preemption during a nuclear crisis, relying on India's quantitative edge in air power and armor.[57] Admittedly, the 1980–1990 period also suggested emerging restraint on both sides. Pakistan did not escalate when India captured Siachen Glacier in 1984, and India did not attack Pakistan conventionally despite abundant evidence of Pakistani support for Punjabi and Kashmiri rebels. These exceptions took place under conditions of evolving nuclear capability on both sides. At Kargil, unlike the response to *Operation Gibraltar* in 1965, India did *not* escalate across the LoC or international border even though it eventually had clear evidence that the attackers were Pakistani troops, rather than insurgents.

India mobilized troops in 1999 for attack. The army canceled leaves and moved elements of mechanized units to the borders of Gujarat, Rajasthan, and Punjab, but it refused to escalate.[58] This matched Pakistani expectations. As Shaukat Qadir noted, the Pakistan army plan at Kargil assumed that India lacked the capability to escalate successfully to all-out conventional war. While nuclear deterrence was "an underlying

---

[56] Brian Cloughley, *A History of the Pakistan Army: Wars and Insurrections*, 2nd edn (Oxford University Press, 2000), 82; Sumit Ganguly, *Conflict Unending: India–Pakistan Tensions since 1947* (New York: Columbia University Press, 2001), 35–50; Lorne J. Kavic, *India's Quest for Security: Defence Policies, 1947–1965* (Berkeley: University of California Press, 1967), 189–190.

[57] Sidhu, "India's Nuclear Use Doctrine," 136; and Scott D. Sagan, "The Perils of Proliferation in South Asia," *Asian Survey* 41, no. 6 (November–December 2001): 1068–1074.

[58] Raj Chengappa, Rohit Saran, and Harinder Baweja, "Will the War Spread," *India Today*, 5 July 1999, www.indiatoday.com; "Vajpayee Rules Out Assault into Pakistan," *The Weekend Australian*, 26 June 1999; Kanti Bajpai, "Testing the Limits," *Times of India*, 6 July 1999. What distinguished the mobilization of 1999 from that of 2001–2002 is that in 1999 strike corps were not moved to their launch areas. In 2001–2002, they were.

factor," it was not a major concern for Pakistan.[59] Because Pakistan was not reinforcing the NLI posts, horizontal escalation would not have enabled India to dislodge the intruders. In the Pakistani calculus, Indian escalation elsewhere along the LoC would only decrease the number of Indian troops available to assail the Kargil heights. Pakistan also had faith that its defensive formations would prevent easy Indian gains elsewhere. Indian mobilization occurred as a contingency against an improbable rout of Indian forces at Kargil and also to prevent Pakistan from employing its reserve forces in Kashmir. In any event, by the time the mobilization was executed, India's military progress against the Pakistani positions made escalation unnecessary.

Post-Kargil interaction: the nuclear dimension

Indian and Pakistani interactions after the conflict demonstrate that both states are trying to adapt to the lessons of Kargil. These adaptations suggest significantly different interpretations of events by the two countries, which may again lead to contradictory policies and further instability. In the aftermath of Kargil, both sides attempted to influence perceptions of the importance of the nuclear dimension. On 12 July 1999, Prime Minister Sharif stated, "It has been my constant effort that our countries be spared the horror of a nuclear war. Only a desire for collective suicide can prompt us to take such a step. I have no such intention. I believe Prime Minister Vajpayee has no such intention either. However, going by the attitude of India, it did seem to us that New Delhi was moving rapidly towards war ... [T]he number of troops deployed by India on our borders was again war-like. Its naval power was moved close to our shores and its nuclear missiles turned towards us. The Indian air force was put on red alert."[60]

The Kargil Review Committee points out that during the Cold War, each superpower guarded against the tactic of "salami slicing" – taking small amounts of territory that the adversary would not find worth the cost of nuclear escalation. Pakistan attempted this at Kargil, according to the report, but was unsuccessful in making Kargil a nuclear flashpoint.[61] The

---

[59] Shaukat Qadir, "Kargil: What Followed," *Daily Times*, 24 August 2002, www.dailytimes. com.pk/.

[60] Sharif's Address to the Nation, 12 July 1999. Sharif sought to explain to a domestic audience why he traveled to Washington and ordered the troop withdrawal. His speech attempted to defuse public anger as the bodies of slain Pakistani soldiers were being returned home and the military openly gave honors to the war dead and injured.

[61] Kargil Review Committee, *From Surprise to Reckoning*, 242–243. See also Timothy D. Hoyt, "Politics, Proximity and Paranoia: The Evolution of Kashmir as a Nuclear Flashpoint," *India Review* 2, no. 3 (July 2003): 117–144.

initial Indian response, therefore, was to highlight to the international community Pakistan's aggression, and to emphasize its own restraint. Even though there was no real fear of nuclear use during Kargil, one of India's first actions after the crisis ended was to update contingency plans to reflect the threat of nuclear attack.[62]

The international community feared that Kargil might escalate to full conventional war – a concern that prompted increasing US diplomatic participation during the conflict.[63] This intense US involvement positioned the United States – perhaps unintentionally – for a more prominent role in future crises and negotiations.[64] Shortly after Kargil, India reviewed its strategic options so that it would not have to rely on the international community as a bulwark against future Pakistani aggression or miscalculation. In more recent crises, however, India relied even more on international support for its compellence strategy against Pakistan. India's goal after Kargil may have been strategic autonomy; however, in 2002 it leaned on US support.

Lessons each side derived from the Kargil conflict soon appeared in policy debates and pronouncements.[65] Kargil forced India to think seriously about how to operationalize its nuclear deterrent and to reevaluate limited conflict under the nuclear umbrella. One month after Pakistani troops vacated the Kargil heights, India announced its Draft Nuclear Doctrine, which, as Rajesh M. Basrur observes in chapter 12 of this book, was highly publicized for domestic and international purposes.[66] This "draft" was modified and made official policy on 4 January 2003.[67] It established a two-layered National Command Authority, with a political council that determines policy and an executive council responsible for implementation. The National Command Authority already has forced the Indian military to begin development of a nuclear command and

---

[62] "New Delhi 'War Book' Updated for Possible Nuke Attack," *Agence France Presse*, 29 July 1999.

[63] "Kashmir Crisis Was Defused on Brink of War," *Washington Post*, 26 July 1999.

[64] Abdus Sabur, "The Kargil Crisis: An Overview," www.arts.monash.edu.au/mai/savir-tualforum/PaperSabur1.htm.

[65] The rest of the international community derived lessons as well. See, for example, Waheguru Pal Singh Sidhu, "In the Shadow of Kargil: Keeping Peace in Nuclear South Asia," in *Managing Armed Conflicts in the 21st Century*, ed. Adekeye Adebajo and Chandra Lekha Sriram (London: Frank Cass, 2001); and Ashley J. Tellis, C. Christine Fair, and Jamison Jo Medby, *Conflict Under the Nuclear Umbrella: Indian and Pakistani Lessons From the Kargil Crisis* (Santa Monica, Calif.: RAND, 2001).

[66] National Security Advisory Board, "Draft Report on Nuclear Doctrine," 17 August 1999, available at www.indianembassy.org/policy/CTBT/nuclear_doctrine_aug_17_1999.html.

[67] Public Information Bureau, Government of India, "Cabinet Committee on Security Reviews Progress in Operationalizing India's Nuclear Doctrine" (4 January 2003), http://pib.nic.in/archieve/lreleng/lyr2003/rjan2003/04012003/r040120033.html.

control system and increase the number of delivery vehicles available for strategic forces. India also has created a post at the top of its military hierarchy with nuclear weapons responsibility: the Commander-and-Chief, Strategic Forces Command, who will report to the Chief of the Integrated Defence Staff.

In early 2000 Indian political and military figures proclaimed a "limited-war doctrine."[68] This doctrine reasserted the conclusions of General Malik, stating that India believed a "strategic space" existed for low-intensity or limited conventional conflict even under conditions of nuclear deterrence. Both concepts aimed at denying Pakistan any advantage through the threat of nuclear escalation, or through support for Kashmiri rebels.[69] They also aimed to maximize the relative Indian advantages of economic resources, presumably larger stockpiles of fissile material, and quantitatively (and, in some cases, qualitatively) superior conventional forces. In short, India tried to practice, at least at the rhetorical level, a form of escalation dominance: the maintenance of military superiority at all levels of warfare.[70]

Pakistan publicized its new command and control arrangements, ensuring that nuclear weapons would be closely controlled and readily available to military commanders in crisis.[71] This would strengthen the credibility of Pakistan's nuclear deterrent and enable nuclear weapons to be used early in a conflict in response to Indian military gains. Pakistan sought to negate India's efforts at escalation dominance by lowering the nuclear threshold and increasing nuclear risks, a reemphasis of Foreign Secretary Ahmed's efforts during the Kargil crisis.

Pakistan foreign minister Abdus Sattar publicly rejected the concept of limited war.[72] Pakistan continued to stress the danger of war, the aggressive policy of India against Kashmiri insurgents, and the importance of US assistance in resolving the Kashmir issue.[73] The fact that General Musharraf, widely blamed for carrying out the Kargil operation and ruining the Lahore process, became Pakistan's new head of state further complicated Indo-Pakistani relations.

---

[68] "Fernandes unveils 'limited war' doctrine," *The Hindu*, 25 January 2000; "When Words Hurt: No Limits on a 'Limited War,'" *Asiaweek*, 31 March 2000. George Fernandes, "Address to the 2nd International Conference on Asian Security in the 21st Century," Institute for Defence Studies and Analyses, New Delhi, India, 24–25 January, 2000.

[69] Rajesh M. Basrur, "Kargil, Terrorism, and India's Strategic Shift," *India Review* 1, no. 4 (October 2002), 39–56.

[70] V. R. Raghavan, "Limited War and Nuclear Escalation in South Asia," *Nonproliferation Review* 8, no. 3 (Fall–Winter 2001): 1–18.

[71] Hoyt, "Pakistani Nuclear Doctrine," 964–965; Musharraf, *In the Line of Fire*, 288–290.

[72] "Nothing Called Limited War: Sattar," *Times of India*, 2 May 2000.

[73] "'Great Danger' of War with India: Sattar," *Times of India*, 14 March 2000.

On 13 December 2001, terrorists attacked the Indian parliament building, very nearly gaining entrance in what appears to be a plot to hold members of the government hostage. This unprecedented attack on the seat of Indian democracy outraged the government, particularly after Indian intelligence services reported a connection between the attackers and Pakistani intelligence services.[74]

The Indian government responded with military coercion, utilizing lessons learned from Kargil. India initiated an unprecedented military buildup, calling formations from central and eastern India to the Pakistani border. By the end of December, Pakistani intelligence officials identified elements of twenty-three Indian divisions on the border, in addition to 600 aircraft. India moved troops from the border with China (3 Corps) as well.[75] The deployment included three entire "strike corps," each based around an armored division, in Punjab and Rajasthan to threaten strikes at Lahore and the highway that links Lahore with the port city of Karachi.[76] Deployment of these strike corps constituted a significant escalation – even at the height of Kargil, full strike corps were not deployed. India also cancelled the Army Day parade as a signal of serious intent.[77]

India also began a careful campaign to undermine Pakistan's nuclear deterrent. Large exercises testing war-fighting capabilities in a nuclear battlefield were announced.[78] On 25 December 2001, Jana Krishnamurthy, president of the ruling BJP party, warned Pakistan that "its existence itself would be wiped off the world map" if it attempted to use nuclear weapons.[79] On 3 January 2002, Defence Minister George Fernandes stated that nuclear attacks on any Indian troops would be treated as nuclear attacks on Indian soil, prompting a massive Indian nuclear response.[80] CoAS General Padmanabhan then repeated this threat on 11 January 2002: if Pakistan used nuclear weapons against Indian soldiers on the battlefield, "the continuation of the existence of Pakistan as a nation would be in doubt."[81] The testing of the 400–500-mile-range Agni-I missile in January demonstrated for the first time that India was

[74] "Lashkar Responsible for Attack, Says Jaswant," *The Hindu*, 15 December 2001.
[75] "India Builds Up Forces as Bush Urges Calm," *New York Times*, 30 December 2001.
[76] "India Fully Prepared to Meet Exigencies, Says Jaswant," *The Hindu*, 24 December 2001.
[77] "Missiles of Military Diplomacy," *Telegraph* (India), 27 December 2001.
[78] "A Unique Army Exercise," *The Hindu*, 30 December 2001. An earlier exercise in May 2001 had tested similar capabilities. See "Heat and Dust: Exercise Poorna Vijay," *Strategic Affairs* (1 September 2001).
[79] "Pak Would Be Wiped Out if it Uses Nuclear Bomb: BJP," *Hindustan Times*, 26 December 2001.
[80] "Military Option if Diplomacy Fails," *The Hindu*, 4 January 2002.
[81] "Army Ready for War, Says Chief," *Statesman*, 12 January 2002.

creating nuclear delivery systems specifically configured for attacking Pakistan.[82]

Ultimately, this vast mobilization of potential coercive force did not achieve concrete gains.[83] India's public demands were relatively moderate – formulated so that they were easily met, but also easily avoided. India submitted a list of twenty terrorists for Pakistan to extradite, but publicized the names in such a way that the targets could easily go into hiding.[84] India also demanded observable reductions in the infiltration of insurgents into Kashmir.[85]

Musharraf replied with a landmark speech, announcing that Pakistan would no longer be used as a base for terrorism of any kind.[86] Actions, however, speak louder than words, and Musharraf did not live up to this commitment.[87] Infiltration, by its very nature, is difficult to determine, and Pakistan can plausibly claim that determined *jehadis* will make their way over the rugged LoC. As of this writing infiltration has not ceased, although the annual number of deaths related to separatist violence in Kashmir has declined over 70 percent since 2001.[88]

This limitation became obvious in May 2002, when the crisis reemerged in an even more dangerous manner. Infiltration had not stopped, and the attack by terrorist forces on the Kaluchak barracks resulted in the deaths of dozens of innocent women and children. India responded through a series of military acts, including the movement of strike corps, combining India's Eastern and Western fleets in the North Arabian Sea, and placing paramilitary forces in Jammu and Kashmir under formal military command, and reportedly preparing a series of military strikes before the monsoon season began in mid-June.[89]

---

[82] "India Tests Missile, Stirring a Region Already on Edge," *New York Times*, 25 January 2002.
[83] One estimate suggests that the cost for Pakistan was as great as 30 percent of its annual budget. See Jasjit Singh, "December 13: A Year After," *Indian Express*, 16 December 2002. Indian costs were reported as 70 million rupees per day – roughly $750 million for ten months. See "Border Stand-Off Cost India RS 7-Cr a Day," *Hindustan Times*, 19 October 2002, and Rajesh Basrur, "Coercive Diplomacy in A Nuclear Environment: The December 13 Crisis" (unpublished manuscript), 13, n. 85.
[84] "Pakistan's Arrest of Militant is 'Step Forward', India Says," *New York Times*, 1 January 2002.
[85] "India's Leader Continues Accusing Pakistan of Terror," *New York Times*, 30 December 2001.
[86] See "Text of President Musharraf's Address to the Nation," 12 January 2002, www.dawn.com/2002/01/12/top2.htm.
[87] Even after the summer crisis, President Musharraf admitted that militants continued to enter Kashmir from Pakistani territory. "Militants Still Entering India, Says Musharraf," *Daily Telegraph* (London), 21 August 2002.
[88] K. Alan Kronstadt, *CRS Report for Congress RL33529: India–US Relations* (Washington, DC: Congressional Research Service, 13 February 2007), 35–36.
[89] See Peter R. Lavoy, "Fighting Terrorism, Avoiding War: The Indo-Pakistani Situation," *Joint Force Quarterly* no. 32 (Autumn 2002): 31; Rahul Bedi, "The Military Dynamics," *Frontline*, 8 June 2002.

Pakistan's response indicated the increased sophistication of Pakistani nuclear signaling after Kargil. In the 25–28 May period, Pakistan tested three nuclear-capable ballistic missiles. On 29 May, Munir Akram, Pakistan's newly appointed ambassador to the United Nations, stated: "So long as the use of force is outlawed, we will accept no first use of nuclear weapons also. But India should not have the license to kill with the use of conventional weapons while our hands are tied with regard to other means to defend ourselves."[90] He further commented: "We do not wish to expend our limited resources on building up a conventional defense which will completely debilitate our development ... We have to rely on our means to deter Indian aggression. We have that means and we will not neutralize it by any doctrine of no first-use."[91] Akram said the nuclear crisis demonstrated the need for international political intervention to resolve the Kashmir issue. He also stated that Pakistan considered "punitive economic measures" to be a form of aggression that might justify nuclear retaliation.[92]

Pakistan also revised its perceptions of the role of nuclear weapons in the subcontinent. In December 2001, Pakistan "informally" detailed a set of potential nuclear red lines, in order to limit India's conventional options in limited war. These guidelines include significant losses of territory, destruction of large parts of the army or air force, efforts at economic strangulation including controlling the flow of the Indus waters or sea blockade, and significant Indian support for domestic destabilization in Pakistan.[93]

Shortly after India released its nuclear doctrine, Pakistan stated that its command and control procedures would ensure that its weapons could quickly move to operational military control, and more readily be used in a crisis.[94] In an interview with *Der Spiegel* in April 2002, President Musharraf stated that Pakistan would continue to rely on conventional means for national security, but that nuclear use was an option, particularly if Pakistan were threatened "with extinction."[95] Pessimistic analysts

---

[90] "Pakistan Won't Rule Out Use of Nuclear Arms if Attacked," *Channel News Asia*, 29 May 2002.

[91] "At UN, Pakistan Defends First-Strike Nuclear Policy," *Agence France Presse*, 29 May 2002.

[92] "Pakistan Asks UN Council for Action on Kashmir," *New York Times*, 30 May 2002.

[93] See the remarks attributed to General Khalid Kidwai, Commander of the Strategic Plans Division, in "Nuclear Safety, Nuclear Stability and Nuclear Strategy in Pakistan" (Como, Italy: Landau Network, Centro Volta, January 2002), http://lxmi.mi.infn.it/~landnet/Doc/pakistan.pdf.

[94] "NCA to Decide on Use of N-weapons," *Dawn*, 7 January 2003.

[95] "Musharraf Warns India He May Use Nuclear Weapons," *The Times* (London), 8 April 2002, available at www.nci.org/02/04f/08-06.htm.

believe that Pakistani nuclear doctrine is based on a policy of deliberate vulnerability and instability, in order to convince India and the United States that any escalation to the conventional level might lead immediately to a nuclear response.[96] However, Pakistan's "vulnerability" is a fact and cannot realistically be viewed as a "deliberate policy." Similarly, instability is a consequence of political animosity and military tensions between two nuclear-armed neighbors, especially since Pakistan has deliberately kept its nuclear doctrine ambiguous.

Conclusion

The nuclear lessons of Kargil are simple in at least one respect. The Kargil experience verifies that nuclear weapons do not automatically create positive results, particularly when underlying political conflicts remain unresolved. Development of new nuclear forces does not necessarily lead to regional stability – although it may play an important role in limiting conflicts or crisis escalation when they occur. Nuclear deterrence in a crisis-prone region requires the development of new doctrines, weapons, and red lines, all of which increase military involvement in strategic affairs. Pakistan's more militarized nuclear decision-making system lends itself more easily to these changes. This induced India to work hard at creating doctrine, command and control capabilities, and nuclear release authority procedures since the end of the Kargil crisis.[97]

Theoretical assertions that small nuclear arsenals are amenable to easy, uncomplicated command and control were not borne out in this crisis. Command and control is not just a function of who possesses the weapons, or who can authorize their use. It also is a function of who can speak with authority in a crisis, and who can make public threats of escalation or retaliation. Both India and Pakistan had poor control over signaling during the crisis, significantly increasing the risk of misperception, miscommunication, and escalation.

Nuclear weapons are a symptom of ongoing regional hostility, and are utilized by both sides in pursuit of political advantage. Each side assumed that the nuclear demonstrations of 1998 would work to its advantage, and that the other side would be unable to adapt and respond to a new nuclear environment. Both were wrong.

---

[96] Michael Ryan Kraig, "The Political and Strategic Imperatives of Nuclear Deterrence in South Asia," *India Review* 2, no. 1 (January 2003): 35–38.

[97] An outstanding recent study of Indian nuclear developments is Rajesh M. Basrur, *Minimum Deterrence and India's Nuclear Security* (Stanford University Press, 2006).

Kargil induced each side to take significant steps away from previous policies of opaque deterrence.[98] India's nuclear capability and policy is moving, slowly but perceptibly, in pursuit of the ability to wage limited conventional wars in a nuclear environment, to dominate escalation in event of a conflict, and to create a legitimate, usable, and survivable nuclear force that can exercise a range of possible military options in order to enhance deterrence. India seeks escalation dominance – substantial military superiority at most or all potential levels of conflict – and the ability to attack Pakistani command and control capabilities with air and missile forces. India is following a path similar to those of the superpowers during the 1950s, although the pace remains slow and the trajectory could change given significant political direction.[99]

Pakistan also revised its perceptions of the role of nuclear weapons in the subcontinent. Kargil demonstrated the limitations of the stability–instability paradox. Salami slicing with regular troops resulted in the cementing of the LoC as an informal status quo accepted by the United States and the international community – a result firmly at odds with Pakistani policy objectives. Further Pakistani efforts to change this status quo will be difficult, particularly at a time (post-9/11) when the international community rejects the notion of terrorism, of redefining borders through force, and views South Asia as an extremely likely location for a nuclear war in the future. Pakistan moved from a vague doctrine of retaliation to more detailed nuclear red lines, and Pakistani command and control procedures also shifted to ensure that the weapons could be quickly devolved to operational military control, which permits early use in a crisis. South Asian nuclear behavior is somewhat similar to the early Cold War era in Europe. India can be said to follow the Soviet model of using conventional force superiority under the nuclear umbrella, whereas Pakistan's posture closely resembles the NATO model of utilizing nuclear weapons as an equalizer to a conventional force imbalance.

Small, recessed nuclear arsenals and unsophisticated nuclear doctrines cannot stabilize the subcontinent. Although the Lahore Declaration optimistically looked forward to substantial cooperation on nuclear risk reduction, the Kargil conflict scuttled its most promising efforts. Neither side has tested nuclear weapons since 1998, and both continue to provide prior notification of missile tests. But cooperation on doctrine, arms

---

[98] Rodney W. Jones, *Minimum Nuclear Deterrence Postures in South Asia: An Overview*, report for the Defense Threat Reduction Agency (October 2001), www.dtra.mil/about/organization/south_asia.pdf.

[99] For a discussion of possible nuclear posture options and the limitations of nuclear compellance in the subcontinent, see Basrur, *Minimum Deterrence and India's Nuclear Security*, 80–101, 169–184.

control, physical security, and confidence building continues to lag. "Composite Dialogue" talks initiated after the Lahore meeting have reopened, but progress remains slow. The Kashmir issue remains an unresolved obstacle in Indo-Pakistani diplomatic relations generally, and the security issues surrounding this dispute continue to push both sides towards larger nuclear arsenals.[100]

This continuing competition, like the Cold War, also eliminates the theoretical cost-effectiveness of nuclear arsenals. Pakistan's use of proxy forces in Kashmir, India's quest for escalation dominance, and the increase in "other" security requirements for both states due to the war on terrorism contribute to a continuing *conventional*, as well as nuclear, arms competition.[101] Until the underlying political disputes are resolved, there will be no "peace dividend" from the nuclearization of the subcontinent.[102]

This does not mean that nuclear war is inevitable – for example, there was no crisis or significant military mobilization after the Mumbai terrorist bombing of 11 July 2006, despite Indian certainty that the authors were Pakistan-backed groups. However, Kargil undermined the nuclear optimist position that nuclear powers will never go to war.[103] The theoretically stabilizing aspects of non-deployed, opaque nuclear forces failed in practice to prevent regional aggression with a substantial potential for nuclear escalation. If anything, Pakistan and India have taken greater risks *after* the 1998 nuclear tests than at anytime in the previous two decades. Nevertheless, they have avoided full-scale conventional war.

As each side alters its doctrines and forces to changing realities, the need to control possible escalation and maintain credible deterrent forces will influence India and Pakistan to pursue larger arsenals and more careful military planning for nuclear use.[104] Increasing readiness and dispersion also increase the risk of accidental or unauthorized use. What

---

[100] On the Kashmir issue, see Musharraf, *In the Line of Fire*, 297–309; and Sumit Ganguly, "The Kashmir Conundrum," *Foreign Affairs* 85, no. 4 (July/August 2006): 45–56.

[101] Emerging Indian perspectives on the conventional and nuclear trends can be found in N. S. Sisodia and C. Uday Bhaskar, eds., *Emerging India: Security and Foreign Policy Perspectives* (New Delhi: Institute for Defence Studies and Analyses, 2005), esp. 15–148.

[102] See, for example, T. V. Paul, ed., *The India–Pakistan Conflict: An Enduring Rivalry* (Cambridge University Press, 2005).

[103] Paul S. Kapur, "India and Pakistan's Unstable Peace: Why Nuclear South Asia Is Not Like Cold War Europe," *International Security* 30, no. 2 (Fall 2005), 127–152; and Paul Kapur, "Nuclear Proliferation, the Kargil Conflict, and South Asian Security," *Security Studies* 13, no. 1 (Autumn 2003), 79–105.

[104] Evidence of this may be found in public discussions of the number of warheads necessary for India's "minimum nuclear deterrent." Before the 1998 tests, the notional arsenal size was usually discussed in terms of dozens of warheads. More recently, an upper limit of

some analysts have referred to as an "arms crawl" in the subcontinent is now turning into an "arms lurch" – quicker, less predictable, and relatively more capable of causing harm to both. Kargil was the first "true" Indo-Pakistani nuclear crisis, but as the events of 2001–2002 suggest, it is unlikely to be the last.

300–400 warheads has been publicly discussed and reported. Several years ago, this would have been considered an exaggeratedly hawkish number. See Tellis, *India's Emerging Nuclear Posture*; and Basrur, *Minimum Deterrence and India's Nuclear Security*.

7 Why Kargil did not produce general war: the crisis-management strategies of Pakistan, India, and the United States

Peter R. Lavoy

The theory of nuclear revolution holds that states armed with nuclear weapons should not fight conventional wars against each other. The risk of military escalation is supposed to produce such caution among decision-makers that the opposing sides in a crisis will curtail their coercive behavior well short of war. Pakistan partially defied this logic in the spring of 1999 by sending fighters to secretly seize mountainous territory near the strategically important Srinagar–Leh highway in Indian-held Kashmir. Pakistani military planners considered this to be a limited, tactical operation, and calculated that war could be averted through the time-tested combination of military *fait accompli*, international political pressures, deterrence threats, and Indian restraint. Viewing the territorial intrusion as a blatant act of aggression and a strategic threat, India launched a ferocious military campaign to oust the "invaders," but stopped short of attacking Pakistani territory or even striking Pakistani military positions across the Line of Control (LoC) separating the Indian- and Pakistani-controlled parts of Kashmir.

During the Cold War, and especially after the 1962 Cuban missile crisis, the United States and the Soviet Union developed elaborate crisis-management strategies to gain advantages over one another during military crises and in their overall strategic competition while at the same time trying to influence domestic and international reactions and attempting to control military escalation.[1] In South Asia's first military crisis since May 1998, when India and Pakistan each conducted nuclear explosive tests and declared themselves nuclear weapons states, New Delhi and Islamabad were forced to practice Cold War-like crisis management during the summer of 1999. With considerable help from the international

---

[1] See Alexander L. George, *Managing US–Soviet Rivalry: Problems of Crisis Prevention* (Boulder, Colo.: Westview Press, 1983). A path-breaking examination of Soviet crisis management during the Cuban missile crisis is William F. Scott, "The Face of Moscow in the Missile Crisis," *Studies in Intelligence* 10 (Spring 1966): 29–36.

community, Indian and Pakistani officials managed to keep the Kargil conflict limited and ultimately resolved the crisis.

A combination of several factors prevented the Kargil conflict from escalating into the fourth major Indo-Pakistani war: India's eventual battlefield success in the Kargil and Dras sectors combined with its reluctance to accept the military and diplomatic risks of a wider war; Pakistan's decision not to enlarge the conflict and to accept the loss of its territorial gains, which was practically unavoidable because Islamabad initiated the land-grab operation without any plans or preparations for military escalation; official and back-channel negotiations between India and Pakistan; and international diplomacy involving many countries and several state leaders, most notably the US president.

This chapter analyzes the conflict-management strategies that Pakistan, India, and the United States adopted during the Kargil conflict in order to understand how close India and Pakistan came to general war in 1999, why war was averted, and what lessons can be learned about the roles nuclear weapons, crisis diplomacy, and deterrence stability play in South Asia and beyond.

South Asia's nuclear revolution

A new strategic environment emerged in South Asia with the secret production of nuclear bombs by India and Pakistan in the mid-1980s and the creation of full-fledged nuclear-deterrence postures after each country openly conducted nuclear explosive tests in 1998. Most significant about the advent of nuclear arsenals in the region is the predicament of *mutual vulnerability*. Waging the first three Indo-Pakistani wars proved very costly, even to the side that won. In a future war, however, the side that is losing would be able to inflict as much destruction on the winning side as the winner could on the loser. Further, the potential speed and scope of destruction in a future war would far surpass that of previous wars. Indian and Pakistani leaders no doubt realize the seriousness of this strategic condition. But did they correctly understand its implications and accordingly adjust their political and military objectives, expectations, and strategies during the Kargil conflict?

As discussed by the author in chapter 1 of this book, a review of Indian and Pakistani conflict-management behavior during the spring and summer of 1999 produces mixed results with regard to the theory and practice of nuclear deterrence.[2] On the alarming side, Pakistan tried to achieve a

---

[2] On nuclear-deterrence theory, see Robert Jervis, *The Meaning of the Nuclear Revolution* (Ithaca: Cornell University Press, 1989). For an early application of this theory to South

Pakistan's calculations

The assumptions and motivations that led Pakistan to mount the Kargil operation are covered extensively by Zafar Iqbal Cheema in chapter 2 and by Khan, Lavoy, and Clary in chapter 3, but it is important here to highlight Pakistan's strategy for translating this campaign into lasting territorial and political gains. Pakistan's "exit strategy" evolved over three phases. The first began in November 1998 when commanders of the army's FCNA division and 10 Corps crafted plans for a "defensive maneuver" in an area where Indian aggression was deemed a real possibility.[15] The resultant strategy resembled India's 1984 secret military occupation of the Siachen Glacier region. At this point, Pakistani planners focused entirely on the tactical level of warfare – deploying Northern Light Infantry (NLI) troops in a small covert surveillance and post occupation operation across the LoC near the towns of Dras and Kargil to seize superior heights along the watersheds (mountain crests, or water-parting ridgelines) of the local mountain complexes.[16] Little thought was given to the wider, strategic implications of the operation despite the presence of nuclear forces in the region.[17] In mid-January, the army leadership approved the FCNA–10 Corps operation.

The rugged NLI soldiers penetrated across the LoC and set up several posts along the originally identified watersheds without detection. The operation then "grew bigger than planned" when they were authorized to push even further into Indian territory.[18] With the NLI troops well on their way to occupying more than 100 posts (each with ten to twenty soldiers), in depth ranging from 4 to 9 miles inside Indian-held Kashmir across a 75-mile stretch of mountain peaks, a new phase of the operation had begun, and Pakistani military *and civilian* officials had to figure out how to manage the reactions of India and the international community.[19]

---

[15] Pervez Musharraf, *In the Line of Fire: A Memoir* (New York: Simon and Schuster, 2006), 90.

[16] *Ibid.*

[17] One reason for the mistaken predictions the Kargil planners made about the likely reactions of India, the United States, China, and other concerned powers to the 1999 land grab was their relative unfamiliarity with strategic weapons. During the 1998 nuclear tests and the subsequent nuclear restraint dialogue with US Deputy Secretary of State Strobe Talbott, Gen. Musharraf was serving as the Mangla Corps Commander; Lt. Gen. Aziz was director of the Inter-Services Intelligence Directorate (ISID); Lt. Gen. Mahmud was commandant of the National Defence College; and Maj. Gen. Javed Hassan was assigned as FCNA Commander. Musharraf became Chief of Army Staff (COAS) and then appointed Aziz as CGS and Mahmud as Rawalpindi Corps Commander, all in October 1998. The planning for Kargil began soon thereafter.

[18] Shaukat Qadir, interview with the author, Islamabad, Pakistan, January 2003.

[19] Musharraf, *In the Line of Fire*, 90.

Pakistan's conflict-management strategy in this phase rested on strong confidence in the ability of the NLI units to hold their newly acquired positions across the LoC and on India's inability to wage a successful counterattack to reclaim this territory – beliefs that turned out to be based more on wishful thinking than careful military planning.

The third phase of the conflict began after Indian forces captured four key posts near the Indian village of Dras in mid-June. After these military losses, tensions between Pakistani prime minister Nawaz Sharif and army chief General Musharraf deepened and evidently exacerbated already disjointed diplomatic efforts to arrange a negotiated settlement to the conflict. The United States and other international parties also stepped up their crisis-management diplomacy during this period. The high point of this phase was a 4 July meeting between Sharif and US president Bill Clinton, when the prime minister reluctantly agreed to pull Pakistani troops from the Kargil heights. Shortly thereafter Pakistan began to with- draw most – but not all – of its forces. The crisis lasted until the end of July when remaining Pakistani troops either were killed or withdrew back across the LoC.

Phase 1: planning Pakistan's covert military operation

In January 1998 10 Corps Commander Lt. Gen. Mahmud Ahmed and FCNA Commander Maj. Gen. Javed Hassan, with the support of Chief of General Staff (CGS) Lt. Gen. Muhammad Aziz, sought permission from Gen. Musharraf to send NLI troops to secretly occupy mountain posts on the Indian side of the LoC in areas that Indian forces typically vacate during the harsh winter season. The stated military objective of the plan, which was drafted in November 1998,[20] was to plug the gaps between Pakistan's military posts along the LoC and to improve the FCNA defen- sive alignment by occupying the dominating positions on the watershed along and across the LoC.[21] Because the scheme's success required strict secrecy (otherwise India would easily detect the intrusion), the prime minister was the only civilian official to be informed. According to Musharraf, the "defensive maneuver" was briefed to Nawaz Sharif in Skardu on 29 January and in Khel on 5 February.[22] Because the NLI forces ultimately penetrated so deep across the LoC, however, the army

---

[20] Qadir, "An Analysis of the Kargil Conflict 1999."

[21] Musharraf, *In the Line of Fire*, 90.

[22] *Ibid.* 90, 96. Nawaz Sharif denies this claim, insisting that Indian prime minister Vajpayee told him about the incursion. See Sharif's interviews with Raj Chengappa in *India Today*, 26 July 2004, www.indiatoday.com/itoday/20040726/cover.shtml&SET=T, and Tahir Siddique in *The Herald* (Karachi), June 2006, 38–39. The army's claims are confirmed

leadership began to envision more ambitions goals, such as undermining India's control over the Siachen Glacier region by interdicting its principal supply route, the Srinagar–Leh highway.

Even if the Pakistan army did not oust its rival from Siachen, it intended to raise the cost for staying there, as India had done since 1994 by interdicting Pakistan's military line of communications through the main Neelum Valley road, an action that greatly complicated life for the valley's 150,000 civilian population and impaired 10 Corps' military operations throughout Pakistan-administered Kashmir.[23] Musharraf's predecessor as army chief, Gen. (retd.) Jehangir Karamat, confirmed that after India stepped up attacks on Pakistani forces and local civilians in the Neelum Valley, Pakistan responded in 1996 with sustained cross-LoC firing on India's most exposed positions, which were around Kargil and Dras. Karamat writes that well before the 1999 cross-LoC operation, "Indian interdiction of roads and villages in the Neelum Valley area of Azad Kashmir … forced Pakistan to interdict the movement on the Dras–Kargil road by fire to obtain leverage that could stop Indian actions in the Neelum Valley."[24] The 1999 gambit was a more elaborate and ambitious bid to exploit India's glaring vulnerability in the Northern Areas (before India itself redressed the situation), and to make permanent an even stronger tactical troop alignment along the northern reaches of the LoC.

India's official Kargil Review Committee acknowledges that the 1999 intrusion was a continuation of Indian and Pakistani efforts to improve their military positions along the LoC: "up to 1990, Pakistan had made 12 such attempts and taken an area of just over 11 square kilometers in adverse possession." It states that "the Indian side had suitably responded," but does not specify how.[25] Referring specifically to Indian military deployments in the Siachen Glacier region, Lt. Gen. (retd.) V. R. Raghavan describes this general condition as an "unending urge to take on next ground" with each side driven by "the belief that if one does not take on the next higher ground, the enemy will."[26] However, the Kargil

---

by Dr. Maleeha Lodhi, Pakistan's ambassador to the United States and the United Kingdom, and former army chief Gen. (retd.) Aslam Beg. Maleeha Lodhi, "Act Now, Think Later," *Newsline*, August 1999, 33; Aslam Beg, "The Kargil Denouement," *Frontier Post*, 14 July 1999. See also Shireen M. Mazari, *The Kargil Conflict 1999: Separating Fact from Fiction* (Islamabad: Ferozsons, 2003), 57. Further, Lt. Gen. Mahmud Ahmed told the author that he briefed the prime minister in January and February.

[23] Information provided in a Pakistan defence attaché briefing document, dated 14 June 1999, Washington, DC.

[24] Jehangir Karamat, "Learning from Kargil," *Daily News*, 5 August 1999. See also Malik, *Kargil: From Surprise to Victory*, 41–46.

[25] Kargil Review Committee, *From Surprise to Reckoning*, 49.

[26] Lt. Gen. V. R. Raghavan, *Siachen: Conflict Without End* (New Delhi: Penguin, 2002), 41.

land grab was the first such military operation to take place after the overt introduction of nuclear arms into the regional competition, which not only raised the stakes of future conflict, but also focused international attention on India and Pakistan like never before.

At this early stage, the planners of the Kargil operation apparently believed they could control the risk of escalation by presenting India with a military *fait accompli* through surprise and deception, as India had done in Siachen in 1984.[27] However, they severely underestimated the determined Indian military and diplomatic reaction, the extensive military capability required to defend their over-stretched positions, and the anxious international reaction. The false optimism of the architects of the Kargil intrusion, colored by the illusion of a cheap victory, was not only the main driver of the operation, and hence the crisis; it also was the cause of Pakistan's most damaging military defeat since the loss of East Pakistan in December 1971.[28]

Phase 2: deterring escalation and seeking political gains

The Kargil maneuver was a victim of its own success. NLI troops captured many more mountain posts than required in the initial plan, which targeted a set of key heights along the mountain ridgelines (watersheds) just across the LoC. Indian surveillance was so lax that NLI soldiers managed to set up military posts well into enemy territory and smaller surveillance and firing positions still farther forward. A Pakistani officer associated with the operation told the author that during the initial surveillance phase, one soldier infiltrated all the way to the town of Kargil and brought back a goat without being detected. A junior officer came across this soldier and his mates feasting on an unlikely barbeque high atop a mountain post in the Tiger Hill area, and, expressing skepticism at the soldier's explanation for the meal, demanded proof of this remarkable feat. The soldier set out for Kargil again the following day and returned with a local

---

[27] For a Pakistani analysis of the centrality of surprise, deception, and psychological warfare to military victory, see Maj. Noshad Hamid, "Surprise and Deception: An Instrument of Win," *Pakistan Army Journal* 33, no. 4 (December 1992): 81–87.

[28] False optimism in cheap victories through asymmetric strategies has been a recurring theme in Pakistani strategic culture, as described by Hasan-Askari Rizvi in chapter 13 of this book and by Altaf Gauhar in "Four Wars, One Assumption," *The Nation*, 5 September 1999, reproduced at http://pakistanlink.com/Opinion/99/Sept/10/01.html. Of course, this problem is not unique to Pakistan; Stephen Van Evera identifies false optimism in military victory as the leading cause of wars. See Stephen Van Evera, *Causes of War: Power and the Roots of Conflict* (Ithaca: Cornell University Press, 1999), 14–34. James J. Wirtz and Surinder Rana develop this point further in the context of the Kargil crisis in chapter 8.

newspaper to prove that Indian defenses were at an extraordinarily low state of preparedness.[29]

With surveillance reports like this one exceeding all initial expectations, FCNA and 10 Corps lobbied the army leadership to authorize a much more ambitious military penetration. NLI troops ultimately occupied over 500 square miles of territory across the LoC.[30] Now that Pakistani troops were in position to threaten a vital Indian interest – the strategic Srinagar–Leh highway – new concerns emerged in Rawalpindi: how to influence India's eventual military response, prevent the conflict from escalating to full-scale war, and translate the tactical gains along the heights overlooking Kargil and Dras into lasting territorial and political advantages. To work through these issues, which had not been analyzed earlier, more people had to be brought into the planning process. Sometime in March 1999, Musharraf informed the Director General of Military Operations (DGMO), Maj. Gen. Tauqir Zia, of the situation and instructed him to devise a strategic plan that would translate military gains across the LoC into lasting political benefits.[31] Early on, the need for secrecy, stealth, and surprise was so important that the CGS, Lt. Gen. Aziz, kept the DGMO, who reports directly to him, completely out of the decision-making loop. Ironically, Pakistan's battlefield success forced a redefinition of the strategic plan, and not the other way around. By April, the air force and the navy were informed of the operation, as were other concerned elements of the government.[32]

Because of the dominance of army war fighters in all planning phases, it is not surprising that Pakistan's approach to escalation control and conflict management relied mainly on military means – in contrast to the unprecedented fusion of political, diplomatic, media, and military elements in India's war effort. The prevailing view inside army headquarters was that India would not be able to oust the well-defended NLI forces sitting in superior positions atop key mountain peaks, and that a significant shift of Indian troops toward the Kargil-Dras sector would erode their ability to conduct offensive operations elsewhere along the LoC or the international border. Further, the newly exposed areas would be vulnerable to Pakistani counterattacks and possibly a renewed insurgency in the Kashmir Valley. "Evaluating this buildup at headquarters,"

---

[29] The Pakistan army awarded the NLI unit that performed this daring feat and also presented its highest military award, the *Nishan-e-Haider*, to the unit's commanding officer, Captain Karnal Sher Khan, who perished in the fight for Tiger Hill on 5 July 1999.

[30] Musharraf, *In the Line of Fire*, 91.

[31] Qadir, "An Analysis of the Kargil Conflict 1999"; and author's interviews with several serving and retired Pakistan army officers, 2003–2006.

[32] *Ibid.*

Musharraf recalls, "we realized that India had created a serious strategic imbalance in its system of forces. It had bottled up major formations inside Kashmir, leaving itself no capability to attack us elsewhere, and, most seriously, had left the field open for a counteroffensive with which we could choke the Kashmir Valley."[33]

The author's interviews with Pakistani officers involved in military deliberations reveal there were a few dissenting voices within the army, at least one of whom criticized the Kargil plan for being overly provocative to India and the world community while lacking any inherent means to apply further military pressure on New Delhi to accept such a large loss of territory. This officer argued that if Pakistan intended to engage India in combat and threaten its strategic interests in the Northern Areas, then it should pursue more militarily meaningful targets, such as the vital Zojila Pass. In this view, the Kargil plan risked too much for too small a military payoff. Another army officer interviewed by the author argued that the only way to compel India to capitulate was to open up additional military fronts against newly vulnerable Indian positions, but in that eventuality the government had to be ready for a wider war. Not having intended or prepared for a major war, the army leadership had no interest in significantly escalating hostilities, and quickly rejected this idea.[34] Hoping that the hardy NLI forces could retain their posts until the winter weather suspended military operations, the army still believed it could keep its new positions across the LoC, force India to withdraw from Siachen, and perhaps even win a favorable political settlement to the Kashmir dispute – all without resort to war.[35] India, however, interpreted Pakistan's actions as a strategic threat, and determined to overcome them at any cost.[36] Given the length and breadth of occupation by NLI forces, it is difficult to see how India could have reacted differently.

There was another weakness inherent in the Kargil plan that probably was not well understood by its planners. The NLI troops had spread themselves far too thinly across the mountains, and their new defensive positions were not arrayed in mutually supportive firing positions nor well

---

[33] Musharraf, *In the Line of Fire*, 93.
[34] Author's discussions in June 2006 with recently retired senior army officers who wish to remain anonymous.
[35] The Pakistan army leadership believed at the time – and probably still does – that it needed greater military and diplomatic leverage to force India to take the Kashmir negotiations seriously. It was particularly concerned in March 1999 that the Lahore peace process was spiraling out of control. Nasim Zehra, "Anatomy of Islamabad's Kargil Policy," *Defence Journal* (August 1999), www.defencejournal.com/aug99/anatomy.htm.
[36] Malik, *Kargil: From Surprise to Victory*, 124–127.

coordinated from a logistical standpoint. Maj. Gen. Nadeem Ahmed, who took command of FCNA after the Kargil conflict, admitted that because operational commanders had a "compulsion" to push patrols forward, "we got a little overstretched." "In the mountains, you cannot do anything more than is planned," Nadeem remarked.[37] The resultant "mission creep" posed two major problems. First, it provided sufficient space for Indian forces to maneuver to surround and isolate the NLI posts. Second, because these isolated posts could not be supplied with reinforcements, ammunition, or basic provisions, they could not hold on indefinitely under relentless firepower from aircraft, artillery, and advancing troop formations.[38]

Pakistani planners did not anticipate that India would detect the NLI presence so early in May and they also assumed that India's strategic Zojila Pass would remain closed until the end of May or early June. But Indian troops discovered NLI forces in the Shyok sector on 2 May, and the pass opened up shortly thereafter because the snows melted several weeks earlier than normal.[39] The opening of Zojila facilitated the induction of troops, supporting units, more than 19,000 tons of ammunition, and logistics needed for sustained attacks against the NLI positions. Despite this good fortune, during the first three weeks of May, the Indian army launched numerous missions to oust the intruders but failed to take any post and suffered major losses in the process. The Pakistani plan seemed to be working.

On 17 May, an upbeat army leadership arranged for DGMO Tauqir Zia to brief the prime minister and his top advisors "in detail" about the LoC situation in a formal Defence Committee of the Cabinet (DCC) meeting.[40] Sharif's defence secretary, Lt. Gen. (retd.) Chaudhry Iftikhar Ali Khan, told the author in a January 2003 interview that this was the first briefing on Kargil he and other cabinet members had received.[41] Seven senior army officers attended the meeting, which took place at the ISID office complex in Rawalpindi (Ojri camp): COAS Musharraf, CGS Aziz, 10 Corps Commander Mahmud, Director General of ISID Lt. Gen. Ziauddin, DGMO Tauqir Zia, FCNA Commander Javed Hassan, and

---

[37] Briefing by FCNA Commander Maj. Gen. Nadeem Ahmed to CCC research team, 12 January 2003.
[38] Discussions with Pakistani military officers familiar with the Kargil terrain and operations.
[39] Nadeem briefing, 12 January 2003.   [40] Musharraf, *In the Line of Fire*, 96.
[41] Interview with Lt. Gen. (retd.) Iftikhar Ali Khan, Rawalpindi, Pakistan, 19 January 2003. Iftikhar and Musharraf did not get along well, and by all accounts the army chief never invited the defence secretary for a GHQ briefing. Iftikhar said that he was not aware whether the prime minister was briefed about the operation in early 1999, as the military claims, but did state that Sharif claimed that he did not know about the plan prior to the 17 May meeting.

head of ISID Special Operations Shamsher Gul. Five civilians joined the prime minister: Foreign Minister Sartaj Aziz, Cabinet Minister Lt. Gen. (retd.) Majid Malik, Foreign Secretary Shamshad Ahmad, Defence Secretary Iftikhar, and Sajid Mehdi, principal secretary to the prime minister. The DGMO provided some details about the military situation and reportedly said that the aim of the operation was to boost the freedom movement in Kashmir. According to Iftikhar, after the briefing was over, Lt. Gen. Aziz then said to the prime minister: "Sir, it was the Quaid-i-Azam and the Muslim League that made Pakistan. Their names are enshrined for all time. Now your name and your Muslim League will be associated with the liberation of Kashmir and the completion of Pakistan." Iftikhar said that these remarks made the prime minister "feel very good about the whole operation."[42]

The following week, the Indian Cabinet Committee on Security (CCS) authorized the use of air power against enemy positions in Kargil and Ladakh in support of ground operations. Air combat operations began on the morning of 26 May. The next day, India lost a MiG-27 over the Batalik sector due to engine failure, and then a MiG-21 was shot down by a surface-to-air missile while searching for the ejected MiG-27 pilot. The following day, another missile downed an Indian MI-17 helicopter.[43] "If more planes will come," an upbeat Nawaz Sharif declared on 29 May, "their fate will be no different from the two downed yesterday."[44] That very day, Sharif called Vajpayee to say that he was sending Foreign Minister Sartaj Aziz to New Delhi for talks to "defuse the current situation and to pave the way for a peaceful settlement of the J&K issue."[45] Aziz denied any military involvement in the intrusion, even after he was informed that India had recovered a body of a Pakistani soldier with army documentation and identity papers on him.

At the end of May, there was a mood of "euphoria" in Islamabad.[46] When the DCC met again on 3 June nearly every military and civilian participant praised the operation. According to then defence secretary Iftikhar Ali Khan, "most people thought that something great was about to be achieved. There was no trace of worry or concern within the army or senior political leadership." Iftikhar said he was the only person in the

---

[42] *Ibid.*

[43] For information on various aspects of the Indian air campaign in Kargil, see the Indian air force report on *Operation Safed Sagar* (as the air operation was called), available at http://indianairforce.nic.in/afsqnmain1.htm.

[44] Cited in Naziha Ghazali, "Down from the Peaks," *Newsline*, July 1999, 28.

[45] Jaswant Singh, *A Call to Honour: In Service of Emergent India* (New Delhi: Rupa, 2006), 206.

[46] Iftikhar Ali Khan interview, 19 January 2003.

India's military buildup and troop movements with impunity.[80] In particular, had India's 56 Mountain Brigade not won the week-long hand-to-hand contest for Tololing – which turned the tide of the battle because Indian forces were then able to operate inside of Pakistan's defense perimeter and recapture several other military posts – India would have been forced either to acquiesce to Pakistan's territorial gains across the LoC or escalate the fighting and run the risk of nuclear war and international opprobrium.

Although Kargil did not erupt into the fourth major Indo-Pakistani war, New Delhi and Islamabad did not do a good job of reading each other's capabilities and intentions. First, the Indians never contemplated that Pakistan was capable of launching such a bold move involving high levels of surprise and deception. Second, after its initial disbelief and disorientation, the Indian political and military leadership read far more into Pakistani motives and objectives than the planners of the Kargil operation ever intended. Consequentially, New Delhi responded with extreme force after initial hesitation. Third, Pakistani planners did not accurately assess India's resolve and capacity to respond to their cross-LoC operation. The tenacious Indian reaction in June shocked the Pakistanis who were ill prepared for a major military conflict. Thus by early June the conflict had escalated vertically beyond each side's expectations. Finally, each party came to drastically different conclusions regarding the likelihood and possible consequences of horizontal escalation. Pakistan's military leadership did not expect the Indian army to take the war across the LoC or the international border because of its focus on Indian vulnerabilities in Kashmir.[81] But we now know that Indian officials planned exactly the opposite of what Pakistani army planners expected. In the end, had Indian forces not succeeded at the tactical level, they undoubtedly would have crossed into Pakistan's unprotected territory, thus creating a very real possibility of escalation to full-scale war and possibly even a nuclear exchange.

Political action

Just as major military operations along the LoC were commencing, New Delhi initiated three parallel diplomatic processes to resolve the crisis on favorable terms. First, Prime Minister Atal Behari Vajpayee engaged Pakistani prime minister Nawaz Sharif over the telephone in private

[80] Interviews with senior Indian defense officials, New Delhi, May 2005; and Malik, *Kargil: From Surprise to Victory*, 148–149.
[81] Musharraf, *In the Line of Fire*, 96.

front-channel talks. Vajpayee also conveyed more sensitive messages through discrete back-channel communications involving trusted Indian journalist R. K. Mishra and Pakistan's retired foreign secretary Niaz Naik, which had been set up during the February Lahore summit to facilitate the negotiations over Kashmir. Third, Indian diplomats were sent to seek understanding and support in major world capitals for New Delhi's position regarding Pakistan's cross-LoC "treachery" in the immediate aftermath of the Lahore talks. In all of these fora, India insisted that all Pakistani intruders must be withdrawn from Indian-held Kashmir before any formal bilateral talks could be held to normalize relations or resolve the Kashmir territorial dispute.

The Indian DGMO formally briefed the prime minister about the Kargil intrusion on 18 May. As the high-altitude combat for control of the Kargil and Dras peaks intensified over the next several days, the Indian government became increasingly aware that Pakistani troops were involved in the cross-LoC incursion. At this point Vajpayee spoke directly to Nawaz Sharif by telephone telling him that Pakistan's role had been discovered, that it was totally unacceptable, and that India would take all necessary steps to evict the intruders.[82] At this early stage in the crisis, Delhi's instinct was to make it as painless as possible for Pakistan to withdraw. Given the bonhomie developed between Vajpayee and Sharif during the recent Lahore Summit, the Indian government tried to give Sharif a face-saving way to end the crisis. By blaming the intrusion on Pakistan's army and by indicating its willingness to consider "safe passage" for the intruders to withdraw, the Indian leadership tried simultaneously to de-escalate the crisis and preserve the Lahore peace process.[83] This was risky because the BJP government was coming under intense criticism at home for having been double-crossed by Pakistan, and it would not be long before the September elections would determine the party's fate.[84] This tactic failed, however, when Sharif not only refused to blame his army for mounting an unauthorized operation across the LoC, but also denied any Pakistani responsibility for the rising violence on the Kargil heights.

As the crisis deepened still further, Sharif telephoned Vajpayee again the following week, stressing the need not only to defuse the Kargil situation but also to work out a peaceful settlement of the Kashmir dispute, and said that he would send his foreign minister to Delhi to commence this process. Having by that point lost three aircraft and scores

---

[82] Singh, *A Call to Honour*, 203–205.
[83] C. Raja Mohan, "Non-military Option 'Open,'" *The Hindu*, 2 June 1999.
[84] "Government Under Attack for 'Safe Passage' Idea," *The Hindu*, 3 June 1999.

of troops, the Indian government was in no mood to negotiate, and refused Sharif's request. After further entreaties, Minister of External Affairs Jaswant Singh finally relented to receive Foreign Minister Sartaj Aziz on 12 June. But the Singh–Aziz talks failed to bring the two sides together. Aziz proposed a military ceasefire and new negotiations about the status of Kashmir and the LoC; but Singh rejected this approach out of hand, insisting that the Pakistan army immediately withdraw from the Kargil heights. Direct talks between the belligerents apparently had reached an impasse; but a parallel, more discrete channel of communications between Sharif and Vajpayee still held out the possibility of a summit between the two prime ministers to resolve the crisis.

The secret diplomacy between Vajpayee's emissary, R. K. Mishra, and Sharif's representative, Niaz Naik, was well underway before the discovery of the Kargil occupation shelved the post-Lahore dialogue on Kashmir. Rather than canceling the back-channel talks, however, Vajpayee instructed Mishra to talk to Nawaz Sharif discretely about Kargil. According to Naik, who gave the most complete account of the back-channel dialogue to scholar Robert Wirsing, Mishra traveled to Islamabad for the seventh round of private diplomacy on 17 May, privately communicating Vajpayee's concerns about the Kargil intrusion and asked whether Sharif had known of the Kargil plan during the 20 February Lahore Summit.[85] Sharif was noncommittal, and there were no further meetings between Naik and Mishra for five weeks.

Mishra returned to Islamabad on 25 June to warn that India and Pakistan were "one inch away from war." Sharif responded by giving Mishra a note for Vajpayee urging India to cease hostilities and resume the Lahore peace process. After receiving the message, Vajpayee instructed Mishra to invite Naik to Delhi to discuss Sharif's proposal. Naik and Mishra arranged for Sharif to stop in Delhi that very night and negotiate an end to the conflict face to face with Vajpayee. However, Indian officials that very day concluded that with the ground situation and international diplomacy shifting decisively in their favor, there was no longer a need to strike a hasty deal with Sharif, who certainly would have seized the opportunity to preserve Pakistan's territorial gains across the LoC and reopen the Kashmir issue to international scrutiny.[86] Indian officials thus leaked the secret talks to the Indian press and abruptly cancelled Sharif's visit.[87]

[85] Wirsing, *Kashmir in the Shadow of War*, 30.
[86] Information from interviews with Indian diplomats based in New Delhi and Washington, 2003–2006.
[87] Wirsing, *Kashmir in the Shadow of War*, 31–33.

If Sharif and Vajpayee had met to diffuse the crisis (and if there were a military stalemate on the ground), a bilateral meeting could well have triggered an agreement, withdrawal of troops, and possibly restoration of the Lahore peace process. Should that have happened, the course of South Asian history might be very different. But three factors worked against an outcome of this sort. First and foremost, Pakistani forces could not hold on to key tactical posts across the LoC and ultimately were defeated militarily. Second, Sharif's dash to China and Islamabad's increasingly discombobulated crisis-management efforts may have indicated to India there was panic in the Pakistani camp; hence India would do well not to abandon its hard-line negotiating position. Third, by this stage, the United States had openly sided with India's position.

In late June US president Bill Clinton called Nawaz Sharif to convey that the United States knew that the occupiers were Pakistani troops and that it viewed Pakistan as the aggressor. The very day that Naik and Mishra were choreographing the Sharif–Vajpayee meeting, Clinton sent US envoy Gen. Anthony Zinni, Commander-in-Chief of US Central Command (CENTCOM), to Islamabad to reinforce this message in person and to discuss the steps that Washington believed were needed to end the crisis. Zinni told Musharraf and Sharif in separate meetings that the United States supported India in insisting upon full and immediate withdrawal of Pakistani forces back across the LoC.[88] Zinni's briefing partner, Deputy Assistant Secretary of State Gibson Lanpher, proceeded on to New Delhi to apprise the Indians of the discussions in Pakistan. Jaswant Singh recalls that the US assessment was that because the Indian army was now enjoying real battlefield success, the "balance of power" had shifted decisively in India's favor.[89] These factors encouraged India to back away from direct diplomacy with Pakistan.

The Zinni visit to Islamabad was especially significant because the CENTCOM chief traditionally has had a special relationship with the Pakistan army, and Zinni's soldier-to-soldier talk with Musharraf was critical to the latter's eventual decision to de-escalate the crisis. The Zinni visit also represented the culmination of India's aggressive political diplomacy to encourage the United States, China, Russia, G-8, the United Nations, and others to pressure Pakistan to withdraw its forces. Further, Indian diplomats worked with the US Congress and opinion-makers in the United States and elsewhere to promote India's case against Pakistan and to build support for its position in Washington and other capitals. This too was a risky strategy because New Delhi wanted to ensure

---

[88] Talbott, *Engaging India*, 159.   [89] Singh, *A Call to Honour*, 224.

at all costs that the matter did not go before the Security Council, for this would have presented Pakistan with a golden opportunity to tie the Kargil withdrawal to the favorable resolution of the Kashmir dispute.[90]

International diplomacy

Ever since the 1971 war between India and Pakistan, the international community was by and large not proactively engaged in trying to reverse Indo-Pakistani tensions. Earlier crises in the 1980s and early 1990s over the Siachen Glacier occupation, the Kashmir uprising, and general border skirmishes along the LoC did not draw international intervention and concern to the level that the 1999 Kargil crisis did. The partial exception was when a US presidential envoy, National Security Advisor Robert Gates, intervened in the spring of 1990 when the George Bush administration feared military escalation of the Kashmir crisis. What made the Kargil conflict different from other recent Indo-Pak crises was the overt demonstration of nuclear weapons a year earlier. The international community was concerned about the strategic behavior of newly declared nuclear powers that had rapidly deteriorating relations with each other. The foremost fear was the possibility of horizontal escalation of the conflict into a full-scale war that could possibly result in a nuclear exchange.

May 1999: early international pressure on Pakistan and India

Washington became actively involved in trying to manage the Kargil crisis when fighting on the mountains near Kargil broke out in May. Initially and throughout the crisis, the overriding American concern was the possibility that India would mount a massive counterattack across the LoC and that nuclear weapons might be used should full-scale war occur.[91] According to Bruce Riedel, who during the crisis managed South Asian affairs for the US National Security Council, "the nuclear scenario was very much on our minds."[92] Once US officials appreciated the gravity of the situation in late May, they concluded that war could be prevented only if Pakistan withdrew its troops behind the LoC. Private diplomacy was pursued first. Assistant Secretary of State for South Asian Affairs Rick Inderfurth and Under Secretary of State Thomas Pickering

---

[90] *Ibid.* 227.
[91] Talbott mentions that Washington also was concerned that China and various Arab states would side with Pakistan and that Israel and Russia would side with India in a dangerous "international free-for-all" if full-scale war broke out. Talbott, *Engaging India*, 157.
[92] Riedel, chapter 5.

expressed the US position privately to the Indian and Pakistani ambassadors in Washington. Secretary of State Madeleine Albright reinforced the message to Nawaz Sharif, and Gen. Anthony Zinni did the same with Gen. Musharraf.[93]

As noted above, the Pakistani leadership consistently told US officials that the Kargil fighters were *mujahideen*, not Pakistani soldiers, and that if the United States truly desired to play a constructive role in resolving the crisis, it should mediate the Indo-Pakistani dispute over Kashmir, which it maintained was the root cause of all the past and present trouble along the LoC. On 28 May, State Department spokesman James Rubin categorically ruled out any mediatory role on Kashmir, stating that this was a bilateral diplomatic matter between India and Pakistan. The following day, Assistant Secretary Inderfurth told a *New York Times* reporter that the intruders who had seized territory in the Indian-held Kashmir would have to leave: "Clearly the Indians are not going to cede this territory that these militants have taken. They have to depart, and they will depart, either voluntarily or because the Indians take them out."[94] The same day UN Secretary General Kofi Annan stated, "Pakistan is violating the Line of Control" and offered to send UN observers to the two countries. Four days later, France issued a thinly veiled warning to Pakistan to stop creating trouble along the LoC.[95] At the end of May, the international community was lining up in support of India's position that the onus of ending the conflict rested squarely on Pakistan.

June 1999: international diplomacy targets Pakistan

As Indian troops intensified their campaign to oust the intruders in June, international diplomatic pressure mounted on Pakistan to withdraw its forces and put an end to the fighting that Washington feared could rapidly escalate at any point. As Raja Mohan observed at the time, "The Clinton administration believes that the rules of engagement in the subcontinent have fundamentally changed with the advent of nuclear weapons."[96] On 3 June President Clinton sent letters to Prime Ministers Sharif and Vajpayee calling on both sides to "take steps to defuse the crisis and respect the Line of Control," and also indicated that the withdrawal of Pakistani forces was a precondition for a settlement and the price Islamabad must pay for US

[93] Talbott, *Engaging India*, 158.
[94] Inderfurth's remarks are cited in Philip Shenon, "US Fears Miscalculation," *New York Times*, 30 May 1999.
[95] "France, Annan Say LoC Must be Respected," *The Statesman* (India), 2 June 1999.
[96] C. Raja Mohan, "The US and Kargil," *The Hindu*, 10 June 1999.

diplomatic involvement on the larger Kashmir question.[97] Indian government officials were pleasantly surprised with the "paradigm shift" that was taking place in American foreign policy; because throughout the Cold War and the post-Cold War periods, Washington rarely sided with India in Indo-Pakistani disputes.[98]

As the crisis intensified, US officials mobilized other international parties to add their support for Pakistan's unilateral withdrawal from Kargil. Apart from the G-8 nations, it was deemed especially important to encourage Saudi Arabia and China to make their views known to Islamabad. As Pakistan's steadiest strategic partner, China's lack of support for the Kargil operation was a crushing blow. Beijing probably calculated that Pakistan was engaging in excessively risky military behavior, which ultimately would weaken its position in the competition with India; and many Chinese believe that "it is not rational for India to confront China before its rivalry with Pakistan is resolved."[99] Observing the clear US tilt toward India during the crisis, Beijing also might have decided to improve its own relations with New Delhi to prevent it from moving still closer to Washington.

On 5 June, Russia joined in the fray. Predictably siding with India, Moscow asked Pakistan to restore the status quo on the LoC that existed before Pakistan's military intrusion and stated that the Kashmir issue should be resolved through political dialogue between New Delhi and Islamabad. Russia also tried to apply pressure on Pakistan by issuing a stern warning through its embassy in Islamabad and official envoys that Pakistan's forces must immediately withdraw – but to no avail.[100] Pakistani officials and commentators criticized the reaction of these world powers, accusing them of looking at the Kargil crisis in isolation. Abdul Sattar, who later would become Pakistan's Foreign Minister, wrote: "emphasis on the Line of Control misses the larger issue of Kashmir and the need for its settlement ... Not until then can peace prevail in Kashmir or relations between India and Pakistan become stable."[101]

---

[97] Talbott, *Engaging India*, 158; and Shakil Shaikh, "Clinton Asks Nawaz, Vajpayee to Defuse Volatile Situation," *News International*, 5 June 1999.

[98] Brajesh Mishra, then principal secretary to the Indian prime minister, used the term, "paradigm shift" when talking to reporters in early June about the change in US–Indian relations. See C. Raja Mohan, *Crossing the Rubicon: The Shaping of India's New Foreign Policy* (New York: Palgrave Macmillan, 2003), 98, 284, n. 10.

[99] Zhang Guihong, *US Security Policy toward South Asia after September 11 and Its Implications for China: A Chinese Perspective*, Occasional Paper No. 50 (Washington, DC: The Henry L. Stimson Center, 2003), 17.

[100] "Russia Rejects Pakistan Version of Kargil Crisis," *The Hindu*, 2 July 1999.

[101] Abdul Sattar, "Crisis with Deep Roots," *News International*, 13 June 1999.

President Clinton telephoned Prime Minister Vajpayee on 14 June reportedly to suggest that India hold talks with Pakistan to resolve the military standoff. Vajpayee rejected this proposal and maintained that there can be no "meaningful dialogue" until the infiltrators vacated the occupied land. The following day, Clinton asked Nawaz Sharif to withdraw his forces back to Pakistan's side of the LoC, saying that this was a necessary step to end the fighting. Because his army was still reporting positive developments on the mountainous battlefield, Sharif was not about to trade away his best bargaining chip for a favorable settlement on Kashmir, so he continued to resist US pressure.

On 20 June the Group of Eight industrialized nations (G-8) issued a communiqué calling for India and Pakistan to respect the LoC, work for an immediate cessation of fighting, and return to the negotiating table in the spirit of the Lahore Declaration.[102] This communiqué received mixed reactions in both India and Pakistan. New Delhi was pleased that the G-8 identified the Kargil intrusion as the root of the crisis and did not urge mediation of the Kashmir dispute as the solution, but it was unhappy that Pakistan was not labeled as the aggressor. Although Pakistani diplomats failed in their bid to obtain support for their position on Kashmir, Islamabad must have been satisfied with the call for a ceasefire.[103]

US officials became even more concerned about the prospect of full-scale war erupting when President Clinton received a letter from Prime Minister Vajpayee in mid-June explaining that India might have to attack across the LoC or international border if Pakistani troops did not withdraw immediately.[104] From Washington's perspective, the ball was now in Pakistan's court. This is what led the White House on 22 June to dispatch Gen. Zinni and Gibson Lanpher to Islamabad. Two days later, they met with Gen. Musharraf at the Joint Staff Headquarters. The next day, 25 June, after considerable foot-dragging by the prime minister's office, they met with Nawaz Sharif. In each meeting, Gen. Zinni told his interlocutors in no uncertain terms that Pakistan must withdraw its forces or

---

[102] The exact text of the communiqué reads: "We are deeply concerned about the continuing military confrontation in Kashmir following the infiltration of armed intruders which violated the line of control. We regard any military action to change the status quo as irresponsible. We, therefore, call for the immediate end to these actions, restoration of the line of control and for the parties to work for an immediate cessation of the fighting, full respect in the future for the line of control and the resumption of dialogue between India and Pakistan in the spirit of the Lahore declaration." "G-8 condemns Violation of the LoC," *The Hindu*, 21 June 1999.

[103] See Joseph A. Mallaka, "The Kargil Crisis and the G-8," in Krishna and Chari, eds., *Kargil: The Tables Turned*, 233–241.

[104] Thomas W. Lippman, "India Hinted at Attack in Pakistan," *Washington Post*, 27 June 1999.

face international isolation and the possibility of war. According to Zinni, he argued, "If you don't pull back, you're going to bring war and nuclear annihilation down on your country. That's going to be very bad news for everybody."[105]

More positively for Islamabad, Zinni reportedly said that the United States would press India to ensure safe passage of Pakistan's troops back across the LoC.[106] Although Pakistan's leadership did not reject this offer, it did insist that it needed a "face-saving" way out of the mounting crisis. According to Zinni, "What we were able to offer was a meeting with President Clinton, which would end the isolation that had long been the state of affairs between our two countries, but we would announce the meeting only after a withdrawal of forces."[107] Zinni's proposal appealed to Gen. Musharraf, who by now certainly recognized that the Pakistan army and NLI troops clinging to their mountaintop positions with dwindling food, water, and ammunition could no longer withstand the onslaught of Indian ground and air forces, and thus withdrawal was the only choice.[108] Musharraf encouraged Prime Minister Nawaz Sharif to accept this deal, but Pakistan's military and civilian leadership alike wanted to obtain some tangible gain for withdrawing their troops. In Zinni's words, Nawaz Sharif "was reluctant to withdraw before the meeting with Clinton was announced (again, his problem was maintaining face); but after I insisted, he finally came around and he ordered the withdrawal."[109]

Soon after Zinni left Islamabad, the Pakistani government convened a meeting of the infrequently used Defence Committee of the Cabinet (DCC). According to former army chief Aslam Beg: "Through this meeting, the need to restore the spirit of the Lahore Declaration was brought into focus and unequivocal assertion was made that LoC would be respected and soon it proved a prelude to what was to come into effect through the Washington Declaration."[110] In other words, although when Lanpher flew to New Delhi the next day and had to report that no conclusive diplomatic solution was reached in Islamabad, he was able to explain that the resolution to the crisis that India had wanted all along was very near at hand.

---

[105] Tom Clancy with Tony Zinni and Tony Koltz, *Battle Ready* (New York: G. P. Putnam's Sons, 2004), 347.
[106] Nasim Zehra, "Zinni's Islamabad Mission," *News International*, 25 June 1999; and "A One-Sided Approach Will Not Work," *Dawn*, 26 June 1999.
[107] Clancy with Zinni and Koltz, *Battle Ready*, 347.
[108] Zinni confirmed this point in an interview with Joseph McMillan and Rodney Jones. See chapter 14 of this book.
[109] *Ibid.*
[110] Gen. (retd.) Aslam Beg, "The Kargil Denouement," *Frontier Post*, 14 July 1999.

July 1999: success

The apparent inability of the Zinni–Lanpher mission to finalize Pakistan's withdrawal from the Kargil heights resulted in even more international pressure on Pakistan. On 2 July Russia rejected another Pakistani request for outside mediation over Kashmir.[111] That very day, a very desperate Prime Minister Nawaz Sharif telephoned President Clinton to request his personal intervention in resolving the Kashmir dispute and the Kargil crisis. Clinton said that he would consider the request if Pakistan withdrew its forces back across the LoC immediately and unconditionally. Still Sharif would not give in.[112] But on the following day, Sharif telephoned the president again and asked if he could come to Washington on 4 July to discuss the Kargil military crisis and the broader political problem of Kashmir. Clinton said that he would meet Sharif, but only with the understanding that Pakistan would withdraw its forces and that he would "not agree to intervene in the Kashmir dispute, especially under circumstances that appeared to reward Pakistan's wrongful incursion."[113] Sharif still did not accept these conditions, but said that he was packing his bags and would be on the next flight. As President Clinton put it to Strobe Talbott, "This guy's coming literally on a wing and a prayer."[114]

Inside the United States, meanwhile, congressional opinion was building solidly against Pakistan, thanks largely to an intense and well-orchestrated Indian lobbying effort. On 3 July, the day that Nawaz Sharif departed for Washington, a US congressional panel rejected a plebiscite as a possible solution to the Kashmir problem. By a vote of 20 to 8, the House International Relations Committee defeated an amendment sought by the Republican Congressman Mr. Dana Rohrabacher. This all set the stage for the eventful 4 July meeting between Clinton and Sharif.

Strobe Talbott has since written that both on the eve and on the very day of Sharif's arrival, the US intelligence community provided new reports that Pakistan had taken steps to improve the preparedness of its nuclear forces for deployment and possible use.[115] This information strengthened the administration's resolve not only to impel the Pakistani prime minister to agree to an immediate military withdrawal but also to take a hard line on Sharif's request for US mediation on Kashmir. Bill Clinton described his perspective on the 4 July meeting in an interview that aired on American television in 2003:

---

[111] Nawaz Sharif's special envoy Khursheed Mehmood made this request during talks with his Russian counterpart, Secretary-General Alexander Losyukov.
[112] Talbott, *Engaging India*, 160.
[113] Bill Clinton, *My Life* (New York: Knopf, 2004), 864–865.
[114] Cited in Talbott, *Engaging India*, 160.   [115] Talbott, *Engaging India*, 161.

Given the fact that these two countries were nuclear powers, I did not believe that I could be in any way, shape, or form part of reacting to a power play by throwing all these soldiers over the Line of Control and running ... increasing the risk of nuclear war, and therefore I was going to be put in a position of going to the Indians and saying, because the Pakistanis have done something wrong, we now have to do what they want us to do. I couldn't do that.[116]

As it turned out, Sharif came to Washington with the clear understanding that Pakistan's remaining contingent of forces still occupying mountain peaks across the LoC would have to withdraw, but he desperately wanted to gain some tangible achievement on the Kashmir issue in exchange for agreeing to the withdrawal. Strobe Talbott recounts the details of this meeting in his book. Bruce Riedel also was personally involved in the president's negotiations with Sharif and his delegation, and offers a rare, candid description of those tense hours at Blair House in chapter 5 of this book. The final statement that Clinton and Sharif agreed to is the following:

President Clinton and Prime Minister Sharif share the view that the current fighting in the Kargil region of Kashmir is dangerous and contains the seeds of a wider conflict. They also agreed that it was vital for the peace of South Asia that the Line of Control in Kashmir be respected by both parties, in accordance with their 1972 Simla Accord. It was agreed between the President and the Prime Minister that concrete steps will be taken for the restoration of the line of control in accordance with the Simla Agreement. The President urged an immediate cessation of the hostilities once these steps are taken. The Prime Minister and President agreed that the bilateral dialogue begun in Lahore in February provides the best forum for resolving all issues dividing India and Pakistan, including Kashmir. The President said he would take a personal interest in encouraging an expeditious resumption and intensification of those bilateral efforts, once the sanctity of the Line of Control has been fully restored. The President reaffirmed his intent to pay an early visit to South Asia.[117]

Pakistani forces did not withdraw immediately after the 5 July joint statement issued by President Clinton and Prime Minister Nawaz Sharif. What took months to occupy in that terrain could not have been vacated overnight. In the meantime, Indian troops captured additional peaks – including Tiger Hill – from the demoralized Pakistani troops that had not been resupplied with food, water, or ammunition in weeks. On 9 July Pakistan's DGMO called his Indian counterpart on the hotline to discuss Pakistan's withdrawal back across the LoC. Two days later, the two DGMOs met on the Indian side of the border and ironed out procedures

---

[116] "Nuclear Nightmares: Losing Control," *Avoiding Armageddon*, videocassette (Washington, DC: Public Broadcasting Service, 2003).
[117] Joint Statement by President Clinton and Prime Minister Sharif, 5 July 1999, available at www.fas.org/news/pakistan/1999/990704-pak-wh1.htm.

for the return of Pakistani forces to their side of the LoC. It took several days for the message to reach Pakistan's forward-deployed troops. And after the deadline for the agreed ceasefire had lapsed, Indian and Pakistani troops again resumed the fighting, which made Pakistan's withdrawal a confused and dangerous affair. As Pakistani troops vacated their positions, Indian troops pushed ahead, while artillery and small-arms firing continued all around.

One reason for the intense post-ceasefire drama was that the Pakistan army wanted to keep the posts it gained in the initial phase of the operation along the ridgelines, which it will be recalled was the initial territorial objective of the Kargil intrusion. After all of the intense fighting, high-level diplomacy, and risk of nuclear escalation, there was no desire on the party of the Kargil planners to give up the high ground that they desperately wanted in the first place. So as late as 20 July, Pakistani troops remained in occupation of several strategic positions on the Indian side of the LoC. Indian sources said that the Pakistani forces had not moved out of their bunkers near point 5060 in the Mushkoh Valley, the base of Marpola in Dras, and the Shangruti top in the Batalik sector. The intruders reportedly still were getting cover from Pakistani artillery fire. The United States continued high-level diplomacy through July, with President Clinton expressing his "understanding" for India's position that Pakistan had to take specific steps to reaffirm the sanctity of the LoC, including cessation of cross-border terrorism. This American "understanding" was conveyed to India during a twenty-minute conversation on 20 July between Clinton and Prime Minister Vajpayee. Then on 25 July the United States told Pakistan to withdraw all its troops from the remaining areas of Kargil and push for the Lahore process, as India made it clear that the resumption of Indo-Pak dialogue depended on the stoppage of cross-border terrorism by Pakistan. By the end of the month virtually all Pakistani forces had either been killed or withdrawn back to Pakistan-controlled territory.

Even during the withdrawal stages of Kargil, the United States remained actively involved with both India and Pakistan. The situation was analogous to a referee trying to stop and separate two physically and emotionally entangled boxers from continuing to fight on well after the bell's toll indicating the round was over.

Conclusion

This analysis of Indian, Pakistani, and international conflict-management efforts during the Kargil crisis yields mixed results concerning the theory and practice of nuclear deterrence. It is troubling that Pakistan tried to use military force to alter the territorial and political status quo in Kashmir. It

8 Surprise at the top of the world: India's systemic and intelligence failure

James J. Wirtz and Surinder Rana

Although there is much unique about the Pakistani effort to present their Indian rivals with a *fait accompli* along the frozen ridges and mountain outposts near Kargil, the incident is a textbook case of both the *success and failure* of military surprise. The Pakistani armed forces succeeded in infiltrating members of the Northern Light Infantry (NLI) undetected into disputed territory, but initial tactical success led to an overall strategic humiliation that culminated in the coup against Pakistani prime minister Nawaz Sharif. Much like the Japanese navy at Pearl Harbor or the German attack through the Ardennes forest in December 1944, Pakistani officials and soldiers were unable to turn operational success into a strategic victory against a vastly superior opponent. This Pakistani success, however, still haunts Indian intelligence analysts, officials, and officers. Indian and Pakistani forces had been exchanging fire in Jammu and Kashmir for years. Both sides had a clear idea about the other's intentions. Nevertheless, Indian officers and intelligence analysts were surprised by Pakistan. Much in the same way the surprise suffered by Israel in the October 1973 war produced a major reassessment of what went wrong and lingering doubts about future intelligence,[1] Kargil shook the entire Indian defense establishment and led to several official inquiries into the sources of the intelligence failure.[2]

---

[1] Uri Bar-Joseph, *The Watchman Fell Asleep: The Surprise of Yom Kippur and its Sources* (Albany, NY: State University of New York Press, 2005).

[2] The Kargil Review Committee (KRC) Report and a report compiled by India's Institute for Defence Studies and Analyses (IDSA) are prominent efforts in this category. Constituted on 29 July 1999, the KRC comprised four members: K. Subrahmanyam (Chairman), Lt. Gen. K. K. Hazari (retd.), B. G. Verghese, and Satish Chandra, Secretary of India's National Security Council Secretariat (NSCS). The committee was charged with reviewing the events leading up to Pakistani intrusions in Kargil. The KRC submitted its 265-page report on 15 December 1999, entitled, *From Surprise to Reckoning: The Kargil Review Committee Report* (New Delhi: Sage, 2000). The IDSA report is: Jasjit Singh, ed., *Kargil 1999: Pakistan's Fourth War for Kashmir* (New Delhi: Knowledge World, 1999).

What is unusual about the Kargil incident is the fact that a relatively inconsequential military move posed potentially horrific consequences for all concerned. Not since the Cuban missile crisis had a nuclear-armed country attempted to surprise a similarly equipped opponent with a military *fait accompli*. There was a clear sense of nuclear danger in the air once this enduring rivalry erupted into open hostilities. Surprise under these circumstances is extraordinarily dangerous because it can prompt the victim to react with emotion, which amplifies the victim's military imperative to escalate the conflict to overturn the *fait accompli*.[3] Exploring the Pakistani motivations for attempting to achieve a *fait accompli* and the Indian response to surprise can generate important insight into the stability of the nuclear balance in South Asia and, for that matter, other situations in which nuclear powers find themselves in an asymmetric military rivalry.[4] Kargil also highlights an important observation about the phenomenon of surprise: despite variations in culture, history, geography, and the issues under dispute, instances of strategic surprise are fundamentally the same phenomenon and produce similar military results.[5] Kargil, Pearl Harbor, and the 11 September terrorist attacks contain striking similarities.

To illustrate the similarities that exist in all instances of strategic surprise, to explain the Pakistani decision to present India with a *fait accompli*, and to explain the surprise suffered by Indian analysts and officers, this chapter elaborates a theory of surprise. The theory is a structural explanation that links both actors' positions in a strategic interaction with their perceptions of information about what the opponent is likely to do under a given set of circumstances. It deals primarily with major instances of surprise, events that suspend the dialectic of war, thereby turning combat into a matter of mere administration by removing an active opponent from the battlefield. Kargil is unusual in the history of warfare because the stronger party was surprised when the weaker party occupied positions that the former had abandoned due to weather and altitude conditions

---

[3] Fred Ikle has brought this escalation dynamic inherent in the response to surprise to our attention.

[4] T. V. Paul, *Asymmetric Conflicts: War Initiation by Weaker Powers* (Cambridge University Press, 1994).

[5] The idea that the phenomenon of surprise transcends history and culture is reflected in the classic works on the subject. See Richard Betts, *Surprise Attack: Lessons for Defense Planning* (Washington, DC: Brookings Institution, 1983); Alex Hybel, *The Logic of Surprise in International Conflict* (Lexington, Mass.: Lexington Books, 1986); Robert Axelrod, "The Rational Timing of Surprise," *World Politics* 31, no. 2 (January 1979): 228–246; and Michael Handel, "Intelligence and the Problem of Strategic Surprise," *Journal of Strategic Studies* 7, no. 3 (September 1984): 229–230.

that barely permitted human habitation.[6] In other words, India inadvertently suspended the dialectic of war on the Kargil heights: Pakistani officers saw India's inattentiveness as an opportunity worth exploiting.

Because the theory does not deal with the use of surprise as a force multiplier at the operational or tactical level of warfare, those who see Kargil as a minor tactical operation that escalated out of control might object to the idea that those behind the operation intended it to have strategic consequences. Nevertheless, the theory can explain why the weaker party in a conflict often becomes mesmerized by a specific operation at the expense of making realistic strategic calculations about its prospects in the overall campaign. As the theory would predict, Pakistan's military leadership, which represented the weaker side in the conflict, was attracted to surprise because it would allow Pakistani troops to achieve immediate objectives that could be expected to lead to major gains at the expense of India, its far stronger opponent. The theory also would predict that India, as the stronger side in the conflict, not only would be surprised by the *fait accompli*, but also would go on to redouble its efforts, regain the initiative, and win eventual victory.

The chapter begins by briefly describing the theory of surprise. It then applies the theory to explain the Pakistani decision to present India with a *fait accompli* at Kargil. It then explains the reasons for the failure of Indian intelligence. The chapter concludes by offering some observations about the impact of surprise on the stability of enduring rivalries given the incentives and perceptions involved in asymmetric conflict.

The theory of surprise

The theory of surprise does not seek to explain all instances of military surprise, but it does explain the events that alter history by punctuating the beginning of conflicts, or events that can inflict catastrophic damage. Kargil thus represents a somewhat muted instance of surprise in the sense that the *fait accompli* Pakistan achieved did not provoke large-scale conventional combat or a nuclear exchange. As Peter R. Lavoy explains in chapter 7 of this book, outside diplomatic intervention on the part of the United States and the failure of China to take sides with Pakistan in the conflict – exogenous factors in terms of the theory – helped to prevent escalation of the conflict. As discussed in chapter 3 by Feroz Hassan Khan, Peter R. Lavoy, and Christopher Clary, the Pakistani officers who planned the operation,

---

[6] Combat between Japanese and US forces in the Aleutian Islands in the Second World War had a similar quality. The harsh weather prevented effective reconnaissance and conditions on the islands made them nearly uninhabitable. Both sides staged amphibious operations, only to find, after suffering numerous casualties, that they were unoccupied by the enemy.

however, apparently expected that the *fait accompli* would produce great results by altering the military balance in the theater of operations by cutting the ability of India to resupply its forces to the Ladakh region.

Three key propositions make up the theory of surprise.

Proposition 1: surprise temporarily suspends the dialectical nature of warfare by eliminating an active opponent from the battlefield

Surprise transforms war from a situation in which the outcome is determined by an interaction between two combatants into a matter of accounting and logistics, an event whose outcome can be controlled by one side. Probability and chance still influence administrative matters and friction still can bedevil any evolution, whether it is conducted in peacetime or in war. But surprise eliminates war's dialectic: achieving a military objective no longer is impeded by opponents who can be expected to make one's life miserable. This has a profound effect on military operations. For example, the amount of time it might take to arrive at and seize an objective can be derived from simple calculations about how fast a unit can drive down some highway (of course, more sophisticated analyses might be undertaken to determine the effects of equipment breakdowns, road conditions, or crew fatigue to estimate probabilities of likely arrival times). No account need be made for delays caused by roadblocks, blown bridges, preregistered artillery, or major enemy units astride one's path. Needless to say, the fact that Pakistani forces encountered no opposition as they occupied positions that Indian units had abandoned greatly facilitated their movement into mountaintop positions in Kargil, even though weather and terrain remained major obstacles.

Although surprise often is described as a force multiplier, something that increases the effectiveness of one's forces in combat, it can transform war as it approaches its ideal type. Surprise, and the asymmetric attacks it facilitates, thus can yield spectacular results. In other words, by placing combatants in critical places where they face no opposition, strategic outcomes can be achieved at an extraordinarily low price in blood and treasure. Weaker parties in a conflict thus become mesmerized by the prospect of suspending war's dialectic because it allows them to contemplate operations that are beyond their reach in wartime. By avoiding the military forces of their opponent, weaker parties use surprise to avoid the attrition and opposition that is inevitable in war to inflict some sort of setback on their stronger opponents. Stronger parties prefer more predictable and less risky strategies based on attrition to achieve their objectives; they are extremely unlikely to risk a battle, to say nothing of an entire campaign, on achieving surprise.

Proposition 2: the weaker party in a conflict is far more likely
than the stronger party to adopt strategies that require the element
of surprise to succeed

Proposition 2 applies to actors that rely on surprise for success, not as a mundane force multiplier. This is an important qualification because strategists everywhere recognize the benefits of surprise. Across cultures and history, military doctrines have encouraged soldiers to incorporate surprise, along with other force multipliers such as the use of cover or maneuver, into their military planning and operations. In ritualistic fashion, for instance, US officials and officers often report that some attack has achieved surprise, even though the United States rarely attempts to surprise opponents in a significant way. As the stronger party in the conflict, it generally seeks to intimidate, coerce, or deter its opponents without fighting by telegraphing its intentions to fight and the general size and severity of the blow that is about to land.[7] Prior to the Second Gulf War, for instance, US Defense Department officials provided many details about the "shock and awe" campaign that would unfold if Saddam Hussein failed to cooperate with UN mandates to disarm.

The weaker party in a conflict, by contrast, generally cannot engage in coercive strategies to intimidate its opponent into complying with its wishes or in attritional combat to eliminate the stronger party from the field. In fact, even the potential threat the weaker party poses is often not recognized by the stronger opponent. Japan had been engaged in a war in Asia for nearly a decade prior to Pearl Harbor. It had abandoned the international arms-control regime governing naval deployments and had joined the original "axis of evil" with Germany and Italy. Yet, US officers and officials never really took the Japanese threat seriously, although they believed it likely that the Japanese might attack someone else. Similarly, Indian officers and analysts probably believed that the advent of open nuclear competition as well as Prime Minister Vajpayee's Lahore initiative signaled an improvement in relations between India and Pakistan, but not a final settlement of the enduring rivalry between the two countries. What is clear to Indian officials in *hindsight*, however, is that the Pakistanis remained willing to exploit any opportunity that came their way to deliver a military or political setback to New Delhi.

The leaders of the weaker side in a conflict are more likely to risk all in attacks that depend on surprise to succeed because they lack credible alternatives to defeat their stronger opponents. They cannot

---

[7] James J. Wirtz and James Russell, "US Policy on Preventive War and Preemption," *The Nonproliferation Review* 10, no. 1 (Spring 2003): 113–123.

win force-on-force engagements so they become preoccupied with using surprise to deliver a devastating blow to an unsuspecting enemy. The weaker party begins to focus on what might be possible in war if military operations could unfold without opposition. By contrast, the stronger party in the conflict remains focused on the attritional nature of warfare and thus fails to perceive the opportunities created by surprise. Moreover, even if the stronger party detects evidence of the weaker party's initiative, it will dismiss the threat as extraordinarily reckless or simply too fantastic to be taken seriously.

Proposition 3: strategies based on surprise appear to all concerned as extremely risky ex-ante and often turn out to be reckless and ill advised

A paradox inherent in surprise is that both sides generally share the same perception of the risk inherent in relying on surprise in some sort of war-winning strategy. For example, Roberta Wohlstetter, in her classic study of Pearl Harbor, noted: "Japanese and American estimates of the risks to the Japanese were identical for the large-scale war they had planned, as well as for individual operations. What we miscalculated was the ability of the willingness of the Japanese to accept such risks."[8] Because the stronger party assesses any potential threat of surprise attack as doomed to eventual failure, it tends to dismiss evidence of an impending threat. Michael Handel captured this phenomenon in the "risk paradox" that is at the core of the theory of surprise: "The greater the risk, the less likely it seems, and the less risky it becomes. In fact, the greater the risk, the smaller it becomes."[9] At this point the structure of the conflict becomes linked to the perceptual biases of the parties involved. The weaker party plays down the extreme risks inherent in the effort to benefit from surprise because of the prospect of achieving gains that otherwise are beyond its grasp. The stronger party, armed with an attritional perspective, focuses on the real impediments – the balance of military capabilities – the weaker party faces in achieving any gain at all. Both parties' perceptions of risk also are validated. The weaker party generally succeeds in surprising its more capable opponent; while the more capable opponent usually goes on to defeat the weaker party.

Propositions 2 and 3 thus link the structure of the conflict that two opponents find themselves in to the perceptual biases they embrace in

---

[8] Roberta Wohlstetter, *Pearl Harbor: Warning and Decision* (Stanford University Press, 1962), 355.
[9] Michael Handel, "The Yom Kippur War and the Inevitability of Surprise," *International Studies Quarterly* 21, no. 3 (September 1977): 468.

assessing their preferred strategy and likely outcomes of a potential conflict. When combined, these propositions do not bode well for those whose job it is to detect denial and deception. What it suggests is that weak opponents perceive great incentives to surprise their stronger opponents using asymmetric attacks and that the stronger opponents will probably dismiss evidence of these emerging threats as harebrained. The stronger party views a potential conflict through the lens of war's dialectic: conflict will involve a clash of wills and combat on some battlefield. This attritional view of war shapes the stronger side's evaluation of information about potential initiatives by the weaker side. By contrast, the weaker side focuses on what might be possible if the opposition turns out to be a "no show." The strategic planning undertaken by weaker opponents, however, also shares another common attribute: it often becomes extremely vague when it comes time to explain how initial tactical or operational success will produce overall success in some campaign or even victory in the overall conflict. Japanese plans for the Pearl Harbor attack itself, for example, were extraordinarily precise, but their plans for the rest of the war were fuzzy.[10] Wishful thinking tends to intrude on the weaker side's estimates of its stronger opponent's response to surprise and the way the entire operation eventually will produce in a favorable outcome. The ex post debate among Pakistani officials and officers about the objectives behind Kargil, for example, reflects the lack of strategic clarity that bedeviled the operation from its inception. Hasan-Askari Rizvi discusses this point in great detail in chapter 13 of this book.

The *fait accompli* at Kargil

Although the Pakistan government had supported an insurgency in Kashmir since 1990, it had failed to spark a mass movement that could be exploited to settle the Kashmir issue in its favor. Given India's military superiority, an all-out military offensive in Kashmir would have ended in disaster for Pakistan. To overcome this stalemate, which was shifting increasingly in India's favor, Pakistani military leaders devised a plan to surprise the Indian military with a *fait accompli* that, in their thinking, would rejuvenate the waning insurgency in Kashmir and provide them strategic leverage against the Indian army's deployment along the so-called Line of Control (LoC) in Kashmir.[11] Because of its preoccupation with the Kashmir insurgency, India's defense and intelligence

[10] Wohlstetter, *Pearl Harbor*, 349.
[11] Since the late 1990s, numerous indicators showed that the Pakistani-aided insurgency in Kashmir was waning. The Indian security forces had most of the insurgents on the run.

establishments did not believe that the Pakistan army was capable of significant offensive activity in the region, especially in light of the earlier failed Pakistani attempts to capture Indian territory in Siachen. Since India had secured the Saltaro ridgeline in 1984, its strong defensive positions and longer-range artillery – most notably the Bofors gun – had been consistently able to defeat Pakistani offensives.[12] When local operatives working for the Jammu and Kashmir government intelligence agencies reported in early May 1999 that the Kargil heights were being occupied by Pakistani regulars and not by a few stray militants, Indian army officials scoffed at the idea that the Pakistan army was on the move around Kargil.[13]

Planning the *fait accompli*: the view from Pakistan

Pakistani military officials grew increasingly frustrated in the mid-1980s with their inability to respond to the Indian occupation of the Siachen Glacier, its capture of a string of Pakistani posts along the LoC in the Northern Areas, and its artillery harassment of the Neelum Valley area. The idea of launching a "Kargil-like" operation in response to India's activities had been floating around for over a decade, but Pakistani leaders had rejected this kind of gambit as too risky. For their part, Indian intelligence agencies had no prior knowledge of any such plans.[14] As Khan, Lavoy, and Clary indicate in chapter 3, the idea of launching an operation during the winter months was championed by the Headquarters of the Force Command Northern Areas (FCNA) and the Headquarters of 10 Corps, the commands respectively charged with conduct of military operations in the mountainous region toward the Siachen Glacier and along the entire Kashmir LoC.

The operation probably had the immediate tactical objectives of infiltrating through the gaps in Indian defenses that were created by winter

For details, see Navnita Chadha Behera, *Demystifying Kashmir* (New Delhi: Pearson Education, 2006), 83–84; and Sumit Ganguly, *Conflict Unending: India–Pakistan Tensions since 1947* (New York: Columbia University Press, 2001), 121.

[12] For the role of artillery in this terrain, see Lt. Gen. V. R. Raghavan, *Siachen: Conflict Without End* (Delhi: Penguin Books, 2002), 94–97.

[13] Author's interview with a senior Jammu and Kashmir state government official during his visit to Monterey, California in August 2002. According to this official, the Jammu and Kashmir state government agencies, based upon information gathered through their own sources, indicated to the army that Pakistan's army regulars, and not militants, were active in the Kargil heights.

[14] The statement by a former Indian Chief of Army Staff (COAS) during an interview in New Delhi on 26 February 2002 that the origin of Pakistan's plan dates back to the late 1980s is an afterthought. Indian intelligence was not aware of any such plans prior to April 1999.

redeployment, and seizing dominating terrain features.[15] Pakistani officials apparently calculated that due to difficulties imposed by terrain and weather, the positions once occupied would be extremely difficult to recapture. If they could be held until the following winter, when large-scale military operations would become impossible, these limited gains might become permanent. John H. Gill indicates in chapter 4 that Pakistani officers might have hoped that Kargil would deliver a shock to Indian officials, enable Pakistan to garner international support for its position, and permit Pakistani officials to enter into negotiations with India from a position of strength.

Even in hindsight, however, these goals appear ill defined and far-fetched. Why would China, the United States, or the European Union, for instance, intervene in a dispute over some mountaintop outposts? Some have suggested that the operation was intended to generate the threat of nuclear escalation, which would have prompted an international response to the crisis.[16] But if one wanted to gain international notoriety, why stage the operation in such a remote and harsh location? This type of failure to link tactical or operational success to victory in a given campaign is actually quite common in the history of surprise and constitutes a phenomenon that transcends history, culture, and the specific points in dispute in a given conflict. Much like Nikita Khrushchev believed that the Americans simply would learn to live with the deployment of nuclear-armed surface-to-surface missiles in Cuba, Pakistani officers simply believed that Kargil would generate significant international support from the great powers in their enduring rivalry with India.[17] From the

---

[15] There were eight Indian posts in the Kargil sector that in earlier years had been vacated in the winter. Sensing the possibility of Pakistan attempting to capture them, Indian military commanders had decided to continue holding these posts during the winter of 1998–1999. Some observers thus believe that Pakistani officials had planned to send forces to infiltrate through gaps between Indian defenses not necessarily with the intention of capturing vacated outposts. See V. P. Malik, *Kargil: From Surprise to Victory* (New Delhi: HarperCollins, 2006), 90.

[16] Shahbaz Hussain Khokhar, "Management of the Kargil Crisis: A Systemic Approach," M.Sc. Dissertation, Department of Defence and Strategic Studies, Islamabad: Quaid-i-Azam University, Pakistan, 2001.

[17] When Polish leader Władysław Gomułka learned in the summer of 1962 of the Soviet decision to present the United States with a *fait accompli* in Cuba, for example, he warned Khrushchev that the Americans would respond vigorously. "Khrushchev assured him," according to Ned Lebow and Janice Stein, "that all would turn out well. He told Gomulka the story of a poor Russian farmer who lacked the money to buy firewood for the winter. He removed his goat into his hut to provide warmth. The goat was incredibly rank but the man learned to live with its smell. 'Kennedy would learn to accept the smell of the missiles.'" Richard Ned Lebow and Janice Gross Stein, *We All Lost the Cold War* (Princeton University Press, 1994), 77.

perspective of the Pakistani officials, apparently only positive consequences would flow from the effort to surprise India in Kargil.

Exactly how the planning for the operation unfolded remains somewhat obscure. The planning initially was limited to four senior officers: Lieutenant General Javed Hassan (FCNA); Lieutenant General Mahmud Ahmed, Commander 10 Corps; Lieutenant General Muhammad Aziz Khan, Chief of General Staff (CGS); and Chief of Army Staff (COAS) General Pervez Musharraf. Lieutenant General Mahmud Ahmed reportedly briefed the initial plan to General Musharraf in mid-November 1998. Prime Minister Nawaz Sharif probably was informed about the operation sometime between January and March 1999.[18] The planners' preoccupation with secrecy resulted in centralized decision-making, which prevented the plan from being vetted and staffed before a larger group of officers and analysts.

Although the secrecy surrounding the operation probably was justified in terms of operational security (if Indian intelligence organizations had detected the operation, they could have scuttled it before it started by reoccupying the mountain positions) and not as a necessary requirement of some sort of conspiracy, the internal security surrounding the operation had unintended consequences. By preventing individuals not involved with devising the Kargil operation from testing its assumptions and estimating its likely consequences, the handful of planners cut themselves off from an honest appraisal of the risks they were about to undertake. Once again, this failure on the side contemplating a surprise attack against a vastly superior opponent is quite common in the history of surprise and is a phenomenon that transcends culture. Planners at the Central Intelligence Agency, for instance, relied on émigré reports when they estimated that the Cuban people would simply revolt at the first news that a few hundred liberators had landed at the Bay of Pigs. They ignored a fact that might have been readily apparent to those with fewer vested interests in the operation: the émigrés themselves had a keen hatred for the Castro regime and a profound interest in seeing the operation go forward.

The secrecy surrounding the planning of the Kargil *fait accompli* might have interfered in the execution of the operation. The movement of Pakistani forces was initially directed to four areas on the Indian side of the LoC that made a good deal of strategic sense: Mushkoh, Dras, Kaksar, and Batalik. The most important positions were located in the Dras sector because they allowed direct observation of National Highway 1A,

---

[18] Shaukat Qadir, "An Analysis of the Kargil Conflict 1999," *Journal of the Royal United Services Institute of Defense Studies* 147, no. 2 (April 2002): 24.

permitting Pakistani artillery to target the road and surrounding Indian facilities. The Dras positions also could serve as a base for patrols and raids to supplement artillery interdiction of the road. But Zafar Iqbal Cheema has noted that the overall scope of the operation might have doomed it to failure: by late spring 1999 Pakistani forces had occupied over 100 outposts covering an expanse of over 50 square miles in depth ranging from 4 to 9 miles inside Indian-held Kashmir.[19] It was impossible for Pakistan to meet the logistical needs of such a large and far-flung force once Indian units responded to the incursion. Also, to achieve surprise, Pakistani planners used local, NLI troops for the operation, rather than moving additional troops from outside the region. As a result, the Pakistan army limited its options for reacting to India's offensive response when the element of surprise was lost.[20] It is impossible to determine if this oversight was the product of bad planning or overzealous implementation on the part of local commanders or militants. But from an operational perspective, Pakistani forces never severed NH-1A, which would have isolated Indian forces in the Leh Garrison.

Ripe for surprise: the view from India

Although several elements are unique about the surprise suffered by India at Kargil, from the Indian perspective, many phenomena common to strategic surprise can be identified in the incident. The fact that Indian officers themselves created the opportunity for surprise by abandoning their positions in winter is somewhat unique. The fact that they set a pattern of activity that was recognized and exploited by Pakistan (i.e., generally rotating units out of fixed positions in winter) is more common to instances of intelligence failure. The fact that the gambit adopted by Pakistan had similarities to the Indian military occupation of the Siachen Glacier in 1984 should have sensitized them to the possibility that Pakistan might try to avenge Siachen.[21] The inability of Indian analysts to recognize their vulnerability, however, is not surprising, given their

---

[19] Zafar Iqbal Cheema interviewed by James Wirtz, 2 June 2003. Cheema's account is corroborated by the leader of this operation, General Pervez Musharraf, in his recently published memoirs. See Pervez Musharraf, *In the Line of Fire: A Memoir* (New York: Simon and Schuster, 2006), 90.

[20] In response to India's summer offensive to dislodge the infiltrated positions, the Pakistan army failed to reinforce, counterattack, or make any other diversionary maneuvers to lessen the pressure upon the infiltrating troops when they were attacked.

[21] Evidence of Pakistani movement into the mountain positions was not a unique event in the annals of history, making it far easier to recognize it for what it was compared to events that have no precedent, especially within living history. See Walter Laqueur, *The Terrible Secret* (Boston: Little Brown, 1980).

apparently low opinion of their opponent. If Indian forces found it too difficult to garrison mountaintop positions in the dead of winter, it was deemed unlikely that Pakistani forces would be willing or able to occupy the same positions.[22]

Indian intelligence officials, whose analyses of possible Pakistani moves seemed to reflect classic cost-benefit calculations, believed that political circumstances did not support a hostile move by Pakistan.[23] The Lahore initiative suggested that political relations between India and Pakistan were improving and it made little sense to upset the diplomatic apple cart. Pakistani efforts to stir up unrest in Indian territory adjacent to Kargil also had met with little success.[24] And as for strategic logic behind the move, it might be possible to occupy the mountain positions, but significant military activity in the mountains in the dead of winter was extremely problematic.[25] Indeed, the severity of the conditions along the ridgelines slowly wore down Indian troops and officers who were supposed to patrol the mountains vigorously once positions were vacated for the winter. These patrols were supposed to detect signs of Pakistani activity in the mountains so that aerial reconnaissance could be undertaken at the first sign of trouble.

Problems with India's intelligence organizations

India's civilian and military intelligence organizations were tasked with detecting and analyzing Pakistan's military movements along the LoC. The Intelligence Bureau (IB), which had its origins in British police efforts to combat thuggery at the start of the twentieth century, is the oldest

---

[22] According to an account written by the former Pakistani minister of information Altaf Gauhar, an operational plan for the occupation of the Kargil heights in 1987 was dropped by the former Pakistani president Zia ul-Haq because of a briefing by then-Foreign Minister Sahibzada Yaqub Khan. According to Gauhar, in this briefing Yaqub Khan was able to convince Zia that due to the difficulty of terrain, and treacherous weather, the plan for the occupation of the Kargil heights was militarily inappropriate. Extracts taken from Altaf Gauhar, "Four Wars One Assumption," *The Nation*, 5 September 1999; as quoted in *Kargil 1999: Pakistan's Fourth War for Kashmir*, ed. Jasjit Singh (New Delhi: Knowledge World, 1999), 133.

[23] Nitin A. Gokhale and Ajith Pillai, "The War That Should Never Have Been," *Outlook*, 6 September 1999, as quoted in P. R. Chari, "Introduction: Some Preliminary Observations," in *Kargil: Tables Turned*, ed. Ashok Krishna and P. R. Chari (New Delhi: Manohar, 2001), 18.

[24] This implies that in 1999 there were apparent signs of decline in Kashmir insurgency (Pakistan called it Kashmiri struggle). Editorial in *Friday Times* (Pakistan), 5 August 1999, in Kargil Review Committee, *From Surprise to Reckoning*, 18.

[25] The envisaged significant military activity included logistic support to maintain those heights; also, sending out protective and early warning elements around the occupied heights. Kargil Review Committee, *From Surprise to Reckoning*, 17.

civilian intelligence organization in India.[26] The IB focuses its efforts on internal security and is at the center of the Indian intelligence community. It is staffed primarily by police officers. Its international affairs divisions are staffed by active-duty or retired military officers. The army, air force, and navy each maintain their own independent intelligence agencies. The IB tracks terrorist or insurgency-related activities, conducts counter-espionage, detects economic crimes, and helps solve serious violent crimes. The IB also is required to gather information on the issues having long-term national security implications, such as demographic changes and ethnic or communal tensions. IB officials are posted in all Indian states, and stations are located along the border with Pakistan. IB officials work in close cooperation with the respective state police and other law-enforcement agencies. The IB also possesses its own communications intelligence (COMINT) collection capability.[27]

A second agency, the Research and Analysis Wing (RAW), was created in September 1968 as an external intelligence division of the IB. It was placed under the control of the Cabinet Secretariat of India. RAW is staffed by active-duty and retired military officers, police personnel, and civilian professionals with expertise in the fields of economics and infor-mation technology. Over time, RAW expanded its military intelligence capability by strengthening its coverage of technical and aviation intelli-gence and by creating a military intelligence group, which is headed by a senior army officer. RAW monitors foreign developments using a variety of sources: human intelligence (HUMINT) gathered from Field Intelligence Posts (situated along the border with China, Pakistan, Nepal, Bangladesh, Bhutan, and Burma) and officials posted in the foreign diplomatic missions; imagery intelligence (IMINT) using aerial and satellite assets; electronic intelligence (ELINT) generated by mon-itoring electromagnetic emissions; and communications intelligence (COMINT) produced from intercepted signals communications. The main consumers of the intelligence products provided by RAW are the Ministry of External Affairs, the Home Ministry (including the IB, and the Border Security Force), the Defence Ministry, the National Security Council Secretariat and the intelligence organizations maintained by the three military services.

Several smaller organizations also form part of the Indian intelligence community. The Border Security Force (BSF) is charged with policing

---

[26] See B. Raman, *Intelligence Past, Present and Future* (New Delhi: Lancer Publishers, 2002), 1.
[27] For the role and capabilities of the IB, see Kargil Review Committee, *From Surprise to Reckoning*, 112–113.

the border during peacetime and with collecting information using HUMINT, ELINT, and COMINT networks. The Directorate General of Military Intelligence (DGMI) gathers intelligence relevant to army operations from divisional and brigade intelligence units. The Joint Intelligence Committee of the National Security Council Secretariat serves as the central intelligence organization for senior government officials. It gathers relevant inputs from all national and state intelligence agencies for review by representatives of all intelligence agencies and concerned ministries during fortnightly meetings.[28]

Collection failures

A proximate cause of the surprise suffered by India at Kargil was the failure of reconnaissance efforts to collect information about the movement of Pakistani units. Between November 1998 and April 1999, Indian and Pakistani forces adopted a winter posture in the Kargil region and vacated some mountain posts.[29] For India, however, winter deployments were purely an administrative matter, not an operational imperative. To keep watch over areas controlled by border outposts, units were required to send winter reconnaissance patrols to areas vacated during the winter.[30] Reconnaissance patrols were not sent to Mushkoh from 10 January to 30 March, Yaldor from 1 February to 5 April, and Kaksar from 3 March to 11 April 1999.[31] Even though Brigadier Surinder Singh, the Commander of the 121 Independent Brigade (the unit responsible for the defense of Kargil), is said to have visualized a serious Pakistani threat in his areas of responsibility, he did not organize reconnaissance patrols during the winter because he feared that he would be held responsible if

---

[28] *Ibid.* 114.

[29] In adopting winter posture, the concerned units vacated those posts that were considered hazardous and would result in exposing troops to the unacceptable risks from extreme weather conditions and avalanches. Certain posts were classified as winter cutoff posts, which were maintained throughout the year after adequate winter stocking. The units made decisions to vacate or maintain certain posts as winter cutoff posts, based upon tactical and logistical factors. In the winter of 1999, by thus adopting the winter posture, the Indian army had left large gaps in defenses astride the LoC in Kargil. See *ibid.* 83.

[30] These patrols reconnoiter the unit's area of operational responsibility with a view to check any hostile movement in those areas, and liaise with the local civilian population of that area. During his active-duty tenure with the Indian army in Kashmir the author, Colonel Surinder Rana (retd.), participated in such winter patrolling.

[31] The then-District Magistrate of Kargil, Shaleen Kabra, reportedly told the Kargil Review Committee in September 1999 that army patrols hired civilian porters for these patrols. According to Kabra, no porters were hired for patrolling during the 1998–1999 winter. Praveen Swami, "Kargil Questions," *Frontline,* 1 September 2000, 13.

these patrols suffered weather casualties.[32] The Kargil Review Committee absolved Singh by saying that under these conditions of uncertainty, his decision not to risk his troops was rational. The decision by unit commanders not to send ground patrols during winter months had been approved by higher authority.

In hindsight, the failure to mount ground patrols carried its own risks. Pakistani army planners apparently had identified patterns in the Indian army's operations, and sent troops into the very areas that were not kept under ground surveillance by the Indian army. Pakistan had begun to move units into the region in December 1998, and by March 1999 the Pakistani military had established 132 posts inside Indian territory covering an area of 60 miles in width and 4 to 9 miles in depth.[33] It is difficult to explain why even the limited ground and aerial reconnaissance carried out by India that winter failed to detect such large-scale intrusions. It is possible that Indian army personnel deployed on these reconnaissance missions did not venture out of their immediate winter locations and instead chose to send false reports indicating that "patrols" had detected no activity.

The Indian army's aviation corps carried out Winter Air Surveillance Operations (WASO) to supplement ground reconnaissance during the winter. Local commanders often fly in the aviation corps helicopter sorties under WASO to reconnoiter their areas of responsibility. The aviation corps' Leh squadron was charged with undertaking WASO operations in the Kargil and Mushkoh sectors. Records show that six WASO sorties flew between 10 November 1998 and 4 May 1999 over the area occupied by Pakistani units. Brigadier Surinder Singh was on board during four of the six sorties, and the remaining two sorties carried the Commander of the Leh Division Major General V. Budhwar. During the same period, five additional operational sorties were undertaken for ground observation missions and thirteen training sorties also flew over the same area. Of all the sorties flown, only the personnel of the WASO mission on 31 March 1999 observed some footprints in the snow within the Mushkoh sector.[34] Subsequent sorties flown over this area did not detect evidence of any activity.

---

[32] Brigadier Surinder Singh stated this to the Kargil Review Committee during his testimony. See Kargil Review Committee, *From Surprise to Reckoning*, 158. In hindsight some reports suggest that Singh's decision not to send winter patrols was influenced by negative response from the Leh (3 Infantry Division) HQ, to his earlier suggestions of enhancing ground and aerial surveillance in 121 Brigade. Journalist Praveen Swami has quoted official correspondence between the HQ 121, and HQ 3 Infantry Division, in which Singh's request for increased aerial surveillance of Kargil region had been rejected by his superior HQ. See Praveen Swami, "The Kargil Story," *Frontline*, 10 November 2000.

[33] Shaukat Qadir, "An Analysis of the Kargil Conflict," 26.

[34] Kargil Review Committee, *From Surprise to Reckoning*, 86.

The Kargil Review Committee report observed that WASO patrols suffered from several shortcomings. The sound of approaching helicopters warned of their movement and allowed ground forces to move into camouflaged positions before the helicopters arrived on the scene. In-flight vibrations made it difficult for crews to use binoculars for observation. Additionally, peacetime restrictions prevented low-altitude operations and overflight of the LoC.

The Kargil Review Committee's explanations, however, do not stand up to close scrutiny. Operational experience suggests that in the rugged, mountainous terrain found in Mushkoh and Kargil, individuals on the ground will be able to hear an approaching helicopter when it is about 7 miles away. A helicopter flying at 90–120 miles per hour covers that distance in less than five minutes, not enough time for personnel to hide extensive operations or large amounts of equipment and supplies. During winter, operations are even easier to detect because activity makes distinctive disturbances on the snow-covered terrain. Even though Pakistani personnel wore white clothes to camouflage themselves against the snow-covered background, they were supported by large columns of load-carrying mules, which could not have remained hidden from aerial observation.[35]

In contrast to the Review Committee's report, a more compelling reason can be suggested for the failure of WASO operations. Without contact reports forwarded by ground patrols, WASO observers lacked the data needed to direct them toward areas of interest. An analysis of WASO flight activity thus suggests that most sorties were being used to ferry commanders from one location to another, not to search for insurgent activity. Even if one of these transportation sorties flew close to the LoC, observers were probably scanning Pakistani territory, not looking for signs of activity on the Indian side of the LoC.

The Kargil Review Committee also placed blame on the intelligence community's collection capabilities. It noted that if India had a half-meter-resolution satellite imagery capability, unmanned aerial vehicles (UAVs), and better HUMINT, then the Kargil intrusion might have been detected earlier. The Kargil Review Committee reported that RAW had reduced the assets it targeted against Pakistan in the Kargil region due to the Indian government's general budgetary cut imposed in 1978, and those cutbacks continued to affect its surveillance capabilities in the region over twenty years later.[36] These deficiencies noted by the

---

[35] Major General Ashok K. Krishna, "The Method Followed at Siachen Is Irrelevant in Kargil," 18 August 1999, www.rediff.com.

[36] *Ibid.* 159

Review Committee, however, are rooted in something other than strategic culture, bureaucratic inertia, or the limitations of existing collection systems. These shortcomings could have been remedied quickly if only RAW or the Indian army identified the Kargil-Dras sector as a region of immediate strategic importance. But without the strategic and analytical decision to focus intelligence assets on Kargil, satellite imagery, HUMINT, or UAVs would not have detected activity in the region because they probably would have been focused on some other target. Indian intelligence and military organization had ruled out a Pakistani threat in the Kargil region, and once this was done, it was unlikely that significant collection assets would be targeted against this region.

Institutional failures and failures of analysis

The official and semi-official inquiries into the failure of the Indian intelligence community to foresee the *fait accompli* at Kargil often suggest that the intelligence failure could have been avoided. The Kargil Review Committee suggested that a series of war games conducted by officers, diplomats, and intelligence specialists who study Pakistan might have anticipated the Pakistan cross-LoC operation.[37] But this observation fails to reflect the realities of India's defense and foreign policy formulation process. War gaming is common in the Indian army, but national defense strategy and consideration of fundamental strategic issues lie within the exclusive domain of elected officials and civilian administrators. Rarely are outside academic experts asked to participate in policy deliberations.

Army intelligence analysts were attuned to the prospect of a large-scale conventional operation in the Kargil region of the LoC. To detect a conventional offensive, army intelligence would be on the alert for various indications and warning signs. These include: mobilization of infantry and artillery units; an increase in logistical activity (e.g., creation and replenishment of ammunition dumps); the construction of roads, bridges, helipads, or airstrips; or a sharp improvement in the quantity and quality of opposing combat and support units (e.g., medical infrastructure). Indian analysts were quick to detect indications of conventional operations. In March 1999, for instance, analysts had picked up some signals of Pakistani military activity in the town of Gilgit.[38] The intelligence inputs available to the Indian army during the first half of 1999 indicated that one additional unidentified infantry battalion was in Gultari (opposite the

---

[37] Kargil Review Committee, *From Surprise to Reckoning*, 152.   [38] *Ibid.*

Mushkoh sub-sector), that Pakistanis were dumping 100 tons of artillery ammunition in gun positions opposite Kargil, that 500 pairs of new snow boots had been provided to forward units, and that about 2,000 militants were present in the Gilgit region.[39] The Indian army did not respond to this information because it did not suggest that Pakistan was about to mount a major conventional operation. One additional infantry battalion did not pose a significant threat (besides, it also was impossible to confirm the presence of a new unit in the region using other sources). The presence of 100 tons of munitions constituted less than 2,000 rounds of field artillery ammunition, which Indian army sources correctly assessed as replenishment of winter stocks and ammunition expenditures in previous artillery exchanges. The three Pakistani army brigades stationed in the area also could have utilized 500 pairs of new snow boots.

RAW in its six-monthly reports submitted on 6 October 1998, had mentioned that in order to offset India's military advantage in the Lipa and Neelum valleys, Pakistan appeared "hell bent" on interdicting the Dras-Kargil Highway (NH-1A), and targeting the local population for vengeance.[40] The report said that the Pakistan army was inducting more troops and guns from Mangla, Lahore, Gujranwala, and Okara to reinforce its units located on the Pakistani side of Kashmir.[41] The report further added that during the period March–September 1998, the Pakistan army had launched massive preparations to improve field defenses and stock ammunition. The report had concluded that a "limited swift offensive threat" with possible support of alliance partners (an apparent reference to militants) could not be ruled out. RAW had shared this report with the IB, DGMI, and the JIC. However, when the HQ DGMI raised queries about the basis of RAW's inference of a "limited swift offensive threat," according to the HQ DGMI, the RAW officials failed to give a satisfactory reply. Also, RAW had omitted a similar assessment from their next six-monthly report sent in April 1999.[42]

In hindsight, this evidence might be seen as a clear indicator that something was brewing in Kargil, but the interpretation of this information at the time by India's intelligence analysts was reasonable. Nothing about these reports suggested that a major initiative was about to unfold. In fact, these reports generally reinforced prevailing Indian images of

---

[39] *Ibid.* 153.

[40] A majority population of the Dras-Kargil region is Shia. They had been noncooperative in Pakistan's efforts of spreading militancy in the region, which has, since 1997, made them targets of the Pakistan army's punitive artillery bombardment. M. K. Akbar, *Kargil: Cross-Border Terrorism* (New Delhi: Mittal Publications, 1999), 63–64.

[41] Mangla, Lahore, Gujranwala, and Okara are major army cantonments in Pakistan.

[42] Kargil Review Committee, *From Surprise to Reckoning*, 128–129.

conflict in the region. Among Indian army officers and intelligence analysts, Kargil was seen as a quiet military front. The fact that the infiltrators
wore civilian clothes and that their radio transmissions were in Pashtu and
Balti languages, which are often spoken by militants, apparently helped to
reduce concern when a few stray communications were detected. The
Kashmir Valley generally was viewed as the center of low-intensity conflict
along the LoC, and the Siachen Glacier generally was believed to be the
most likely location for high-intensity conventional combat. The difficulty
of the terrain and the predominance of the Shia population in the area
suggested to Indian analysts that there were better places for Pakistan to
launch an attack. Army officers and analysts responsible for the defense of
the Kargil-Dras sector of the LoC planned to plug possible militant
infiltration routes; however, they did not anticipate that Pakistan army
units actually would use these routes to occupy the region.

Some Indian defense analysts, such as Jasjit Singh, believe that an
objective analysis of the geopolitical situation and developments in the
months leading up to the Pakistani effort to present India with a *fait
accompli* should have alerted the Indian government and military to
impending action in Jammu and Kashmir. They point to General
Musharraf's emergence as the Chief of the Pakistan army. According to
these analysts, General Musharraf's ethnic origin as a Muhajir, his strong
anti-India bias, his known, strong linkages with the militant organizations
in the past, and his antipathy toward the Shia population, should have
raised concerns about new military developments in the region.[43]
Immediately after becoming the Pakistan army's COAS, Musharraf had
visited Gilgit in November 1998 and March 1999.[44] Although
Musharraf's background and preferences do not provide a clear signal of
what was about to happen in Kargil, they should have alerted Indian
officers and analysts to the possibility that a significant departure in
Pakistani policy was possible.

In the months before Kargil, the Lahore process also raised high expectations that peace between India and Pakistan might be at hand. Yet, in the
aftermath of the Lahore peace process, there was no cessation of
Pakistan's artillery attacks across the LoC and Islamabad continued to
offer military support to Islamic militants operating in Jammu and
Kashmir.[45] Not much was made of the fact, however, that Pakistani

---

[43] Singh, ed., *Kargil 1999*, 137.   [44] Nawaz Sharif also visited Gilgit in January 1999.
[45] Kargil Review Committee, *From Surprise to Reckoning*, 157. General V. P. Malik has also
mentioned that when the Indian prime minister asked him about the pattern of cross-LoC
infiltration in the aftermath of his Lahore visit, his reply was that there was no let up in the
pattern of this infiltration. See Malik, *Kargil: From Surprise to Victory*, 98.

military operations along the LoC failed to match the spirit of the Lahore process. If an alarm had been raised, Indian officers and analysts might have realized that the supply route to the Ladakh region along the Srinagar–Leh road was the most vulnerable sector along the LoC. Nowhere else in Jammu or Kashmir had the Indian army left such wide gaps in its defenses.

Conclusion

Once Indian officers and officials overcame the shock produced by the realization that they had been presented with a *fait accompli* by Pakistan, they slowly brought their superior military capability to bear against their opponents, and drove them out of their mountaintop positions. As the theory of surprise would predict, Pakistani forces achieved great success when they did not face an active opponent, but the dialectic of war returned to the Kargil heights before the overextended Pakistani units could cut the Srinagar–Leh road. The much hoped-for help from the international community also failed to materialize for Pakistan, leaving their units in Kargil isolated and dependent on inadequate lines of supply.

In spite of inherent weaknesses in the Indian intelligence system on the eve of the Kargil operation, the basis of the Pakistani surprise can be found in a pervasive idea generated by India's position as the stronger party in the enduring conflict with Pakistan. Indian officials and officers believed that it made little military sense for Pakistan to launch an operation in the dead of winter in the mountains along the LoC. After all, if Indian units were withdrawn from their mountain outposts in winter due to the incredibly harsh conditions, it would make little sense for Pakistani units to attempt to occupy the vacated positions. Instead of many misinterpreted signals or faulty analyses, the story of Indian intelligence during the winter of 1998–1999 is really a story of an absence of signals. Indian intelligence only had a few extremely faint hints of what was transpiring on the Pakistani side of the LoC. Indeed, most of the information it had about Pakistani activity supported preexisting beliefs that Kargil would remain a quiet sector of the LoC. Needless to say, because they did not suspect Pakistani activity, Indian officers and analysts did not concentrate collection efforts to discover Pakistani infiltration into Kargil. When activity was detected, India's military commanders at first were unsure about the identity and intentions of the intruders or the seriousness of the threat.[46]

---

[46] During a meeting of the Cabinet Committee on Security (India's highest decision-making body) on 21 May 1999, the NSCS said that 70 percent of intruders were militants and 30 percent were Pakistani regular soldiers. See Malik, *Kargil: From Surprise to Victory*, 111.

The first confirmation of the Pakistani army's complicity in the operation apparently occurred on 26 May 1999 when Indian intelligence intercepted a telephone conversation between General Musharraf and his deputy Lieutenant General Muhammad Aziz Khan.[47] In the annals of intelligence failure, Kargil is thus a rare instance of surprise in two respects: an action taken by the victim (i.e., withdrawal from the mountain outposts) suspended war's dialectic; and an absolute minimum number of signals (i.e., accurate indications of what was about to transpire) were within the Indian intelligence pipeline at the moment when the Pakistani *fait accompli* was discovered.[48] Kargil is probably best considered a failure of intelligence collection, not a failure of intelligence analysis. Indian complacency was so pervasive that it effected the entire intelligence cycle, beginning with the identification of intelligence collection requirements.

When fully alerted, Indian intelligence analysts and officers responded quickly and effectively to indications that Pakistani units were on the move on their side of the LoC. This would suggest that Indian intelligence and command and control were capable of responding relatively quickly to indications of Pakistani operations once the possibility of movement across the LoC became salient. As John Gill notes in chapter 4 on military operations during the crisis, reports of unusual Pakistani helicopter activity along the LoC in the Turtok area were received in late April and between 6 and 19 May, and Indian patrols identified small intrusions at five locations near the LoC. Two battalions from 102 Brigade were dispatched to the area and quickly captured these positions, and arrested a score of local inhabitants who were suspected of plotting to attack Indian troops and assist the intruders.[49] Psychology (i.e., the fundamental assumption used in the planning of the defense of Kargil in the winter of 1998–1999), not bureaucratic or technical weaknesses, is the primary cause of the Indian failure to detect the movement of Pakistani forces across the LoC.

Those who planned the Kargil operation also displayed much evidence of the cognitive bias that affects the weaker party in a conflict, the bias that makes the idea of using surprise to present their stronger rival with a

---

[47] According to General V. P. Malik, when this conversation was intercepted, the Indian army was fairly certain about the collusion of the Pakistani military. Until this intercept, however, most intelligence reports had continued to point to the *Jehadi* militants. See *ibid.* 99.

[48] For an effort to explain Pearl Harbor as an instance of surprise caused by a lack of signals see Ariel Levite, *Intelligence and Strategic Surprise* (New York: Columbia University Press, 1987).

[49] Y. M. Bammi, *Kargil: The Impregnable Conquered* (Noida: Gorkha Publishers, 2002), 361–370.

fait accompli seem like an attractive option. Pakistanis became mesmerized by the possibility of generating a significant setback to India, so much so that they apparently failed to turn initial success into a local battlefield advantage by failing to hold the infiltrated heights, and using their positions to cut the Srinagar–Leh road. Pakistani ideas about how success in a region would translate into overall strategic and political gains were particularly vague and apparently based on wishful thinking.

The theory of surprise applied to the *fait accompli* at Kargil also offers a rather unsettling observation about Pakistani officials' behavior during the conflict. Instead of being deterred or reassured by the defensive dominance implied by a mutual nuclear-deterrence relationship, they instead looked for ways to inflict a setback on a much stronger opponent. They saw surprise and the ability to suspend war's dialectic as a way to obtain meaningful gains. As the theory of surprise would suggest, Kargil confirms the prediction that the weaker party is attracted to surprise, and this attraction does not seem to have reduced the specter of nuclear war.

9   Militants in the Kargil conflict: myths, realities, and impacts

C. Christine Fair

Background: origins of the myth

In the spring of 1999, Pakistan executed a broad incursion across the Line of Control (LoC) in Kashmir using 3–4,000 men equipped primarily with small arms from the then-paramilitary organization the Northern Light Infantry (NLI).[1] Ostensibly, the Pakistani forces sought to make small territorial gains at tactically significant locations near the Indian town of Kargil. Initially, Indian reports characterized these intruders as *mujahideen*, or *ghusbhaitiyan*.[2] Indian authorities later believed that a composite force of militants and Pakistani regulars executed the incursion. After the fighting intensified, however, Indian officials learned that this infiltrating force was comprised not of civilian militants, but rather nearly entirely of NLI troops supported by civilian porters, or *razakars*.[3]

---

[1] The research for this chapter draws from several research trips to Pakistan and India between 2000 and 2006, some of which were conducted explicitly for this research. Initial fieldwork in Pakistan was undertaken during the winter of 2000, during which the author interviewed serving and retired army officers, academic and think-tank analysts, journalists, political leaders, and non-state actors. See Ashley J. Tellis, C. Christine Fair, and Jamison Jo Medby, *Limited Conflicts under the Nuclear Umbrella: Indian and Pakistani Lessons from the Kargil Crisis* (Santa Monica, Calif.: RAND, 2001). During a second CCC research trip to Pakistan in January of 2003, the CCC team, including this author, met with a number of retired and serving army officers, intelligence officials, civil servants, journalists, and analysts. I also conducted extensive interviews with serving and retired army officers, intelligence officials, journalists, and analysts in India and Pakistan in the winter of 2000, the fall of 2002, the summers of 2003 and 2004, and the falls of 2005 and 2006. This chapter was written in 2003 and updated in 2007 to reflect changed events and the feedback from external reviews. The opinions expressed here are solely attributable to the author.

[2] This is the plural of *ghusbhaitiya*, which is the Hindi neologism for "intruder."

[3] Civilian *razakars* (volunteers) were used mainly as porters. They may have carried light arms. See Shaukat Qadir, "An Analysis of Kargil," *RUSI Journal* 147, no. 2 (April 2002), 26. See also Ashok Krishna, "The Kargil War," in *Kargil: The Tables Turned*, ed. Ashok Krishna and P. R. Chari (New Delhi: Manohar, 2001), 102; V. P. Malik, *Kargil: From Surprise to Victory* (New Delhi: HarperCollins, 2006), 42–46, 82–83, 92–97, 110, 116, 344; Y. M. Bammi, *Kargil 1999: The Impregnable Conquered* (Noida, India: Gorkha Publishers, 2002), 180–183; Tellis, Fair, and Medby, *Limited Conflicts under the Nuclear Umbrella*, 20.

Curiously, many popular accounts of Kargil still sustain the myth that the operation was executed by *mujahideen* either operating alone or in tandem with Pakistani troops.[4] This misperception about the intruding force has persisted for a number of reasons. First, the initial reporting of the incursion characterized these forces as *mujahideen* or *jehadi* militants and those accounts formed the basis of most subsequent analyses of the conflict. Second, and related to the first, Pakistan did not deny for many years after the crisis the Indian reports that these intruders were irregular fighters. Third, the international community did not publicly discount these claims even when the NLI's involvement was discerned. Finally, prior to January 2003, Pakistan did not issue a publicly available, authoritative, and credible account of the operation, its planning and objectives, as well as a thorough and detailed account of the force employed.[5]

There is some dispute over whether Pakistan intended to use the *mujahideen* cover story from the conception of the operation or whether the Pakistan army simply found it expedient to permit the Indian mischaracterization to persist. Major General Nadeem Ahmed, Commander, Force Command Northern Areas (FCNA), during a January 2003 briefing to the Center for Contemporary Conflict (CCC) Kargil team, indicated that the Indians made this claim and that Pakistan found it beneficial to continue letting the Indians believe this was the case rather than disclosing that the land grab was executed by the NLI.[6] CCC research shows this to be a correct statement. After the initial Indian contacts with the intruding forces occurred in early May, Indian authorities assessed that the intruders were *mujahideen*. The Pakistan army had anticipated that the true identity of the intruders would be discovered sometime during the spring, but because the Indians believed the deception, the Pakistani military leadership decided to continue with it as long as possible. Lt. Gen. (retd.) Chaudhry Iftikhar Ali Khan, the former Chief of General Staff of the army and Defence Secretary to Nawaz Sharif, related

---

[4] P. R. Chari, "Some Preliminary Observations," in Krishna and Chari, eds., *Kargil: The Tables Turned*, 13; and Shireen M. Mazari, *The Kargil Conflict 1999: Separating Fact from Fiction* (Islamabad: Ferozsons, 2003), 33–34.

[5] The use of NLI rather than civilian militants was conceded during a briefing by Maj. Gen. Nadeem Ahmed, Commander, FCNA, on 12 January 2003. Also see Mazari, *The Kargil Conflict 1999*, 46. The Indian government previously released evidence of the involvement of the NLI in Kargil: identity cards and paybooks of captured NLI sepoys. See V. P. Malik, "Terrorism and Limited War with Kargil Backdrop" (presentation to the Near East South Asia Center, National Defense University), personal communication. In addition, there is substantial inferential evidence attesting to the direct involvement of the Pakistani regular army in the planning, execution, logistical support, and artillery coverage for the operation, as these functions could not be adequately supplied by the NLI.

[6] This point is reiterated in Mazari, *The Kargil Conflict 1999*, 46.

to a CCC team member that during a 17 May 1999 briefing, Pakistan army officials explained: "To the outside world, the information given will be that *mujahideen* are operating, not the Pakistan army."[7]

CCC interviews with another senior retired army officer offer the most lucid account of how the *jehadi* story enjoyed such staying power within and outside of Pakistan. He explained that the Pakistan army planned to use the locally based NLI as a fundamental element of its initial denial and deception strategy. He, and others interviewed over the course of this research, averred that these troops were sent across the LoC without their uniforms with the explicit intention of concealing their NLI affiliation. This contributed to the perception that the intruders were Kashmiri militants, or *mujahideen*.

The NLI troops transmitted military communications in Pashtu, Balti, Shina, and other local dialects. Some of these transmissions were "intercepted" by Indian intelligence networks, giving further credence to the Indian hypothesis that the intruders were civilian militants, not Pakistani soldiers. This aspect of the Pakistani deception plan probably was fortuitous, because even though Pakistani military officers generally use Punjabi or Urdu for communications, the enlisted NLI soldiers under them speak to one another in their native dialects, including Pashtu, Balti, and Shina, and generally have poor command of Urdu or Punjabi. It is possible that Pakistan's deception plan included the element of local-dialect communications, but it is more likely that the planners of the Kargil operation assumed that if Indian intelligence picked up any military communications, all that they would hear would be the local dialects, which are routinely used by both the NLI troops and the civilian militants that operate along the LoC.

The Pakistan army hoped that the *mujahideen* façade would last long enough to obtain some territorial gains even if eventually the truth would be discerned. However, the Pakistan army was surprised by the subterfuge's success, due in good measure to India's inability to properly identify the intruders.[8] Once Indian sources reported that there were *mujahideen* ensconced in the Kargil-Dras sector, according to one officer interviewed by the CCC team, the Pakistan army developed the *mujahideen* story more thoroughly. By the time that the international community ascertained that the intruders were NLI soldiers, the Foreign Office, specifically the Foreign Secretary, argued against conceding the involvement of the NLI and the Pakistan army in the operation. He insisted, "We must stick to this story." In his view, admission would have been

---

[7] Lt. Gen. (retd.) Chaudhry Iftikhar Ali Khan interview, 19 January 2003.
[8] See discussion in Malik, *Kargil: From Surprise to Victory*, 42–46, 82–83, 92–97, 110.

tantamount to confessing that Pakistan deliberately committed an act of war. Prime Minister Nawaz Sharif agreed with the Foreign Office's advice and persisted with the *mujahideen* fabrication. The Pakistan army, for the first time, admitted the exclusive use of NLI soldiers (perhaps with logistical support from *razakars*) during the January 2003 CCC meeting, convened at the FCNA Headquarters. Former President Pervez Musharraf later admitted use of the NLI in his autobiography in 2006.[9]

India too faced several incentives to sustain the *mujahideen* story, despite its embarrassment at the lack of veracity of initial reports. First, political strategists in New Delhi found it expedient to allow the myth to persist as it provided the Indian prime minister Atal Behari Vajpayee and his Bharatiya Janata Party (BJP) some degree of political cover for engaging Prime Minister Nawaz Sharif in the Lahore process of late 1998 and early 1999. If *mujahideen* were responsible, Nawaz Sharif arguably could have engaged Vajpayee in good faith, potentially mitigating Vajpayee's personal loss of political capital. The *mujahideen* infiltration likely generated a more tempered public outcry in India. Had the public become immediately aware of the Pakistan army's deliberate seizure of Indian-administered territory, popular demands to punish Pakistan might have been even more forceful than it was. Given the Government of India's need to temper escalation, this could have been politically destabilizing for the weakened BJP-led government. Indian intelligence officials also had a bureaucratic incentive to cling to their initial assessments that the entirety, or at least the majority, of the intruders were civilian militants, not Pakistani army soldiers.

When the international community finally intervened to restore the status quo and to compel Pakistan to restore the sanctity of the LoC, the United States and others also were content to permit Nawaz Sharif to sustain the fiction of a *mujahideen*-led initiative. This provided Pakistan with an honorable exit if Nawaz Sharif compelled the intruders to return to Pakistan's side of the LoC. In short, none of the key actors – India, Pakistan, or the United States – had much incentive to decisively put to rest the farcical claim that civilian militants executed the Kargil intrusion.

Pakistan's ploy to make India and the rest of the world believe that the intruders were *mujahideen* struggling to liberate Kashmir from Indian control worked brilliantly at the outset of the crisis. However, Pakistan clung to this canard well after the direct involvement of Pakistani troops

---

[9] Pervez Musharraf, *In the Line of Fire: A Memoir* (New York: Free Press, 2006), 87–98. Musharraf denies that the Pakistan army engaged in an offensive seizure of ground, contending Pakistan's actions were defensive in nature in anticipation of Indian offense. See the Introduction to this volume for more on this Pakistani allegation.

residents took on a very different color when the Pakistan government began asserting that the conflict was a militant operation. One resident told Khan, "When I first heard in the Pakistani media that the Kargil was being fought by the *mujahideen*, I was shocked ... My children were being killed, but the laurels went to Qazi Hussain Ahmed [The Amir of Jamaat-e-Islami]."[19]

Most of the residents of the Northern Areas are not Sunni Muslims, the sect represented by most of the militant organizations taking credit for the incursion. This caused considerable outrage because the loss of life was born disproportionately by Shia and Ismaili fighters while the Sunni groups took credit for the territorial gains.[20] Social unrest was further exacerbated because many of the Sunni militant groups support a militantly anti-Shia ideology and advocate violence against them.

The sectarian concern in the Northern Areas is important because the Shia there and elsewhere have been the victims of sanguinary communal violence for decades. Zia ul-Haq's government was accused of complicity in a three-day rampage against Shia in Gilgit (a town in the Northern Areas), perpetrated by Sunni militants in May 1988. In that anti-Shia violent episode, official estimates claim that 150 Shia were killed although unofficial estimates put the figure much higher. In addition, numerous villages were razed, herds slaughtered, and millions of rupees of property damaged.[21] The military also relies upon anti-Shia militias such as Sipah-e-Sahaba-e-Pakistan in areas like Kurram Agency, where Shia are concentrated. Presumably, this is done to thwart or offset Iranian influence in those areas.[22] Thus it is important to understand that while Shia, Ismaili, and Sunni fighters wage Pakistan's external war with India in unison within Pakistan's armed forces, domestically the Shia and other minorities have been and continue to be victimized and targeted by Sunni militant groups. In some cases, this anti-Shia violence has taken place with significant degrees of state complicity. While Zia's patronage of these groups is most notorious, other Pakistani military and civilian governments have courted and even formed alliances with these Sunni sectarian organizations.[23]

---

[19] *Ibid.* 28.

[20] The Ismailis are the second largest Shia community. Ismailis dispute the proper succession from the sixth to seventh Imam, and supported the eldest son of the sixth Imam, Ismail. A majority of Shia accepted the younger son, Musa al-Kasim. That line of succession would be broken with the disappearance of the Twelfth Imam.

[21] International Crisis Group, *The State of Sectarianism in Pakistan*: Crisis Group Asia Report no. 95 (Brussels and Islamabad: International Crisis Group, 2005), 12, 19–20. Also see A. H. Sorbo, "Paradise Lost," *The Herald*, June 1988, 31.

[22] Personal communication with Husain Haqqani, March 2007.

[23] Vali R. Nasr, "International Politics, Domestic Imperatives, and Identity Mobilization: Sectarianism in Pakistan, 1979–1998," *Comparative Politics* 32, no. 2 (January 2000), 175–179, 183–187.

Residents of Skardu also told Khan that militants associated with violence in India's Kashmir Valley began establishing a presence in Skardu by late May to give credence to Pakistan's assertion that Kargil was a militant operation. Citing the account of a senior police official in Gilgit, Khan reports that these militants forcefully took over a house for use as their office. An exchange of fire ensued between local residents and the militants. In a further bizarre twist of events, a captain of ISID threatened the Superintendent of Police for favoring the Skardu residents.[24] To quell the groundswell of unrest, top state officials began touring the Northern Areas and provided the families of martyrs with "extravagant awards" in an effort to buy out their discontent.[25]

Impact on domestic militant and Islamist groups

The Pakistani press and the Pakistani populace remained unaware of the nature of the infiltration, the use of the NLI, and the orchestration of the operation by army leaders. As discussed in detail by Saeed Shafqat in chapter 11 of this book, the domestic press coverage of Kargil persisted in its depiction of the invading forces as the work of a few hundred *mujahideen*. Several militant groups were – and are at present – based in and around Muzaffarabad, capital of Pakistan-held Kashmir. One June 1999 report in *The Herald* writes with some suspicion that "if the statements from the political camps of the various militant groups in Muzaffarabad are to be believed, members of at least four such organizations are involved in Kargil. Initially, it was Tehrik-e-Jihad which openly claimed that their men had taken control of large parts of Kargil. Later, three more groups, Al-Badr, Harkatul Mujahideen, and Lashkar-e-Taiba came out with similar statements."[26] The militant organizational leadership claimed to be operating collectively in the Kargil effort.[27]

Such pronouncements and public posturing by militant groups are consistent with interview data obtained from Lt. Gen. (retd.) Chaudhry Iftikhar Ali Khan, who suggested that at a later stage limited *mujahideen* were incorporated. (Iftikhar was the Defence Secretary to Prime Minister Sharif during the Kargil crisis.) Likely, these *mujahideen* statements were encouraged to lend credibility to Pakistan's assertion that this was a

---

[24] Ilyas Khan, "Life After Kargil," 27–28.
[25] For more information about these visits, see *ibid*. 29.
[26] Zaffar Abbas, "Back from the Brink," *The Herald* (Karachi), June 1999, 46–48.
[27] *Ibid*. 48.

completely militant-orchestrated and executed operation. However, because ISID was excluded from the initial planning of the operation, coordination with militant elements either within Pakistan or within Indian-held Kashmir was limited initially. It is not clear when ISID director Ziauddin became aware of the Kargil operation, but based on interview material, it appears that while he did not oppose the operation, he did not go out of his way to support it either.[28]

Pakistani press coverage from May to October 1999 reflected a consistent sense of outrage over the way in which the Indians responded. Why would the Indians *need* to introduce air power to confront some bedraggled *mujahideen*?[29] But simultaneously, a sense of pride was evinced because a few *mujahideen* posed such a threat to India that it required such a large mobilization of forces. During the entire time that the Pakistani populace remained in the dark and under the mistaken belief that the *tanzeems* executed the operation, Islamists and militant groups generally were held in high esteem. For example, according to US Department of State data, confidence in religious leaders spiked in July 1999, relative to January and November 1999.[30]

Throughout most of the conflict, the Pakistani press was fairly consistent in its depiction of the Kargil intrusion as the effort of freedom fighters. The lag-time required to produce critical accounts of the government's version of events is odd given that presumably some of the well-connected intelligentsia were aware that the *mujahideen* story was false. Nonetheless, it was not until the end of July and the beginning of August that the domestic audience began to question Islamabad's version of events. For example, in late July, M. P. Bhandara wrote, "We are told incessantly that the Kargil freedom fighters are genuine Kashmiri freedom fighters. However, is it reasonable to believe that freedom fighters can fight at 15,000 feet above sea level without Pakistani rations, clothing, logistics, ammunition and intelligence support? Again, who are we fooling? It is

---

[28] Another complicating factor was the tense relationship between CoAS Musharraf and Director General of ISID Ziauddin, both of whom were appointed on the same day. For more information about this relationship and its significance, see chapter 3 by Feroz Hassan Kahn, Peter R. Lavoy, and Christopher Clary, and chapter 11 by Saeed Shafqat in this volume.

[29] Between 1 June and 1 August 1999, there were twenty-three articles in *Dawn* that held the Indians responsible for escalation. Tellis, Fair, and Medby, *Limited Conflicts under the Nuclear Umbrella*, 14, fn. 19.

[30] The percentage of individuals replying that they had a great deal or "a fair amount" of confidence in Pakistan's religious leaders went from 40% in a survey taken in January and February 1999, to 48% in July, down to 36% in November. Department of State, "In Pakistan, Musharraf Has Broad Public Support; Most Back His Anti-Extremist Reforms" (17 May 2002). Provided by personal communication.

possible for PTV to beguile its captive audience at home but the world does not consists [sic] of retards."[31]

Moreover, as the United States, the G-8, the United Nations, Russia, and even China joined India's call for Pakistan's withdrawal, Nawaz Sharif claimed that he had no control over these independent forces.[32] Such news coverage also attributed to the operations of Pakistan's *tanzeems* a degree of independence that they did not deserve. The truth is quite different: the *tanzeems* have been, currently are, and are likely to remain under the influence and direction of ISID.[33] Despite Musharraf's rhetoric, analysts widely believe that Musharraf had little or no intention to eliminate these *tanzeems* altogether. Rather, he sought to restrain their violence as India and Pakistan engaged diplomatically, while maintaining a core capability that could be ramped up as needed. From 2003, Musharraf, as the anti-status quo actor, was more creative in proposing innovative options to resolve the Kashmir dispute. However, India did not reciprocate and, as the status quo power, had little incentive to move substantially from its current position. (Musharraf gave up Pakistan's long-held demand for a plebiscite and stated that Pakistan would accept any solution acceptable to Kashmiris.) Given presumed – and demonstrated – Indian recalcitrance on the disposition of Kashmir, Musharraf had few options but to retain the *tanzeems* as one of his few coercive options.[34] That said, Pakistani authorities contend that a resolution of the Kashmir dispute will make the *jehadi tanzeems* irrelevant, thus enabling the Pakistan government to marginalize them once and for all. Alternatively, the use of state force against them could produce a domestic backlash that could produce uncontrolled internal violence.

On 4 July 1999 Nawaz Sharif went to the United States seeking a dignified exit strategy from then-President Bill Clinton. While Clinton had no delusions that Kargil was planned and executed by entrepreneurial *mujahideen*, the agreement penned with Nawaz Sharif did not require any

---

[31] M. P. Bhandara, "On the Edge of the Precipice," *Dawn*, 21 July 1999 cited in Tellis, Fair, and Medby, *Limited Conflicts under the Nuclear Umbrella*, 44–45.

[32] See Tellis, Fair, and Medby, *Limited Conflicts under the Nuclear Umbrella*, 22–23; "Pakistan's Sharif Meets with Military over Kashmir," 9 July 1999, www.cnn.com/WORLD/asiapcf/9907/09/india.pakistan.01/; and Sridhar Krishnaswami, "Firm American Demand," *Frontline*, 17 July 1999, www.frontlineonnet.com/fl1615/16150160.htm.

[33] This assessment is based on the author's fieldwork in July and August of 2003, focusing on militant recruitment techniques in Pakistan and the connections between militant groups, the army, and ISID.

[34] See "The Year of Kashmir," *HIMAL South Asian*, February 2007, www.himalmag.com/2007/february/commentary2.htm.

admission of Pakistan army complicity. Rather, the prime minister only pledged to bring the intruders back to Pakistan's side of the LoC. As this withdrawal was executed in July, public sentiment turned against the government for selling out the brave *mujahideen*. The pusillanimity of the Sharif government imposed a defeat on the *mujahideen* that they did not deserve and gave India a victory that it did not earn. Public anger was even more apparent as the so-called *mujahideen* casualties mounted after the withdrawal agreement.

So in many ways, Kargil was a major boon for the reputation of the various Islamist and militant groups. In truth, Pakistan's deception strategy gave the militants a tactical victory they did not earn. During the so-called withdrawal phase, when the *jehadi tanzeems* were at the height of their popularity and the government at the receiving end of the criticism, not a single militant group revealed the mendacity that Kargil was a *mujahideen* affair.

Impact on the militants

Determining the extent to which the Pakistan government's handling of Kargil affected the militant groups is difficult because there is generally considerable opacity surrounding the relationships among the militants and their handlers in the Pakistan army and ISID. Data gathered through field interviews by this author suggest that such impacts were rather indirect.[35] Despite the positive press and numerous accolades for the *jehadi tanzeems*, is it reasonable to suggest that the execution of Kargil without the actual use of militants had an untoward impact on relations between these groups and their handlers in the army and ISID? Presumably, these militants could have reasoned that had Pakistan been serious about affecting the balance of power in the valley, ISID would have coordinated militant activities there as a force multiplier. However, as noted above, Lt. Gen. (retd.) Iftikhar provides the most credible information on this issue: He claimed that there was no formal coordination of, or plan to include, civilian militants initially because ISID was

[35] Another interesting element of the army's motive in pursuing Kargil is the personality and vested interested of Lt. Gen. Muhammad Aziz Khan. Prior to assuming his position as Chairman of the Joint Chiefs of Staff, Aziz was responsible for handling the Kashmir policy within ISID. Aziz is himself a Kashmiri and is passionately devoted to the case, based on the author's interaction with Aziz and based on the views espoused by retired senior Pakistani army officers of his acquaintance. One informant (a retired Lt. Gen. from the Pakistan army) suggested that Aziz may have argued the case that the Kargil operation could provide a fillip to the enervated insurgent movement in Kashmir. Militants could be motivated to resume the fight with renewed vigor if they observed Pakistani troops forfeiting their own lives to make inroads into Indian-held Jammu and Kashmir.

completely excluded from the planning and execution of the Kargil intrusion.[36]

The policy decisions made by President Musharraf subsequent to 11 September 2001 further strained the army's relations with militants and their allied political parties. After Pakistan's decision to participate in the global war on terrorism and the militant attack on the Indian parliament on 13 December 2001, Musharraf was under intense – if episodic – pressure to rein in Pakistan-based militants operating in Indian-held Kashmir and within India. To the extent that Pakistan has been consistent in its application of restrictions upon *jehadi tanzeems*, these policies were effective. For example, it has been more difficult for groups to openly raise funds and recruit and train new cadres. However, this appears to be at best a tactical decision on Islamabad's part. Pakistan likely has made no strategic decision to move away from the reliance upon militants in the pursuit of its policy of proxy war in Indian-held Kashmir. Militants and the regime appear to have struck a sort of bargain whereby they agree to keep operations at a minimum and maintain a low profile in exchange for which they will be allowed to continue to recruit and train new cadres and raise funds.

There is little doubt that the relationship has suffered since 11 September 2001 when Pakistan withdrew its support for the Taliban and al Qaeda. Moreover, the militants were dealt a significant setback when they lost vast training infrastructure in Afghanistan, and a number of large camps were closed in Pakistan.[37] Initially, some groups may have speculated that Pakistan's overnight willingness to abandon its decades-old policy in Afghanistan may have implied a willingness to abandon its Kashmir policy – with the right combination of sticks and carrots from the international community. However, the *jehadi tanzeems* remain operational despite various bans and limitations placed on them.[38]

Impact in the Valley of Kashmir

Because ISID has responsibility for coordinating militant operations in Indian-held Kashmir and because ISID was left out of the planning and

---

[36] Peter Lavoy's interview in January 2003 with Lt. Gen. Chaudhry Iftikhar Ali Khan.

[37] See C. Christine Fair, "Islam and Politics in Pakistan," in *The Muslim World After 9/11*, Angel Rabasa, Cheryl Benard, Peter Chalk *et al.* (Santa Monica Calif.: RAND, 2004), 247–295; Amir Mohammad Rana, "Jehad Inc – Back In Business," *Friday Times* (Pakistan), 16 January 2003; Amir Mohammad Rana, *Jihad-e-Kashmir Aur Afghanistan* [The Jihad in Kashmir and Afghanistan] (Lahore: Mashaal Books, 2002).

[38] Ilyas Khan, "The Waiting Game," *The Herald* (Karachi), July 2003, 36–41; and Ilyas Khan, "Business as Usual," *The Herald* (Karachi), July 2003, 38–39.

execution of the Kargil intrusion, there was no coordinated effort to mobilize militants on either side of the LoC before or during the Kargil operation. Senior Pakistani military officers indicated in interviews that there likely were civilian militants operating on the Indian side of the LoC, but without any formal coordination with the Pakistan army or the FCNA. This assertion is confirmed by data obtained from the Indian army's 15 Corps Headquarters based in Srinagar, which indicates that the Jammu and Kashmir Valley did not experience any significant increase in militant activities at the time of the Kargil conflict.[39] This is one of the stranger elements of the execution of the operation since one of the often-posited purposes for the operation was to give a fillip to the lagging insurgency within the valley. It is not obvious how this operation would energize the insurgency if they were abandoned in the planning and execution phases. Presumably, Pakistani planners reasoned that if soldiers were willing to die for the Kashmiri cause, militant morale might be boosted. However, given that Pakistan did not concede NLI presence in Kargil, the efficacy of this tactic may have been limited.

Prima facie, it would not be unreasonable for militant groups operating in the valley to be surprised that they were excluded from such a significant operation. They may have even drawn their own conspiratorial conclusions as to why Pakistan launched the operation without the use of these civilian combatants at least as a force multiplier. Indeed, had these militants been used in a concerted fashion with the NLI, Pakistan's cover story might have been more credible and durable, and this might have put much more pressure on the Indian counterinsurgency grid in the valley and elsewhere.

During interviews with Kashmiri groups (in Pakistan-administered Kashmir and in Islamabad) in December 2000, individuals communicated with this author a sense that Pakistan repeatedly had demonstrated that it was not a reliable partner. For example, during a meeting with several constituents of the Kashmir Action Committee, one interlocutor expressed concern that Pakistanis and other non-Kashmiris should be fighting in Kashmir.[40] It was this person's view that these guest militants would de-legitimize the Kashmir struggle. The Kargil operation certainly denuded the conflict of any patina of legitimate freedom struggle. This

[39] The author met extensively with 15 Corps Headquarters in September 2002. Additional data were also supplied in interviews with other Indian military officers.
[40] Kashmir Action Committee Pakistan "is a voluntary non-governmental organization of Kashmiris living in Pakistan and their supporters and sympathizers whose objective is to help Kashmiris get their right of self-determination." See http://kacp-pk.com/home.htm.

also was the view espoused by a representative of the All Parties Hurriyat Committee in Pakistan interviewed about Kargil during December 2000.

Interviews conducted in Srinagar in September 2002 and in August 2006 found considerable antipathy with both the Government of Pakistan and the militant groups supported by Pakistan operating in the valley. How much of this is attributable to Kargil *per se* is unclear. Much of this vexation stems from the ongoing violence imposed upon Kashmiris from the militants and Indian security forces as well from the kind of Islam generally pursued by the militants (such as Jaish-e-Mohammed), which is rooted to the Deobandi and Wahhabi strands of thought. Lashkar-e-Taiba, unlike most of the militant groups, espouses the more stringent Ahl-e-Hadith interpretative tradition.[41] On the main, these militant groups embrace forms of Islam that are hostile to the traditional Sufi practices of the residents of the Kashmir Valley. Incidents such as electoral violence (for example, killing poll workers, candidates, and voters) as well as attacks on women who do not observe *purdah* have generated anger and resentment toward these groups in the valley.[42]

The antipathy that has developed among residents of the valley toward Pakistan and its proxies essentially arose from the ways in which Pakistan and its allied *tanzeems* have appropriated and fundamentally transformed

---

[41] The Deobandi, Wahhabi, and Ahl-e-Hadith comprise important Sunni traditions. The Deobandi school of Islamic interpretation originated in the nineteenth century in the Indian town of Deoband. Originally, this school of thought argued for the purification of Islam and called for Muslims to abandon nonorthodox local customs that may have been accretions from Hinduism or which may have been Sufi practices. Deobandis in Pakistan were a small minority until the early 1970s. The ascendancy of General Zia ul-Haq brought political patronage to the Deobandis which precipitated rapid Deobandi growth. They have come to operate the largest share of religious schools (*madaris*) in Pakistan. Deobandi organizations were one of the most important bastions of support for the Taliban, many of whose leaders studied in Deobandi *madaris*. Ahl-e-Hadith is a very conservative Muslim reform movement that also originated in the nineteenth century. It was heavily influenced by the Wahhabi movement, centered in Saudi Arabia. Ahl-e-Hadith rejects the Hanafi interpretive tradition. Ahl-e-Hadith is regarded as one of the most stringent Muslim groups in Pakistan and takes guidance from the ulema in Saudi Arabia. It is hostile to Sufi practices, which prevail in large swathes of Kashmir. Wahhabi refers to the eighteenth-century reform movement founded by Muhammad ibn Abd al-Wahhab and which originated in Saudi Arabia. This reform movement, sharing much in common with the Deobandis of India, argued against accretions to Islam and maintained that they should be expunged. All three of these traditions in Pakistan have become highly associated (with varying degrees of legitimacy) as stringent and all have developed political organizations and militant outfits. For additional information, see Guilian Denoux, "The Forgotten Swamp: Navigating Political Islam," *Middle East Policy* 9, no. 2 (June 2002), 56–81; and Mandavi Mehta and Teresita C. Schaffer, "Islam in Pakistan: Unity and Contradictions" (Washington, DC: Center for Strategic and International Studies, 7 October 2002), http://csis.org/saprog/021007schaffer.pdf.

[42] Based on conversations with students, political figures, and newspaper editors in Srinagar in September 2003.

what was initially an indigenous Kashmir-based struggle for self-determination. Throughout the 1990s, the conflict in the valley increasingly involved Pakistan-backed "guest militants," who come from Arab states, Central Asia, Afghanistan, Pakistan, and elsewhere and who trained in camps in Afghanistan and Pakistan. Concomitant with the changed composition of the fighters, the nature and objective of the conflict in Kashmir changed. These largely non-Kashmiri fighters were less interested in securing Kashmiri sovereignty and more interested in establishing a Sunni-based Islamic regime first in Kashmir and subsequently throughout South Asia.[43]

One of the consequences of this changing nature of the violence and its perpetrators in the valley is that by the late 1990s, the authenticity of the "Kashmir struggle" largely has been rejected. Instead, the conflict in the valley has been characterized as devoid of Kashmiri support and representation and a cynical consequence of Pakistan's execution of proxy war to coerce India to the negotiating table. The conflict in Kashmir was further cast within the broader contours of the much-reviled Islamist violence, which only intensified in the wake of the second Intifada against Israeli occupation of Palestine and in the aftermath of the terrorist attacks against the United States on 11 September 2001. Consequently, Kashmiris in the valley are very interested in regaining the credibility of their grievances against the Indian state within international fora. This likely requires that Pakistan cease supporting Pakistan-based militants operating in Kashmir and cease interfering in the affairs of Kashmiris in the valley.

The deep-seated antagonism toward Pakistan and India among the various areas of Kashmir was evident in a late 2002 survey conducted by A. C. Nielson. Nielson surveyed 574 people between 12 and 16 September in the urban areas of Srinagar and Anantang, in the Muslim-dominated district of Kashmir, and in the cities of Jammu and Udhampur, in the Hindu-dominant district of Jammu. When asked about their preferred political future, not a single respondent in Srinagar, Anantnag, or Udhampur was in favor of the valley joining Pakistan, and only 1% in Jammu wanted to; whereas 48% in Srinagar and 59% in Anantang said independence was the only solution to the Kashmir problem. While 26% in Srinagar and 27% in Anantang said Kashmir should stay with India, they also indicated that the state should be granted greater autonomy. In

---

[43] For more information about this transformation, see Alexander Evans, "The Kashmir Insurgency: As Bad as it Gets," *Small Wars and Insurgencies* 11, no. 1 (Spring 2000), 69–81; and Sumantra Bose, *The Challenge in Kashmir: Democracy, Self-Determination and a Just Peace* (New Delhi: Sage, 1997).

Srinagar (the heart of the valley and with a dominant Muslim majority), 21% wanted the valley to stay with India, and in Anantang (also heavily Muslim) only 5% wanted this.[44]

Returning to the narrow question of Kargil's effects on internal dynamics in the valley, a number of those interviewed in Pakistan believed that while the Kargil operation was mainly a failure, it also was a victory of sorts. Some interlocutors said that because of Kargil and its deep significance within India, New Delhi initiated the ceasefire during Ramadan of 2000 that endured until the spring of 2001. Pakistani interlocutors interviewed by the author in December 2000 explained that Kargil demonstrated to India that a military solution would not prevail and that India could not simply act with disregard to Pakistani and Kashmiri equities. Thus, these individuals believed that Kargil inclined India to pursue nonmilitary solutions such as the Ramazan ceasefire.[45] Whether or not residents of the valley espoused this view is unclear.

It is unclear if the Kargil conflict had specific and isolable impacts upon groups and populations in the valley. However, over time, the valley's residents have come to espouse little or no support for Pakistan and its proxies. Their support for India, while more than that for Pakistan, is still low. Over time, the residents of the valley have expressed a preference for independence from both. Residents also have expressed vexation and exasperation with Pakistan's continued support of non-Kashmiri fighters in the region and the notions of Islam that they seek to exert upon the varied people of Kashmir.

Impact on Pakistan's foreign relations

While the consequences of the Kargil conflict on Pakistan's domestic politics and the valley have perhaps been overshadowed by the events subsequent to 9/11, Kargil had an enormous impact on Pakistani foreign relations for the first several years following the conflict. First, Pakistan was completely isolated because it pursued the destabilizing intrusion and because it persisted in clinging to a falsehood that no one found credible. The United States, the G-8, and even China took positions that were concordant with India's preferred position: that

---

[44] Praveen Swami, "The Game of Numbers," *Frontline*, 14 October 2000, www.flonnet.com/fl1721/17210360.htm; see also "Kashmiris Don't Want to Join Pak: Survey," *Times of India*, 27 September 2002, http://timesofindia.indiatimes.com/cms.dll/articleshow?artid=23409600&sType.

[45] See Tellis, Fair, and Medby, *Limited Conflicts under the Nuclear Umbrella*, 35.

Pakistan was the aggressor and that Islamabad needed to act to restore the LoC.[46]

Kargil left Pakistan internationally isolated, widely perceived as a rogue state, veering dangerously toward becoming a bastion of radicalized Islamists increasingly similar to its neighbor under the Taliban. Whereas in 1998, India emerged as the regional pariah responsible for nuclearizing the subcontinent, Pakistan squandered on the heights near Kargil whatever goodwill it had accumulated in the wake of the nuclear tests. At one point, the US State Department even suggested that sanctions could be imposed upon Pakistan if it persisted with its posture of intransigence.[47] The absurdity of Pakistan's cover story and Islamabad's tenacity in maintaining it further diminished Pakistan's credibility.

This credibility deficit continues to complicate Pakistan's external relations. When Pakistan-based and Pakistan-backed militants attacked the Indian parliament in December 2001, few believed that Islamabad was innocent of the incident. That event precipitated a near-war condition that involved the largest mobilization of troops since the 1971 Bangladesh war. The diversion of Pakistani troops from the western border to the eastern border also complicated US military operations in Afghanistan, which were predicated upon Pakistani fortifications to prevent al Qaeda and Taliban fugitives' escape into Pakistani territory. Pakistan's contention that the parliament attack was "stage managed" by India to diminish Islamabad's renewed international standing was immediately dismissed. Similarly, Pakistan's claim to have no involvement in the Afghanistan insurgency has been met with dubiety given that it is well known that Taliban and al Qaeda operatives enjoy sanctuary in key tribal agencies and Baluchistan. The historical reliance upon deception and deniability has cast a long shadow on Pakistan's credibility with the international community generally and key partners, like the United States, in particular.

Indo-Pakistani relations

Kargil was an important turning point in Indo-Pakistani relations. First, it confirmed India's belief that Pakistan was "a reckless, adventuristic, and

---

[46] For transcripts of the various statements, see "Texts of the G-8 Statement on the Kargil Crisis" and "Text of the Clinton–Sharif Statement, 5 July 1999," in Krishna and Chari, eds., *Kargil: The Tables Turned*, 313, 314. The G-8 is an informal organization comprised of eight countries: Canada, France, Germany, Italy, Japan, the Russian Federation, the United Kingdom, and the United States.

[47] Sridhar Krishnaswami, "Zinni Mission to Pak, Very Productive," *The Hindu*, 29 June 1999. See also C. Raja Mohan, "Will US Match Words with Deeds?" *The Hindu*, 26 June 1999; Amit Baruah, "US Asks Pak to Pull Out Intruders," *The Hindu*, 25 June 1999.

risk-acceptant state, capable of behaving astrategically and irrationally."[48] Second, because Kargil was planned and prosecuted at the same time as the Lahore process, India concluded that it simply could not do business with Pakistan, which was a duplicitous and inherently untrustworthy partner. Third, India assessed that Pakistan's ongoing civil–military rivalry would make normalizations with that state exceedingly difficult. This conclusion stems at least in part from the regrettable tendency within India to view the Kargil operation as the design of the army imposed upon an unwitting civilian leadership under Nawaz Sharif. This was an important division of onus because it allowed India's political leadership to justify squandering political capital on the Lahore process because it held that Nawaz Sharif was duped as well.

These conclusions influenced how India tended to deal with Pakistan in the few years following Kargil. First, despairing of reaching any viable agreement with Pakistan, India preferred to avoid substantive engagement with Pakistan. Distinguishing between "substantive" and "procedural" engagement, India preferred to engage Pakistan procedurally, not substantively.[49] The Agra Summit exemplified such procedural engagement.[50]

The Kargil conflict raised questions about the basis for substantive engagement with Islamabad. Even if India did manage to reach an agreement with Islamabad, India has little guarantee that such an accord could endure. Rather, any such agreement would be hostage to the vicissitudes of Pakistan's ever-changing internal dynamics. For several years following Kargil, India believed that it could only deal with Pakistan by not dealing with it – particularly on the issue of Kashmir. India found that its best strategy was to continue to marginalize Pakistan on this issue while mobilizing the specter of Islamist terrorism emerging from this state. During and after Kargil, the Indian press made explicit references to al Qaeda and Osama bin Laden and the various deep connections with Pakistan in an effort to cast Pakistan as an ignominious, unstable, nonsecular, and increasingly Islamist neighbor.[51] In contrast, Indian media managers early on sought to drape about India an aura of responsibility and trust by exercising restraint against crossing the LoC – and by

---

[48] Tellis, Fair, and Medby, *Limited Conflicts under the Nuclear Umbrella*, 16.

[49] *Ibid.* 62.

[50] One could certainly argue that there was little hope for any productive outcome at Agra because neither side was anywhere near convergence. In some ways, Agra could be seen as a tool to distract the international community from the serious development in Indo-Pakistani relations: the termination of the 2000 Ramadan ceasefire.

[51] See "Delhi Plans Publicity Blitz to Expose Direct Role of Pakistan," *Hindustan Times*, 30 May 1999; "Kargil Infiltrators Are Fundamentalists: Russia," *Hindustan Times*, 29 May 1999; and B. Raman, "Is Osama bin Laden in Kargil?" *Indian Express*, 26 May 1999.

publicizing its efforts to do so.[52] India emerged from Kargil as a front-line state against Islamist terror, a mantle that it has further claimed in the aftermath of the 11 September terrorist attacks. Thus, India has tried to resolve Kashmir without any recognition of Pakistan's putative equities in the dispute. This would entail cutting a deal with the Kashmiris and presenting to Islamabad a *fait accompli*, forcing Pakistan to either abide by or rubbish its often-stated commitment to honor the wishes of the Kashmiris.

Following 11 September 2001 and the formal end of the 2001–2002 military crisis in October 2002, India and Pakistan embarked upon a "peace process" of sorts. This round began in early January 2004, when then-Prime Minister Vajpayee and then-President Musharraf met on the sidelines of the South Asian Association for Regional Cooperation (SAARC) meeting in Islamabad. This process has endured despite shocks such as the 2006 terrorist attacks on the Mumbai transit system.

In varying degrees, the conclusions that Indian authorities drew from the Kargil conflict continue to hold. The current Indo-Pakistan detente has yet to yield substantial progress on the core issue of Kashmir's political and territorial disposition. While many Indians may believe Musharraf was the only available leader to push through some deal on Kashmir, there was little reason to believe that future leaders would not renege. This conclusion was strengthened by Musharraf's ever-eroding domestic and international standing. Indeed India's behavior suggests that it prefers to maintain the status quo of reduced violence while it finds an internal solution to present to Islamabad as a *fait accompli*. India has good reason to believe that its position on Kashmir will strengthen over time as a key ally of the United States while Pakistan's will weaken for myriad reasons related to terrorism, democracy, and nuclear proliferation. This confidence diminishes any incentive to accommodate Pakistani equities provided that the violence in Kashmir and elsewhere in India remains at a tolerably low level. Pakistan's ability to expand the violence may be limited by the international community's waning tolerance for violence as a means to achieve political means.

The Kargil conflict also prompted massive changes within India's defense and intelligence infrastructures, which are transforming India as an adversary of Pakistan. Because of Kargil, India undertook a sweeping review of its entire defense infrastructure in an effort to explain how such an intrusion could have happened without detection and how "future Kargils" might be avoided. The Kargil Review Committee and the

<hr />

[52] Arpit Rajain, "India's Political and Diplomatic Response to the Kargil Crisis," in Krishna and Chari, eds., *Kargil: The Tables Turned*, 181–203.

subsequent Ministerial report on the matter proposed many wide-ranging reforms. As this topic is covered elsewhere in this volume, the discussion here focuses specifically on those concerns relating to the problems of infiltration, the desire to monitor activities along the LoC, and the development of improved methods of countering Pakistani disinformation.

Pakistan's deception campaign and use of intruders in mufti clearly led to an Indian intelligence failure. The Kargil Review Committee report argued for a reorganization of all of its communication and electronic intelligence efforts under one organization, similar to the US National Security Agency. It also suggested establishing an integrated defense intelligence agency to ensure a coherent system of intelligence collection, collation, and assessment.[53] Kargil also made painfully obvious that India needed new intelligence hierarchies to ensure "the flow of intelligence from tactical elements to strategic agencies, the analysis of the many pieces of information coming in from different sectors, the communication among the various agencies, and the necessary technology upgrades for early warning surveillance equipment."[54] In addition, India realized the imperatives of an effective strategic warning system: broad investments in better technology, a commitment to better intelligence assessment, and dissemination procedures at the highest diplomatic and political levels.[55]

To counter the ongoing problem of infiltration, India is making and will continue to make a number of investments to fortify its forward defenses to mitigate the possibility of future Kargil-like adventures. Kargil made painfully obvious to Indian defense managers the degree of vulnerability that exists along the porous and rugged mountain terrain of the LoC. To mitigate these vulnerabilities, India is hungrily acquiring a range of technologies that will augment India's thermal, infrared, acoustic imaging as well as image-intensification capabilities. This includes the acquisition of high-endurance unmanned aerial vehicles and pace-based systems, along with their concomitant ground-based command and control and image-processing facilities.[56] The army also needs long-range artillery for

---

[53] *Ibid.*   [54] Tellis, Fair, and Medby, *Limited Conflicts under the Nuclear Umbrella*, 71.

[55] Kargil Review Committee, *From Surprise to Reckoning*, 253–256; for a general discussion of this, see also Ashley J. Tellis, *India's Emerging Nuclear Posture: Between Recessed Deterrent and Ready Arsenal* (Santa Monica, Calif.: RAND, 2001), 623–625, 660–662.

[56] Tellis, Fair, and Medby, *Limited Conflicts under the Nuclear Umbrella*, 70–71. See also Tellis, *India's Emerging Nuclear Posture*, 623–625, 660–662; "Israeli UAVs: Forces of the Future," *Vayu Aerospace Review* 4 (2000), 50–52; "Imaging Capability," *Aviation Week and Space Technology*, 22 November 1999, 17; "'Spy Satellite' Launch by Year-End," *The Hindu*, 2 July 2000.

deployment along the LoC to effectively target militant formations across the LoC. It also wants to acquire ground sensors.[57]

In addition to these hardware and weapons systems acquisitions, India is also actively seeking military training to better confront the challenges it faces in Jammu and Kashmir. This has been made apparent in the emphasis that India has paid to Special Operations within the Indo-US army-to-army training exercises. Some Indians even have suggested that future restructuring of the Indian army could include the creation of a Special Operations Command similar to that of the United States. The Indian army also has been active in obtaining Special Forces-specific equipment such as night-vision goggles, special rifles, assault vehicles, kayaks, masks, and protective gear for operating in nuclear, biological, and chemical (NBC) warfare environments. It also seeks enhanced and more secure communications (such as secure hand-held communications) as well as an increased ability to intercept militant communications. Night-vision equipment is a priority because it would allow the army to insert teams under the cover of night.[58]

As is apparent from the above discussion, the Kargil conflict has motivated India to rethink its entire strategy for dealing with Pakistan. It has altered the Indo-Pakistani bilateral relationship as well as how Indian officials portray Pakistan in multilateral fora. Kargil also ushered in a wide-ranging and thorough review of India's entire defense and intelligence infrastructures. Much of India's current defense-reform initiatives stem from Kargil. Finally, India's ambitious pursuit of more robust forward offensive capabilities has motivated India's defense acquisitions as well as defined the type of combat training that it hopes to gain in its bilateral army exercises with other nations. In short, because of Kargil and its sequelae, the kind of adversary that Pakistan will face in future conflicts has evolved in manifold dimensions.

Pakistan–US relations

Pakistan was generally cast as the transgressor by various international commentators of the conflict and, as noted above, its reliance upon the *mujahideen* cover story did little to advance a sympathetic interpretation of Pakistan's actions in multilateral fora. To a great extent, the damage to Pakistan's credibility has been irreversible despite President Musharraf's

---

[57] The paramilitary forces have been using the Israeli sensor (Elop-manufacted LORROS) on a test basis with unsatisfactory results. See R. K. Jasbir Singh, ed., *Indian Defence Yearbook 2003* (Dehra Dun: Natraj Publishers, 2003), 196, 206.

[58] C. Christine Fair, "Indian Army-to-Army Relations: Prospects for Future Coalition Operations," *Asian Security*, 1, no. 2 (April 2005), 157–173.

heroic decision to join the war on terrorism, in part, because he had little choice in the matter – as Musharraf himself acknowledges.[59]

Moreover, after 2005, considerable doubt arose over Musharraf's commitment to aid the United States in the war on terrorism, particularly with respect to the insurgency in Afghanistan. Pakistan also has made numerous commitments to completely cease cross-LoC infiltration under pressure from the United States and others. Indian officials grant that while infiltration is reduced compared to pre-2001 levels, it is widely accepted that Pakistan has not abandoned the use of proxies altogether for reasons discussed above.[60] The availability of militant training facilities in Pakistan continues to imperil Pakistan's foreign relations, as evidenced in the aftermath of the July 2005 London terror attacks. Several bombers made several trips to Pakistan and are believed to have met with Deobandi militant groups. One of the suicide bombers, Mohammad Sidique Khan, forged connections with al Qaeda in Pakistan and filmed his suicide video in Pakistan.[61] As long as Pakistan retains camps, the potential for such crises will persist.

While the Kargil conflict had a wide-ranging ensemble of corrosive impacts upon Pakistan's foreign relations, its untoward significance was particularly notable in its relations with the United States. Kargil opened the door for the expansion in Indo-US relations that began in 2000 with President Clinton's March 2000 summit visit to India.[62] With the presidency of George Bush, the pace in bilateral engagement surpassed the expectations of even the most optimistic observers of the Indo-US relationship. Kargil was catalytic in these regards for two reasons.

First, the stance that the United States adopted during the Kargil crisis toward Pakistan was very much appreciated in New Delhi. India had

---

[59] President Bush reportedly told Musharraf after 11 September that he could either be an ally in the war against terrorism or a target. C. Christine Fair, *The Counterterror Coalitions: Cooperation with Pakistan and India* (Santa Monica, Calif.: RAND, 2004). Musharraf agrees he had little or no choice. Musharraf writes in his autobiography that US Deputy Secretary of State, Richard Armitage, explained "in what was the most undiplomatic statement ever made" that should Pakistan demur, it "should be prepared to be bombed back to the Stone Age." Musharraf, *In the Line of Fire*, 201.

[60] See Ilyas Khan, "The Waiting Game," 36–41 and Ilyas Khan, "Business as Usual," 38–39. Author interviews with the Indian Home Ministry in September 2006 and interviews with police officials in Srinagar in September 2006.

[61] See "7 July Bombing: The Bombers," BBC News online, http://news.bbc.co.uk/2/shared/spl/hi/uk/05/london_blasts/investigation/html/bombers.stm; "Bomb Trail Goes Cold on Pakistani Ties," BBC News online, 11 May 2006, http://news.bbc.co.uk/2/hi/south_asia/4761659.stm.

[62] He was the first president to visit India since President Carter did so in 1978. Prime Minister Atal Behari Vajpayee made a reciprocal visit in September of that year. This was the second occasion in the two states' history when reciprocal state visits were made within the same year.

previously assumed that if the United States intervened in a bilateral dispute between India and Pakistan that it would take Pakistan's side. In light of the prolonged estrangement between the United States and India and the intense pressure that the United States applied to New Delhi regarding its nuclear weapons and missile programs, India was both surprised and delighted that the US position posited Pakistan as the aggressor and insisted upon its withdrawal. Kargil demonstrated to New Delhi the potentially positive regional role of the United States.

Second, the Kargil crisis gave the United States a window of opportunity to strategically realign its priorities in South Asia both by providing a convenient "excuse" to distance itself from Islamabad and by demonstrating to India that the two democracies had several shared strategic interests. Pakistan made this movement toward an "India first" policy even easier with the October 1999 military coup, which invoked Section 508 sanctions.[63] Both India and the United States emerged from Kargil with a clear sense that they both shared a growing convergence of strategic interests, including containing the global threat of terrorism, and stabilizing and rehabilitating Afghanistan, as well as mutual interest in Pakistan's stability. One of the key dimensions of this new US relationship with India was the resumption in and expansion of military-to-military relations that began in the spring of 2000 under the Bush administration's new approach to South Asia popularly known as "de-hyphenation."[64]

Since the events of 11 September 2001 and commencement of military action in Afghanistan, the Indo-US relationship has continued to strengthen and has taken on hitherto unimaginable dimensions inclusive of a US–Indian civilian nuclear agreement and a commitment to help India become a global power among other initiatives.[65] The fate of

---

[63] The term "India first" derives from Stephen Cohen, "Moving Forward in South Asia," Brookings Institute Policy Brief no. 81 (May 2001), www.brookingsinstitution.org/comm/policybriefs/pb081/pb81.htm. Under Section 508 of the 1999 Foreign Operations Appropriations Act, no US assistance may be given to any country "whose duly elected head of government is deposed by military coup or decree." However, after 11 September, Congress gave waiver authority to the president until the end of the fiscal year 2005. See Dianne E. Rennack, "India and Pakistan: Current US Economic Sanctions," *CRS Report*, no. RS20995 (Washington, DC: Library of Congress, Congressional Research Service, updated 12 October 2001) and K. Alan Kronstadt, "Pakistan–US Relations," *CRS Issue Brief* (Washington, DC: Library of Congress, Congressional Research Service, updated 2 December 2003).

[64] This policy shift calls for a decoupling of US relations with India and Pakistan ensuring that bilateral relations with both states is not held hostage by their security competition. Fair, *The Counterterror Coalitions*.

[65] See Ashley J. Tellis, *India as a New Global Power: An Action Agenda for the United States* (Washington, DC: CEIP, July 2006) and Faaiza Rashid and George Perkovich. "A Survey of the Progress in US–India Relations," in Tellis, *India as a New Global Power*, available at www.carnegieendowment.org/publications/index.cfm?fa=view&id=17079&prog=zgp&proj=zsa.

US–Pakistan relations remains very much indeterminate and will likely depend upon future decisions that Pakistan takes with respect to supporting proxy warfare in Kashmir and Afghanistan in an effort to project its equities in these two regions. Notably, Pakistan's cooperation in the global war on terrorism concentrated the attention of the newly elected, Democrat-led Congress. Both the Senate and the House explored ways of exacting greater accountability from Pakistan, moves which the Bush administration opposed.[66] Further, A. Q. Khan's network's nuclear assistance to Iran, Libya, and North Korea continues to create policy dilemmas as concerns persist over the responsibility of Pakistan as a reliable and responsible custodian of nuclear weapons.[67]

Conclusion

This chapter takes as its starting point that civilian combatants were not used in the execution of Kargil. Pakistan's use of the deception strategy has had a number of consequences for Pakistan's domestic internal dynamics, the various groups operating in the valley as well as large swathes of the civilians there, and upon its foreign relations – particularly with the United States and India. Initially, the Pakistan public took great pride in believing that a handful of ragtag *mujahideen* could have effectively tied up the Indian army and inflicted such heavy causalities. This occasioned a brief, but important improved opinion of the religious leadership of Pakistan among the Pakistani polity. While the deception may have provided a boost to the insurgency in Indian-held Kashmir as well as to the popular perception of religious leadership and militant groups in Pakistan, the deception campaign appears to have had very negative consequences in Pakistan's Northern Areas. Unfortunately, research cannot shed much light on the ways that Kargil may or may not have influenced the relationships and the interoperability of the militant organizations and their Pakistani handlers in the army and ISID. It seems likely

---

[66] The US House of Representatives introduced H.R. 1, which seeks greater accountability from Pakistan. See "H.R. 1: Implementing the 9/11 Commission Recommendations Act of 2007 (Referred to Senate Committee after being Received from House)," available at http://thomas.loc.gov/cgi-bin/query/D?c110:3:./temp/~c110t9AF0T. For an official statement from the White House opposing the measure, see Office of the President, Statement of Administration Policy: H.R. 1 – Implementing the 9/11 Commission Recommendations Act of 2007H.2007, January 9, 2007, available at www.whitehouse. gov/omb/legislative/sap/110-1/hr1sap-h.pdf.

[67] See William J. Broad, David E. Sanger, and Raymond Bonner, "A Tale of Nuclear Proliferation: How Pakistani Built His Network," *New York Times*, 12 February 2004, A1; and David E. Sanger, "Threats and Responses: Alliances; in North Korea and Pakistan, Deep Roots of Nuclear Barter," *New York Times*, 24 November 2002, A1.

that decisions relating to the global war on terrorism undertaken by the Pakistan government may have posed more far-reaching challenges to these relationships. What has become apparent is that these *jehadi* groups are still very much in operation and still largely under the scrutiny and perhaps even control of the Pakistan army and ISID.

Turning to the consequences that the Kargil conflict may have had upon actors in the Kashmir Valley, with the passage of time it is difficult to isolate trends that are directly attributable to Kargil. Rather, over time, Kashmiris in the valley appear to have grown dissatisfied with Pakistan and its militant proxies. For sure, they also appear exhausted with New Delhi and many in the valley seem to prefer an option of independence.

The impact of Kargil on Pakistan's foreign relations has been most apparent. Because of Kargil, Pakistan will face a completely transformed foe in future conflicts with India. Kargil was a clarion call to New Delhi's security managers and has prompted India to make broad investments to fortify its forward offensive capabilities, to seek enhanced technology and combat training to contend with the insurgency in the valley, and to launch a major defense and intelligence restructuring. Second, because of Kargil, India and the United States found an opportunity for rapprochement. This process began anew in 2000 and has continued to develop momentum and gravity since then. Whereas India is the new US strategic partner, the future of US–Pakistan relations remains very much in question. Concerns over democracy, support of militancy in Kashmir and in Afghanistan, as well as missile and nuclear proliferation continue to pose policy challenges to Washington. Prospects for Islamabad to assuage Washington's concerns on these fronts appear ever dim.

10   The impact of the Kargil conflict and Kashmir on Indian politics and society

Praveen Swami

A person in the Indian state of Bihar had offered 111 coconuts and intended to offer 10001 … A large Corporate House and the local unit of the Bhartiya Janta [sic] political party in the city of Bombay offered prayers at the celebrated Siddhivinayak Temple and distributed sweets. A youth in Gujarat went on a fast unto death. No, none of the above commitments were for the well being of the Indian soldiers but for the Indian cricket team.[1]

Naresh Arya's irate assault on his fellow Indians – widely circulated on the Internet during the Kargil war – was sparked off by what he believed to be their outrageous lack of wartime patriotism.

On 7 June 1999, troops of the 56 Brigade were preparing to take the key heights of Tololing and point 4590-meters. These were the first major Indian victories of the Kargil war, and were to come about six days later.[2] At about the same time, Indian television viewers were preparing to watch the showdown between their team and that of Pakistan in the 1999 Cricket World Cup at the Old Trafford ground in Manchester. In the event, India won a low-scoring and generally unremarkable match, beating Pakistan by forty-seven runs. Journalists in the United Kingdom, bored with lamenting the early exit of the British team, had billed the event as something of a war in itself. Sadly for them, the enthusiastic crowds of emigrants from the subcontinent chose to enjoy the match peacefully, and went home quietly afterwards. "A few modest rockets notwithstanding," noted one British commentator, "the game was firework-free and the only serious injury was a knock to Indian golden boy Jadeja's pride when he

---

[1] Naresh Arya, "Cricket Fever," *Goinside.com*, 14 June 1999, http://goinside.com/99/6/cricket.html.

[2] Amarinder Singh, *A Ridge Too Far: War in the Kargil Heights 1999* (Patiala: Motibagh Palace, 2001), 100.

258

tripped over the boundary rope attempting to make a quick return to the pavilion and fell on his backside."[3]

This chapter examines the impact of the Kargil conflict on India's political life. Contrary to received wisdom on the subject, India's wartime victory did little for the political prospects of the Bharatiya Janata Party (BJP), the principal partner in the ruling National Democratic Alliance coalition government. Commentators often point to the enormous, often hyper-patriotic, cultural production that the Kargil war generated. But although the war suffused mass culture, a phenomenon the first part of this chapter documents, it did not have any demonstrable impact on the configuration of Indian politics. In the election that followed the Kargil conflict, which is discussed in the second part of the chapter, the BJP actually *lost* two percentage points of its pre-victory national vote-share. My purpose here is to examine the disjunction between the impact of Kargil on mass culture and on India's electoral politics – to suggest, as it were, that the strategists who planned the BJP's postwar Lok Sabha election campaign ought to have paid more attention to the mood at the wartime cricket match.[4] In the third part of the chapter, I argue that the BJP's failure to capitalize on its war triumph may have been because of the sharp escalation in violence in Jammu and Kashmir that followed India's military victory – a larger conflict that was, in the public imagination, inextricably interwoven with the Kargil war itself. In conclusion, I suggest that this conflict contributed to the growth of Hindu chauvinism, a political process that may be of considerable significance for Indian political life in years to come.

Popular culture

It was perhaps understandable that politicians would overestimate the political consequences of the Kargil conflict. Arya may have been wrong in suggesting that the bulk of Indians were unmoved by the battle in the Himalayas. "For two and a half months," Geeta Seshu has pointed out, "wargames occupied television viewers and readers of newspapers and magazines."[5] As a consequence, the official Kargil Review Committee's

---

[3] Alex Balfour, "Scorecard," *Cricinfo.com*, 7 June 1999, www.cricket.org/link_to_database/ ARCHIVE/WORLD_CUPS/WC99/SCORECARDS/SUPSIX/ IND_PAK_WC99_ODI-SUPSIX4_08JUN1999_CI_MR.html.

[4] The Lok Sabha is India's directly elected lower house of parliament.

[5] Geeta Seshu, "Media and Kargil: Information Blitz with Dummy Missiles," *Economic and Political Weekly (Mumbai)*, 9 October 1999.

report approvingly recorded, "media coverage, especially over television, bound the country as never before."[6]

Violently nationalist television and newsprint reporting, and support from film and sport celebrities for the soldiers fighting on the Kargil heights, ensured the war received a mass response on an unprecedented scale and intensity in India.[7] One of the few scholarly studies of the war suggests a conscious effort was made by the Indian media to valorize soldiers fighting in Kargil by focusing on them as individuals; more than one article in six focused on war-related human-interest stories.[8] Significantly, the study found, the Hindi-language media, which caters to the largest linguistic region in India, carried more articles than the English-language media. Although no scholarly work is available to substantiate the proposition, Kargil is routinely referred to in India as the country's first television war, a reference to the round-the-clock broadcasting of events there by a welter of new satellite-television channels.

Some caveats are due here. Certainly, images of the conflict beamed into Indian homes would have contributed to patriotic feeling. However, in the absence of primary research material, and given the fact that Indian satellite-television reach is principally urban, it would be rash to draw firm conclusions. No comprehensive attempt at content analysis has so far been attempted. There is an identical lack of scholarship on the print media during the Kargil war. Much of the little work that exists focuses on the English-language press, and, marginally, writing in Hindi. It is important to note, in this context, that not a single English-language newspaper figures among the ten most widely circulated newspapers in India; only half of these giants, moreover, are Hindi-language.[9] As such, studies of their content can at best provide some illumination of elite opinion. It is near impossible, moreover, to gauge the precise impact of this media output, too, since no reader-attitude surveys are available.

However, other indices do exist that support the argument that the Kargil conflict had an enormous impact on public consciousness. The prime minister's Relief Fund alone received an estimated 5,000 million rupees for Kargil-war-related expenditure, a record figure believed to be considerably higher, even inflation adjusted, than gold and cash donations

---

[6] K. Subrahmanyam, B. G. Verghese, and K. K. Hazari, *From Surprise to Reckoning: The Kargil Review Committee Report* (New Delhi: Sage, 2000), 139.

[7] For further information on Kargil and the media see, Colonel S. C. Tyagi, *The Fourth Estate: A Force Multiplier for the Indian Army* (New Delhi: Gyan Publishing, 2005), 67–111.

[8] Jaishri Jethwaney and Shivaji Sarkar, *Information War: Media a Victim or a Tool?* (New Delhi: Indian Institute of Mass Communication, 14 August 1999).

[9] National Readership Studies Council, *NRS 2006: Key Findings* (Mumbai: Audit Bureau of Circulations, August 2006), www.auditbureau.org/nrspress06.pdf.

made to the National Defence Fund during the 1962 China–India war. By way of contrast, the prime minister's Relief Fund received only 1,000 million rupees of public donations after the Orissa cyclone of October 1999, and 2,300 million rupees after the even more devastating Gujarat earthquake of 26 January 2001.[10] This, of course, excludes nongovernmental charitable contributions, and private initiatives by businesses and individuals. There are no authoritative records available of the numbers of municipal and private memorials built to the memory of those who fought in the Kargil war, but these are more evident, at least to my eye, in small-town and rural India than for any other conflict of the past.

No war of the past had quite such an impact on mass culture either. India's film-industry celebrities, often criticized during the 1990s for their lack of social conscience, pitched in energetically. Many visited forward positions, joined in charity sports matches, and organized fundraisers. The first week of July alone saw two major concerts in Mumbai, featuring top movie stars like Govinda, Sunil Shetty, and Raveena Tandon.[11] Shortly afterwards, four separate film projects were announced on the war and allied themes, two by top directors Mani Ratnam and J. P. Dutta. Images of the war suffused calendars, popular iconography, and even the popular Yatra theatre form of Bengal, which turned out a long-running play called *Rakte Ranga Kargil* [Bloodstained Kargil].[12] At least some of these media productions had an unconcealed political agenda. Impresario Amir Raza Husain's light-and-sound spectacular *The Fifty Day War* had Pakistani generals plotting the start of the Kargil war even as the first Atal Behari Vajpayee-led government fell on 15 April 1999.[13] This liberty with the historical record – essays elsewhere in this volume elucidate the infiltration started when Vajpayee was still in power – served an obvious ideological purpose. By mid-2002, there were so many of these kinds of media productions in circulation that one critic acidly observed that:

For Bollywood producers, it is time to peddle strident jingoism masquerading as pulp patriotism to an audience tired of tearjerkers on the small screen and choc-olate boy romances on the big screen. And laugh all the way to the bank.[14]

This pop-culture deluge, of course, came well after the 1999 elections, but does give some indication of the cultural climate of the time. One means through which Kargil's impact on popular culture expressed itself

---

[10] Ramesh Menon, "Nobody Knows How Much Money Has Come to Gujarat," *Rediff.com*, 14 April 2001, www.rediff.com/news/2001/apr/14spec.htm.
[11] "Out and About," *Indian Express* (Mumbai), 2 July 1999.
[12] Tapash Ganguly, "Its Yatra, Folks," *The Week* (Cochin), 13 February 2002.
[13] K. Sunil Thomas, "Kargil Plot Theatre," *The Week*, www.the-week.com/20jan30/enter.htm.
[14] Zia-us-Salaam, "Peddling Patriotism," *The Hindu* (New Delhi), 15 March 2002.

was through an upsurge of recruitment applications for the Indian army. At one rally in Amritsar, in the state of Punjab, 20,000 men turned up for the 650 military jobs on offer; many were relatives of soldiers killed in the Kargil conflict. Recruitment rallies in the adjoining state of Haryana also drew similar numbers. On one occasion, the enormous rush for recruitment into the army actually led to fatalities. On 17 July 1999, twenty people were killed at rallies in Bihar's districts of Darbhanga and Chappra, three when the police opened fire on rioting applicants, and seventeen in a stampede. In the state of Gujarat, applications were reported to be up by 30 percent from previous years, often from potential recruits whose families had no tradition of military service.[15] Much media commentary from the time attributes this rush to patriotic sentiment. Alternative explanations were, however, also offered. One skeptical media commentator, Pritam Bhullar, attributed the recruitment surge to the belief of "unemployed young men ... that with the Army having suffered a large number of casualties, it will be easier to get in now." He wrote:

That patriotism has stung them to some extent cannot be denied. But more than this is the large scale unemployment in the country that is responsible for the heavy rush at recruitment centers. Some of the poor say that it is better to get killed in a war than to sleep on empty stomachs.[16]

In a thoughtful analysis of Indian soldiers' funerals, the scholar Max-Jean Zins has pointed to the army's own institutional role in giving birth to popular cultural expressions of sentiment on the Kargil war. The Indian army's decision to bring back bodies from the battlefield provided "an excellent opportunity to stage a spectacular extravaganza, a sort of meticulously choreographed funereal ballet."[17] As represented in the media and in popular discourse, Zins has argued, the Kargil martyr was a pan-India hero, who transcended region, caste, or religion; the funerals of Muslim soldiers killed in combat were given special emphasis. Typically, very large numbers of villagers gathered to watch these funerals.[18] A similar response was seen in urban areas. One cremation procession in New Delhi, for example, saw a five-mile-long line of mourners file past for four and a half hours.[19] Interestingly, perhaps, a battle martyrs' funeral occupies no special place in Hindu tradition. As such, the funerals

---

[15] *Hindustan Times* (New Delhi), 25 June 1999, cited in Max-Jean Zins, "Symbolism of the Kargil War Funerals," *Faultlines* 13 (New Delhi: Institute for Conflict Management, 2002), 61.

[16] Pritam Bhullar, "Fauji Beat: Economical Option for the Army," *Sunday Tribune* (Chandigarh), 8 August 1999.

[17] Zins, "Symbolism of the Kargil War Funerals," 71.

[18] "Havildar Cremated," *The Hindu* (Chennai), 18 June 2004.

[19] Zins, "Symbolism of the Kargil War Funerals," 73.

witnessed during the Kargil war were an act of cultural praxis unprecedented in past India–Pakistan conflicts, one that helped to make concrete the patriotic tenor of media reportage and popular-culture production.

Prime Minister Atal Behari Vajpayee made clear his party's intention to instrumentalize this cultural climate: to make political capital from what he believed to be a historic battlefield victory. On one notable occasion in Karnal, in the state of Haryana, he addressed a campaign rally from a platform decorated with portraits of the Indian armed forces' three services chiefs. When outraged opposition politicians protested, the prime minister disassociated himself from the organizers of the rally. Similar motifs, however, became a recurrent theme of the election campaign.[20] Earlier, the injured war hero Yogendra Yadav had been asked to touch the feet of the Vishwa Hindu Parishad (VHP: World Hindu Council, an ideological affiliate of the BJP) senior vice-president, Giriraj Kishore. Yadav was asked to perform the traditional Hindu gesture of submission and respect while Kishore was visiting an army hospital. When he was found to be physically unable to comply, his wife made the gesture in his stead.[21] Members of the women's wing of the VHP marched to army headquarters carrying lotus-shaped *Rakhis*, a ritual symbol of brotherhood, made in the form of the BJP's symbol, further advertising the supposedly organic relationship between the army that represented the nation and the party that claimed to represent the essence of Indian nationhood.[22] The 20,000-odd *Rakhis* were refused on logistical grounds, but the VHP–BJP cadre were granted access elsewhere.[23]

The Kargil election

Kargil, contrary to popular perception and some scholarly wisdom, did not win the 1999 election for the BJP. Indeed, the BJP actually received a smaller share of the popular vote than it had in the previous General Elections – and sometimes in the very states where popular mobilization on Kargil war themes was strongest.

Delivering his annual address to the nation on its independence day on 15 August 1999, Prime Minister Vajpayee launched an unusually acid broadside against Pakistan. Over half the speech was devoted to conflict between that country and India. There was no hint here of the prime

[20] "Kargil Mural at PM's Meet Irks Oppn," *Indian Express* (New Delhi), 22 August 1999.
[21] Seema Mustafa, "The Politicization of Kargil," *Asian Age* (New Delhi), 21 August 1999.
[22] Gaurav Sawant, "Army Chief Says No to VHP's 20,000 Rakhis," *Indian Express* (New Delhi), 23 August 2002.
[23] Kanwar Sandhu, "Not by Homilies Alone," *Indian Express* (New Delhi), 3 September 1999. For further information, see, Tyagi, *The Fourth Estate*, 67–111.

minister who, not that many months in the future, would seek a ceasefire with terrorist groups, and invite Pakistan's military ruler, Pervez Musharraf, to India. "For peace," he said, "we need trust. Has trust increased on account of all that happened in Kargil? Does the path of armed intrusion lead to friendship? Terrorists are being trained in Pakistan. Camps are being run for them. Hordes of terrorists are being sent into India. They are killing innocent people. They are targeting women and children. How can meaningful dialogue take place in this atmosphere?"

On the eve of elections, the prime minister went on to categorize the Kargil war as a defining moment in the making of Indian nationhood:

The Red Fort and its world-renowned ramparts are not merely a geographical spot. The very heartbeat of India's freedom struggle is linked to this fort and its ramparts. In the First War of Independence of 1857, this is where Bahadur Shah Zafar was held a prisoner. Netaji Subhash Chandra Bose made this very fort the target of his campaign in 1943 and, blowing the bugle of Independence, gave the stirring call to his countrymen: *"Dilli Chalo, Chalo Lal Kile"* [March to Delhi, March to the Red Fort]. It is from this very fort that our first Prime Minister, Pandit Jawaharlal Nehru, hoisted for the first time the tricolour of Free India in 1947. More than half a century has passed. Today, we stand at the threshold of a new era. Come, let us enter this new era united in step and united in resolve.[24]

Voters were united in that postwar election, but only for the purpose of single-mindedly rejecting Kargil as its central issue. The BJP came out with no more seats than it had in 1998, while its share of the popular vote declined by almost two percentage points. While the main opposition grouping, the centrist Congress (I),[25] lost a large number of seats, this was the product of local factors and India's first-past-the-post election system. The Congress (I)'s share of the popular vote and that of the Communist Party of India (Marxist) actually grew somewhat. The center-left Samajwadi Party, accused by the BJP of being "pro-Muslim," lost a part of its popular vote, but significantly increased its representation in parliament. Thus, the BJP remained as dependent on regional allies after 1999 as it had been in 1998: allies often hostile to its core Hindu-nationalist ideological positions (Table 10.1).[26]

---

[24] Atal Behari Vajpayee, "Prime Minister's Independence Day Speech, 1999," http://pmin-dia.nic.in/infocentre/curr_speeches.htm.

[25] The Congress (I) is referred to in official election data as the Indian National Congress, or INC. In most media and academic discourse, however, it continues to be referred to as the Congress (I). In deference to practice, I use the term Congress (I) throughout my chapter, while using the initials INC in all data derived from official records.

[26] These data, and that pertaining to elections not otherwise specifically footnoted, are derived from the *Statistical Report on General Elections 1999 to the 13th Lok Sabha* and the *Statistical Report on General Elections 1998 to the 12th Lok Sabha*, both published by the Election Commission of India, New Delhi, available online at www.eci.gov.in.

Table 10.1 *Results in the 1998 and 1999 General Elections for major parties*

Party	Percentage of votes polled			Number of seats obtained		
	1998	1999	Change+	1998	1999	Change
Bharatiya Janata Party	25.59	23.75	−1.84	182	182	0
Indian National Congress	25.82	28.3	2.48	141	114	−27
Janata Dal (United)*	3.24	3.1	−0.14	6	21	15
Janata Dal (Secular)		0.91	0.91		1	1
Bahujan Samaj Party	4.67	4.16	−0.51	5	14	9
Communist Party of India (Marxist)	5.16	5.4	0.24	32	33	1
Communist Party of India	1.79	1.48	−0.31	9	4	−5
Samajwadi Party	4.93	3.76	−1.17	20	26	6

+ In percentage points
*Figures for 1998 are for both factions of the Janata Dal, then a single entity
Source: Election Commission of India

Such aggregate data can often be misleading, since India is diverse and voting patterns can vary sharply along regional lines. I have, therefore, chosen four states for detailed scrutiny (Table 10.2). Punjab has a long association with the Indian army and a considerable presence in its ranks. It also experienced a decade of Pakistan-backed terrorism. Moreover, its border villages have suffered the consequences of India–Pakistan wars in the past, and would have done so again had the conflict in Kargil generalized. For all these reasons, the state may have strongly responded to any political manifestation of the Kargil conflict. Gujarat, like Punjab, is on India's western border, but the Rann of Kutch, a vast stretch of marsh and desert that makes up the bulk of its border with Pakistan, is unsuitable for heavy warfare. As a consequence, the state has never seen real battle. It is, however, a stronghold of the Hindu right, and is often described as a laboratory for the forging of *Hindutva*, Hindu nationalism. Maharashtra is not a border state, but has a long tradition of association with the Indian army. More important, it was in 1999 considered a key base of the Hindu Right, having been the birthplace of both the Rashtriya Swayamsevak Sangh (RSS) and Shiv Sena. Finally, Uttar Pradesh is the political heart of north India, and sends the largest number of representatives to the Lok Sabha of any Indian state. In all but one of these states, the BJP and its allies saw an erosion of their command of the popular vote in the 1999 elections.

For the purposes of this chapter, the question of why Gujarat was the only state to give the BJP a majority of the popular vote is not germane.

Table 10.2 *Voting patterns in four key states, General Elections 1998 and 1999*

State	Party	Percentage of votes polled			Seats obtained		
		1998	1999	Change*	1998	1999	Change
Gujarat [26 seats]	Bharatiya Janata Party	48.29	52.48	4.19	19	20	1
	Indian National Congress	36.49	45.44	8.95	7	6	−1
Maharashtra [48 seats]	Bharatiya Janata Party	22.49	21.18	−1.31	4	13	9
	Indian National Congress	43.64	29.71	−13.93	33	10	−23
	Shiv Sena	19.66	16.7	−2.96	6	15	9
	Nationalist Congress Party	did not exist	21.58	21.58	did not exist	6	6
Punjab [13 seats]	Bharatiya Janata Party	11.67	9.16	−2.51	3	1	−2
	Bahujan Samaj Party	12.65	3.84	−8.81	0	0	0
	Indian National Congress	25.85	38.44	12.59	0	8	8
	Shiromani Akali Dal	32.93	28.59	−4.34	8	2	−6
Uttar Pradesh [85 seats]	Bharatiya Janata Party	36.49	27.64	−8.85	57	29	−28
	Bahujan Samaj Party	20.9	22.08	1.18	4	14	10
	Indian National Congress	6.02	14.72	8.7	0	10	10
	Samajwadi Party	28.7	24.06	−4.64	20	26	6

*In percentage points
Source: Election Commission of India

Journalists and social scientists there have energetically debated the question in the context of the recent violence. A variety of local factors, notably the peculiar development of caste relationships and alliances in the state, have been offered by way of explanation. However, the focus to note here is that the growth of the Congress (I)'s share of the popular vote, in percentage points, was more than twice that of the BJP. Whatever took place in Gujarat in 1999, then, cannot simply be attributed to any mass endorsement for the party's management of the Kargil conflict.

Neighboring Maharashtra offers a study in contrast. Here, both the BJP and its electoral ally, the Shiv Sena, registered a significant increase in their representation in Parliament, from ten in 1998 to twenty-eight in 1999. The share of the popular vote of both parties, however, fell markedly. So did that of the Congress (I), which also ended up losing twenty-three of the Lok Sabha seats it held in 1998. The reason for this was quite simple. A key Congress (I) figure in the state, former Indian Defence Minister Sharad Pawar, had left the party to set up a new organization, the Nationalist Congress Party (NCP). Pawar's stated reason for forming the NCP was his opposition to the prospect that the Congress (I) president Sonia Gandhi, a former Italian citizen, might become India's prime minister. In the event, the decision spelt disaster for both parties, although in parallel elections to the state's legislature, the Congress (I), NCP, and a welter of center-left and center allies succeeded in forming a government. One analysis by the Centre for the Study of Developing Studies (CSDS) pointed out that:

A simple arithmetical calculation shows that if a split had not taken place in the Congress (I) and the various [other] parties had got the same vote share they did in this election, the Shiv Sena and the Bharatiya Janata Party would have won just nine Lok Sabha seats from Maharashtra, and the Congress (I) alliance's tally would have been 39, instead of the final figures of 28 and 11[27] respectively. This alone would have changed the majority equation in Parliament, with the national verdict looking much different from what it does today. This demonstrates once again how an electoral verdict is as much an artifact of party managers and the first-past-the-post system as it is a product of the changing mood of the electorate.[28]

---

[27] The figure "11" should read "16," and seems to be a typographic error. The figure 16 is used in the Election Commission of India data and in figures provided in a graphic within the CSDS study itself.

[28] CSDS Team with Suhas Palshikar, "Split Factor decides the Outcome," *Frontline* (Chennai), 19 November 1999. India, like the United States and the United Kingdom, has a first-past-the-post system, where the party that gains the largest share of the vote wins power in a given constituency. Thus, a party that actually commands a minority of the popular vote may end with a majority in the legislature. Proportional representation systems, of the kinds practiced in Europe, use various means to avoid this anomalous situation.

Pawar, then, appears more central to the making of the Union government in 1999 than anything that happened in Kargil!

Punjab offers another example of such localized factors playing a key role in shaping the electoral result. In the 1998 elections, the state's main party of the religious right, the Shiromani Akali Dal (SAD), had fought in alliance with the Bahujan Samaj Party (BSP), a formation which claims to represents the state's large Dalit, or lower-caste, population. For a variety of reasons, notably its desire to undermine the Congress (I)'s command of urban Hindu voters, the SAD chose to ally with the BJP this time around. The tactic, as the data make clear, backfired. The Congress (I) dramatically increased its representation in the Lok Sabha, while the BJP, SAD, and BSP were decimated. I am not suggesting here that the change in tactical alliances was the sole reason for the result – allegations of corruption directed at the state SAD–BJP alliance government, economic mismanagement, and Hindu discontent with the increasing stridency of the Right within the SAD all had a role. But it is clear that local factors unconnected to the grand theme of the Kargil conflict were central in shaping the electoral outcome.

Finally, Uttar Pradesh may have been expected to be a major theater of gain for the BJP had the Kargil war generated a religious-chauvinist political response. The state has a long history of communal violence between Hindus and Muslims, and is at the center of the explosive Babri Masjid dispute. The confrontation, which has claimed hundreds of lives over the years, was initiated by the Hindu Right, which laid claim to, and subsequently demolished, a historic mosque in northern India. As the figures make clear, claims to have won the Kargil war did little for the party in this communally fragile state. Prime Minister Vajpayee, who had won the 1998 elections from this state by a margin of over 215,000 votes, won again in 1999, but with a considerably smaller margin of only 123,000 votes. His Congress (I) opponent, Karan Singh, is the son of the royal family that ruled Jammu and Kashmir before independence. Interestingly, Singh has for long been a voice of the Hindu Right within his state, and his presence may have been intended to make clear to voters that the Kargil victory had done little to address the suffering of the Hindu community there. The BJP overall suffered a very sharp loss in its share of the popular vote and in its representation in the Lok Sabha from Uttar Pradesh. The journalist Venkitesh Ramakrishnan offered this analysis of the BJP debacle:

Five major factors contributed to the BJP's defeat. The strong anti-incumbency mood against the Kalyan Singh-led BJP coalition government; the shift in upper caste votes, particularly that of Brahmins and Jats, from the BJP to the Congress (I) and its alliance partner, the RLD; the anti-BJP, pro-SP campaign by former BJP MP Sakshi Maharaj, who was denied the ticket, and its impact on large sections of the Lodh Rajput backward caste community who were BJP supporters; the vote arithmetic factor that is bound to give an edge to the party coming second in the previous election; and the tactical voting of Muslims, who more or less successfully identified the secular party capable of defeating the BJP in each constituency.[29]

It is important to note that these multi-state reverses carried on from a long line of BJP defeats after that other great display of ultra-nationalist fervor, the Pokhran-II nuclear tests of 11 May 1998. Less than a month later, the BJP suffered severe losses in the elections and by-elections of 3 June, spread across three Lok Sabha and fifty-one Assembly seats. Senior BJP leader Pramod Mahajan had expressly claimed the nuclear tests would be the central issue in these elections, and that their outcome would "prove that the BJP has conclusively replaced the Congress (I) as the main national party."[30] In the event, the BJP lost ground, registering some gains along with its allies in the states of Uttar Pradesh, Himachal Pradesh, Punjab, and Jammu and Kashmir, but losing in other crucial states, particularly in southern India.[31]

Even sharper decline in the BJP's electoral fortunes was evident by the time the 25 November 1998 Assembly elections came around. In Madhya Pradesh, where the BJP won 119 seats to the Congress (I)'s 172, its vote share fell from 46 percent in the 1998 Lok Sabha elections to 41 percent. Similarly, the BJP's vote share in Rajasthan fell from the 1998 figure of 42 percent by ten percentage points, meaning it could win just 33 seats to the Congress (I)'s 150. In Delhi, long considered something of a pocket borough for the Hindu Right, the BJP's vote share fell from 51 percent in 1998 to 33 percent in November 1999.[32] This fall was, by any standards, precipitate. It is possible to argue that the Kargil war did help the BJP by preventing the even more calamitous decline that might otherwise have come about by the time the 1999 Lok Sabha elections came around. The proposition seems reasonable, since the rhetoric unleashed in the 1999 elections seems to have been built around the belief that Indian victory would, at the very least, rally the party faithful. The fact that hate campaigns against Christian missionaries in Gujarat and Orissa began soon

[29] Venkitesh Ramakrishnan, "Patterns and Pointers: A State-Wise Round-up of Verdict 99," *Frontline* (Chennai), 5 November 1999.
[30] Venkitesh Ramakrishnan, "Ominous Signs for the BJP," *Frontline* (Chennai), 3 July 1998.
[31] *Ibid.*
[32] Sukumar Muralidharan, "A Debacle in 9 Months," *Frontline* (Chennai), 18 December 1998. For detailed state results and data, see Venkitesh Ramakrishnan, "A Fresh Polarisation in Delhi," T. K. Rajalakshmi, "A Crippling Blow," and V. Venkatesan, "A Surprise Victory," all in the same issue of *Frontline*.

after the November defeat do suggest the Hindu Right was aware of the need to galvanize its core constituency. There is, however, no real way to validate this kind of speculation empirically, at least in the absence of detailed surveys of the impact the Kargil conflict had on voters. What is clear, however, is that patriotism alone did not serve to deflect attention from other issues.

The Kargil war and the conflict in Kashmir

If Kargil figured little in the shaping of the 1999 electoral verdict, the obvious question to ask is why. I argue here that any successes in Kargil were undermined by escalating levels of violence within Jammu and Kashmir, of which the war was, in popular consciousness and in fact, merely a part.

Several possible answers exist for this question. The first is what might be called the Arya Cricket Thesis: that Indians are more concerned with the transient glory of the game, be it cricket or politics, rather than the abiding glory of the battlefield. A second, more serious proposition might be that local factors of caste, class, ethnicity, and religion so deeply suffuse Indian politics that meta-events like the Kargil war have no real impact. This proposition, however, is demonstrably untrue. In several elections of the past, grand themes have dominated campaigns and shaped outcomes. From Indira Gandhi's triumphant post-1971 war campaign, through the anti-Emergency wave and on to Vishwanath Pratap Singh's crusade against Congress (I) corruption, grand issues have at least covered over, if not completely subsumed, the local politics of caste, region, or religion. Better reasons, then, have to be found to explain the evident absence of impact the Kargil conflict had on Indian political life in 1999.

A third explanation might lie in the growing suspicion, among both politicians and the media, that Official India was being economical with the truth about just what had happened on the Kargil heights. By late July, several commentators were suggesting that the Pakistan withdrawal was not just the consequence of overwhelming Indian military superiority, but the United States' pressure on Pakistan. Soon, senior politicians joined the skeptics. One former prime minister, Chandra Shekhar, flatly said that:

In the beginning, the Defence Minister [George Fernandes], talked about considering the idea to give safe passage to the intruders. It was ridiculed and rejected. Now the same is being implemented. Whatever may be the claim, in reality it is a ceasefire and safe passage.[33]

[33] "Kargil Has Witnessed an Invasion," *Hindustan Times* (New Delhi), 18 July 1999.

Chandra Shekhar's views may not have been finely nuanced, but they were buttressed in the public imagination by the Union defence minister's bizarre wartime assertions. On 13 May 1999, Fernandes described the shelling in Kargil as "sporadic," a somewhat odd description of artillery fire that had claimed the 121 Independent Infantry Brigade's ammunition dump and several other installations. A day later, he promised that the intrusion would be vacated "within two days." As late as 29 May, he peddled the outright lie that Indian troops in Dras had flushed out infiltrators, and "restored the Line of Control."[34] No one could blame either journalists or the public for being somewhat skeptical when victories in the area were, this time truthfully, announced later. By September, news had also broken that the disgraced commander of the 121 Brigade, Surinder Singh, had months prior to the war issued repeated warnings of large-scale infiltration into the sector, which his superiors chose to ignore.[35] The army denied there had been any such warnings. Soon afterwards, the documents appeared in facsimile form, along with reports that Singh's superior, Major General V. S. Budhwar, had been busy at about the same time using his troops to hunt for wildlife to inhabit a zoo he was determined to build in Leh.[36] Stories that troops were ill equipped for high-altitude warfare also circulated widely.

As I noted earlier, there are no existing compilations of mass-media reports across languages and regions, nor scientific studies of their impact. We therefore have no way of judging whether reports of this kind had any presence outside the confines of the English-language press. Nor are there any empirical data on how widespread skepticism about official claims of comprehensive victory was. Other damaging media exposés – the Indian failure to recapture point 5353-meters in the Dras sector and, above all, the *Tehelka.com* sting operation which covertly videotaped top politicians receiving bribes in return for helping journalists posing as arms agents to gain contracts – were yet to occur. It is possible, then, that criticism of the official conduct of the war was peripheral to public discourse in the 1999 elections. Fernandes or some army officials may have been reviled, but that in itself does not mean there was any widespread belief the Kargil conflict had been mishandled.

---

[34] "Govt. Double Speak on Kargil," *The Tribune* (New Delhi), 5 June 1999. The article contains an excellent collection of Fernandes' increasingly erratic wartime proclamations.

[35] Nitin A. Gokhale and Ajith Pillai, "The War that Should Never Have Been," *Outlook* (New Delhi), 6 September 1999. The official denial of this report was enabled by the fact that it incorrectly referred to a briefing note as a letter, a somewhat frivolous ground for objection.

[36] Praveen Swami, "The Kargil Story," *Frontline* (Chennai), 10 November 2000.

One undeniable fact was however at the forefront of public conscious-ness, imprinted there by daily newspaper and broadcast reports on con-tinued killings in Jammu and Kashmir. Troops had to be withdrawn from both the two principal zones of the state of Jammu and Kashmir during the war.[37] This enabled a generalized escalation of terrorist violence. Second, the summer of 1999 was pockmarked by a series of ugly mass killings of Hindus, both in the Jammu region and in Kashmir. Twelve brick-kiln workers from Madhya Pradesh and Uttar Pradesh were killed at Sandu, near Anantnag, on 29 June.[38] Then, on 1 July, five more Hindus were killed near Mendhar, as retaliation for a Hindu man marrying a Muslim woman. This was followed in quick time by the killing of fifteen more at Lihota, in the district of Doda. All this was punctuated by the first major *fidayeen* (suicide squad) attack, on the Border Security Force sector head-quarters in Bandipur on 23 July.[39] These killings had an immediate political impact on the Hindu-dominated areas of Jammu, particularly within the city from which it takes its name and the rural regions south of the Chenab. The existence of a national mass media ensured that the impact of the rising levels of violence did not stay contained in this region alone.

Mass killings were, of course, not new. The summer of 1998 had witnessed the massacre of 104 Hindus in four major attacks.[40] What was different this time around was that the killings came not as a counterpoint to an otherwise unexceptional security situation, but amidst a general collapse of the internal security system and claims of an overwhelming victory against Pakistan. Newspaper readers did not in general have access to official data, but they must have drawn their own conclusions from the reports before them. What the data show is that in the summer and autumn of 1999, more civilians and security force personnel were being killed by terrorists than at any point in the past. The terrorist offensive was facing little resistance, since these killings were being achieved in fewer acts of violence than before. Worst of all, from the point of view of Indian security, the number of terrorists killed for every security force trooper killed had declined to all-time low levels. Kargil and Kashmir were, in popular imagination and in fact, inextricably linked together. The victory in Kargil, unequivocal, qualified, or imagined, had clearly not brought an end to the war in Kashmir; quite the opposite had come to pass (Table 10.3).

---

[37] Praveen Swami, *The Kargil War* (New Delhi: Left Word, 1999), 76.
[38] Praveen Swami, "Another Summer of Killings," *Frontline* (Chennai), 30 July 1999.
[39] Praveen Swami, "Massacres and Cold Facts," *Frontline* (Chennai), 13 August 2002.
[40] *Ibid.*

Table 10.3 An overview of the "pro-active" policy

Period	Attacks on security forces	Security forces killed	Non-Muslim civilians killed by terrorists	Muslim civilians killed by terrorists	Terrorists killed	Terrorists killed per security force killed
1988	6	1	0	29	1	1.00
1989	49	13	6	73	0	0.00
1990	1098	132	177	679	183	1.39
1991	1999	185	34	549	614	3.32
1992	3413	177	67	747	873	4.93
1993	2573	216	88	891	1328	6.15
1994	2593	220	104	635	1851	8.41
1995	2253	258	97	1013	1338	5.19
1996	2433	241	114	1175	1194	4.95
1997	2116	203	64	717	1177	5.80
1998	1211	230	159	678	1045	4.54
1999 Jan	78	17	5	33	43	2.53
1999 Feb	87	24	29	43	106	4.42
1999 Mar	91	20	4	41	85	4.25
1999 Apr	86	14	2	76	69	4.93
1999 May	97	27	8	48	71	2.63
1999 Jun	95	32	13	85	71	2.22
1999 July	72	14	32	86	58	4.14
1999 Aug	143	70	5	81	114	1.63
1999 Sep	153	28	0	80	145	5.18
1999 Oct	257	18	0	57	127	7.06
1999 Nov	97	46	0	36	104	2.26
1999 Dec	111	46	0	57	89	1.93
Total 1999	**1367**	**356**	**98**	**723**	**1082**	**3.04**

Source: Union Ministry of Home Affairs, New Delhi. Note that these data are the Ministry's internal data, and vary marginally from the data published in its Annual Report, which is in fact compiled from legal records maintained from the Jammu and Kashmir Police. The Police records are skewed by a variety of reporting errors, which the Ministry of Home Affairs seeks to audit and correct in its in-house data.

BJP claims of triumph may have also been read against its earlier claims of impending victory in the larger war in Kashmir. Former Prime Minister P. V. Narasimha Rao managed to take credit for a decisive Indian victory in the war against terrorism in Punjab. His main tactic was to maintain a stoic silence on these issues, and had he failed in Punjab, few would have known he had attempted something in the first place. The BJP's problems were the outcome of its louder approach to terrorism. Even as Pakistani troops had started to build up positions in Kargil, the party had begun proclaiming it was well on the way to a Punjab-style victory in Jammu and Kashmir. Union Home Minister L. K. Advani was advertised as a warrior who would cast aside decades of effete liberal policy, and crush Pakistan-backed terrorism. The RSS house journal, *The Organizer*, argued that:

After the Valley being virtually cleansed of the Hindu Kashmiri Pandits by the Pakistan secret service ISID, the Kashmiri Muslims' ego having been satisfied, there is less sting in their estrangement with the Central Government. Added to this is a new breed of terrorist mercenaries whose inhuman treatment of their women-folk has further intensified their ire at the aliens. And the collapse of their main bread-earner, the tourism industry, due to the scaring away of all tourists by the senseless killings of foreign tourists by the Pakistan-controlled terrorist organizations which in turn robbed the common Kashmiri people of their livelihood. Home Minister L. K. Advani's pro-active Kashmir policy effectively checked trans-border influx of troublemakers. All these have helped the Kashmir Valley to steadily, though not quite so fast, return to their earlier pleasant days of a "Happy Valley."[41]

"Happy Valley" needs no comment; other elements of this polemic demand attention. The term "pro-active" had been introduced into official discourse in the context of the Pokhran-II tests, when Advani for the first time made express a linkage between India's nuclear capabilities and its counter-terrorist objectives in Jammu and Kashmir. After a party meeting, he announced a new "pro-active" approach to "deal firmly and strongly with Pakistan's hostile designs and activities in Kashmir." "India's decisive step to become a nuclear weapon state has brought about a qualitatively new stage in Indo-Pak relations, particularly in finding a lasting solution to the Kashmir problem," he said, demanding that "Islamabad should realize the change in the geo-strategic situation." The VHP near simultaneously announced plans to build a *Shakti Peeth* (shrine to cosmic power) at Pokhran.[42] Advani again picked up the theme at a conference of Chief Ministers in Srinagar a week later. This time, a

[41] Shrikant Joshi, "Call of Jammu Kashmir," *The Organizer* 50, no. 34 (New Delhi), 24 March 1999.
[42] Federation of Atomic Scientists, "17 Days in May: Chronology of Indian Nuclear Weapons Tests," http://fas.org/nuke/guide/india/nuke/chron.htm.

"pro-active" policy was defined as consisting of four principles: the strengthening of democratic process in the state; the isolation of terrorist groups from the people; pro-active response to neutralize the terrorists; and, finally, galvanizing developmental activity.[43] The meeting came two days after the minister had visited Premnagar to address an all-Hindu rally, held to condemn the massacre of twenty-six members of a wedding procession at Chapnari, near Doda.[44] At that meeting, Advani asserted, "a ruler who cannot protect his people has no business to govern." He was careful not to make plain whether he meant himself, the prime minister, or Jammu and Kashmir Chief Minister Farooq Abdullah.

Kargil rudely interrupted the warm nuclear glow that clouded the Hindu Right's imagination. Wide sections of the Indian public appeared bewildered by just why a weapon that had been guaranteed to subdue Pakistan appeared to have done nothing to either prevent or end the Kargil war. Among the Hindu Right, the sentiment was even more intense. At one wartime rally led by Advani, the party faithful chanted a slogan at once anti-Muslim and anti-Vajpayee, demanding that members of the minority religious community leave for Pakistan by the New Delhi to Lahore bus service initiated by the prime minister.[45] Stung by early Indian reverses, and the prospect of a lost war, the RSS journal *Panchjanya* drew on Hindu mythology to demand that Vajpayee use the ultimate weapon:

The time has come again for India's Bheema to tear open the breasts of these infidels and purify the soiled tresses of Draupadi with blood. Pakistan will not listen just like that. We have a centuries-old debt to settle with this mindset. It is the same demon that has been throwing a challenge at Durga since the time of Mohammad Bin Qasim. Arise, Atal Behari. Who knows if fate has destined you to be the author of the final chapter of this long story? For what have we manufactured bombs? For what have we exercised the nuclear option?[46]

If the victory at Kargil allowed the Hindu Right some salve for the wound inflicted by the failure to use nuclear weapons, many Indians were less than relieved at the way events were moving. By January, any euphoria about Kargil was dissipated by the release of three top terrorists, Mohammad Masood Azhar, Syed Omar Sheikh, and Mushtaq Zargar for

---

[43] "Center Formulating Four-Pronged Strategy for Jammu and Kashmir: Advani," *Press Trust of India*, 24 June 1998.

[44] "Pakistan Sponsored Terrorism must be Crushed: Advani," *The Hindu* (New Delhi), 23 June 1998.

[45] Asghar Ali Engineer, "Communalism and Communal Violence 1999," *Economic and Political Weekly* (Mumbai), 4 February 2000, www.epw.org.in/showArticles.php?root=2000&leaf=01&filename=2838&filetype=html. The slogan was "Lahore bus *se* Lahore *jao*" (Go to Lahore on the Lahore bus).

[46] Editorial, *Panchjanya* (New Delhi), 20 June 1999.

the safety of passengers on board a hijacked Indian Airlines flight. The New Year's Eve hijacking illustrated that the stated official concern about the need for an aggressive anti-terrorist policy had not translated into coherent practical measures. Its significance transcended the immediate. Azhar and Sheikh were to engage in a series of terrorist attacks on India, as well as the subsequent kidnapping and murder of the *Wall Street Journal's* Daniel Pearl. For India, the real issue was that Kargil notwithstanding, Pakistan-backed terrorists seemed able to hold the Indian state hostage. India, for its part, seemed to have no means available at its disposal to inflict retaliatory costs on Pakistan. The country's best-known police officer pointed out that:

the specific reverses that India suffered as a consequence of the blunder at Amritsar, and the subsequent and sub-optimal resolution of the hijacking crisis at Kandahar, have limited significance. To the extent, however, that a nation fails to correct the lapses of the past, the basic flaws in its strategic perspectives and institutions, it is condemned to repeat its mistakes at incremental costs to the national interest. At some point of time, the processes of attrition will carry it beyond the point of return or recovery, and the cumulative consequences, then, would be disastrous.

The evidence available suggests that we are currently set upon this course to catastrophe and lack the will and the vision to institute satisfactory correctives.[47]

The word "Kargil" figured only twice in Prime Minister Vajpayee's Independence Day speech of 2000. Perhaps the electoral reverses of the previous year had sunk home; perhaps he believed the "pro-active" approach had failed. The speech contained a drastic discontinuity from the BJP's post-Pokhran-II polemical aggression on Jammu and Kashmir. Drawing on the Urdu-language poet Sahir Ludhianvi, Vajpayee now laid the grounds for a Jammu and Kashmir policy that would place emphasis on domestic and international diplomacy. "This is the age for resolving differences, not for prolonging disputes," the prime minister said. "The people of Jammu, Kashmir, and Ladakh are tired of violence and blood-shed. They are craving for peace. We need to apply the salve of brother-hood on the wounded body of Jammu and Kashmir. That is why I recently said that India is prepared to apply the balm for Kashmir's agony within the framework of *Insaniyat* (humanity)."[48] The term *Insaniyat* was a self-conscious departure from past Indian insistence that any dialogue with

[47] K. P. S. Gill, "Terrorism, Institutional Collapse & Emergency Response Protocols," *Faultlines* 4, www.satp.org/satporgtp/publication/faultlines/volume4/Fault4-kps.htm.

[48] Atal Behari Vajpayee, "Prime Minister's Independence Day Speech, 2000," http://pmindia.nic.in/infocentre/curr_speeches.htm.

secessionist or terrorist groups be conducted within the framework of the Indian constitution.

Put simply, a hard-line posture on Pakistan had not delivered dividends. With that lesson learned, the decks had been cleared for alternative strategies to be attempted.

Conclusion: war, terrorists, and temples

Elections notwithstanding, no one in India can plausibly deny that the conflict in Jammu and Kashmir has acquired a centrality to Indian national consciousness it perhaps did not have two decades ago: this, perhaps, is the most abiding political legacy of the Kargil war. This consciousness has manifested itself through a variety of media. At least four major films have been made on the Kargil war since 2003, including the Hindi-language *LoC: Kargil, Dhoop*, and *Lakshya*, and the Malayalam-language *Keerthi Chakra*. Less visible, but no less significant, are the large numbers of streets and public squares named after war heroes in major Indian cities and towns.

What is more difficult to document, but no less evident, is the permeation of the conflict in Jammu and Kashmir into the everyday content of Indian political life. Conversations on the 2002 violence in Gujarat were peppered with references to events in Jammu and Kashmir; university seats in several areas are reserved for refugees from the state; the steady flow of pilgrims to the shrine at Amarnath each summer, a pilgrimage twice attacked by terrorists, speaks for itself. In a country gripped by the multiple fissures and tensions brought about by rapid integration in a global capitalist economy, it is easy to argue that both Indian nationhood and Hindu identity are at stake in Jammu and Kashmir. This, predictably, is a terrain of engagement the Islamic Right is eager to widen. Two competing communalisms, both of which have appropriated the Kashmir conflict for their own ends, feed and inform each other.

It is possible the BJP-led government that took power in the Kargil election sensed this sharpening of communal tensions, and hoped to capitalize on them. In December 2001, after terrorists stormed India's Parliament House building, Prime Minister Vajpayee ordered a military mobilization that brought both countries to the edge of war. Without being certain that such action had mass legitimacy, it is unlikely that the government would have risked this course of action. For Hindu neo-conservatives, there was little doubt what the core issue in fact was. In March 2002, in the midst of the India–Pakistan military standoff, two terrorists stormed the Raghunath Temple in Jammu, one of the shrines most venerated by Hindus. A few days later, on 4 April, the VHP's Giriraj

Kishore made an extraordinary and unprecedented express linkage between conflict in Jammu and Kashmir and broader communal questions in India:

> Acharya Giri Raj said first they cleared the Valley of the Hindus and now they want to terrorize the Hindus of Jammu by making attempts to strike at the shrines like Vaishno Devi and Raghunath temple. He warned those behind this game plan that they should also understand that they too had many shrines related to their religion in [the] rest of the country which can be made target[s] in case terrorists continue with the attack on Hindus' religious places in J&K [Jammu and Kashmir].[49]

An unstated line was crossed here. Even Bal Thackeray, who routinely abuses Muslims at large, only said of communal massacres in India that if "Hindus are going to be massacred in Hindustan, then let the government declare emergency in the country, or at least martial law in Jammu & Kashmir."[50] Since Kishore's statement was made, Muslims have repeatedly been threatened by the Hindu Right with collective reprisals for communal killings in Jammu and Kashmir. VHP president Ashok Singhal, for example, told journalists on 23 July 2002, that "Jehadis should keep in mind that today Hindus are united and competent enough to protect the honor and dignity." "What happened in Gujarat," he continued, "is a clear indication for the *jehadis* that Hindus will not tolerate atrocities any more."[51]

I have argued elsewhere that hate polemic of this kind can be debunked by simple recourse to publicly available data: Muslim civilians in Jammu and Kashmir have, in fact, been the principal victims of the *jehadi* groups fighting in their name.[52] But the important issue here is not fact *per se*, but fact as it is perceived to be. There is little doubt that massacres of Hindus have contributed to the legitimization of the extreme right postures represented by figures like Kishore. I believe these massacres, and continuing Pakistan-backed violence in and outside Jammu and Kashmir, have had an impact that transcends the extreme right.

Interestingly, the rise of Hindu chauvinist tendencies has been mirrored by the growth of Islamist forces within Jammu and Kashmir, as also elsewhere in India.[53] Despite the forward movement evident in the ongoing peace processes within Jammu and Kashmir and between India and Pakistan, Islamists too have strengthened their constituency by

---

[49] "VHP to Observe April 8 as Nation-Wide Black Day," *Indian Express / Himalayan Mail* (Jammu), 5 April 2002.
[50] "Thackeray Calls for Martial Law," *Hindustan Times* (New Delhi), 15 August 2000.
[51] Praveen Swami, "A Massacre and a Message," *Frontline* (Chennai), 16 August 2002.
[52] *Ibid.*
[53] Praveen Swami, "A Taliban-coloured Dawn," *The Hindu* (Chennai), 11 July 2006, www.hindu.com/2006/07/11/stories/2006071104630800.htm.

representing India as a predatory Hindu entity. Although the rise of the Ram Janambhoomi movement had little street-level impact in the state, it is reasonable to suppose that the consolidation of the Hindu-nationalist neoconservatism may have led some in India's only Muslim-majority province to question their future in a mainly Hindu India. Sheikh Mohammad Abdullah, who made the fateful decision to bring Jammu and Kashmir into the Indian Union, had anticipated the possibility as early as 1951:

Certain tendencies have been asserting themselves in India, which may in the future convert it into a religious state wherein the interests of Muslims will be jeopardized. This would happen if communal organization had a dominant hand in the Government and the Congress ideals of the equality of all communities were to give way to religious intolerance.[54]

Are we heading, then, toward an inevitable sundering of Hindu from Muslim, a finishing of the unfinished business of partition many have long sought? The fact is that Jammu and Kashmir has increasingly figured as a motif in all-India communal violence. In July 2000, Muslim homes and businesses in Gujarat were torched after terrorist attacks on Hindu pilgrims visiting the shrine of Amarnath, near Pahalgam in Kashmir.[55] At the end of that year, the funeral of an Indian army soldier killed in Jammu and Kashmir sparked off similar violence in Maharashtra.[56] Through the summer of 2002, we have seen what a Hindu-fundamentalist India might look like. The terrible violence in Gujarat was not provoked by events in Jammu and Kashmir, but it is foolish to pretend events there have not fed, informed, and legitimized the fascism we are now witness to. War might not win elections, a lesson that was demonstrated when the BJP-led government was voted out of office in 2004 despite its aggressive posture on Pakistan and use of communal mobilization. However, continued violence has legitimized Hindu neoconservatism, a fact with potentially fateful consequences for Indian politics notwithstanding the defeat of the BJP.

Perhaps the time has come, then, to concern ourselves with not just what Jammu and Kashmir means to Pakistan or the world, but also to ask what it means to India. This is not, after all, just a game of cricket.

[54] Sheikh Mohammad Abdullah, "Inaugural Address to the Jammu and Kashmir Constituent Assembly," cited in *The Report of the State Autonomy Commission* (Jammu: Government of Jammu and Kashmir, 1999), 150.
[55] Asghar Ali Engineer, "Communal Riots 2000," *Economic and Political Weekly* (Mumbai), 27 January 2001, www.epw.org.in/showArticles.php?root=2001&leaf=01&filename=2109&filetype=html.
[56] Asghar Ali Engineer, "Communal Riots: Review of 2001," *Economic and Political Weekly* (Mumbai), 12 January 2002, www.epw.org.in/showArticles.php?root=2002&leaf=01&filename=3919&filetype=html.

11   The Kargil conflict's impact on Pakistani politics and society

Saeed Shafqat

The Kargil conflict evokes contradictory images and responses among Pakistani elites and the public. Although precious few people in Pakistan understand what actually occurred on the frigid heights in the Kargil-Dras sector of Indian-held Kashmir, popular perceptions of the conflict have profoundly affected politics and civil–military relations in Pakistan. Seven years after the Kargil conflict, in his memoirs General Pervez Musharraf claimed that the prime minister Nawaz Sharif was fully informed about the operation, that Kargil was a successful operation, and that the prime minister showed a lack of statesmanship by running to Washington and quickly yielding to US pressure to withdraw troops from Kargil.[1] Nawaz Sharif was quick to refute Musharraf's claims. He categorically denied any knowledge about the operation and claimed that he learned about the incursion from Indian prime minister Vajpayee.[2] This controversy led political leaders to demand investigation by a Parliamentary Committee. Some retired generals alleged that Kargil compromised Pakistan's position on Kashmir.[3] These allegations notwithstanding, the evidence about Kargil remains murky and both civil and military elites continue to contest the facts.

This chapter provides four main observations about the impact of the Kargil crisis on Pakistani politics and society. First, elite opinion in Pakistan remains fractured. Analysis of the Kargil operation – its purpose, its conduct, and its resolution – varies widely in press accounts and commentary, allowing different commentators to use selective media coverage to articulate their messages for their audience. The government's insistence on the *mujahideen* cover story significantly complicated not only the Pakistani media's reporting of the conflict but also Pakistan's

---

[1] Pervez Musharraf, *In the Line of Fire: A Memoir* (London: Simon and Schuster, 2006), 95–98.
[2] Nawaz Sharif's interview with Tahir Siddique, *The Herald* (Karachi), June 2006, 38–39.
[3] Raja Zafar ul-Haq, Chairman PML-N, www.dailytimes.com.pk/default.asp?page=2006%5C10%5C20%05Cstory 20-10-2006.

media-management strategy. Because Kargil was a clandestine operation, the Pakistan army was not in a position to provide the national media access to the war zone.[4] In contrast, the Indian media was much more unified and coherent, and played an effective part in the Indian government's public relations strategy after it recovered from its early surprise.

Second, the Kargil conflict had an enormous impact on Pakistan's domestic politics. The mainstream political parties – the ruling Pakistan Muslim League (PML-N) and the opposition Pakistan Peoples Party (PPP) – were conspicuously silent during the crisis. In contrast, the religious right exploited the crisis to mobilize public opinion and generate political support. The religious parties attacked the civilian government and occasionally made spiteful comments about the military's role. Pakistani religious groups insisted that the military and the *jehadi* groups had waged a successful war, but that their valiant gains were lost on the political front by Prime Minister Nawaz Sharif who caved in to Indian-influenced US pressures and ordered the withdrawal of forces from tactically superior positions. After the Washington Declaration, the religious parties became more strident in demanding Prime Minister Nawaz Sharif's removal.[5]

The third argument is that the Kargil crisis widened the gulf between the civilian and military leadership, and that ultimately led to the October military coup. Apparently, Kargil did not generate any serious discontent within the army's junior officer corps or *jawans* (soldiers) against the senior military command, but it does appear to have caused resentment against the civilian leadership – further discrediting political parties and the democratic process in the eyes of the Pakistan military.

Finally, the conflict increased the discomfort already apparent in Washington and other foreign capitals regarding Pakistan's ability to become a responsible nuclear weapons power. Conversely, it heightened India's reputation as a moderate, responsible nuclear state, and marked a

---

[4] The nearest media reporters could access the military front was by the nearby garrison of Skardu, about 60 miles from the battlefield, almost a day's journey by road.

[5] Addressing a protest rally at Nasir Bagh, Lahore on 24 July 1999, Qazi Hussain Ahmad demanded: "it is imperative for the resolution of Kashmir issue and for the safety and solidarity of the country that Nawaz Sharif be removed from the office of the Prime Minister." Qazi charged that Nawaz had committed "an unforgivable crime by showing cowardice against a besieged army in Kashmir. It was shameful for the head of the only nuclear Muslim state to accept becoming a satellite state of India, despite having a historical and tactical edge over the enemy. The accord is nothing except to implement American New World Order with Indian hegemony in the region." Quoted in *The Nation* (Lahore), 25 July 1999. For more on this theme, see, Zahid Hussain, "Beating a Hasty Retreat," *Newsline*, July 1999, 21–23.

vivid enhancement in Indo-US relations, while Pakistan struggled to recover its reputation.

This chapter analyzes the tensions and contradictions that emerged in Pakistani politics and society in the wake of the Kargil conflict. The first section analyzes the literature and print media narratives of Pakistani commentators. The second section explains Kargil's impact on Pakistani domestic politics. The third section explains how and why national and religious political parties, *jehadi* groups, and the military perceived and responded to the conflict and its aftermath. The fourth and fifth sections analyze how the mismanagement of the crisis resulted in the military coup and created further civil–military tensions after the coup.

The Pakistani print media's Kargil

A review of Pakistani journalism on the Kargil affair reveals that elite opinion is fractured. There were and still are divergent, albeit overlapping, views on the causes and conduct of the Kargil operation and, even more so, on its outcome. The outcome of the war came under more public scrutiny and debate than the actual conduct of the war itself because the media had (and still has) little access to reliable information about the actual conduct of the war. Thus journalists had to confine themselves to reporting on the tangible results of the conflict. As the crisis unfolded, domestic criticism increased as the international media uncovered Pakistan's involvement in the conflict and as the international community intensified calls for Pakistan to completely withdraw its military forces back across the Kashmir Line of Control (LoC). Several Pakistani groups expressed their disapproval: the *jehadi* groups and religious parties who felt that Prime Minister Nawaz Sharif had given in to the Americans; the English print media for the government's ill-conceived operational and diplomatic planning; and the armed forces after the prime minister tried to blame them for the whole Kargil episode.

A qualitative distinction must be drawn between the Urdu and English print media and the mindsets they reflect and promote.[6] However, it needs to be recognized that the dominant discourse in Pakistani print media with regard to the conflict has been Islamist and realist. The liberal worldview is marginal and largely confined to the English print media. Urdu print media tend to be more sensational, less investigative, and also have a tendency to portray the views and demands of religious groups with

---

[6] This interpretation is based on several conversations with Pakistani journalists, particularly Khaled Ahmed of the *Friday Times* (Lahore) and I. A. Rehman and Altaf Hasan Qureshi of the *Urdu Digest*.

great passion and strong rhetoric. Despite these limitations, the Urdu media do mobilize public opinion in Pakistan.

The English print media has matured considerably. It is more critical and less sensational than the Urdu media. It also tends to be progressive, liberal, conscious of its credibility, and generally more responsible. While the analysis and commentary in the English-language press are of high quality, most English-language journalists are not investigative reporters. This is evident in the lacunae in the commentary presented in the English-language media, although it is notable that by July 1999, several credible and highly critical pieces on the Kargil operation had appeared in several of the country's English-language newspapers and monthlies.[7]

Two related factors significantly constrained the ability of the Pakistani media to report and make educated commentary on the Kargil operation. First, the government had made it quite clear that this was a *mujahideen* operation, with only the political and moral support of the Pakistan government. Some commentators ran with this analysis, even after it became apparent that this was simply a government cover story for an entirely military operation. Second, the government restricted access to the Northern Areas – though it is unclear how eager the press was to travel and report from Skardu or elsewhere in this remote part of Pakistan. These governmental limitations were critical to keep the *mujahideen* cover story alive, and they necessarily limited investigative reporting. Kargil war coverage was downplayed in the Pakistani media. This contrasts markedly with India's media coverage of the conflict, which was able to bring the campaign onto the televisions in millions of Indian homes. Kargil became India's first "media war," which helped create more support among people for the Indian government's actions. Consequently, the media-management strategies of India succeeded and those of Pakistan failed.

Urdu- and English-speaking journalists have different mindsets. They reflect two different worldviews and voice the concerns of different constituencies in Pakistani society. English journalists are better educated and informed, and therefore are more professional in their approach. Nevertheless, Urdu newspapers have a much wider audience: almost 90 percent of the newspaper-reading population read an Urdu newspaper. The Urdu print media play a crucial role in shaping public opinion and

---

[7] See, for example, Maleeha Lodhi, "The Kargil Crisis: Anatomy of a Debacle," *Newsline*, July 1999, and Ardeshir Cowasjee, "Lesson Learnt," *Dawn*, 11 July 1999; "Endgame," *Dawn*, 18 July 1999. M. Ilyas Khan has written several pieces critical of Kargil's handling. See "Life After Kargil," *The Herald* (Karachi), July 2000, 24–30; "The Waiting Game," *The Herald* (Karachi), July 2003, 36–41; and "Business as Usual," *The Herald* (Karachi), July 2003, 38–39.

informing the public on a very wide variety of issues. The Urdu media do feature some diversity of views; however, their sensational style on occasion can inflame emotions. How effectively do they promote democratic norms versus authoritarian tendencies? Opinions differ, but by and large academics and policymakers agree that the Urdu print media have developed to a level that their voices cannot be muzzled – even though they are a little more susceptible to manipulation, regulation, disinformation, and control as compared to the English print media.

The degree of freedom of the Pakistani press can be measured by analyzing the wide variety of coverage the print media gave to India's May 1998 nuclear-test explosions, the February 1999 Lahore peace process, and the Kargil conflict. Urdu media reporting on the May 1998 Indian nuclear tests was very outspoken and placed tremendous pressure on the Pakistan government to respond in kind.[8] There was a healthy debate on the Lahore Declaration.[9] But the Urdu media discourse on Kargil mainly reproduced the *jehadi* euphoria that had become so prevalent throughout Pakistani society.[10] These episodes showed that the print media had become an important barometer of public opinion and also an effective instrument used to influence public opinion on specific issues. Ironically, the civilian and military governments in Pakistan continue to control, regulate, and suppress independent voices, but both the Urdu- and English-language journalism communities have shown considerable vigor and vitality in defending freedom of expression. The coverage of the Kargil crisis was a good test case of freedom of journalistic expression in Pakistan.

Kargil revealed two facets of the Pakistani print media. On the one hand, investigative reporting is still weak. The journalism community had neither the resources nor the will to report on the actual conduct of the war. It is obvious that the government was not keen to provide any opportunity for journalists to report on the nature and conduct of the military operations, especially in the early weeks of the crisis. The investigative role was covered largely by the Western and Indian media. On the other hand, many Pakistani political commentators were strident in presenting a critical appraisal of the conflict. For purposes of convenience and brevity, the commentators will be divided into three categories: liberals, Islamists, and realists.

Liberal commentators took the lead in criticizing the country's civil–military leadership, informing the citizens, and also defining the public

[8] See especially the stories appearing in *Daily Jang* and *Nawa-I-Waqat*, 8–30 May 1998.
[9] See *Nawa-I-Waqat*, 15 February to 15 March 1999.
[10] See *Daily Ausaf* (Lahore) and *Daily Pakistan* (Lahore).

discourse. Most liberal narratives revolved around the theme of injury to national pride, humiliation, bankruptcy of ruling elites, and betrayal of the people. They were critical of faulty military planning and incompetent civilian leadership. Thus, it was not the war, but the manner of withdrawal that was perceived as humiliating and compromising to "national dignity."[11]

Liberal commentators articulated the outrage against the Washington Declaration in terms of injury to national pride, rather than military or diplomatic defeat. From the perspective of most of these journalists, the dominance of the military in Pakistan's political system and the military elite's attitude toward politics have been the primary causes of Pakistan's problems. The Kargil intrusion was portrayed as yet another manifestation of this unending story. The liberal commentators echoed the popular question: will Pakistani elites ever shed their adventurous and reckless policies? Inadvertently, these narratives also gave boost to anti-American sentiment among the English-speaking classes in the country. These writings produced skepticism about any sympathy from the Clinton administration toward Pakistan's position.[12] The liberal journalists thus criticized the military's handling of the Kargil operation, the incompetence of the civilian leadership, and the American "tilt" toward India. However, they offered no suggestion about how to escape the quagmire; nor did they provide an alternate vision of crisis management.

Interestingly, the Western media, particularly the British Broadcasting Corporation (BBC), provided some credible early reports that exposed the Pakistani military's support of the *mujahideen*.[13] Upon these reports, the Indian media launched a blistering attack on Pakistan as a state

---

[11] Ayaz Amir wrote in *Dawn* on 9 July 1999: "Kargil intrusion was a blunder, there was no reason to panic. Pakistan still had options before it which, if sensibly exercised, could have brought out a withdrawal without a minimum loss of national dignity." He repeated the same theme a month later: "humiliated in that crisis [Kargil] and subsequently humbled in Washington, our circumstances are now so reduced that India thinks it can push us around and get away with anything. So not only does it shoot our aircraft, it also has the gall to send in helicopters and steal the wreckage. It is a measure of our helplessness that we cannot completely stop the theft." *Dawn*, 13 August 1999. For a similar critique, see Irfan Hussain, "The Cost of Kargil," *Dawn*, 14 August 1999; Ardeshir Cowasjee, "Lesson Learnt," *Dawn*, 11 July 1999; "Endgame," *Dawn*, 18 July 1999; and "Non-official Component," *Dawn*, 19 September 1999.

[12] According to one June 1999 commentary, "Pakistan's misfortunes" climaxed when the US House Foreign Relations Committee, "adopted with an overwhelming majority [22–5 vote] an anti-Pakistan resolution accusing it of precipitating the Kargil conflict and urging President Clinton to consider opposing the release of financial assistance to Pakistan from lending agencies unless the Pakistani forces were withdrawn." Hasan Ali Shahzeb, "Clueless in Washington," *Newsline*, July 1999, 23.

[13] The BBC reporting is available at www.bbc.co.uk/hi/English/world/south_asia/05July1999.

sponsor of terrorists, particularly targeting the military as "rogue," adventurous, and out of the control of the civilian leadership.[14] The Indian media and commentators were skillful in appealing to the sensibilities of the West that the military in Pakistan was the real culprit as it defied and deceived the civilian leadership. From the Indian perspective, success would mean "taming the Pakistan army" and convincing others to declare Pakistan a "terrorist state."[15]

Islamist commentators, mostly in the Urdu press, focused their attention not on domestic factors in Pakistan, but rather on the perceived hostility of India and the United States. Urdu commentaries argued that a growing Washington–New Delhi conspiracy had targeted Islamic forces, which in their view were gaining momentum in Pakistan, particularly with the emergence of the Taliban in Afghanistan.[16] The Islamists advocated moral and material support to various Muslim groups, from Chechnya to Kashmir, which were combating the ruthlessness of the repressive states. They believed that the United States perceived the rise and success of these pan-Islamic movements as a challenge to its global hegemony.

---

[14] J. N. Dixit made a similar assertion, "Pakistan cannot be trusted ... The objective should be to exhaust Pakistan and convince it that its military /terrorist misadventures will not be allowed to succeed." In "A Defining Moment," *Guns and Yellow Roses: Essays on the Kargil War*, ed. Sankarshan Thakur (New Delhi: HarperCollins, 1999), 205.

[15] For example, Gurmeet Kanwal, a retired Indian army officer then still in uniform, expressed this anti-Pakistan-military sentiment: "India's problems in Kashmir will remain until Pakistan's army is tamed ... the real problem between India and Pakistan is the Pakistan army and its abnormal influence in Pakistan's affairs and not Kashmir or any other issue." Gurmeet Kanwal, "Nawaz Sharif's Damning Disclosures," *Pioneer*, 16 August 2000.

[16] The Islamist viewpoint was reflected by Urdu columnists such as Abdul Qadir Hasan in *Daily Jang*, Altaf Hasan Qureshi in *Urdu Digest*, Hamid Mir in *Daily Ausaf*, Mujeeb-ur-Rehamn Shami in *Weekly Zindigi*, and editorials of *Nawa-I-Waqat*. *Monthly Baidar Digest (Urdu)*, a self-declared mouthpiece of intellectual and philosophical activities of the Mujahideen-e-Islam, extensively reported on the *jehadi* groups, their political and military connections, and stories of jihad. Its editorials portrayed Osama bin Laden as a holy warrior, the Taliban as a model Islamic government, and America as a "great Satan" bent on destroying them. See the issues of June 1998, October 2000, December 2000, January 2001. The trader-merchants of Lahore apparently support the *Monthly Baidar Digest*. For fascinating coverage of the views of Pakistani opinion builders on Kargil, particularly the perceptions of a leader of Lashkar-e-Taiba and the editors of *Nawa-I-Waqat* and *Ausaf*, see Bharat Bhushan, "In the 'Enemy Country,'" in Thakut, ed., *Guns and Yellow Roses*, 95–122. For an enthusiastic depiction of the military-*jehadi* connection and claims of how "*Mujahideen* humbled the might of India" and why "*Mujahideen* of Kargil" and "*Mujahideen* of Afghanistan" have been denied the fruits of their struggles, see an interesting interpretation by the former chief of the Pakistan army, General (retd.) Mirza Aslam Beg, "Kargil Withdrawal and Rogue Army Image," *Defence Journal* (September 1999).

Islamist commentators were so convinced about the righteousness of their cause that they asserted the *mujahideen* were successful in imposing heavy casualties upon the Indian military fighting in the Kargil heights and elsewhere in Kashmir. To undermine the impending victory, this reporting maintained that the United States applied pressure on Pakistan and rescued India from an inevitable military defeat. The Islamist narratives constructed an anti-Islamic "axis of evil" led by the United States, India, and Israel. These narratives were conjectural at best. Yet, they had a profound impact on public consciousness in Pakistan. A significant number of Pakistanis believe that the United States and India cooperate in ways that are inimical to Muslim interests. This belief has grown even stronger in the aftermath of the US-led military campaigns in Afghanistan and Iraq and unrelated statements by American and Indian officials of the US–Indian strategic partnership.[17]

The realist position has been expressed mostly by former civil servants and academics who analyzed Kargil from the perspective of the endemic conflict between India and Pakistan. These commentaries highlighted the centrality of nuclear weapons, and implied how deterrence worked in keeping the conflict confined, and yet projected Kashmir as a potential "nuclear flash point." Some realists took an alarmist position and argued that the risks of strategic misperceptions, brinkmanship, and miscalculation could trigger a nuclear war between India and Pakistan. It is in this context that they weaved a link between Kashmir and nuclear weapons, and claimed the United States and India were conniving to weaken Pakistan's national security and nuclear program.[18]

Between the Kargil conflict and the terrorist attacks on the United States in September 2001, the liberal, Islamist, and realist narratives all reinforced the anti-American sentiment among the Pakistani populace. In the post-Kargil phase, the liberal, progressive, tolerant, and democratic

---

[17] See, for example, Maulana Tufail Muhammad, "Events September 11 and the Real Objectives of America," *Jang*, 12 April 2004, www.jang.com.pk/jang/apr2002-daily/09-04-2002. The former Jamaat-e-Islami chief contends that American Zionists who supported the Bush administration are promoting India to contain the Islamic world, while he also draws parallels between the conditions of Palestinians and the plight of the Kashmiris.

[18] See the realist views expressed by former Foreign Service officers Afzal Mahmud ("Seeing Kargil in Perspective," *Dawn*, 18 July 1999, and "India's Aggressive Posture," *Dawn*, 31 January 2000) and Tanvir Ahmad Khan ("Kashmir: The Global Context," *Dawn*, 13 July 1999). For a hawkish, deterrence-driven assessment of the Kargil conflict, see Shireen Mazari, "Low Intensity Conflicts: The New War in South Asia," *Defence Journal*, July 1999, and "Re-Examining Kargil," *Defence Journal*, June 2000. For a more full-blown account, see Shireen M. Mazari, *The Kargil Conflict 1999: Separating Fact from Fiction* (Islamabad: Ferozsons, 2003), esp. 42–63.

dispensations of Pakistani civil society were further constrained. The reporting on Kargil and its aftermath also brought to the surface the absence of consensus among the highest echelons of political and strategic decision-makers. At both the national and global levels, the intricate relationship between the Pakistani state and the Islamic militants became a matter of concern and debate. Kargil also roused speculation about the nature of the relationship between the mainstream religious political parties, such as Jamaat-e-Islami and Jamiat-ul-Ulema-e-Islam, and the *jehadi* groups. At the elite level, Kargil struck at the very roots of the government's relations with Pakistani religious groups. At the societal level, it showed how potent the religious groups had become in defining the parameters of public discourse in Pakistani society. However, once Prime Minister Nawaz Sharif visited Washington, DC on 4 July 1999 and accepted the regime's involvement in the conflict by agreeing to order a full withdrawal from the Kargil heights, the full public debate ensued.

It could be argued that Kargil provided the political elites and the mainstream national political parties with a great opportunity to build consensus and redefine relations with the military and the religious groups. However, the political leadership could not rise to the occasion and seize the moment. Had Prime Minister Nawaz Sharif after the Washington Declaration reached out to the political parties, various Islamic groups, and also the military perhaps a process could have been initiated to improve decision-making mechanisms in the Pakistani institutions and power elites. There was a real possibility – and a real need – to rebuild trust among the state institutions after the Kargil conflict and to focus the system on how to avoid the recurrence of such a debacle. Instead, the civilian leadership, obsessed with threats to its continued rule, spent most of its energy on devising ways to sort out the military.[19] This brought to the fore not the system-corrective but system-reactive responses from the liberal media: how to sort out the military. Kargil revealed an intense need in Pakistan to rebuild linkages between different institutions. However, there was no way to begin such a discussion without one side attempting to implicate the other for the "failure" of the Kargil operation. After the crisis, the relationship between Nawaz Sharif and the military was irreparably damaged.

---

[19] It is possible that the political fallout from the Kargil conflict was more of an excuse than a reason for the prime minister to reduce the influence of the military. After all, prior to this crisis, Nawaz Sharif successfully stripped all meaningful power from the office of the president and also the institution of the judiciary of Pakistan. He also forced Pervez Musharraf's predecessor, Jehangir Karamat, to resign as army chief.

The domestic political impact

Kargil was a clandestine operation, and the secret nature of the operation compelled the government to remain tight-lipped about it. Partially, but not entirely, as a consequence, the government had great difficulty in explaining the rationale of the intrusion and the subsequent fighting. In other words, the war itself had little or no effect on public consciousness, nor did the Pakistan government seem to have made any conscious effort to take the people into its confidence about the war effort – probably because the government never contemplated a war. The planners of Kargil never anticipated the profound impact the operation could have on the domestic politics and external relations of Pakistan.

First, the Pakistani public came to believe that the junior officers and *jawans* (soldiers) of the Pakistan army fought valiantly under adverse environmental conditions and the flawed war plans of the "generals." Kargil did produce skepticism among the populace about the war-winning strategies of the senior military leadership. Second, it brought the relationship between Pakistan-based *jehadi* groups and the Pakistani state under serious review and public scrutiny by the national and international media. Especially after 11 September 2001, the international community became more vigorous in exposing the links between the military and the *jehadi* groups and forced President Musharraf to reexamine its alleged involvement with some of these groups. Third, Kargil also revealed the disarray of pro-democracy and liberal forces in Pakistani civil society, which failed to realign and capitalize on the variance of interest between the *jehadi* groups and the military. Both the PML and the PPP found it difficult to build any bipartisan consensus on the after-effects of Kargil or to counter the rising tide of *jehadi* groups and their impact on society and politics. Fourth, following Kargil, the military was under pressure not only to redefine its relationship with the *jehadi* groups, but also to alter the entire framework of Pakistan's Kashmir policy, which was defined by the military. Since 1989, Pakistan had supported the uprising in Indian-held Kashmir by not constricting the *jehadi* groups in cross-border violations. In the post-Kargil phase, the United States asked Pakistan to curb what it viewed as "cross-border terrorism" and restore a peace process. By September and October 1999 Nawaz's government was showing indications of a future crackdown on *jehadi* groups, while simultaneously preparing to "sort out" the army chief. This sorting out ultimately precipitated the military takeover. No tears were shed over the ouster of Sharif; in fact, the government's credibility had sunk so low that the Pakistani public showed signs of relief and many welcomed the coup. Finally, the planners of Kargil had not imagined how its outcome would drastically alter US–Pakistan relations. Kargil brought a paradigm shift in the US–India relationship and redefined the terms of engagement for the United States in South Asia.

What follows is an assesment of how Kargil influenced the behavior of the religious political parties, the national political parties, and the armed forces. Each pursued an extremely narrow and partisan agenda, failing to evolve a coherent strategy or develop a national vision in a situation of national crisis. As noted at the outset of the chapter, the conflict exposed the absence of elite consensus, proportionately raised the dominance of the military in decision-making, and revealed that the civilian government's control over national security issues and the military was cosmetic and precarious. In particular, it examines how the religious political parties outmaneuvered their mainstream counterparts during and after the Kargil conflict, and also analyzes how the crisis – and subsequent blame game – exposed and then exacerbated the civil–military divide in Pakistan.

The religious parties outflank the mainstream

In early 1999, as the government of Prime Minister Nawaz Sharif embarked on the Lahore peace process, it was obvious to most observers that he had not built sufficient consensus to carry along the political parties, particularly the religious right. Consequently, when the Kargil episode unfolded in May–June 1999, the religious political parties were already on a warpath with the government. They seized the opportunity and were quick to project Kargil as a *jehadi* affair – yet another holy war. They adopted a dual strategy of mobilizing the masses and confronting the government. Their political approach in the summer of 1999 actually was an extension of the steadily increasing political role they had played in Pakistani politics and society, especially during the last decade of civilian rule in Pakistan, from 1988 to 1999.

The political and ideological usage of Islam – and Islamization – has gained momentum in Pakistan since the country's independence in 1947. More than a belief system, Islam became a particularly potent instrument of mass mobilization in the Pakistani polity and society to protest the creeping authoritarianism of the Zulfikar Ali Bhutto government of the 1970s. It is in this context that the religious parties have structural roots, as well as cultural and political legitimacy. On the domestic front, religious political parties have propounded and sought to reform society and political institutions by demanding the implementation and enforcement of Shariah (Islamic laws). During Pakistan's most recent period of civilian rule from 1988 to 1999, the Pakistani religious right also had gained greater influence in the government's deliberations on foreign policy matters, especially on India and

Table 11.1 *Party share of votes: all-Pakistan National Assembly elections*

	1988		1990		1993		1997	
	% of votes	Seats won	% of votes	Seats won	% of votes	Seats won	% of votes	Seats won
PML-N/IJI	30.16	54	37.37	106	39.86	72	45.88	134
PPA/PDA	38.52	93	36.83	44	37.85	86	21.80	18
MQM	5.37	13	5.54	15	-	-	3.55	12
JUI (F)	1.84	7	2.94	6	2.40	4	1.61	2
ANP	2.09	2	1.68	6	1.67	3	2.31	9
JWP/BNA	0.36	2	0.61	2	0.27	2	0.29	2
BNP	-	-	-	-	-	-	0.66	3
PKMA/PMAI	0.24	0	0.35	1	0.49	3	0.33	0
Others	1.92	6	4.38	5	12.46	21	9.20	2
IND	19.50	27	10.30	22	7.40	15	14.37	22
Total	100	204	100	207	100	206	100	204

Afghanistan. It is ironic that the parties in charge – both the PPP and the PML-N – faced slow erosion in their influence and increasing difficulty in defining their policy goals toward their northern and eastern neighbors – an opportunity that was seized by the religious right.

In the elections from 1988 to 1997, the voting strength of religious parties remained no more than 3 percent, as shown in Table 11.1.[20]

[20] This table is taken from *The Herald*, March 1997. PML-N/IJI is the Pakistan Muslim League (Nawaz Sharif faction). In 1988 when Islami Jamhuri Itehad (IJI) was formed, the two League factions were PML-N and the Pakistan Muslim League (Junejo). IJI was formed on 8 October 1988, and on 10 October Jamaat-e-Islami also joined. PPA/PDA is the Pakistan Peoples Alliance/Pakistan Democratic Alliance, an alliance dominated by the Pakistan Peoples Party (PPP), then led by Benazir Bhutto. It has a national support base as a mainstream liberal party. MQM was originally called Muhajir Qaumi Movement, and is now called the Muttahida Qaumi Mahaz. It has a predominantly Karachi–Hyderabad base and claims to represent the interests and voice of Urdu-speaking and Muhajirs – those who migrated to Pakistan after 1947. JUI-F Jamiat-ul-Ulema-e-Islam has two factions, one headed by Maulana Fazal-ur-Rehman, the other by Maulana Sami-ul-Haq (JUI-S). These two factions of Jamiat traditionally have been popular in two provinces of Pakistan: the North-West Frontier Province (NWFP) and Baluchistan. Explicitly religious political parties, they do have support bases in Punjab and Sindh. JUI factions are the backbone of the Muttahida Majlis-e-Amal (MMA), the six-religious-party coalition. ANP is Awami National Party, a Pashtun nationalist, secular party with socialist orientation, with primarily support from NWFP and to a lesser extent Baluchistan. JWP is Jamhuri Watan Party, a Baluchistan-based regional party. BNA is Baluch National Alliance, another Baluchistan-based regional party. BNP is Baluchistan National Party, another Baluchistan-based regional party. PKMA/PMAI is the Pakistan Kissan Mazdur Alliance (Peasant, Labour) Pakistan and Mazdur Awami Itehad, which are small leftist/ Marxist movements that participate in elections for symbolic reasons. IND means independent candidates who have traditional constituencies and after electoral victory make bargains with the political parties that would best serve their interest/agendas.

The weak electoral showing of Pakistan's religious parties cannot provide an accurate indication of their true political power. It is not the small support base of religious parties or their failure in elections, but the clamor they make in raising demands for Islamization of laws that projects them as a large force on the national scene. More importantly, they have created an environment of trepidation in which espousing liberal causes could be equated with rejecting Islamic Shariah. Most of the religious parties have a small but loyal following cadre of committed workers who possess an enormous capacity to mobilize mass support for religious issues or ignite agitation on issues that they oppose.

Pakistan's two largest religious political parties – the Jamaat-e-Islami (JI) and the Jamiat-ul-Ulema-e-Islam (JUI) – reacted strenuously to the Kargil conflict. The JI, led by Qazi Hussain Ahmed, is the only religious political party in the country that has a small but strong party cadre, whose members are recruited through a rigorous process, and which holds elections for top party positions. The JI has a support base among the traders, public officials, and semiliterate groups in the urban centers of Punjab, the North-West Frontier Province (NWFP), and in urban Sindh, especially in the cities of Karachi and Hyderabad. Since late 1960s, the JI has been able to win support from sympathizers and develop ideological linkages with the Pakistan army and governmental bureaucracy. These connections peaked when Zia ul-Haq was president in the late 1970s and 1980s.

The JI and the JUI are mainstream religious political parties. They have participated consistently in the electoral process and have taken part in coalition governments in various phases of Pakistan's history. These religious parties also have supported and at times made alliances with the military regimes in Pakistan; yet from the sidelines they have also shown forbearance for the electoral process. As noted above, these religious political parties have built coalitions in situations of crisis and pursued mass mobilization and regime confrontation. During and after the 2002 elections, these religious parties have demonstrated considerable coalition building skills and pragmatism. They have sustained the Muttahida Majlis-e-Amal (MMA) coalition and also retained power in the two provinces of NWFP and Baluchistan. The MMA did not approve of Pakistan's abandoning of the Taliban and President Musharraf's pro-US tilt, but they refrained from launching a full-scale confrontation with the Musharraf government, recognizing that such a confrontation likely would lead to the dissolution of the provincial governments.

The JUI has two factions. Maulana Fazal-ur-Rehman leads JUI-F and Maulana Sami-ul-Haq leads the other, JUI-S. Both of these factions have a strong support base in Baluchistan and the NWFP, and also have a significant following among the trade-merchant classes in Punjab. The

JUI ulema (religious hierarchy) consider themselves to be the guardians of and successors to the Deobandi tradition in Islam. The Pesh Imams (prayer leaders) of the two factions of JUI dominate and control mosques in rural and urban Pakistan. The JI has been marginal in controlling the mosques and therefore has a predominantly urban support base.[21]

The JUI-F and JUI-S gained the status of spiritual and political mentors of the Taliban movement. The JUI madrassas (religious schools) in the NWFP and Baluchistan were prominent breeding grounds for the Taliban. Emerging from these madrassas, the Taliban rose and swept through Afghanistan in 1994.[22] In 1993, while the JUI-F was a coalition partner to the Benazir Bhutto government, Maulana Fazal-ur-Rehman was chosen as the chairman of the Senate Foreign Relations Committee in the Parliament of Pakistan. He held that largely ceremonial but highly visible position until 1996 – during the very years that the Taliban grew and captured Kabul. It was an important trendsetter and morale booster for the religious right. It established that religious leaders could have a role in voicing their concerns on foreign policy issues and also closely observe, if not influence, the formulation of foreign policy. Major General (retd.) Naseer Ullah Baber, who was interior minister in the cabinet of Prime Minister Benazir Bhutto from 1993 to 1996, played a key role in coordinating Pakistan's Afghanistan policy and developing ties with the JUI. Under the Interior Ministry's supervision, JUI–Taliban connections were nurtured. Thus the JUI-F and JUI-S assumed the role of defenders of the Taliban and also become more vocal in advocating a Taliban-like Islamic government for Pakistan. Interestingly, however, the JUI-F supported the Lahore peace process in 1999, even while the JI protested against it. It reluctantly began to distance itself from the government of Nawaz Sharif when the prime minister grew antagonistic toward the Taliban and showed inclination to support the deportation of Osama bin Laden from Afghanistan. Between July and October 1999, as the Nawaz Sharif government began to adopt what the religious right saw as "anti-Kashmir *mujahideen*" and "anti-Taliban" measures, the religious parties began to explore ways to minimize their differences and built coalitions to combat these hostile policies, which they perceived were driven by the "American agenda."

---

[21] For details and an overview of the JUI, see Sayyid A. S. Pirzada, *The Politics of the Jamiat ulema-i-Islam 1971–77* (Oxford University Press, 2000).

[22] Kamal Matinuddin, *The Taliban Phenomenon: Afghanistan 1994–97* (Oxford University Press, 1999), 17–27; and Ahmed Rashid, "The Taliban: Exporting Extremism," *Foreign Affairs* (November/December 1999): 22–35.

A significant change that occurred in the post-Kargil phase and does not seem to have received adequate attention was that the conflict brought the JI, the JUI-F, and the Taliban closer to one another. Interaction among the three groups intensified in an unusual manner when the provincial *naib ameer* (vice-president) of JI, Dr. Yaqub, visited Afghanistan in August 1999.[23] Prior to this visit, relations between the JI and the Taliban had remained cool and tense because of the Taliban's hostile attitude toward Gulbuddin Hekmatyar (who had been closely allied with the JI during the Afghan war against the Soviets in the 1980s), and his forced exile in Iran after the Taliban came to power. In their public pronouncements, the leaders of the three religious parties vociferously denounced the United States and also criticized the Pakistan military's role in agreeing to support the withdrawal of *mujahideen* from Kargil and for turning their backs on the Taliban for not handing over Osama bin Laden to America.[24] These religious parties felt that the military was simply succumbing to the US pressure to appease India, which they believed was on the run but was favored by Washington.

In their perception, the ejection of "the *jehadis*" from Kargil was an American action. Adding insult to injury, this policy was portrayed as being done at the behest of India. The JI, JUI, and the *jehadi* groups believed that the United States and India put pressure on the Sharif government to curb fundamentalism and sought Pakistan's help in capturing Osama bin Laden. To counter this perceived threat, groups on the religious right began to form a broad coalition. The religious groups raucously maintained that the military and the *jehadi* groups had waged a successful war, but that their valiant gains were lost on the political front. Obviously, the religious groups downplayed – and still downplay – the Pakistan military's complete involvement. Indeed, many in the Pakistan armed forces hold similar views. Anti-American sentiments are common in the military not just because of US sanctions on Pakistan in 1990 owing to nonproliferation concerns, in 1998 because of the nuclear tests, and in 1999 because of the military coup, but also because of a widespread perception of Washington's heavy-handed and uneven pressure on Pakistan during the Kargil affair.[25]

Professor Khursheed Ahmed propounded the Jamaat-e-Islami position on Kargil: "after conquering the peaks of Kargil, the climb down and

---

[23] Behroz Khan, "For the Love of Islam," *Newsline*, August 1999, 43–44.
[24] Ismail Khan, "For the Love of Islam," *Newsline*, August 1999, 57–58.
[25] Shireen Mazari's book, *The Kargil Conflict 1999*, is especially revealing as a reflection of anti-American sentiment within senior military circles in Pakistan.

humiliation of the Washington declaration and retreat of the *mujahideen* has created a complex situation which has made the old wounds bleed again and has endangered the very existence of the country and the freedom of its people." Khursheed lamented that the withdrawal from Kargil "has distorted the Kashmir issue and has stabbed the Jihad movement in the back. It has rendered even our nuclear deterrence ineffective and has very adversely affected our defense capability and morale of the fighting forces."[26] Interestingly, the JI view coincided with and somewhat reflected what many in the Pakistan military felt then. There was no real partnership between the JI and the military leadership at the time, but such views published mostly in the Urdu press were widely read by soldiers, followers of *jehadi* groups, religious party supporters, and ordinary citizens. This narrative did have a profound impact on public consciousness and partly explains the continuing mystique of the *mujahideen* role in Kargil even today.[27]

After the Kargil withdrawal, Khursheed Ahmed questioned the personal integrity and "patriotism" of Nawaz Sharif, declared the prime minister a "security risk," and called for the overthrow of the government. An editorial in the Jamaat's official mouthpiece, *Tarjuman ul Quran*, echoed the same theme. It exhorted "all the *jehadi* forces to hold on their positions on this point firmly with resolve and unity." Then in a style characteristic of JI, the editorial, without any shred of evidence, harped that "some American and Jewish circles wish to take advantage of India's imbroglio and drag it into a war so as to secretly target the nuclear installations of Pakistan."[28] Islamists have been prolific in splashing and echoing this convoluted message. One editorial ran, "America is the sworn enemy of Osama bin Laden. In order to get him, the United States could commit any terrorist act in any Muslim state. In order to curb and disband religious organizations, it is necessary to flare up sectarianism – we cannot rule out the role of the American Central Intelligence Agency (CIA), Indian Research and Analysis Wing (RAW), and Israeli Mossad in converting sectarianism into terrorism to discredit the *mujahideen*."[29]

---

[26] Professor Khursheed Ahmed, "The Washington Declaration and Retreat from Kargil," www.Jamaat.org/Isharat/index/htm/sept.1999.

[27] C. Christine Fair observes in chapter 9 in this book that this lauding of the militant groups and neglect of the NLI soldiers' efforts had its own impacts.

[28] *Tarjuman ul Quran* editorial, July 1999.

[29] Author's translation of editorial from *Takbeer*, 13 October 1999, 5. Also see the many statements by Qazi Hussain Ahmed, Maulana Fazal-ur-Rehman, Maulana M. Ajmal Khan (JUI-F), and Senator Abid Hussain al Hussaini, secretary (Wahdat-e-Islami), insinuating CIA and RAW involvement in sectarian killings in Pakistan to discredit the religious parties, *Takbeer*, 13 October 1999. Strangely, a few years ago such writings

Maulana Fazal-ur-Rehman readily articulated the JUI-F position: "JUI was of the opinion that the withdrawal from Kargil would put an end to the Kashmir issue once and for all." Rehman condemned the Washington Declaration because he felt that it "betrayed the people and *mujahideen* of Kashmir where [the] freedom movement had received a great setback." He asserted that the Pakistani people want to change the government and replace it with a "new system based on Islamic principles." In a conjectural way, the JUI leader weaved a linkage between Kargil and the Taliban "and warned that a withdrawal from Kargil will lead to a US attack on Afghanistan and will be a blow to jihad."[30] In the post-Kargil phase, JUI-F has relentlessly defended the Taliban and advocated Taliban-style Islamic government in Pakistan.[31]

The religious parties played off the Kargil withdrawal to redefine the country's political discourse and subsequently became more vocal in promoting Islamization. The Kargil episode also enabled these religious groups to develop an effective strategy of regime confrontation and mass mobilization against the Nawaz Sharif government. That experience came in handy during the October 2002 election campaign in the two provinces of NWFP and Baluchistan. At that time, the religious parties formed a six-party coalition called the MMA. They mobilized mass support in opposing both the US-led war in Afghanistan and the Musharraf government for supporting the US campaign against terrorism. This strategy proved fruitful. For the first time in Pakistan's electoral history, a coalition of religious parties emerged as the third largest party in Pakistan's national assembly, winning fifty-two seats and 11 percent of the total votes polled.[32]

Political management and mismanagement

By the summer of 1999, Nawaz Sharif was the leader of the party that dominated the Pakistani parliament, and in turn dominated Pakistani civilian institutions. It was his party that, upon Sharif's wishes, was able to emasculate the office of the President and the Supreme Court. But the Sharif government suffered a fatal flaw: it was highly personalized in its

would have been considered comical and devoid of any validity or serious research. However, growing Indo-Israeli ties and the expanding US–India strategic partnership have helped these messages to register in the public consciousness.

[30] Statement by Maulana Fazal-ur-Rehman, *Dawn*, 12 July 1999.

[31] Amir Meer, "Crusade," *Newsline*, October 1999, 65–69. Also see Dr. Inam Ullah Khan, "Taliban Movement: Analysis and Suggestions," *Monthly Baidar Digest* (Urdu), January 2000: 31–34.

[32] The PPP won 25 percent, and the Pakistan Muslim League (Quaid-i-Azam) (PML-Q) earned 24 percent of the total votes cast.

decision-making. When a real crisis appeared, Sharif and his cadre of advisors were unable to overcome the breakdown between Pakistani institutions that had occurred in the 1990s. This inability to formulate a coherent message not only weakened Pakistan's position internationally, it also weakened the Pakistan Muslim League (Nawaz) in its competition with the religious parties and, to a lesser extent, the Pakistan Peoples Party, and ultimately set the stage for a future civil–military showdown.

The PML-N and its leadership could do little to explain why the Kargil operation was imperative for Pakistan. It opted to put the blame on the army at a time when charges of civilian corruption and mismanagement were on the rise. At the same time, the PML-N's chief mainstream competitor, the PPP, also failed to capture the public sentiment or develop a coherent strategy to challenge the Nawaz Sharif government. As a result, Kargil marginalized the national parties, and the incompetence of their leadership severely damaged and constrained the liberal and progressive voices in Pakistan. It is in this context that we may look at the support base of these national parties and how their leadership responded to the crisis.

Pakistan's two major national political parties, the PPP and PML, have amorphous and uneven support bases, cutting across all regions of the country. Their leadership hails from different areas and they have office-holders and branches in every province. National political parties accept elections as a vital condition for democracy. Therefore, the leadership of national parties and their candidates participate vigorously in the electoral process and make promises to strengthen governance through democracy. In the 1990s, the PPP and the PML maintained themselves as national political parties. Both acquired power twice, forming governments at the federal level as well as in the provinces. Ironically, both did little to promote conditions for good governance and democracy. They violated the rule of law, failed to tolerate dissent, encouraged confrontations rather than consensus-building, and ultimately failed to strengthen the country's representative institutions – the parliament, autonomous groups, and civil society – which are essential for efficient governance and democracy. Both political parties have remained elitist: landlords, tribal chiefs, business groups, and a few urban professionals dominate their leadership. These parties were so occupied with acquiring and perpetuating power and preserving the status quo that they failed to comprehend the scale of *jehadi* fervor that Pakistan's religious groups and *jehadi* networks had produced. The domestic hue and cry over Kargil came as a complete surprise: the PML-N and PPP were practically paralyzed and unable to respond.

The immediate political consequences of Kargil are best analyzed by focusing on the second term of Prime Minister Nawaz Sharif, which may be divided into three phases. In the first phase, from October 1997 to May 1998, Sharif sought to consolidate power. On the one hand, he revealed democratic dispensations, pursued politics of accommodation and coalition-building, and constructed a coalition government at the federal level. In the process, he strengthened the federalist spirit in Pakistan.[33] However, these hopeful tendencies contrasted markedly with more vicious and authoritarian moves to seize power. He initiated a series of events that were designed to emasculate the presidency and the judiciary.

Following the nuclear tests in May 1998, the prime minister and his close associates began to suffer from delusions of invincibility and adopted a do-it-alone policy, gradually wrecking the national coalition and consensus. During the second phase, from May 1998 to the beginning of the Kargil conflict in May 1999, Prime Minister Sharif decided to assert his newly consolidated power. Having removed the chief justice, replaced the president, and done away with the federal and provincial coalition governments that he had so skillfully built in the first year, he also replaced the chiefs of the navy and air force. Finally, in October 1998, he forced the resignation of General Jehangir Karamat, the army chief, only three months before his scheduled retirement date. As brought out by Feroz Hassan Khan, Peter R. Lavoy, and Christopher Clary in chapter 3 of this book, the army did not take such an unprecedented, intrusive move lightly – in particular because of Karamat's very short remaining tenure. The prime minister promoted and appointed General Pervez Musharraf to replace Karamat. Musharraf spent the next week assembling his team and making important appointments. By the end of 1998, Sharif controlled two-thirds of the parliament, and had successfully demonstrated primacy over the presidency, the judiciary, and the army.

The seeds of civil–military distrust were sown at the very outset of General Pervez Musharraf's appointment as Chief of Army Staff (COAS). Three days later, on 10 October, the prime minister removed the chief of the Inter-Services Intelligence Directorate (ISID), Lieutenant General Nasim Rana, and appointed Lieutenant General Ziauddin in his place – a move that was not well received by the army.[34] The army was already wary of the prime minister's intrusive approach in its internal

---

[33] Hasan Askari Rizvi, "Civil–Military Relations in Contemporary Pakistan," *Survival* 40, no. 2 (Summer 1998): 96–113.

[34] As a matter of convention and procedure, the ISID chief is appointed in consultation with the COAS. The Military Secretariat proposes the name to the COAS, who forwards it to the Ministry of Defence, which puts it up to the prime minister for final selection/ approval. The military grudgingly accepted the appointment, but quietly upgraded the parallel Military Intelligence organization. Information based on interviews with senior Pakistan military officers.

affairs and was willing to protect its institutional interests. In any case, it needs to be recognized that the COAS maintains his authority and the functional autonomy of the army by relying on and operating through formation commanders. Thus, even early on, the ISID chief was an "outsider" – a Nawaz loyalist – and later events were to prove that. While pursuing the subordination of the military, had the prime minister and the party in power shown democratic dispensation or taken steps to strengthen the party system and the judiciary, or shown respect for freedom of the press – steps that could have proved conducive for establishing supremacy of the elected leadership over the military – civilian supremacy over the military could have materialized.

Sharif was not content to play a subtle form of power consolidation, however. He sought to curb the media, thus causing uproar and outrage at both the national and the global levels.[35] At the same time, his freedom of maneuver had been dramatically constrained economically and internationally. Sharif's May 1998 decision to reciprocate India's nuclear tests had triggered international sanctions against Pakistan – sanctions that were more damaging to Pakistan than India. Sharif's decision to freeze foreign currency accounts caused serious hardship and resentment among the populace. At the same time, the "Cooperatives Scandal," which had emerged earlier in 1997, was also generating popular concern about the country's financial trajectory.[36] Abroad, Sharif was under intense international pressure to resolve outstanding conflicts and build confidence with India. Foreign secretary-level talks were held in Islamabad in October 1998 on peace and security issues – talks in which the military was engaged and supportive. Outside pressure on Sharif culminated in a December 1998 trip to Washington, DC to meet with US president Bill Clinton.

During the third phase of Sharif's rule – which began with the Lahore peace process, was rocked by Kargil, and ended in October 1999 – Sharif struggled to rescue the government from the various missteps that had been made. The unfolding of Kargil raised several questions: first, did the civilian leadership and the military have a common strategic vision of Indo-Pakistani relations? The Kargil episode, following so shortly after the Lahore peace process, revealed that the two were working at cross-purposes. However, once the events unfolded, the civil and military

---

[35] Amir Mir, "The Midnight Knock," *Newsline*, May 1999, 29–30.
[36] The Cooperatives Scandal was a junk-bond crisis in Pakistan. Companies with close ties to serving politicians, including those in the Nawaz Sharif government, had been selling corporate debt to the public with high rates of return, but when these companies collapsed, thousands of middle-class Pakistanis lost their investments.

leadership put on a brave face and insisted that everyone was on board. Within weeks after the Washington Declaration the unease between civilian and military leaders began to surface. Second, did Pakistan's institutions function properly? Specifically, were institutions such as the Defence Cabinet Committee (DCC) fully and effectively utilized to monitor the operational plan proposed by the army? Most accounts appear to convey at best that the civilian control of the military was precarious and decision-making highly personalized. At the worst, it has been suggested that Nawaz Sharif either had no clue what the army was doing or could hardly comprehend the complexities of the operation, if and when given briefings on the subject.[37]

After Sharif's December 1998 visit to the United States, the momentum for substantive India–Pakistan talks grew rapidly. The peace and security talks between India and Pakistan, which previously had been managed by both countries at a bureaucratic level, were overwhelmed by Indian prime minister Atal Behari Vajpayee's Lahore initiative. The military was increasingly concerned that Sharif's highly personalized and erratic decision-making style was inappropriate for Indo-Pakistani negotiations, which could permanently impact Pakistani national security. The military was concerned that Sharif was getting carried away with the dynamics of the process leading to Lahore. Ground realities could not, in the military's opinion, be altered so quickly.

This institutional disconnect was epitomized in the decision to continue with Kargil. Sharif had visited Skardu for briefings on Kargil on 29 January and the Kel sector on 5 February 1999, nearly simultaneously with the first press reports of Prime Minister Vajpayee's intention to travel to Pakistan during the bus route's opening.[38] In other words, Sharif had approved the progression down two incompatible tracks pursued by the Foreign Office and the armed forces, respectively. Had Sharif institutionalized these decisions, and if the Foreign Office knew about the military's moves, it seems unlikely that these professionals would not grasp the obvious cross-purposes in the two policies. The army's General Headquarters (GHQ), however, knew of both developments, and its

---

[37] Interview with Chaudhry Iftikhar, Rawalpindi, 19 January 2003. Also see, Owen Bennett Jones, *Pakistan: Eye of the Storm* (New Haven, Conn.: Yale University Press, 2002), 34–55, 87–108. Khan, Lavoy, and Clary provide a detailed discussion in chapter 3 of this book.

[38] Discussion of Sharif's trips to the 10 Corps area of operations can be found in Mazari, *The Kargil Conflict 1999*, 55–58. Early press accounts include K. K. Katyal, "PM to Take Bus to Lahore," *The Hindu*, 4 February 1999 and Malina Parthasarathy, "US Sees Potential in Indo-Pak 'Bus Diplomacy,'" *The Hindu*, 6 February 1999. Also see Robert J. Wirsing, *Kashmir in the Shadow of War: Regional Rivalries in the Nuclear Age* (Armonk, NY: M. E. Sharpe, 2003), 18–25.

inability to foresee the implications of these two incompatible tracts was inexcusable – though even key directorates of the GHQ, much less the navy and the air force, were not fully aware of the developments on the Kargil heights.[39] The secret nature of the planning and execution, combined with the belief that the mission would remain limited to 10 Corps, meant that even the military hierarchy had a limited understanding of the ramifications of the Kargil operation. As a result, even though Pakistan launched the surprise operation, initially with success, when it encountered Indian resistance, Pakistan's national security institutions were what were really put into disarray.

This institutional breakdown is highlighted even further in Robert Wirsing's recent account of back-channel talks between India and Pakistan during March and June 1999. Nine rounds of secret talks took place between Nawaz Sharif's representative, Niaz A. Naik, and Atal Behari Vajpayee's delegate, R. K. Mishra. Wirsing appears to convey that the two negotiators not only respected each other's views and sensitivities but were also convinced that in order to have any resolution of the Kashmir dispute the two sides would need to move beyond their stated positions.[40] This account reinforces the view that the relevant decision-making bodies were either out of the loop or that there was no communication among the military, ISID, Foreign Office and prime minister's office on these crucial secret talks.

As Kargil unfolded, the Pakistani national security apparatus was dumbfounded about how to respond. The Foreign Office, prime minister's office, and the military had been pursuing two separate tracks, which diverged further after the Indian prime minister's February visit to Lahore. As Pakistani troops were already in motion to seize territory across the LoC near the Indian town of Kargil, the political breakthrough at Lahore took almost everyone by surprise. Momentum in both directions was growing, and Sharif and the military proved unable or unwilling to reverse the Kargil operation. Perhaps it would have been easier to reverse this operation if it were not proceeding excellently on the ground. Pakistani troops were able to maintain surprise and had begun to seize large swathes of Indian territory.

An arrangement in such tension is unsustainable. Two ripples disturbed the stillness of March, April, and May. On 12 April, India tested its new Agni-2 ballistic missile. This was the first such test since the May 1998 nuclear detonations. More significantly, on 15 April, the BJP-led government in India lost a no-confidence motion in the parliament.

---

[39] Interviews by the CCC research team with senior Pakistani military officers and government officials.
[40] Wirsing, *Kashmir in the Shadow of War*, 25–36.

Finally, though, the stillness was truly shattered when Indian troops discovered intruders on their side of the LoC on 28 April 1999. Although it took India several days to recover from the surprise, India's national security institutions ultimately worked well together to produce a coherent Indian response. Pakistan, however, was at a loss to explain whether independent *jehadis* or its own military forces carried out the operation. It also was at a loss to explain how it would respond to the fighting around Kargil. Fearful from perceived threats on multiple fronts, Nawaz Sharif flew to Washington, DC – uninvited – to seek a way out of his international and domestic crises.

The prime minister's meeting with President Clinton on 4 July 1999 and the signing of the Washington Declaration sealed his fate. In the popular perception, Nawaz Sharif came to be seen as a leader who had no vision or comprehension about Pakistan's strategic interests and vital national goals. A number of accounts reinforce the perception about Nawaz Sharif as a clueless leader. For example, Shaheen Sehbai, then the *Dawn* correspondent in Washington, DC, reported that the prime minister looked "resigned ... unruffled by the enormity of the occasion." According to Bruce Riedel (who took the only notes during the Clinton–Sharif meeting): "The PM was distraught, deeply worried about the direction the crisis was going ... his own hold on power and the threat from his military chiefs who were pressing for a tough stand."[41] In his autobiography even Musharraf asserts that, "International pressure had a demoralizing effect on Prime Minister Nawaz Sharif."[42]

It is widely recognized that Sharif's decision-making style was highly personalized and confined to a few select associates. The cabinet had one or two briefings on Kargil, but there were hardly any discussions on the possible political implications of the conflict. The party leadership was least equipped to evolve a response as the government sought political and diplomatic resolutions to the conflict. In a situation of national crisis, the prime minister was unable to win the goodwill of the main opposition party in the parliament, the PPP, even though earlier, for the Lahore peace process, he was able to carry it along. More importantly, in this hour of crisis, the PML government failed to win the support of its former regional coalition partners, including the Awami National Party, Muhajir Qaumi Movement, and the Baluchistan National Movement. Instead of mobilizing the party leadership to build consensus, the prime minister

---

[41] An early and insightful account of the meeting between President Clinton and Prime Minister Sharif was provided by Shaheen Sehbai, "Blair House to Kargil," *Dawn*, 13 July 1999. See also chapter 5 in this book by Bruce Riedel (quotation on pp. 137–138).

[42] Musharraf, *In the Line of Fire*, 93.

relied on his younger brother, Shahbaz Sharif, the chief minister of Punjab, to defend and rescue his government. It reflected how isolated and nepotistic he had become. Thus, in the post-Kargil phase, Shahbaz Sharif emerged as the crisis manager for the government, which undermined the federal government's credibility, evoked criticism from the opponents, and also diminished the chief minister's management of the provincial government. Since the prime minister kept the defense portfolio to himself, it was widely reported in the Pakistani media that he allowed PML politicians and ministers, such as Choudhry Nisar and Mushahid Hussain, as well as his brother, Shahbaz Sharif, to meddle in the affairs of the military, which was not seen kindly within the armed forces.[43]

Choudhry Nisar and Shahbaz Sharif served as crucial "message carriers" between the prime minister's secretariat and the army GHQ.[44] This view gains further credence by examining the events and circumstances between the Kargil conflict and the October 1999 military coup. Shahbaz Sharif's role as "crisis manager" and "broker" for the federal government reached its climax when he and the ISID chief, Lieutenant General Ziauddin, visited the United States from 14 to 25 September 1999. During their meetings, it appears they offered to take a harder line against the Taliban while also agreeing to provide Pakistani assistance to find Osama bin Laden. At the same time, they apparently expressed their fears to US officials that Sharif was in danger of being overthrown by the Pakistan armed forces. In response, Reuters quoted an unnamed US official in Washington as saying, "We hope there will be no return to the days of interrupted democracy in Pakistan." Further, the official let it be known that Washington would oppose "any extra-constitutional actions" in Pakistan.[45]

[43] Amir Mir, "The Army Strikes Back," *Newsline*, October 1999, 30–34.
[44] Based on private conversations with senior officials in the Punjab bureaucracy.
[45] Quoted in Jones, *Pakistan: Eye of the Storm*, 40–41. In a 12 October 1999 briefing, US State Department spokesman James Rubin repeated the US stance by saying that, "we were concerned about the extra constitutional measure" and that "Pakistan's constitution must be respected not only its letter but spirit." Transcript: State Department Noon Briefing, 12 October 1999. The US Assistant Secretary of State for South Asian Affairs Karl Inderfurth's testimony to the Senate Foreign Relations Committee on 14 October 1999 is equally revealing. While referring to the house arrest of General Ziauddin, Nawaz Sharif, and Shahbaz Sharif, he asserted: "we call upon the current Pakistani authorities to assure their safety and well being." Karl F. Inderfurth, Testimony Before the Senate Foreign Relations Committee, Washington, DC, 14 October 1999, www.fas.org/spp/starwars/congress/1999_h/991014_inderfurth_tst.htm. These pronouncements and degree of interest shown by US officials led many to ask if Nawaz Sharif was seeking US support to remove Musharraf. It seems highly speculative but has led analysts such as Tariq Ali to assert that Musharraf's takeover was "the first time that the army seized power without the approval of Washington." Tariq Ali, *The Clash of Fundamentalisms: Crusades, Jehadis and Modernity* (London: Verso, 2002), 200. Another news report speculated that perhaps a "deal" was struck between the Nawaz government and the Clinton

This statement and the visit by Shahbaz Sharif was celebrated and seen as an important victory for the Sharif government. In reality, it was an ephemeral victory and showed that the government had lost its domestic political support and moral authority to rule. After the visit, a badly bruised and injured Pakistan government took a hard-line position against the *jehadi* groups and the Taliban, and also attempted to distance itself from the religious political parties. However, this action proved to be too little, too late.

The coup and its aftermath

By early September 1999, it was clear to many Pakistanis that a showdown between Sharif and Musharraf was imminent. For both the prime minister's office and the army, it was difficult to imagine blame for Kargil being apportioned without one or the other losing decisively. The military was also increasingly concerned with what it perceived to be Sharif's misrule and poor management. At the same time, as Owen Bennett Jones notes, at a mid-September corps commanders' meeting, "the generals decided that the army could not move without clear justification. But if Sharif tried to sack Musharraf, the corps commanders agreed, then they would act: to lose two army chiefs in the space of a year would be unacceptable."[46]

Shortly after the mid-September meeting of the senior military leadership, Lt. Gen. Tariq Pervez, Corps Commander for Quetta, met privately with Nawaz Sharif and informed the prime minister that if he moved against Musharraf the army would respond. But Sharif, in turn, dispatched Shahbaz Sharif and Lt. Gen. Ziauddin to Washington, and received in return supporting statements by US officials on 20 September. The trip demonstrated only Sharif's domestic weakness. Musharraf was made full chief of the Joint Chiefs of Staff Committee in the first week of October – either to appease Musharraf or as an attempt to provide Musharraf an easy offramp out of the more powerful Chief of Army Staff position. Immediately after receiving this additional position, Musharraf demanded and received Tariq Pervez's resignation, having learned of his back-channel communication with the prime minister. Musharraf then left on a fateful trip to Sri Lanka for a meeting of South Asian military chiefs.

administration that in return for supporting the appointment of Ziauddin as COAS, Pakistan would sign the Comprehensive Test Ban Treaty (CTBT), make peace with India, and curb *jehadi* groups. Amir Mir, "The Army Strikes Back," *Newsline*, October 1999, 33–34. Both interpretations are highly speculative, but what is evident is that the civil–military consensus that was assiduously built in Pakistan at the time of Kargil fell apart by September, when the personal and policy differences between the Nawaz government and the military surfaced and culminated in the October coup.

[46] Jones, *Pakistan: Eye of the Storm*, 39.

The story of the coup itself is not the subject of this chapter; but when Sharif decided to move against Musharraf, the dominos were tipped. The prime minister's groundless attempt to remove Musharraf as army chief was unacceptable – even more so when he was abroad. The army moved quickly to execute a "counter-coup." Sharif's gambit had failed, and he was ousted by the military, making way for Musharraf's safe landing at Karachi airport.

Many Pakistanis, particularly those close to the Sharif government, feel that Sharif was ousted in part because he was demanding a reappraisal of the military's ties with the Taliban regime. Reportedly, the military was concerned that the Sharif government was giving too many concessions to the Clinton administration as it sought to further isolate the Taliban regime and pursue al Qaeda chief Osama bin Laden in Afghanistan. During the September visit by Shahbaz Sharif and Ziauddin, plans to coordinate operations against bin Laden were discussed. By October, the Sharif government had dispatched ISID chief Ziauddin to Kabul to ask for the deportation of bin Laden and, when that failed, Sharif ordered ISID to cease its support of Taliban groups along the Pakistani–Afghan border. The order was issued on 11 October, one day before the coup, and was never implemented.[47] Others argue that the Sharif administration's change of heart about the Taliban had more to do with its fears of an ensuing coup and attempts to receive support from the Clinton administration than anything else. This line of argument concludes that while Musharraf did stop cooperation with the United States on a commando raid to seize bin Laden after the October coup, this was significant, but by no means the cause of Sharif's ouster.[48]

Regardless of its causes, the military coup had several effects on politics and society. First, it further deepened Pakistan's international isolation. Pakistan now triggered almost all possible US sanctions, though it still avoided being listed as a state sponsor of terror. Second, Musharraf's

[47] Jean-Charles Brisard and Guillaume Dasquie, *Forbidden Truth: US–Taliban Secret Oil Diplomacy and the Failed Hunt for Bin Laden* (New York: Thunder's Mouth Press, 2002); and Amir Meer, "The Army Strikes Back," *Newsline*, October 1999, 30–34.

[48] Steve Coll's excellent *Ghost Wars: The Secret History of the CIA, Afghanistan, and Bin Laden, from the Soviet Invasion to September 10, 2001* (New York: Penguin Press, 2004) describes how persistent the United States had been during September and October 1999 in putting pressure on the Nawaz government to abandon the Taliban and help capture Osama bin Laden. This account also explains how the Pakistan military grew suspicious over the way the ISID chief, General Ziauddin, was conducting himself on behalf of Prime Minister Nawaz Sharif. Aside from acting independently of the army high command, in the eyes of the army chief and army top brass, the ISID chief was working against the army's institutional interest; and that was significant enough to disrupt the trust between the civil and military leadership. In short, the prime minister could not persuade the military to revise the government's Afghan policy. See esp. 478–480.

disgust at a decade of PPP and PML-N misrule led him to politically exclude the leadership of these two mainstream parties. From the membership of these two parties, he crafted a "king's party," which would support him in his rule after parliament was reconvened in 2002. In the meantime, the mainstream parties were allowed to wither on the vine. Further, post-9/11, the religious parties were able to take advantage of international events and this domestic-leadership vacuum to gain greater prominence. So while Musharraf opposed and was opposed by the religious parties, he inadvertently aided them. Finally, in the disarray of Pakistani political institutions that typically characterizes a coup, previous military regimes had generally sought partnership with the bureaucracy, particularly the celebrated and powerful Civil Service of Pakistan (CSP). The military regime of General Musharraf departed from the old pattern. The regime decided to uproot the linchpin administrative role of the CSP and its offshoot, the District Management Group (DMG). It demolished the "colonial relic of Deputy Commissioner" and declared its aim to empower the elected public official at the grass-roots level. The regime recast itself as the dominant governor relegating civil bureaucracy to a subordinate role. Like many military rulers, Musharraf was prone to technocratic solutions, and as a result he redefined the role of the bureaucracy in his government.

Conclusion

The Kargil conflict had three principal effects on Pakistani society and politics. First, it revealed profound institutional cleavages within the Pakistani polity. There were gaps within the military (crucial directorates and the other services were left uninformed about Kargil), there were gaps between the military and the prime minister's office, there were gaps between the prime minister's office and his cabinet, and the list could go on further. The press reporting about the conflict and its aftermath reveals the fractured nature of elite opinion in Pakistan. This stands in sharp contrast with the more coherent and unified Indian response.

Second, Kargil set in train a series of events that led directly to the October 1999 coup – possibly in part because the military was increasingly concerned that Sharif was making ill-informed changes in Pakistan's Afghan policy. While blame for Kargil's mishandling can be spread between the military and civilian institutions, it was clear that in Pakistan's political game, determining blame would be a winner-take-all affair. Nawaz Sharif decided he had to move against the military before it moved against him, but he seriously overestimated his strength relative to that of the armed forces. There was no conceivable way the Pakistan army

made by the Saxena Committee, are known.[15] These include the untethering of the IB from the Ministry of Home Affairs, the setting up of a National Technical Facilities Organisation (NTFO) for integrating technical intelligence, and the creation of a Multi-Agency Centre (MAC) for the collation and analysis of all intelligence.

The Indian government took the recommendations of the Kargil Review Committee and the GoM seriously, and numerous changes were initiated. Even before the GoM report had been prepared, India purchased unmanned aerial vehicles (UAVs) from Israel in late 2000 for tighter border surveillance.[16] In October 2001, India launched its Technology Experiment Satellite (TES), which greatly improved intelligence collection because of its relatively advanced 1-meter resolution.[17] While India requested ground sensors from the United States, indigenously produced sensors were deployed along the LoC and border.[18] In March 2002, a new Defence Intelligence Agency (DIA) was created, reportedly with a budget larger than those of RAW and IB together.[19] DIA is a new, joint-service intelligence organization, whereas DGMI was and remains the army intelligence component. NTFO and MAC have been established, but not all the GoM's recommendations have been implemented. IB remains under the control of MHA, apparently because the latter's mandarins, who represent the Indian Administrative Service (IAS), are reluctant to loosen control over the Indian Police Service (IPS), which staffs IB.[20]

Border management

The Kargil experience highlighted the larger problem of border management, which encompasses cross-border flows not only of terrorists, but also of informants, economically motivated migrants, and smugglers. In this respect, India has faced difficulties on all its land borders as well as its coastline. Apart from the army, border regulation involves different paramilitary forces (the Assam Rifles, the Border Security Force [BSF], the

---

[15] Praveen Swami, "Stalled Reforms," *Frontline*, 26 April–9 May 2003, www.frontlineonnet.com/fl2009/stories/20030509002108700.htm.

[16] "India to Induct Unmanned Aerial Vehicles along Borders with Pakistan, China," *Business Recorder*, 30 January 2001. Ironically, wrangling between the army and the air force delayed their deployment by several months.

[17] "Dream Vehicle Gifts Army Dream Eyes in Space," *Statesman*, 24 October 2001.

[18] "Extra Vigil Near LoC, IB after Kargil: Fernandes," *Times of India*, 26 July 2002, http://timesofindia.indiatimes.com/articleshow/17199179.cms.

[19] Praveen Swami, "A New Intelligence Organisation," *Frontline*, 16 March 2002, www.frontlineonnet.com/fl1906/19061240.htm.

[20] Swami, "Stalled Reforms."

Indo-Tibetan Border Police [ITBP], and the Rashtriya Rifles, in diverse locations). Different government departments are involved in border regulation, including the Ministry of Defence (the regular military and some paramilitary forces), the Ministry of Home Affairs (mostly para-military forces), and the Ministry of Finance (narcotics control). Coordination among these different departments is not easy. Aside from vested interests that might benefit from smuggling, interagency rivalry has also been problematic.[21] The Kargil Review Committee recommended that the issue be treated holistically rather than compartmentally, and that a comprehensive border-management policy be formulated.[22]

The appointment of the Task Force on Border Management reflected the seriousness of government concern with the issue. The GoM report, which incorporates the study and recommendations produced by the task force, devoted considerable attention to the issue of border manage-ment.[23] It called for the establishment of a new Department of Border Management within the Ministry of Home Affairs and for the adoption of the principle of "one border, one force," which would reduce conflicts in command and control and improve accountability.[24] The government decided to bifurcate the BSF into East and West forces, place the Assam Rifles, hitherto under the operational control of the army, fully under the control of the Ministry of Home Affairs, and appoint a senior police official as vigilance officer for every paramilitary border force.[25] Reflecting the government's new priorities, the report also pushed for effective training of the army and paramilitary forces in border manage-ment, and improvement in the working and living conditions of the border forces.[26]

Going beyond the Kargil Review Committee's recommendations, the GoM also focused on the need to reinforce border management by enhancing its local component. It called for an increase in the local composition of border forces, the expansion and strengthening of Village Volunteer Forces (VVFs), and the enhancement of the Border Area Development Programme.[27] The comprehensive character of both the Kargil Review Committee and GoM reports reflects lessons well learned. Notably, the latter ordered a process of administrative action, oversight, and review to ensure implementation of the recommended changes.[28] Immediate actions included the decision to focus the army units based in Jammu and Kashmir solely on the management of the LoC, instead of diverting large portions of it to counterinsurgency operations,

---

[21] GoM Report, 61.   [22] Kargil Review Committee, *From Surprise to Reckoning*, 246, 257.
[23] GoM Report, 58–96.   [24] *Ibid.* 61–62.   [25] *Ibid.* 75–77.
[26] *Ibid.* 77–78, 80–81.   [27] *Ibid.* 77, 95–97, 91–95.   [28] *Ibid.* 118–119.

and to augment the strength of the paramilitary forces by adding twenty battalions to the Assam Rifles and twelve to the Rashtriya Rifles.[29] In addition, Home Affairs Minister L. K. Advani announced that local officials had been given automatic weapons and communications equipment, with the expectation of more to follow.[30] In May 2001, control of the ITBP was shifted from the Ministry of Home Affairs to the Ministry of Defence, and the Assam Rifles regiment was shifted in the reverse direction. The Bureau of Immigration was moved from the IB to the direct control of the Ministry of Home Affairs.[31] In Jammu and Kashmir, the fencing of the India–Pakistan border and extending it to the LoC was also taken with fresh impetus.[32]

On the military aspects of border control, some deficiencies highlighted by the Kargil Review Committee's published findings include the need for improved clothing and weapons for troops fighting in cold-weather conditions. Other military lessons remain classified and redacted from the publicly available report.[33] While there is no comprehensive declassified report on the military lessons of Kargil, evidence of these is available from fragmented press reports. A study produced for the US Pacific Command in September 1999 reportedly revealed shortcomings in the Indian army's "intelligence, key equipment, and interservices coordination."[34] Minister of External Affairs Jaswant Singh, later to be a member of the GoM, observed soon after the Kargil conflict that its "simple message ... is that adequate resources have to be made available for national defence, that the kind of relegation of defence needs that we witnessed in the late eighties and nineties is unsound policy, that technological upgradation cannot be postponed."[35] Technological weaknesses such as the absence of night-vision equipment were responsible for a slow and difficult campaign to recover lost territory and caused high casualties. The army had no gun-locating radars, and its British-made Cymbeline mortar-locating radars were ineffective.[36] The air force suffered from

---

[29] Sanjiv Sinha, "Army Will Man Only Borders Now," *Indian Express*, 24 July 1999, www.indianexpress.com/ie/daily/19990724/ige24007.html.

[30] "Curbing Cross-border Terrorism Will Be Our Next Target – Advani," *Indian Express*, 24 July 1999, www.indianexpress.com/ie/daily/19990724/ige24005.html.

[31] Jay Raina, "Kargil-Wary Govt Shuffles Paramilitary Forces," *Hindustan Times*, 17 May 2001.

[32] "Border Fence in Jammu Area," *The Tribune* (India), 21 September 2000, www.tribune-india.com/2000/20000922/j&k.htm.

[33] Kargil Review Committee, *From Surprise to Reckoning*, 231–232.

[34] "Kargil Showed Indian Army's Shortfalls: Report," *Times of India*, 9 August 2002, http://timesofindia.indiatimes.com/articleshow/18590859.cms.

[35] "Kargil and Beyond," Text of Jaswant Singh's Speech at India International Centre, New Delhi, 20 July 1999, http://meadev.nic.in/Opn/kargil/jaswadd-2007.htm.

[36] Pranab Dhal Samanta, "India Can Now Procure Weapon-Locating Radars," *The Hindu*, 29 September 2001, www.hinduonnet.com/thehindu/2001/09/29/stories/02290005.htm.

a paucity of laser-guided munitions, which left most of its targets unscathed.[37] It also lacked helicopter gunships capable of flying at high altitudes, and night-flying equipment.[38] Subsequently, the government undertook a rapid modernization program for the armed forces, increasing its defense budget and importing new equipment of higher technology levels such as gun-locating radar, night-vision equipment, and advanced helicopter gunships. A deal for the purchase of American Firefinder weapon-locating radar systems, signed in 2002, was completed by May 2007.[39] The presence of both the army and the air force in the LoC region was enhanced.[40] Moreover, the army reportedly carried out a comprehensive study to identify areas astride the LoC that could be subjected to Kargil-like intrusions. The army also revised its operational plans for adopting a winter posture in its positions along the LoC. As a consequence, permanent defenses have been prepared and occupied in areas of the Kargil region that were subject to intrusion during the 1999 conflict. Also, as recommended by the Kargil Review Committee, construction of an all-weather route to Ladakh, which would reduce dependence on the vulnerable Srinagar–Leh highway, commenced in August 2002.[41] In May 2007, it was reported that the government had approved a 9-mile-long tunnel to allow winter traffic on the Srinagar–Leh highway at Zojila Pass, which until now has been closed for half the year.[42]

National security management

An important lesson of Kargil was that the management of national security policy required revamping. Besides the failure to integrate the political and military dimensions of intelligence, the Kargil Review Committee emphasized that the armed forces ought to have more than an "operational role" in the formulation of decision-making.[43] As a result of the traditional practice, the military lacked a "staff culture," policy-making was deprived of military inputs, and comprehensive planning suffered. Arguing that civilian control over the armed forces is not "a real issue," the committee advocated "a much closer and more constructive

---

[37] Vishal Thapar, "IAF Planes Failed to Hit Targets in Kargil," *The Hindu*, 11 August 2001.
[38] "Indian Air Force to Upgrade Helicopter Gunships," *BBC Worldwide Monitoring*, 10 June 2001.
[39] "India Acquires 12 Contracted Weapon Locating Radar," *News International*, 3 May 2007.
[40] Atul Aneja, "IAF Punch Enhanced to Foil Kargil-type Intrusions," *The Hindu*, 28 September 2000; V. P. Malik, "India's Initiative," *Times of India*, 2 February 2001.
[41] *Press Trust of India*, 13 August 2002.
[42] "Kargil Winter in Mind, Centre Okays Zojila Pass Tunnel," *Indian Express*, 1 May 2007.
[43] Kargil Review Committee, *From Surprise to Reckoning*, 258–259.

interaction between the Civil Government and the Services."[44] The GoM echoed these concerns, and asked that the service headquarters be integrated into the policymaking structure of the government.[45] Specifically, it called for the designation of the defense headquarters as the "Integrated Headquarters" of the Ministry of Defence, the decentralization of decision-making, and the creation of a Chief of Defence Staff (CDS). The CDS, assisted by a Vice Chief of Defence Staff (VCDS), would be responsible for providing single-point military advice to the government, administering the nuclear forces, and ensuring the "jointness" of the armed forces.[46] The integration of the services with the civilian structure was partially achieved in 2002 by the reorganization of the Ministry of Defence, which was renamed the Integrated Headquarters of the Ministry of Defence. Funds were allocated for the establishment of a National Defence University.[47] The appointment of a Chief of Integrated Defence Staff was announced in October 2001.[48] However, the creation of the CDS remains unimplemented, partly because of interservice wrangling, but also because of the government's reluctance to concentrate power in one military official's person.[49] The integration of military planning passed a significant milestone with the development of a joint doctrine (released in May 2006), but it is questionable how far jointness is workable without single-point decision-making at the top.[50] In light of recent revelations about the quarreling between the air force and army chiefs over the use of air power in Kargil, the problem is clearly not a minor one.[51] At least one lesson of Kargil (among others) appears not to have been sufficiently well learned: the high cost of bureaucratic politics and of exaggerated concerns about the power of the military.

The larger problem of integrating apex decision-making made some progress. The coalition led by the Bharatiya Janata Party (BJP) that came

---

[44] *Ibid.* 259.   [45] GoM Report, 97–104.   [46] *Ibid.* 100–103.

[47] "Defence Ministry Gets a New Name," *The Hindu*, 2 July 2002, www.hinduonnet.com/thehindu/2002/07/02/stories/2002070204761100.htm.

[48] Deepan Dasgupta, "CIDS: Arming the Forces with Synergy," *The Newspaper Today*, 8 October 2001, www.thenewspapertoday.com/.

[49] See "Tipnis Expresses Reservations on CDS," *The Hindu*, 5 August 2001, www.hinduonnet.com/thehindu/2001/08/05/stories/0205000h.htm; and Ashok K. Mehta, "Made in India CDS," *Rediff.com*, 27 April 2001, www.rediff.com/news/2001/apr/27ashok.htm. On civilian distrust of the military in this context, see Harsh V. Pant, "India's Nuclear Doctrine and Command Structure: Implications for Civil–Military Relations in India," *Armed Forces & Society*, 33, no. 2 (January 2007), 252–253.

[50] A. Vinod Kumar, "Will the Joint Doctrine Result in Synergy on the Ground?" Institute for Defence Studies and Analyses, New Delhi, 8 June 2006, www.idsa.in/publications/stratcomments/VinodKumar080606.htm.

[51] Rahul Singh, "Ex-Air Force Chief Alleges Army Botched Kargil War," *Hindustan Times*, 26 October 2006.

to power in 1998 had introduced a number of much-needed organizational changes, including the creation of a National Security Council (NSC) under the prime minister, the establishment of a National Security Advisory Board (NSAB) of nongovernmental experts to advise the NSC, and the revamping of the Joint Intelligence Committee (JIC) as the National Security Council Secretariat (NSCS) to provide inputs for the NSC.[52] The NSC and the full NSAB met for the first time only a month after the Kargil conflict began.[53] However, claiming that the official machinery was too unwieldy, the government called upon a core group of five of its members to advise it on a regular basis.[54] These were former Foreign Secretary J. N. Dixit, former Principal Secretary N. N. Vohra, leading defense analyst K. Subrahmanyam (also a former civil servant), retired Air Chief Marshal S. K. Mehra, and retired Major General Afsir Karim. The fact that all of them were from outside the government, and that three were retired civil servants and two retired military officials, was an encouraging sign of the lessons drawn from Kargil being taken early and seriously. Still, significant deficiencies in the integration of the national security decision-making process revealed by Kargil – and acknowledged by the government – remain, as is evident from the failure to appoint a CDS quickly, and from the lack of a comprehensive strategic doctrine. More importantly, the actual functioning of the system has been erratic. The NSC has not met regularly over the years, while the NSAB's role has been undercut by lack of access to classified data and by limited interaction with the government.[55]

Strategic lessons

In the post-Cold War era, India's external relationships have undergone significant change. On the global scale, the Indian government is no longer chary about major powers, especially the United States. The old "East-India-Company" syndrome has largely given way to a more confident approach to the developed countries and to their strategic interests. Foreign investment is now actively sought, and the presence of American

---

[52] For a critical assessment of the evolving decision-making apparatus, see D. Shyam Babu, "India's National Security Council: Stuck in the Cradle?" *Security Dialogue* 34, no. 2 (June 2003), 215–230.

[53] "Fernandes Restrained by NSC," *Indian Express*, 10 June 1999, www.indianexpress.com/ie/daily/19990610/ige10049.html.

[54] Arati R. Jerath, "Don't Tom-tom Kargil Win, Government Told," *Indian Express*, 24 July 1999, www.indianexpress.com/ie/daily/19990724/ige24061.html.

[55] B. Raman, "National Security Management," *Outlook*, 20 May 2004, www.outlookindia.com/full.asp?fname=raman&fodname=20040520&sid=2.

forces in the region is accepted with equanimity. Closer to home, India's relationship with China, and, to a lesser extent, with smaller neighbors such as Bangladesh, are not unproblematic, but these have not prevented negotiations to upgrade trade relations. Pakistan remains the major exception, with Kashmir at the center of the dispute. The gradual and initially covert process of nuclearization, which dates back more than a decade before Kargil, aggravated the hostility between the subcontinental rivals. Kargil itself marked a turning point, and the lessons Indian policymakers drew from it have had major consequences for Indian strategy.

Contending with Pakistan

Kargil had a powerful impact on Indian thinking about the role of politics and force in relations with Pakistan.[56] It evoked, above all, a deep sense of betrayal over Pakistan's duplicity in welcoming Prime Minister Vajpayee to Lahore in February 1999 even as the Kargil operation was underway. Vajpayee had invested considerable political capital in extending the olive branch to Prime Minister Nawaz Sharif, and Kargil came as a shock. Two years later, the perception of Pakistani perfidy remained powerful in Vajpayee's memory; "We shook hands like friends. It's a different matter that we were stabbed in the back."[57]

Still, Indian anger over Kargil did not immediately lead it to abandon diplomatic and political efforts to improve relations with Pakistan. Though relations for about a year after Kargil remained embittered, India eventually undertook a range of initiatives to improve the political environment through negotiation. In late 2000, a unilateral ceasefire was declared to facilitate talks between the Government of India and Kashmiri secessionists. At the same time, India and Pakistan agreed to revive the hotline between their respective Directors General of Military Operations that had become inoperative a year earlier. Renewed diplomatic efforts subsequently led to the Agra Summit between Vajpayee and Pakistan's new military ruler, President Pervez Musharraf. Thus Kargil was not a turning point in India's relationship with Pakistan: the possibility of negotiations remained. But, seen from the Indian perspective as the beginning of a rising trend of Pakistani interventionism and aggressive provocation over Kashmir, Kargil represents a watershed event in India's

---

[56] This section draws extensively from Rajesh M. Basrur, "Kargil, Terrorism, and India's Strategic Shift," *India Review* 1, no. 4 (October 2002), 39–56.

[57] Harjinder Sidhu, "Ansari Arrest Proves Pak Hand: PM," *Hindustan Times*, 11 February 2002, www.hindustantimes.com/nonfram/110202/detNAT01.asp. India's perception of betrayal initially focused on the Pakistani military, but later became less discriminating. The point became moot after General Musharraf's coup.

recent strategic history. While political efforts failed repeatedly, the depth of Pakistani involvement in the insurgency in Kashmir remained unchanged. Indian policymakers saw Pakistan using its nuclear capability as a cover for generating the pressure of the "stability–instability paradox": while Indian and Pakistani nuclear weapons deterred each other, and India's conventional advantage was neutralized by the risk of escalation to nuclear conflict, Pakistan had ample space for putting India under increasing pressure through covert intervention.[58] Kargil was one example of this paradox. The more widely prevalent form has been the abetting of terrorist violence, a strategy dating back to the 1980s when India's Punjab state was troubled by a prolonged Pakistan-aided insurgency, and is now practiced in Kashmir.[59]

Kargil, the failure of the Agra Summit, and the swelling tide of terrorism deeply embedded Indian distrust toward Pakistan. The terrorist attack on the Indian parliament on 13 December 2001 was the last straw. After Kargil, the hope for a negotiated stabilization had not died. Vajpayee had offered to bury the past and "pick up the threads" and put in place a stable structure of cooperation and address all outstanding issues, including Jammu and Kashmir."[60] Jaswant Singh had affirmed this, ruling out any preconditions for dialogue, but adding, "it is only right for our nation, at this juncture, to expect that Pakistan will repair the damage it has done to trust, that it demonstrates this through concrete and tangible steps."[61] The Indian leadership had planned the Agra Summit in July 2001 perceiving that after a military and diplomatic setback in Kargil, Pakistan would be looking for reconciliation with India, and that it would be prudent to work with Musharraf, who had emerged as a strong leader in Pakistan. However, it became apparent that Pakistan perceived Kargil as a victory, and the call for the summit as a sign of weakness on the part of the Indian leadership. Such perceptual distortions resulted in the failure of the summit and the hardening of attitudes on both sides.

---

[58] The original formulation of the concept is Glenn Snyder, "The Balance of Power and the Balance of Terror," in *The Balance of Power*, ed. Paul Seabury (San Francisco: Chandler, 1965), 194–201.

[59] Peter Chalk, "Pakistan's Role in the Kashmir Insurgency," *Jane's Intelligence Review*, 1 September 2001, reproduced on the website of the RAND Corporation: www.rand. org/hot/op-eds/090101JIR.html, n.d. [14 February 2003]; Sumit Ganguly, "Conflict and Crisis in South and Southwest Asia," in *The International Dimensions of Internal Conflict*, ed. Michael E. Brown (Cambridge, Mass.: MIT Press, 1996), 157; and Tim Judah, "The Taliban Papers," *Survival* 44, no. 1 (Spring 2002), 69–80.

[60] "India: Let's Bury the Past: Vajpayee," *The Hindu*, 14 July 2001, www.hinduonnet.com/ thehindu/2001/07/14/stories/01140002.htm.

[61] Singh, "Kargil and Beyond."

After 13 December Indian leaders had become convinced that Pakistan could not be trusted, and that negotiation was pointless without evidence of Pakistani good faith. Kargil remained the reference point. Recalling that event much later, Vajpayee ruminated: "India wanted peace with its neighbor, that is why I undertook Lahore, but see what I got in return."[62] Thereafter, India made an end to cross-border terrorism a precondition to talks. Given the continuing problem of terrorism, highlighted by the 13 December attack, it followed that the only language Pakistan would understand was force. The result was the 2001–2002 military standoff, though this can only be properly understood by taking into account three other lessons of Kargil: its role in crystallizing the LoC and the border as "red lines," its effect on international opinion, and its stimulus to Indian rethinking about the relationship between nuclear weapons and force.

Red lines and international responses

Since the formal delineation of the LoC after the 1971 war, that marker has played a significant role as the symbolic red line between war and peace. Both sides have contributed to this by abjuring its formal transgression except for occasional skirmishes. Pakistani strategic thought holds that India's seizure of the Siachen Glacier in 1984 constituted a major transgression of the LoC. Kargil is seen in this analysis as a response to the Indian offensive action in Siachen and an extension of the post-jockeying in the Northern Areas that followed. Even in Kargil, however, Pakistan acknowledged the vital role of the LoC as a threshold for war by avoiding an overt violation and maintaining the pretense that the forces that crossed the LoC to occupy territory on the Indian side were "freedom fighters." This was to prove a costly limitation, for it prevented Pakistan from sending in reinforcements to back up its faltering forces. It also avoided flying aircraft close to the LoC during the conflict. In effect, once India decided to respond with massive force, if the LoC was to be treated as sacrosanct, Pakistan was bound to fail. Since the fighting was on the Indian side, the balance of forces was bound to be heavily weighted in India's favor. India could deploy without limitations on its own territory, whereas Pakistan did not have that option. Though much is made about Pakistani military officials being ready to expand the conflict, the fact is that they did not. Instead, they risked losing their much-vaunted image in a political system over which they are universally held to have an iron grip. In short, the entire Pakistani leadership showed a willingness to bear costs

---

[62] C. Raja Mohan, "Let's Walk the High Road to Peace: Vajpayee," *The Hindu*, 26 May 2001, www.hinduonnet.com/thehindu/2001/05/26/stories/01260001.htm.

to preserve what is widely and significantly referred to as the "sanctity" of the LoC.

On the Indian side, the political leadership mirrored this pattern, and the armed forces were under strict orders not to cross the LoC. While the "sanctity" of the LoC was not hard and fast, since Indian forces did resort to heavy shelling across the LoC, India was willing to bear the considerable cost of closing several options. The Indian military avoided tactics such as diversionary attacks across the LoC, the crossing of the airspace over the LoC for approach runs in bombing Pakistani positions, and the enlargement of the conflict along the international border.[63] These restraints were costly, and added considerably to the number of casualties.

The international response to the crossing of the LoC by Pakistan helped crystallize the LoC as a red line. Pakistan received no support from any quarter, not even from its "all-weather" friend, China. On the contrary, while appealing for an immediate cessation of the conflict, the Group of Eight industrialized nations (G-8) called on both India and Pakistan to "respect the Line of Control" and return to the negotiating table.[64] More important, Pakistan, much to its surprise, was widely seen as the transgressor and was isolated by the international community as a result. Above all, the United States pressed Pakistan hard to withdraw to its own side of the LoC. At first, US leaders conveyed private messages to Pakistani diplomats and officials, including Sharif and Musharraf. When this did not work, President Clinton made a public demand that Pakistan respect the LoC, reiterating his position in a letter to Sharif.[65]

The reinforcement of the LoC – and, by extension, the international border – as a strategic threshold by India, Pakistan, and the international community was an important lesson of the Kargil conflict. For all sides, the nuclear potential of the conflict gave the matter much greater weight than might otherwise have been the case. Subsequent Indian behavior confirmed this. As the pressure to act against an intransigent Pakistan grew over time, Indian leaders were caught between the need for a strong response to what was seen as an inveterate adversary and the national and

---

[63] D. Suba Chandran, *Limited War: Revisiting Kargil in the Indo-Pakistan Conflict* (New Delhi: India Research Press, 2005), 56–61. The symbolism of physical presence in a geographic space in defining red lines is significant here. As an Indian army spokesman put it, cross-border shelling was an acceptable tactic, as "we are operating from our territory, we respect the sanctity of the LoC." "Army Takes Fight to Enemy Camp," *Indian Express*, 19 June 1999.

[64] "G-8 Asks India, Pak to Respect LoC, Cease Fighting," *Indian Express*, 11 June 1999, www.indianexpress.com/ie/daily/19990611/ige11044.html.

[65] Bruce Riedel, chapter 5.

international risks of crossing the threshold. This tension was reflected in the internal struggle to shape a strategy that could carve out a strategic space between inaction, on the one hand, and the limitations imposed by the sanctity of the LoC and the border, on the other. For two and a half years, the Indian government strained to develop a strategic vision, until dramatic external and internal developments helped determine its course, giving – for better or worse – substance to the lessons of Kargil. Perhaps the best evidence of the reinforcement of the LoC as a red line is the "dog that did not bark": the absence of its violation even at the height of tension in the 2001–2002 military standoff.

Strategic space and the shift to compellence

As Indian frustration grew, the discourse steadily veered away from a search for political solutions to a quest for the appropriate means of projecting force against an intransigent and malevolent Pakistan. The options aired included hot pursuit of terrorists into Pakistani territory, limited strikes or special operations missions against terrorist camps in Pakistan, and a vague conception of "limited war." During the Kargil conflict itself, India did initiate an initial mobilization for a possible war on a wider scale.[66] But the rapid winding down of the conflict altered the situation, and the prospects of an intensified confrontation receded. Still, influential strategic analysts of moderate persuasion voiced support for the concept. For instance, Jasjit Singh, then director of the government's Institute for Defence Studies and Analyses (IDSA), argued that "the most likely demand on our defense policy in the future would be that posed by a local border war that our own interests may require to keep limited," and that "serious consideration must be given to planning for ways and means of winning such wars."[67] In January 2000, Defence Minister George Fernandes asserted that nuclear weapons "can deter only the use of nuclear weapons, but not all and any war," and that Kargil had demonstrated that Indian forces "can fight and win a limited war, at a time and place chosen by the aggressor."[68] While admitting that under the nuclear shadow there were "definite limitations if escalation across the nuclear

---

[66] V. R. Raghavan, "Limited War and Nuclear Escalation in South Asia," *Nonproliferation Review.* 8, no. 3 (Fall–Winter 2001): 89. See also the subsequent statement by V. P. Malik, who had been India's army chief during the Kargil conflict, in Vishal Thapar, "Pak Nukes in US Custody?" *Hindustan Times*, 30 September 2002, www.hindustantimes. com/2002/Sep/30/printedition/300902/detNAT14.shtml.

[67] Singh, "Beyond Kargil," 226.

[68] C. Raja Mohan, "Fernandes Unveils 'Limited War' Doctrine," *The Hindu*, 25 January 2000, www.hinduonnet.com/thehindu/2000/01/25/stories/01250001.htm.

326 Rajesh M. Basrur

threshold was to be avoided," Fernandes claimed that conventional war "has not been made obsolete by nuclear weapons."[69]

During the Kargil conflict, neither side seriously feared that the fighting, which was restricted to a limited theater, would escalate into nuclear conflict. But there was *awareness* that any significant fighting between Indian and Pakistani forces had the potential to escalate into nuclear conflict. Kargil underscored the sanctity of the LoC and the entire border. In the aftermath, India would have been hard pressed to undertake a serious violation of the LoC or the border without undoing the international goodwill obtained by India's restraint in 1999. Thus, the tension between strategic paralysis and efforts to break out of it remained unresolved. The emergence of a changed global environment and of more compelling regional circumstances pushed India in a more assertive direction.

The dramatic events of 9/11 and the chain reaction they released around the world crystallized the new Indian strategic thinking that had germinated after the Kargil conflict. The new environment was dominated by a global revulsion against terrorism, which enabled India to contemplate stronger anti-terrorist action. Second, Pakistan itself was suspect in the eyes of many because of its role in bringing the atavistic Taliban to power in Afghanistan. Its own emergence as a center of radical Islam added to its negative image and strengthened India's case. The US-led war in Afghanistan facilitated India's shift to a pro-active policy against Pakistan-sponsored terrorism. While the United States and its allies worried about the risk of a nuclear conflagration, they could scarcely deny that India's stand against Pakistan was essentially the same as their position on Afghanistan. Moreover, 11 September was followed closely by intensified terrorist activity inside India. Two specific events – an attack on the Jammu and Kashmir Legislative Assembly on 1 October 2001, and the assault on the Indian parliament on 13 December – galvanized Indian decision-makers into action. The massive military buildup they initiated on the India–Pakistan border and the confrontation that followed embodied a major strategic shift that can be traced directly to Kargil. India grasped the moment to embark on a strategy of coercive diplomacy.[70] The 2001–2002 military standoff is better understood in the context of another aspect of Indian learning from Kargil: the role of nuclear weapons.

---

[69] *Ibid.*

[70] For a detailed analysis of the crisis of 2001–2002, see Rajesh M. Basrur, "Coercive Diplomacy in a Nuclear Environment: The December 13 Crisis," in *Prospects for Peace in South Asia*, ed. Rafiq Dossani and Henry S. Rowen (Stanford University Press, 2005), 301–325.

Nuclear weapons: beyond minimum deterrence

Kargil led Indian policymakers to conclude that their established view of nuclear weapons, especially the notion that mutual deterrence between India and Pakistan would freeze the status quo, was wrong. On the contrary, because mutual deterrence ruled out conventional war, Pakistan was freed to use subconventional strategies, such as abetting terrorism and covert attrition at the LoC. As the Kargil Review Committee observed,

It would not be unreasonable for Pakistan to have concluded by 1990 that it had achieved the nuclear deterrence it had set out to establish in 1980. Otherwise, it is inconceivable that it could sustain its proxy war against India, inflicting thousands of casualties, without being unduly concerned about India's conventional superiority.[71]

Kargil compelled Indian leaders to think more carefully about what nuclear weapons implied for Indian strategy.[72] Oblique Pakistani threats to use nuclear weapons if India resorted to conventional war gave notice that the ground realities of nuclear weapons had been neglected. During Kargil, it has been claimed that India went to the extent of a low-level nuclear alert, preparing warheads for mating with delivery vehicles,[73] but this has not been confirmed. India felt the need to do two things: bolster its deterrent and look for ways to overcome the strategic paralysis imposed by Pakistan's deterrent. The first objective was given an early start. Immediately after the conflict, India redrew its military contingency plans to take the possibility of a nuclear attack into account.[74] In August 1999, only a month after the end of the Kargil conflict, India widely publicized the Draft Nuclear Doctrine produced by the NSAB.[75] Development of the Pakistan-specific mobile Agni-I ballistic missile began soon after Kargil in October 1999 and culminated in a successful full-scale flight test in January 2002.[76] In January 2003, a new command and control system was also established.[77]

---

[71] Kargil Review Committee, *From Surprise to Reckoning*, 241.

[72] Tellis, Fair, and Medby, *Limited Conflicts under the Nuclear Umbrella*, 56–57.

[73] Raj Chengappa, *Weapons of Peace: The Secret Story of India's Quest to Be a Nuclear Power* (New Delhi: HarperCollins, 2000), 437.

[74] "New Delhi 'War Book' Updated for Possible Nuke Attack," *Agence France Presse*, 29 July 1999.

[75] *Draft Report of National Security Advisory Board on Indian Nuclear Doctrine*, 17 August 1999, Embassy of India, Washington, DC, www.indianembassy.org/policy/CTBT/nuclear_doctrine_aug_17_1999.html. The report was already underway when the Kargil conflict occurred, but the fact that it was widely disseminated is indicative of the government's interest in stirring a country-wide debate and bringing nuclear weapons to the forefront as a national strategic issue.

[76] T. S. Subramanian, "The Significance of Agni-I," *Frontline*, 2 February 2002, www.flonnet.com/fl1903/19031300.htm.

[77] C. Raja Mohan, "Nuclear Command Authority Comes into Being," *The Hindu*, 5 January 2003, www.hinduonnet.com/thehindu/2003/01/05/stories/2003010504810100.htm.

The search for strategic space after Kargil led to talk of "limited war" being possible under the nuclear shadow. Indeed, army chief General V. P. Malik recalled in 2002 that he had affirmed the possibility of a limited war even before Kargil, and that "not many people took my statement seriously, till Kargil happened."[78] That space was only conceivable if India had scope to act in such a way as to override mutual deterrence. Eventually, this was achieved by making the argument that mutual deterrence had more to it than a straightforward balance between nuclear adversaries. India now began to argue that the subcontinental equation was not an equal one. On the contrary, India had the advantage. Fernandes put it in stark terms:

Pakistan can't think of using nuclear weapons despite the fact that they are not committed to the doctrine of no first use like we are. We could take a strike, survive, and then hit back. Pakistan would be finished.[79]

Because a nuclear exchange would hurt Pakistan far more than it would India, Indian defense planners reasoned, they had the choice of engaging in some unspecified form of limited war.[80] This in turn enabled India to launch its ten-month-long exercise in compellence in December 2001.

Conclusion: lessons well learned?

The word that best describes the Kargil experience is "shock." The very severity of the shock invited – indeed, necessitated – drastic changes in thought and practice. The drawing of lessons was inevitable and the appointment of the Kargil Review Committee was a logical consequence. But learning is a matter of perception: not everyone extracts the same lessons from an event. Nor need the lessons drawn necessarily be correct. Learning, in short, is not synonymous with wisdom. And finally, learning cannot be complete unless it results in appropriate action. This becomes clearer when subsequent policy is subject to critical questions. How far did Indian policymakers integrate the lessons they drew with their larger understanding of strategy? Did they implement properly the reforms generated by the lessons of Kargil? Did they appreciate that the impetus of Kargil, in modifying their view about the role of force between nuclear adversaries, might alter the basis of India's deterrence strategy?

[78] V. P. Malik, "Lessons from Kargil," *Bharat Rakshak Monitor* 4, no. 6 (May–June 2002), www.bharat-rakshak.com/MONITOR/ISSUE4-6/malik.html.

[79] "We Could Take a Strike and Survive. Pakistan Won't: Fernandes," *Hindustan Times*, 30 December 2001, www.hindustantimes.com/nonfram/301201/detfea06.asp.

[80] Basrur, "Kargil, Terrorism, and India's Strategic Shift," 46–47.

Perhaps the most positive Indian learning from Kargil was the attention given to the organization of security. The jolt of discovering that a large chunk of Indian territory had been occupied by stealth drew attention to technological, organizational, and human failures. During the previous India–Pakistan wars of 1965 and 1971 such postwar analysis and follow-up had not materialized. The government took up the recommendations of the Kargil Review Committee in earnest. Specifically, the GoM report represented a determination to rethink and to reorganize. It recommen-ded the strengthening of the intelligence apparatus through organizational changes, notably the creation of the Defence Intelligence Agency, and by a new emphasis on technical means for border surveillance. The govern-ment also gave attention to the larger problem of border management at all levels: the military, the paramilitary, and the local (village) levels. The revelations of technological weaknesses in the armed forces led to rapid efforts to upgrade technology through new acquisitions suitable for the extreme conditions along the LoC. Finally, the government introduced significant changes in the national security policymaking apparatus. Kargil had exposed the gulf between the armed forces and the civilian apparatus. The decision to bring the military into apex decision-making was calculated to overcome this widely perceived deficiency.

Several problems remain. The upgrading of border security has not been particularly effective. Despite considerable investments in this area, terrorist attacks continue to occur with high frequency, and, by the government's own admission, cross-border terrorism remains significant. Terrorist attacks continue on civilian as well as military targets. On the planning and organizational side, there remains the vexed issue of appointing the CDS, which continues to hinder integrated planning and strategy. The irregular functioning of the reformed national security decision-making apparatus raises doubts about the government's com-mitment to a truly effective, integrated process of policy formulation. Among the criticisms of its functioning: government neglect of the NSC, weak coordination of the numerous bodies that make up the sys-tem, and domination of the NSAB by retired bureaucrats.[81]

With respect to strategy, the primary impetus of Kargil was recognition of the need to *think* about strategy. The suspicion of Pakistan as an irredeemable recidivist traces back to Kargil, but truly was embedded by Pakistan's failure, in Indian eyes, to make amends *after* Kargil. A critical

---

[81] Babu, "India's National Security Council"; Inder Malhotra, "NSA: Lessons from America," *The Hindu*, 9 January 2005; and B. Raman, "National Security Mechanism," Paper no. 1228, South Asia Analysis Group, Noida, 24 January 2005, www.saag.org/papers13/paper1228.html.

question was whether negotiations were at all feasible under the circumstances, and if so, what kind. Initially, Indian leaders were unwilling to talk to a military-run Pakistan government. In June 2000, India rejected Pakistan's proposal for talks on a restraint regime on the ground that it was "essentially propagandist" and that, after the "Kargil misadventure," it was Pakistan's responsibility first to create a proper environment by putting a stop to cross-border terrorism.[82] The diplomatic process was revived, but set back again by the ill-fated Agra Summit and more severely by the 2001–2002 crisis. The lesson of Kargil and the 2001–2002 crisis was that, with nuclear weapons ruling out the use of force and indeed sharply raising its potential costs, there was no option but to talk. This led to the dialogue process that commenced in January 2004.

The search for strategic space in tackling Pakistan was also problematic. Here, Kargil's "lessons" were contradictory. On one hand, Indian leaders felt compelled to act through force projection, because Pakistan could no longer be trusted. On the other, the reinforcement of the LoC and the border as red lines recognized by India, Pakistan, and the global community meant the way in which that force could be projected was necessarily limited: by the threat of war rather than its actual conduct. The muddled lessons drawn from Kargil led eventually to India's 2001–2002 military buildup, which represented the maximum threat projection without war that was possible under the circumstances. Kargil also "taught" Indian policymakers that the United States would intervene early to contain a conflict in South Asia, which perhaps gave them the confidence to discount the risk of war while initiating a massive military mobilization against Pakistan.

The crisis failed to resolve India's Pakistan problem, leaving Indian decision-makers with the same situation they had faced in the aftermath of Kargil. Despite an initial commitment to reversal, Pakistani strategy with respect to Kashmir remained essentially unchanged and continued to exact high costs.[83] The "lesson" of Kargil – that force projection would work better than diplomacy – was a case of "incorrect learning." In practice, the whole argument for limited war came to naught in 2002. Military thinking has not changed. General Malik continues to hold that "limited war was, and still is, a strategic possibility so long as the proxy war continues on the subcontinent."[84] But then, this represents a military professional's thinking, and does not reflect the perspective of political

---

[82] "India Rejects Pak. Proposal, Terms it 'Propagandist,'" *The Hindu*, 15 June 2000, www.hinduonnet.com/thehindu/2000/06/15/stories/01150001.htm.

[83] Basrur, "Coercive Diplomacy in a Nuclear Environment."

[84] V. P. Malik, *Kargil: From Surprise to Victory* (New Delhi: HarperCollins, 2006), 366.

decision-makers, who have been reluctant to return to the limited-war logic that preceded the 2001–2002 crisis. The politicians, at least, seem to have learned the combined lesson of the two crises: that limited war is not a viable option in a nuclear context. This explains the Indian leadership's persistence with efforts to put together a structure of confidence-building on nuclear and nonnuclear issues with Pakistan despite its continuing dissatisfaction with the relationship.

That India began to take nuclear weapons-related issues more seriously was no doubt commendable. The lack of a refined command and control system was a handicap that needed to be overcome. But there are difficulties with India's nuclear posture that actually have intensified as a result of the perceived lessons of Kargil. Most fundamentally, no Indian official has been able to articulate what exactly "minimum deterrence" is, let alone explain what is meant by "*credible* minimum deterrence."[85] That being so, the tension between the political risk element associated with nuclear weapons and the operational aspect of how well they work as weapons of war remains unresolved. Instead, the political facet has been misappropriated, and the operational one misread. Despite Pakistan's failure, Kargil demonstrated that nuclear weapons could be manipulated for political gain. India used this "lesson" later to try, unsuccessfully, to transform Pakistani behavior through a strategy of compellence. While the actual risk of nuclear conflict in 1999 and 2001–2002 may be debated, there is little doubt that the political use of nuclear weapons has severe limitations and significant risk. The military's expanded role in strategic planning is an invitation to develop a more operational conception of nuclear weapons, with a greater concern for numbers, accuracy, reliability, damage expectancy, and the like. Unless Indian policymakers come to grips with the fundamentals of deterrence – which centers around the question "how much is enough?" – the management of nuclear weapons will be difficult.

Kargil's final lesson is that learning requires introspection. What has been learned? And how well? What are the long-term implications of one's learning? Are there alternatives? The process of learning does not – and should not – stop. To return to the point with which this chapter began, learning in complex situations requires "practice," for the process occurs over time. It depends on numerous factors: one's own ability to learn continuously, the responses of others, and the nature of the environment in which learning occurs. This essay provides some judgments that may help in the process of learning. It is evident that of the lessons that were

---

[85] For a detailed critique of the concept and Indian nuclear strategy, see Rajesh M. Basrur, *Minimum Deterrence and India's Nuclear Security* (Stanford University Press, 2006).

drawn from Kargil, some have been of long-term benefit, some had to be rethought in the wake of the subsequent crisis, and some linger in the penumbra of inadequate implementation. Above all, while the consequences of the nuclear revolution have been brought into high relief by Kargil and its succeeding crisis, its intellectual foundations remain weak, though this is hardly unique to the subcontinent. In these respects, the lessons of Kargil have yet to be fully learned.

13   The lessons of Kargil as learned by Pakistan

Hasan-Askari Rizvi

Pakistan has had difficulty learning from its past military failures, but the learning process from the Kargil conflict has been a particularly tortuous and private affair for the country's civilian and military leaders and national security institutions. The Pakistan government's ability to discuss the Kargil operation and ensuing military crisis was – and still is – constrained by its determination to maintain the *mujahideen* cover story.[1] Several nongovernment analysts in Pakistan have questioned the army's official version. However, the official narrative still dominates Pakistani writings on the Kargil conflict. While more thoughtful, internal reviews reportedly have taken place within various organizations of the armed forces, they remain classified and have not been released to the public.[2] For its part, the Nawaz Sharif government did not institute any official or semi-official inquiry of the Kargil operation largely because it feared opposition from the military.

The task of explaining what lessons Pakistan has learned as a result of the Kargil conflict is further complicated by the fact that the military operation and its aftermath became closely intertwined with the nation's civil–military political debate. In the months leading up to the October 1999 coup, and even in subsequent years, military officers and civilian officials from the Nawaz Sharif government have sought to pin the blame

---

[1] See Christine Fair's detailed discussion of this issue in chapter 9 of this book.

[2] Public discussion of Kargil by Pakistani officials began with a conference at the Naval Postgraduate School in 2002, but was far from complete. As the Center for Contemporary Conflict (CCC) research project progressed, the Pakistan government reluctantly concluded that more information had to be made public to present its side of the story. Consequently, Pakistani army officers briefed a CCC team of US and Pakistani scholars in Rawalpindi, Islamabad, and Gilgit in January 2003. The military also allowed the research team to interview some of the senior officers associated with the Kargil operation. A Pakistani version of what transpired emerged with the publication of Shireen M. Mazari's quasi-official account, *The Kargil Conflict 1999: Separating Fact from Fiction* (Islamabad: Ferozsons, 2003). Pervez Musharraf gives a brief account of the Kargil conflict in his autobiography, *In the Line of Fire: A Memoir* (London: Simon and Schuster, 2006), 86–98.

for the Kargil debacle on each other. These obstacles notwithstanding, this chapter analyzes if the Kargil operation was an isolated incident or instead conforms to a broader pattern of Pakistani strategic conduct. I argue the latter. Since its inception in 1947, Pakistan has not shied away from using force to redress grievances, believing that military or para-military means are necessary elements in its tit-for-tat relationship with India, and also that this approach had support in the international community. Pakistan historically has sought small, tactical victories in order to achieve larger psychological dividends. And repeatedly, Pakistan has underestimated the Indian response and overestimated the support its own cause would receive from friends and allies.

This chapter examines four questions. First, what has Pakistan learned from its past crises and wars with India? In particular, why do Pakistani leaders repeatedly fail to anticipate the severity of responses by India and the international community to Pakistani military and paramilitary actions in Kashmir? Second, what were Pakistan's expectations of Indian and international responses to the Kargil crisis and why was it so poorly prepared for the elevated political and military intensity of the conflict? Third, what explains the mistakes Pakistan made at the military opera-tional level that enabled India to recapture the territory that Pakistan had occupied.[3] Fourth, in the aftermath of the Kargil conflict, have Pakistan's civilian bodies and security institutions – particularly within the armed forces – undergone significant shifts in strategic thinking and behavior?

Military learning in South Asia

South Asian states seldom conduct in-depth, public inquiries into military debacles. For example, a military analysis of India's failure in the 1962 border war with China was prepared by Indian army officers Lieutenant General Henderson Brooks and Brigadier P. S. Bhagat, but this report remains classified by the Indian government.[4] Internal assessments of India's problematic peacekeeping operation in Sri Lanka from 1987 to 1990 have not been released. Similarly, there were no public reports of Pakistani miscues in the 1965 war in Kashmir. Following that conflict,

---

[3] In 1984, when India had occupied the Siachen Glacier, the operational conditions made it impossible for Pakistani troops to retake the ground that was lost. Apparently, the Kargil planners believed that the same logic would apply to the 1999 high-altitude military operation. What then explains India's reacquisition of the area at such heights?

[4] However, a British military historian of the 1962 war has described what he claims are the main points of the report. See Neville Maxwell, "Henderson Brooks Report: An Introduction," *Economic and Political Weekly* (14 April 2001): 1189–1193, www.epw.org. in/epw/uploads/articles/5306.pdf.

Zulfikar Ali Bhutto resigned from the Ayub Khan cabinet, threatening that he would expose conspiracies behind the war and the Tashkent ceasefire accord. While the commission chaired by Pakistan Supreme Court Justice Hamood-ur-Rehman did analyze Pakistan's 1971 defeat in its eastern wing (now Bangladesh), its report was suppressed for nearly three decades until the Musharraf government made it public.[5] After the loss of the Siachen Glacier in 1984, no public inquiry was conducted, though the government of Prime Minister Muhammed Khan Junejo came under heavy pressure from the opposition to do so. Given this history, it is not surprising that the Nawaz Sharif government chose not to institute any official or semi-official inquiry of the Kargil operation.

By contrast, almost as soon as the fighting had ended, the Indian government and armed forces undertook a widely publicized set of studies and reports, as discussed by Rajesh Basrur in chapter 12 of this book. New Delhi also was able to use the Kargil operation to garner domestic and international support for its policy on Kashmir and against Pakistan. India conducted two quasi-public reviews of the Kargil operation – a report by the government-appointed Kargil Review Committee and then a report by the Group of Ministers that turned the first report's findings into practical policy initiatives. Such introspection is rare in South Asia, yet the Kargil Review Committee barely apportioned any blame on the military failures. Nor did General V. P. Malik's book on Kargil, which evoked criticism from the Indian intelligence community and led to a subsequent blame game.[6]

As the Kargil experience shows very clearly, to the extent that India and Pakistan do learn from past crises and wars, the lessons that are learned tend to create the conditions for future crises and wars. In their six decades of enduring political–military rivalry, India and Pakistan have yet to learn how to manage disputes without evoking the risk of war. As Russell Leng observes, this has been a persistent problem for the Indian and Pakistan governments from their independence in 1947 to the present: "insofar as the peaceful management of disputes and progress toward the termination of the rivalry are concerned, the lessons drawn by both sides have been largely dysfunctional. Experiential learning that has occurred during the course of the rivalry most often has reinforced behavior that has encouraged the recurrence of crises and

[5] "Report of the Commission of Inquiry: 1971 War as Declassified by the Government of Pakistan," available at www.bangla2000.com/Bangladesh/Independence-War/Report-Hamoodur-Rahman/default.shtm.
[6] General V. P. Malik, *Kargil: From Surprise to Victory* (New Delhi: HarperCollins, 2006).

wars."[7] Because Pakistan has been the party to initiate most of the bilateral conflicts in the past, its learning behavior most starkly bears this pattern.

Why does Pakistan not learn to manage its rivalry with India in ways that reduce the risk of war, yet assure its existence? Sixty years of grappling with this security challenge has eroded Pakistan's overall security and made its foreign policy completely India-centric. Born with a set of grievances – most notably on Kashmir – Pakistan has long sought strategic opportunities to settle the dispute militarily. In 1947–1948, and again in 1965, Pakistan's failure to resolve the Kashmir dispute militarily made the management of relations with India even more difficult. After 1965 Pakistan found itself in a predicament where it could neither grab Kashmir militarily nor give it up politically since Kashmir is an emotive domestic issue. Consequently, Pakistan cannot simply accept the regional status quo and have the confidence that resultant stability would bring in the form of a benign India.[8] In six decades, India and Pakistan have tried to resolve disputes bilaterally, multilaterally, as well as through third-party interventions, but have failed to develop a sustained peace and security architecture.

Further, both India and Pakistan have attributed the notion of success in a crisis or war with the demonstration of resolve. For example, Pakistani military officials believed that their military success in the Rann of Kutch in 1965 indicated that India had insufficient resolve to compete militarily, and thus the Ayub Khan government mounted a major military operation in Kashmir, which ultimately failed to achieve its objectives and worsened bilateral relations considerably. Conversely, India's victory in the 1971 Bangladesh war was seen in Pakistan as proof of a harsh *Realpolitik* lesson that India will exploit any opportunity it has to take Pakistan down a notch. After the 1971 military debacle, Pakistani planners did not make a fundamental adjustment of policies toward India, nor were they willing to accept India's preeminence. Rather, they simply revised their military and paramilitary strategies – to include acquiring nuclear weapons at any cost – so as to compete more effectively in the next round.[9] Pakistani behavior after each setback in crises has been to analyze the causes of failure and resolve to live to fight another day.

---

[7] Russell J. Leng, "Realpolitik and Learning in the India–Pakistan Rivalry," in *The India–Pakistan Conflict: An Enduring Rivalry*, ed. T. V. Paul (Cambridge University Press, 2005), 103.

[8] For a discussion of how Indian and Pakistani perceptions of each other shape behavior in bilateral crises, see Russell J. Leng, *Bargaining and Learning in Recurring Crises: The Soviet–American, Egyptian–Israeli, and Indo-Pakistani Rivalries* (Ann Arbor: University of Michigan Press, 2000), 195–265.

[9] Leng, "Realpolitik and Learning in the India–Pakistan Rivalry," 106.

Pakistan has not learned the lessons of Kargil evenly. On one end of the spectrum, the Pakistan army probably has learned a good deal from the many logistical and tactical errors it made during the Kargil incursion. Military institutions reportedly conducted in-depth, internal reviews of operational failures, although these reports have not been made public.[10] On the other end of the spectrum, it is unclear whether Pakistan will be able to prevent the recurrence of the severe institutional failures that plagued the planning and execution of the Kargil operation. In the 2001–2002 military standoff with India, Pervez Musharraf's dual role as army chief and president brought a semblance of institutional coherence to the government's capacity for crisis management. However, it remains to be seen whether the gaps between civilians and the military, among the armed services, and among different departments within the army – all in evidence during the Kargil conflict – have been reduced, particularly as Pakistan transits from a military-dominated system to a civilian-led, democratic government.

Misperceiving others: Pakistani perceptions of international response

The planners of Kargil bit off more than they could chew. They never envisioned that the Kargil intrusion would be on the front pages of newspapers around the world. Instead, they visualized the operation as being similar to India's 1984 occupation of the Siachen Glacier, which the international community greeted with a collective yawn. This misperception of foreign reactions occurred for three reasons.

First, for decades, the Pakistan military consistently has underestimated Indian responses and overestimated international sympathy for Pakistani actions.[11] Most Pakistanis approach their relationship with India with a strong sense of grievance. In 1948, Pakistani decision-makers did not anticipate the intense Indian military response to the marauding tribal *lashkars* in Jammu and Kashmir, even though the British governor of the North-West Frontier Province, Sir George Cunningham, was concerned that such forays might present India with a *casus belli*.[12] Faith in the

---

[10] Information based on CCC research team members' interviews with Pakistani military officers in Rawalpindi and Islamabad in January 2003 and in subsequent years.

[11] For a broader examination of this topic, see Hasan-Askari Rizvi, "Pakistan's Strategic Culture," in *South Asia in 2020: Future Strategic Balances and Alliances*, ed. Michael Chambers (Carlisle, Pa.: Army War College, Strategic Studies Institute, November 2002), 305–328.

[12] Cunningham is quoted in Brian Cloughley, *The History of the Pakistan Army: Wars and Insurrections* (Oxford University Press, 1999), 14–16.

lashkars was probably misplaced anyway. The tribal warriors ultimately were less concerned with a jihad to free Kashmir, and concentrated more on pillaging and looting along the way. Relying on proxies and under-estimating the Indian response backfired on Pakistani decision-makers in these formative years and again two decades later.

In 1965, the Pakistan military and the Foreign Office both had unfounded faith that the Kashmiri population was ripe for an uprising. A minor victory in the Rann of Kutch, coupled with a perception of Indian vacillation, led to the belief that Pakistani intervention in Indian affairs would not lead New Delhi to undertake significant retaliation. Instead, the Kashmiris did not show up in significant numbers in what Pakistan had intended to be their liberation. But India did react in a big way. The government of Prime Minister Lal Bahadur Shastri responded to *Operation Grand Slam* by escalating militarily along the international border.[13]

There are many parallels between the 1999 Kargil conflict and the 1965 Kashmir war. While President Ayub Khan foresaw the possibility that a desperate India might escalate the conflict in 1965, he assessed, "As a general rule, Hindu morale would not stand for more than a couple of hard blows delivered at the right time and place. Such opportunities should therefore be sought and exploited."[14] In 1999, the Kargil plan was much less ambitious than the sequenced *Gibraltar* and *Grand Slam* operations, and the Pakistani planners calculated that India would not escalate because it did not make military sense to do so. Military escala-tion elsewhere along the Line of Control (LoC) was bound to dissipate available resources and dilute the pressure that could be applied along the Kargil front. Further, Pakistani planners believed that India would be restrained from dramatically escalating the conflict because of Pakistan's new nuclear deterrent, and the expected strong pressure from the interna-tional community to prevent a serious nuclear crisis. While the Kargil planners may have correctly assessed that India would not want to escalate elsewhere in Kashmir or along the border, they were completely incorrect in their belief that India could not achieve local military advantage in the Kargil-Dras and Batalik military sectors.[15] As James J. Wirtz and Surinder Rana point out in chapter 8 of this book, wishful thinking tends to intrude

---

[13] See the discussion by Feroz Hassan Khan, Peter R. Lavoy, and Christopher Clary in chapter 3 of this book.

[14] Directive from President Ayub Khan to General Mohammad Musa, Commander-in-Chief Pakistan army, 29 August 1965, quoted in Cloughley, *History of the Pakistan Army*, 70–71. The directive was drafted by the foreign minister, Zulfikar Ali Bhutto.

[15] It is difficult to judge whether the Indian government would have escalated horizontally had its armed forces been unable to dislodge Pakistan's occupying forces from their

on the weaker side's estimates of its stronger opponent's response to surprise and the way the entire operation eventually will produce in a favorable outcome.

Second, Pakistan's national security elites had yet to internalize the real meaning of the 1998 nuclear explosive tests, which, conversely, were almost the sole prism through which the international community saw the crisis. While the Kargil planners may have had some vague notion of how nuclear deterrence operated, none of them had ever been involved in the nuclear program.[16] While Pakistan's possession of nuclear weapons may well have been one of the factors that discouraged India from expanding the conflict elsewhere, it also led the international community, most significantly the United States, to apply intense pressure on Islamabad to de-escalate and withdraw its forces unconditionally. In other words, while the nuclear factor may have dampened the risk that Kargil would escalate militarily, it certainly guaranteed that the operation would take a far higher profile in Washington and New Delhi.

Third, as Khan, Lavoy, and Clary highlight in chapter 3 of this book, these mistakes might have been reduced had Pakistan's national security institutions not broken down at multiple levels. The Kargil operation was conceived exclusively in terms of an "LoC affair."[17] As a consequence, planning for the operation was confined mostly to the 10 Corps within the Pakistan army. Further, discussions of Kargil were compartmentalized to ensure that the operation would remain secret, a necessary requirement for the success of any high-altitude operation along the LoC. While there is evidence that the Pakistan military did brief Nawaz Sharif in January, February, and March 1999,[18] it also seems apparent that the prime minister's office and the Defence Cabinet Committee (DCC) were

mountain posts in the Kargil-Dras sector. Senior Indian military officers told the book's editor that they were under strict orders to get the job done on the Indian side of the LoC in the Kargil-Dras sector – even though there were strong military reasons to take the fight across the LoC into Pakistani-held territory. However, as discussed by Peter R. Lavoy in chapter 1 of this book, India would have crossed the LoC and probably also the international border had its troops not been able to achieve their objectives in the Kargil-Dras sector in a timely fashion.

[16] Of the senior Pakistani military leaders in command at the time of Kargil, only the Director General of ISID, Lt. Gen. Ziauddin, had significant experience with Pakistan's nuclear weapons program. But he was excluded from planning for the Kargil operation. He had served as Director General, Combat Development Directorate, in the army's GHQ. After the May 1998 nuclear tests, CDC was disbanded, and the Strategic Plans Division was created to oversee Pakistan's nuclear policy and capabilities.

[17] Pakistani officials made this comment repeatedly during briefings to CCC researchers.

[18] General Pervez Musharraf claimed that the army briefed Prime Minister Nawaz Sharif on 29 January 1999, 5 February, 12 March, 17 May, 2 June, and 22 June. Musharraf, *In the Line of Fire*, 96. Nawaz Sharif claimed that Musharraf had "deliberately hidden some aspects of the Kargil war from me." *Daily Times*, 11 April 2007. Earlier he denied getting any briefing from the army prior to May 1999.

unaware of the operation early on and, when they did come to know of it, failed in their coordinating roles. The Foreign Office appears to have been left out of any discussions of the Kargil operation until after the first Pakistani positions were discovered in early May, while the other military services and key directorates within the army were largely marginalized during the contingency planning and initial operational phases. This is reminiscent of the 1965 war, when President Ayub Khan ordered Gen. Mohammad Musa to prepare for possible Indian escalation in response to *Operation Grand Slam*, but went ahead with the plan without ensuring that such preparations took place. As a consequence, the Lahore garrison was unprepared for the 6 September 1965 Indian attack, despite the predictability of such escalation.[19]

The Pakistani planners' misperception of the importance of the Kargil operation – in the eyes of India and as well as the international community – had a significantly negative impact for the outcome of the operation. Although the initial infiltration could not have gone better, when the crisis escalated in May 1999, Pakistan was not ready to mobilize the various components of national power to achieve either military or diplomatic success. As a result, Pakistan found itself isolated and in a disadvantageous position relative to India.

The harsh spotlight

No military expedition can be undertaken without taking into account the totality of the environment, which includes the domestic political scene, the economic environment, and the global and regional diplomatic contexts. The planners of Kargil did not expect the conflict to rise above the level of a large-scale skirmish along the LoC. The army planners in Rawalpindi and Gilgit (which is home to the Force Command Northern Areas Headquarters) prepared for an ambitious, local operation (and possibly more), but Islamabad was not ready for a limited war. When the international spotlight did shine on Pakistan, the government found it was divided domestically, fragile economically, isolated diplomatically, and in institutional disarray.

Pakistan was very much a house divided. There was a military–military disconnect between the army General Headquarters (GHQ) and the Inter-Services Intelligence Directorate (ISID), and also among 10 Corps and the rest of the corps commanders. There was a serious civil–military divide; for the military planned the operation without taking into

---

[19] Owen Bennett Jones, *Pakistan: Eye of the Storm* (New Haven, Conn.: Yale University Press, 2002), 77–78.

its confidence the Foreign Office or other civilian officials – with the sole exception of the prime minister. And there was a civil–civil divide between the Sharif government and the opposition and also between Nawaz Sharif and his cabinet ministers. Each of these divisions severely hampered the ability of the Pakistan government to respond coherently and effectively to the rapidly unfolding Kargil political–military crisis.

The military–military disconnect is discussed elsewhere in this volume.[20] To recapitulate, the army GHQ and ISID appear not to have coordinated on the Kargil operation, so that the insurgency was not orchestrated to disrupt Indian operations. Additionally, planning discussions were confined to 10 Corps and were not held with other corps commanders and military services, both of which were brought in only after the intrusion had been publicly revealed.

Pakistan's domestic political scene was marked by sharp polarization between the civilian government of Nawaz Sharif and the opposition in the wake of the prime minister's efforts to concentrate all powers in his hands at the expense of state institutions and the opposition. The government was unable to mobilize support for the war effort partly because it was bogged down in political wrangling with the opposition and partly because it had made a policy decision not to admit the Pakistan army's involvement in the Kargil operation. How could the government mobilize domestic support for the war effort when it maintained that the army was not fighting a war with Indian troops?[21] Because it clung to the *mujahideen* cover story, it could either express sympathy for the so-called Kashmiri freedom fighters engaged in armed conflict with the Indian army or declare that it would take appropriate action to defend Pakistani territorial integrity if the Indian troops crossed the LoC or the international border.[22]

Further, Sharif appears to have been briefed about the Kargil plan as early as 29 January and 5 February 1999.[23] He reportedly did not, however, inform his cabinet or his closest advisors of the operation until

---

[20] See especially chapters 2, 3, and 9.

[21] Even after agreeing to withdraw its personnel, Pakistan's official spokesmen continued to harp on the theme that there were no Pakistani troops on the Indian side of the LoC. See, for instance, text of Radio Pakistan report, "Pakistani Army Official Rejects Indian Claim of Recapturing Tiger Hill," 5 July 1999, reproduced in *BBC Summary of World Broadcasts*, 7 July 1999. C. Christine Fair examines this issue in detail in chapter 9 of this book.

[22] See, for instance, text of Pakistan Radio report, "Pakistan 'Will Not Tolerate Any Trespass' on Line of Control," 23 June 1999, reproduced in *BBC Summary of World Broadcasts*, 25 June 1999.

[23] Mazari, *The Kargil Conflict 1999*, 57–58. Gen. Pervez Musharraf does not explicitly write in his memoir that Nawaz Sharif attended the briefing, but he displays images in the book showing briefings in the 10 Corps area on 5 February 1999. Musharraf, *In the Line of Fire*.

17 May, when Sharif and his key ministers and secretaries attended an ISID briefing on the operation. At a cabinet meeting on 25 May, Sharif's cabinet still had a poor understanding of the operation, but was largely supportive of giving the military wide latitude in the conduct of what could turn out to be a major foreign policy success. Despite some notable opposition to the operation, in particular from Sharif's defence secretary, Lt. Gen. (retd.) Chaudhry Iftikhar, a cabinet meeting on 25 May ended without any decisions being made. By mid-June, however, as media reports appeared worse and worse for Pakistan's ground position, the divide within Sharif's cabinet began to shift, with increasing numbers of ministers becoming pessimistic about the operation's outcome.[24]

Furthermore, the official statements gave exaggerated accounts of the exploits of the Kashmiri freedom fighters in the face of Indian attacks. The Pakistani media generally carried forward these accounts without verification through their own professional sources.[25] The government's denial strategy and the exaggerated accounts of the successes of the freedom fighters made the Nawaz Sharif visit to Washington to sign a withdrawal agreement even more jarring to the Pakistani public. If the earlier success stories of the freedom fighters were true, a sudden decision to withdraw did not make much sense. Thus it was not surprising that the news of Nawaz Sharif's meeting with President Bill Clinton and his willingness to work toward the withdrawal of Pakistani elements from the Indian side of the LoC in Kashmir caused much disappointment throughout the Pakistani population. Several political leaders described Nawaz Sharif's action as a national betrayal.[26] And as Saeed Shafqat points out in chapter 11 of this book, Pakistan's Islamic parties and political groups were particularly critical of the decision to withdraw from the heights around Kargil.[27] Some analysts raised the issue that if the personnel fighting Indian troops were not under Pakistani control, how could Nawaz Sharif promise their withdrawal?[28] By agreeing to pull back and restore the sanctity of the LoC, Nawaz Sharif confirmed what India and others had been saying: that the Pakistan army or paramilitary forces had secretly occupied the Kargil-Dras heights.

---

[24] Information based on interviews by the CCC research team with Pakistani political and military officials.

[25] For a brief review of the role of Pakistan's press during the Kargil crisis, see Rashed Rahman, "Media's Role during the Kargil Crisis," *The Nation*, 1 February 2000.

[26] See "Opposition: Sharif–US Deal a Major Setback," *The Nation*, 6 July 1999.

[27] See, for instance, "Imran: Washington Pact 'Betrayal' of Mujahideen," *Dawn*, 12 July 1999.

[28] Some *mujahideen* groups continued to take credit for the defense of Kargil even after the withdrawal of Pakistani forces commenced. See "Mujahideen Vow to Open New Fronts," *Ausaf* (Islamabad), 22 July 1999, translated, *FBIS report no. FTS19990723000321*.

Not only was Pakistan domestically divided, but also its international standing was very weak, with far from satisfactory economic conditions in mid-1999. Its foreign exchange reserves were down to less than 1 billion US dollars and the annual growth rate had been in decline for several years. Direct foreign investment and domestic investment also were deteriorating. Pakistan was under numerous economic sanctions. In October 1990, the United States had terminated all economic assistance and financial transactions with Pakistan when it invoked the Pressler Amendment in response to advances in Pakistan's nuclear weapons program. The United States, Japan, and the European Community imposed additional economic sanctions after the May 1998 nuclear explosions. Given the troubled state of the economy, it was an inopportune time for Pakistan to engage in a military expedition against a bigger and more powerful neighbor.

The Pakistan army launched the Kargil operation without fully taking into account the regional and global contexts and the possible diplomatic fallout of what was sure to become a big military crisis. Pakistan already had an image problem at the international level dating back to 1992, when it narrowly escaped being designated as a terrorist state by the United States for its alleged involvement with transnational militant Islamic groups that were an outgrowth of the Afghan resistance movement against Soviet military presence in Afghanistan from 1979 to 1989.[29] Few international observers believed that Kashmiri militants could mount or sustain a decade-long insurgency of such magnitude on their own.

Several states responded to the Pakistani intrusion near Kargil by decrying Islamabad's violation of the "sanctity of the LoC." The international community was especially concerned about the risk of nuclear escalation. In the eyes of foreign policymakers, Pakistan recklessly had started a conflict between two war-prone states locked in a new and unstable nuclear rivalry.[30] All this proved detrimental to Pakistan's long-standing strategy of trying to build support at the international level with respect to its position on Kashmir and the overall political competition with India.[31]

---

[29] Pakistan also narrowly avoided being declared a state sponsor of terrorism in August 1998. See *The 9/11 Commission Report* (Washington, DC: US Government Printing Office, 2004), 122–123.

[30] Availing of the negative sentiments about Pakistan's role in triggering the Kargil conflict, an unknown British-based pro-India group, the India League, had a full-page advertisement published in the *New York Times* describing the Pakistan army as a "rogue army" that had "its finger on the nuclear button." *New York Times*, 1 July 1999.

[31] For background on Pakistan's Kashmir strategy, see Robert G. Wirsing, *Kashmir in the Shadow of War: Regional Rivalries in a Nuclear Age* (Armonk, NY: M. E. Sharpe, 2003), esp. 168–169.

After the outbreak of the Kargil crisis, Pakistan was more isolated than ever.[32] No country came out openly in support of Pakistan. Most advised both sides to exercise restraint. Pakistan's top civil and military officials, including the prime minister and the army chief, visited China during the course of the Kargil conflict. While reiterating China's traditional friend-ship to Pakistan, Chinese leaders advised Pakistan to de-escalate the situation because they did not want to see the two neighbors engaged in a full-fledged war, leading to further regional instability. The Musharraf and Sharif visits to Beijing proved as fruitless as the visit to Beijing of Zulfikar Ali Bhutto during the 1965 war.[33] The United States and other Western countries ultimately held Pakistan responsible for the war and advised the withdrawal of its troops back to its side of the LoC.[34]

Finally, there was poor policy coordination among different parts of the Pakistan government. While the army briefed Prime Minister Sharif on the operation, the consultative institutions of government had broken down. The Foreign Office was not made aware of the operation until May 1999, well after India first discovered Pakistani troops in late April. During the crisis-management stage, after the operation had been revealed, communication between civilian and military institutions was still incomplete. The civilian government, overwhelmed by international diplomatic pressure, engaged in numerous diplomatic moves to cope with the situation without keeping the army high command fully informed of these moves. Most significantly, Nawaz Sharif flew to Washington for a withdrawal agreement on 4 July without discussing the details of this option with the army staff or his cabinet. The DCC met on 2 July, but the Washington visit reportedly was not discussed at this meeting. It appears that Sharif arranged the visit hastily *after* this meeting, catching

---

[32] As one Pakistani political commentator wrote, "A year after the conflict we are still feeling sharp twinges to remind us of the high costs and risks of ill-conceived military adventure ... Whatever yardstick we use, Kargil has been an unmitigated disaster." Irfan Husain, "Kargil: The Morning After," *Dawn*, 29 April 2000.

[33] For background on Bhutto's September 1965 visit to Beijing, see Jones, *Pakistan: Eye of the Storm*, 79. Western scholars speculate that President Ayub Khan accompanied Bhutto, based on an account by Altaf Gauhar, though this is a matter of considerable debate. See Altaf Gauhar, *Ayub Khan: Pakistan's First Military Ruler* (Lahore: Sang-e-Meel, 1993), 351–353 and also Dennis Kux, *The United States and Pakistan, 1947–2000: Disenchanted Allies* (Washington, DC: Woodrow Wilson Center, 2000), 163 and 397, fns. 70–71. Musharraf's 1999 visit was pre-scheduled and was not an attempt to elicit Chinese support. His visit took place in late May, when Pakistan was still denying involvement in the operation.

[34] See "G-8 Statement on Regional Issues," Cologne Summit, 20 June 1999, www.g7.utoronto.ca/summit/1999koln/regional.htm; and the Clinton–Sharif 5 July 1999 statement in chapter 7, p. 203, also available in "US–Pakistan deal calls for withdrawal of Kashmir fighters," *CNN.com*, 4 July 1999, www.cnn.com/WORLD/asiapcf/9907/04/kashmir.04/.

US officials in Washington just as much by surprise as most of his own colleagues. Musharraf saw the prime minister off at the airport, and reportedly this is when the two men discussed the terms of Sharif's negotiating position; but this strategy was not more broadly coordinated within the Pakistan government.[35]

Two other incidents demonstrated problems in policy management and coordination. When the Indian government released the transcripts and audio recordings of several mid-June telephone conversations between General Pervez Musharraf, while on a visit to Beijing, and his Chief of General Staff, Lieutenant General Muhammad Aziz Khan, to show the involvement of the Pakistan army in Kargil, Pakistani civil and military authorities could not offer a credible response except to argue that the tapes were fabricated.[36] When an unknown Indian group published an advertisement in the *New York Times* on 1 July 1999, describing the Pakistan army as a "rogue army," Pakistan's Ministry of Information prepared a counter-advertisement, but it could not be published in the United States or elsewhere due to bureaucratic lethargy and a lack of governmental coordination.[37]

As discussed in further detail by Peter R. Lavoy in chapter 7 of this book, the international community played a crucial role in ending the Kargil conflict and stymieing significant military escalation. In Pakistan, however, the international community's intervention was not viewed as particularly helpful or friendly. Instead, the perception inside Pakistan is that international pressure for Pakistani withdrawal, and the eventual acquiescence of the Sharif government, robbed the Pakistan military of a brilliant tactical victory. In particular, many Pakistanis believe that pressure from Washington short-circuited a promising back-channel dialogue between long-time Pakistani diplomat Niaz A. Naik and influential Indian journalist R. K. Mishra.[38] The collapse of the Naik–Mishra talks discredited the back-channel process in the eyes of Pakistani elites, as a result of India's conclusion that it could achieve better results outside of private negotiations with Pakistan. Pakistani decision-makers viewed US diplomats and officials as doing India's bidding. Furthermore, the absence of a ceasefire guarantee in the Washington Declaration of 4 July 1999 ensured

---

[35] Information based on CCC interviews with Pakistani civilian and military officials, January 2003. Because this turn of events happened so quickly over an American holiday weekend, the normal policy coordination measures were bypassed in Washington as well as in Islamabad.

[36] See "Ever More Dangerous in Kashmir," *The Economist*, 19 June 1999.

[37] Mazari, *The Kargil Conflict 1999*, 65–67.

[38] The most detailed discussion of this back-channel process is in Wirsing, *Kashmir in the Shadow of War*, 29–36.

that Pakistani troops would take dozens, if not hundreds, of unnecessary casualties during the withdrawal phase.[39] While US policymakers believe they averted a potential catastrophe,[40] Pakistani policymakers are decidedly more negative in their assessment of the role Washington and other concerned parties played in managing the crisis.

Operational lessons

The Pakistan military had conducted planning for a Kargil-type operation for over a decade before 1999, as it considered responses to India's 1984 occupation of the Siachen Glacier.[41] However, the Kargil operation, as it unfolded, diverged from this planning. Kargil's planners sought to use readily available paramilitary troops and military equipment for "preemptive defense." Using these capabilities ensured the secrecy of the operation, but by no means did it guarantee that Pakistani forces would be able to hold off a sustained and coordinated Indian counterattack.

Kargil's planners were overly ambitious. As discussed above, they calculated that the operation would arouse little international attention or, if it did, that the international attention would put pressure on both parties to negotiate their way out of the conflict. The United States and other concerned parties did not view Pakistan's "preemptive defense" in such a light. The analogy with India's 1984 occupation of the Siachen Glacier could not be maintained in a nuclearized South Asia, and was particularly incompatible with the *mujahideen* cover story. In the Northern Areas, both parties had minimized their vulnerabilities through aggressive, forward-leaning operations since at least 1984.[42] In many ways, Kargil was the *reductio ad absurdum* of this strategy. It remains to be seen whether the Kargil episode will transform a strategic culture in the Northern Areas, which had prized aggressiveness and punished defensive vulnerabilities. Discussions with Pakistani officers who have served in

---

[39] This was emphasized repeatedly in interviews by and briefings to the CCC research team.

[40] Concern over the potential of the Kargil conflict to escalate to a nuclear exchange is evident in the accounts of almost all key US policymakers. See Bruce Riedel, chapter 5 of this book; statements by President Clinton, Deputy Secretary of State Strobe Talbott, and Assistant Secretary of State Karl F. Inderfurth in "Nuclear Nightmares: Losing Control," *Avoiding Armageddon*, videocassette (Washington, DC: Public Broadcasting Service, 2003); and Strobe Talbott, *Engaging India* (Washington, DC: Brookings Institution, 2004), 161–168.

[41] Javed Nasir, "Kargil: The Bitter Hard Facts," *The Nation*, 30 August 2004. See also chapter 3 of this book by Khan, Lavoy, and Clary.

[42] India crossed the LoC at Chorbat La even earlier in 1972, though jockeying for posts was fairly mild in the Northern Areas until India's occupation of Siachen in 1984. Mazari, *The Kargil Conflict 1999*, 24.

these areas since the Kargil misadventure indicate a heightened degree of caution, maintained through top-down pressure to avoid cross-LoC provocations. Jockeying for posts, however, appears to continue to some degree, as evidenced by a high-profile border incident near the Anzbari feature in the Gurez-Machal sector in July 2002.[43]

Further, the operation was overly ambitious in its use of defensive troops (the Northern Light Infantry) to achieve offensive objectives. It is one thing to move defensive troops into forward locations a few hundred yards across the LoC; it is quite another to use these same forces to capture several hundred square miles of territory and interdict the adversary's key strategic highway. In the minds of Kargil's planners, interdicting the Srinagar–Leh highway (NH-1A) was roughly equivalent to the Indian interdiction of the Muzaffarabad–Kel road in the Neelum Valley. Interdiction combined with a cross-LoC intrusion was understandably far more provocative to India and the international community. Further, while Pakistan had grown used to the Neelum "pain" – after all, Indian dominance of the Neelum Valley had existed off and on since 1948 – NH-1A had been subject to indirect fire from Pakistan only since 1996. Heightening the provocation further, NH-1A is strategically much more significant to India – it is the only strategic artery that reaches Leh and Indian forces in the Siachen Glacier region. Beyond that, the Kargil operation was taking place within months of the nuclear tests.

The analogy of Kargil and the Neelum Valley seems attractive, particularly in the context of the numerous other examples that Pakistani decision-makers cite of Indian violations of the LoC. However, the combination of a cross-LoC intrusion, targeting a more significant strategic artery, and a nuclear environment made the Kargil operation far more provocative. This would have been apparent if Kargil's planners had broadened the discussion to include other corps commanders and directorates of GHQ. While 10 Corps viewed Kargil in tactical terms, as soon as the intrusion was discovered the other corps commanders and service chiefs were surprised they were not consulted before such a strategic action was taken.[44] This failure to anticipate the strategic significance of the operation was a large reason that Pakistani national security institutions were unprepared to manage the unfolding crisis. The obvious lesson

---

[43] See Josy Joseph, "CO Removed for Allowing Pak Troops to Occupy LoC Position," *Rediff.com*, 15 August 2002, www.rediff.com/news/2002/aug/15josy.htm; and Praveen Swami, "When Pakistan Took Loonda Post," *Frontline*, 31 August 2002, www.frontlineonnet.com/fl1918/19180220.htm.

[44] Discussions with Pakistani officers by the CCC research team.

for Pakistani decision-makers is that changes to the status quo with respect to India can quickly jump from tactical to strategic significance.

Third, the Kargil operation quickly became a victim of "mission creep." As Maj. Gen. Nadeem Ahmed indicated in his official briefing to the CCC research team on the Kargil operation, there was a "compulsion to push forward," which led to troop positions becoming "overstretched."[45] Closely related to this, the fog of war was compounded by high-altitude operations. In high-altitude, mountainous terrain, commanders are never sure if their orders are executable and, if they are, if their orders actually were executed as desired. The terrain conditions precluded effective oversight of orders.[46] Initiatives by low-level officers to obtain better tactical location to improve their defensive position are encouraged, but if they extend too far, they make lines of communication untenable. Controlling for the exuberance of low-level officers is the task of more senior officers, and this apparently did not adequately occur in 1999. The terrain, altitude, and size of the territory seized presented logistical and command challenges to the operation, which FCNA ultimately never overcame. As brought out by Khan, Lavoy, and Clary in chapter 3 of this book, this remains one of the most important unanswered questions: whether overextension was caused by the exuberance of younger officers and terrain conditions that made oversight difficult or by the decisions of operational commanders who might have pushed the incursion deeper for their glory and ambition.

As noted by John H. Gill in chapter 4, there were gaps among Pakistan's five sectors (Mushkoh, Dras, Kaksar, Batalik, and Turtok), between sub-sectors, and between posts within sub-sectors. These gaps, brought about by the overstretch of forces and the fog of war, allowed Indian forces to progressively isolate Pakistani positions. An outpost-based offensive of this type is unsustainable. Positions cannot be readily reinforced, particularly during combat. Similarly, they cannot retreat hastily, particularly when they are under fire.[47] All the while, the counterattacking side is able to continuously increase its forces. Compounding these difficulties were mistakes made in properly locating weapons, sending out patrols, and other issues of field-craft.[48] The Pakistan army has studied these

---

[45] Briefing by Maj. Gen. Nadeem Ahmed, FCNA, Gilgit, Pakistan, 12 January 2003.

[46] Nadeem briefing; and interview with Lt. Gen. Javed Hassan, Islamabad, Pakistan, 17 January 2003.

[47] This second point was not adequately considered when Western leaders demanded, and Nawaz Sharif agreed to, unilateral withdrawal.

[48] Marcus P. Acosta, "High Altitude Warfare: The Kargil Conflict and the Future," Master's thesis, Monterey, Calif.: US Naval Postgraduate School, June 2003), www.ccc.nps.navy.mil/research/theses/Acosta03.asp.

problems, with internal reviews having transpired in FCNA, GHQ, and the army staff college.

Assessment of the conflict

Pakistan made errors on three levels during the Kargil operation. First, it made errors in perception. It miscalculated the strategic significance of this limited cross-LoC operation. This mistake fed into the second level: Pakistan was not prepared for a strategic standoff with India. It was divided internally, isolated diplomatically, and weak economically. Finally, Pakistan made errors in the execution of the Kargil campaign, from operational and tactical mistakes, down to problems in proper field-craft for the Pakistani soldiers.

By all accounts, Pakistan's soldiers fought with great bravery under incredibly difficult conditions. Pakistan still has a great deal of strategic introspection to do. While this chapter has hinted at logical lessons to be drawn from the Kargil affair, many of Pakistan's strategic questions have no one correct answer. There are at least three questions that Pakistan needs to more fully consider in the light of the Kargil conflict, and, more recently, the 9/11 and the 2001–2002 composite crises.

First, what role should Pakistan expect other parties to play in a crisis? Apparently, both Pakistan's civil and military leadership failed to antici-pate the US position during the spring 1999 crisis. The United States had grown increasingly frustrated with Pakistan's Afghan and Kashmir poli-cies, and in particular felt that such actions were incompatible with the responsibility required of a nuclear weapons state. Did Nawaz Sharif realize what he was getting into as he traveled to Washington, DC unin-vited? Sharif did not gain anything from his American visit; he only had to codify what already had been agreed to during the visit by United States Central Command (CENTCOM) Commander General Anthony Zinni to Islamabad a week before. However, Sharif's behavior during the Washington visit precipitated the fragile civil–military relationship that awaited him when he returned home.[49] Sharif gained nothing from Washington, while he gained only sympathy from Beijing. Pakistani decision-makers must learn that it is difficult to predict how outsiders will view their interests in an Indo-Pakistani crisis.

Second, what lessons has the military leadership learned about its role in regional security policy? For more than a decade, the military had dominated Pakistan's Kashmir and Afghan strategies, both of which

---

[49] Talbott, *Engaging India*, 166.

collapsed dangerously for Pakistan by late 2001. Should GHQ and ISID continue to have hegemony over the regional security policies? What division of labor should civilian and military officials have over these policies? During the Kargil crisis, institutions designed to regulate these policies failed. The Defence Cabinet Committee was ignored during the formulation of the Kargil plan and proved utterly ineffective in reaching coherent and purposeful decisions in handling the crisis.

Third, the Pakistan government was particularly maladroit in its public diplomacy and media management. While government spokesmen persisted with the *mujahideen* cover story, the GHQ briefed foreign military attachés about the Northern Light Infantry's role in the conflict.[50] India's coherent message enabled it to play the victim and portray Pakistan as the aggressor – a message made easier to convey given the facts on the ground. While Pakistan's handling of the 2001–2002 military standoff with India indicates it has learned a great deal since Kargil, it still has a long road to travel.

Conclusion: has Pakistan learned?

As a new state, Pakistan was born without any state infrastructure. The evolution of Pakistan to a point of modernity in itself has been in the face of crises. Normally, a state would learn to survive by drawing critical lessons from each crisis that it faced to meet the next. Therefore, the evolution of a state's functioning system is directly dependent on the environment in which the state survives. Pakistan's evolutionary history to a modern state has taken place in an environment of domestic insecurity, regional conflict, and global power politics. Pakistan had to move carefully in all three areas and faltered primarily because of the serious and diverse nature of threats to its polity. Under these circumstances, Pakistan had to structure and restructure its security institutions and decision-making apparatus. Second, its strategic thought process also evolved within the context of repeated military failures and increasing insurmountable challenges from the Indian military. Third, the failure to evolve civil–military relations was also caused by the first two factors. Resultantly, classic civilian control of the military – an essential ingredient in a modern state – has, as of yet, failed to evolve in Pakistan. Nevertheless, Pakistani attempts in all three areas have been made progressively over several decades – especially after the 1971 war.

---

[50] See chapter 14 of this book by Rodney W. Jones and Joseph McMillan.

First, following the 1973 constitution and the conclusion of the Hamood-ur-Rehman Commission, the civilian government of Zulfikar Ali Bhutto established the higher defense organization to manage the security affairs of the country. Most notably, the Defence Cabinet Committee (DCC) was a key institution for strategic and defense decision-making. The functioning of this institution regrettably has been either a rubberstamp or ineffective throughout Pakistan's existence. For one, the military takeover made these committees redundant, but even during the democratic regimes the civilian governments seldom used this forum effectively. Because the DCC does not have a functioning secretariat where constant analysis and inputs are regularly made, and also because no national secretariat exists in the country, the national security problem has remained within the domain of the Pakistani armed forces – most significantly the GHQ of the army.[51] After the army takeover in 1999, and despite some restoration of the domestic political process, the system remained dominated by the army. Therefore, the roles of security institutions are meaningless. Thus it is unclear if Pakistan has learned the lesson of institutional decision-making. The management of the 2002 crisis was done under military rule where all state institutions were functioning under the unity of command. How will this system form in a future crisis, should full democracy return?

Has there been a learning process in Pakistan's strategic thinking? Evidently, the answer to this question is difficult because very little public debate on national security thinking is done in Pakistan. Traditional military thought in Pakistan has been that Pakistan would be able to fair better in a limited war as compared to a total war where the superior Indian economy, military industry, and fighting force eventually would prevail. The Kargil operation has underscored that this strategy did not work. As a result, it is possible that Pakistani security institutions may be reevaluating their core strategic assumptions and calculations.

The key institutions in Pakistan that are the cradles of strategic thought are the National Defence University in Islamabad and the Command Staff College in Quetta. The former focuses on policy and strategy at a high strategic level, whereas the latter focuses on operational and tactical issues. The analysis conducted by these institutions and within the military headquarters remains classified. There is not a system, as of yet, of declassifying documents for public inquiry. In the past couple of years, under the Musharraf regime, civilian government officials, parliamentarians, and selected journalists have been inducted in various courses and

---

[51] The Joint Services Headquarters (JSHQ) has existed since the mid-1970s but has more of a ceremonial function and not enough power to replace the dominance of the GHQ.

workshops at the National Defence University. It is therefore expected that new inputs and contributions from civilian thinking will occur, but when this will happen remains to be seen.

As the new dynamics in Pakistan's political system evolve, it is yet to be seen how civilian control of the military will evolve in the future. The role of the Pakistani military in the National Security Council (NSC) is a matter of controversy in the political system. It is unclear how the civil domination of the military will evolve when the civilian, political, and bureaucratic institutions are weak in comparison. One way ahead would be for the Pakistan government to establish reforms in three critical areas: (1) to initiate structures and organizations within the civilian bureaucracy, for example in the ministries of foreign affairs, defence, and interior, where security threats are assessed in a joint civil–military endeavor; (2) to create independent civilian think tanks to understand the predicaments of the military and independently assess the threat perceptions and their responses; and (3) to establish and reform political–strategic organizations (such as the NSC and the DCC) in a manner where they have a functioning secretariat that provides a continuous security analysis to the country's political leadership.

14 The Kargil crisis: lessons learned by the United States

Rodney W. Jones and Joseph McMillan

The Kargil crisis was the first direct military conflict between two "new" nuclear weapons-capable states. It put a spotlight on widely held theories about the stabilizing, or destabilizing, properties of nuclear deterrence, at least at the low levels of nuclear arms and recessed deployment postures India and Pakistan were believed to have after their May 1998 nuclear tests. By the end of the Cold War, based on several decades of US–Soviet experience, most Western policymakers and military experts had become accustomed to the view that nuclear-armed adversaries would go to great lengths to avoid direct conventional military provocations for fear of escalation to a nuclear exchange. Pakistan's armed intrusion across the "line of control" (LoC) separating Pakistani and Indian forces in the disputed territory of Kashmir, and India's response, especially its moves to ready itself for horizontal military escalation, seemed to defy this conventional wisdom, generating new questions about the propensity of new nuclear states for risk-taking under the "nuclear shadow."

What lessons did US policymakers debate or take away from the Kargil crisis? In retrospect, the danger that the local conflict might spark a serious nuclear crisis was a key rationale for the US diplomatic intervention that defused the conflict, but how has that concern been translated since? Key US concerns since Kargil include the possibility that Pakistan and India have taken their own, quite different, lessons from their Kargil experience, storing up yet more dangers for the future.

Although the Kargil conflict garnered little public attention within the United States when it took place, and although its effects on US relations with South Asia have since been overshadowed by the attacks of 11 September and the ensuing US operations in Afghanistan, Kargil marked an important turning point in the evolution of US policy toward South Asia. The lessons drawn by Washington from the respective roles of Pakistan and India in the crisis had a significant effect in the direction of its overall relations with both countries. Further, the Kargil experience consolidated a reorientation of the US approach to the advent of nuclear weapons in the subcontinent. Beyond the substantive policy lessons, the episode also offered important lessons about the effectiveness of different methods of influencing the parties to a conflict. Whether these lessons of diplomatic intervention and leverage in crisis are as clear as the substantive policy lessons is open to question. The purpose of this chapter is to examine the lessons that the US government took away in these three aspects of South Asia foreign and security policy, namely, lessons on: (1) direction, scope, and quality of relations with Pakistan and India; (2) efforts to contain the nuclear risks and nuclear weapons capabilities in both countries; and (3) diplomatic efforts to overcome the hostility and tension between the two countries.

Lessons for US relations with India and Pakistan

The most widely remarked change in US policy to come out of Kargil was probably the most exaggerated. This was the strategic shift from a pro-Pakistan to a pro-India orientation in relations with the subcontinent. During the decades of the Cold War, both India and Pakistan had come to expect the United States to tilt reflexively toward Pakistan, its ally against Soviet pressure on the region. Against that backdrop, both may have been surprised to find the US position on the Kargil conflict unequivocal in condemning the Pakistani intrusion of armed units across the LoC and in demanding their unconditional withdrawal. In the past, the most the United States would have done would have been to react "even-handedly" by holding both sides partially to blame, urging both to take steps to resolve their differences and de-escalate the confrontation. In this case, however, the United States was not evenhanded; it openly favored India's position. This gave added impetus to Indian as well as US initiatives to deepen the nascent strategic bilateral relationship.[1]

Kargil influenced the strategic shift toward India and brought it into the open, but did not cause it. The Clinton administration had already put a high priority on improving relations with India long before the Kargil operation.[2] This improvement was not intended to come at the expense

---

[1] These points were made in an early interview with Donald Camp, Country Director for South Asia, Department of State (and during Kargil, serving on the NSC staff as deputy to Bruce Riedel), on 27 December 2002. They have been amplified since by then-Deputy Secretary of State Strobe Talbott, in his book, *Engaging India: Diplomacy, Democracy, and the Bomb* (Washington, DC: Brookings Institution Press, 2004), with its chapter 8 devoted to the US response to the Kargil crisis.

[2] Bruce Riedel, chapter 5 of this book.

of Pakistan. In fact, improving relations with both countries was one of the foreign policy priorities of the second Clinton term. The formal enunciation of this objective came out of an interagency policy review in 1997, which called for greater engagement with both countries, building to an early presidential visit. At the September 1997 meetings of the United Nations (UN) General Assembly, the president held three bilateral meetings. One was with Russian prime minister Primakov; the other two were with Indian prime minister I. K. Gujral and Pakistani prime minister Nawaz Sharif.[3] However, even though the United States sought to improve relations with both countries, the post-Cold War historical context combined with India's natural weight as an emerging power made progress with New Delhi appear more important and substantial. The same urgency and depth of concern was not present in US relations with Pakistan, at least as seen from Islamabad.

The Indian decision to test nuclear weapons in May 1998 was a serious impediment to the evolving US–Indian relationship, but did not stall it altogether. In fact, the continuing bond between Deputy Secretary of State Strobe Talbott and the then-Indian minister of external affairs Jaswant Singh, which was so important in US–Indian coordination throughout the Kargil crisis, actually originated in the bilateral discussions on nonproliferation issues that began after the nuclear tests.[4]

To ascribe the change in the US perspective on South Asia entirely to the Kargil episode is therefore incorrect.[5] Rather than improving India's standing in Washington, Kargil dramatically worsened Pakistan's. This can be understood only in the context of recent developments in the region. The US policy community, operating in a frame of reference shaped by its own Cold War experience with nuclear brinksmanship, had long been seized of the dangers presented by the acquisition of nuclear weapons by two rivals who were conducting regular military and covert actions against one another. Thus when Indian prime minister Atal Vajpayee and Pakistani prime minister Nawaz Sharif met to establish a process for moderating tensions between the two new nuclear states at an unprecedented summit in Lahore on 20–21 February 1999, the US government strongly supported that effort and was hopeful that progress

---

[3] Interview with Hon. Karl F. Inderfurth, former Assistant Secretary of State for South Asian Affairs, 7 November 2002.

[4] Inderfurth interview. Talbott has since told this story of his interchanges with Jaswant Singh in intimate detail in his *Engaging India*.

[5] Interview with Hon. William B. Milam, former US ambassador to Pakistan, 25 November 2002.

in resolving the underlying causes of Indo-Pakistani conflicts might finally be possible.[6]

It therefore came as an unpleasant surprise when the US government began picking up indications of Pakistani incursions across the LoC into the Kargil sector hardly two months after the apparent success of the Lahore Summit.[7] By mid-May, South Asia-focused officials in the Clinton administration had clarified to their own satisfaction that the Pakistani intruders were not merely armed militants, but consisted mainly of government-trained military forces,[8] and were concerned that Kargil had the makings of a fairly serious military and political crisis. At a minimum, it jeopardized the progress made at Lahore. Worse, it had the potential to escalate to a wider military conflict. In response to US inquiries about what was going on, Pakistani authorities claimed the intruders were volunteers and denied official sponsorship, claims the United States knew to be untrue.[9] This confirmed Washington's assessment that Pakistan was responsible for the provocation near Kargil, which was building into a major confrontation.

The message that the Clinton administration would place the blame on Pakistan was privately but firmly conveyed to the Pakistani ambassador by Under Secretary of State Thomas Pickering on 27 May. Pickering told Ambassador Riaz Khokhar in very clear terms that it was up to Pakistan to take steps to ratchet down the brewing confrontation. Secretary of State Madeleine Albright conveyed a similar message by phone to Nawaz Sharif, and also spoke by phone with Jaswant Singh and British foreign secretary Robin Cook. President Clinton turned his attention to the crisis in the first week of June, sending private letters to Sharif and Vajpayee, making clear his view that Pakistan's withdrawal was a precondition for a settlement.[10] When private démarches failed to persuade the Pakistanis to withdraw, the administration began to state publicly in early June its view

---

[6] Former State Department official Walter Andersen noted that the initiative for the Lahore Summit appeared to come from the Indian side and that this made a favorable impression in Washington. From his comments on the manuscript in July 2003, after retiring to Johns Hopkins University School of Advanced International Studies.

[7] Camp interview.

[8] According to our informants, the US had indications in the latter half of April that some form of infiltration from Pakistan across the LoC was underway, but was unable at the outset to determine that this was officially organized and distinct from the militant-group infiltration through the LoC of *mujahideen* ("freedom fighters" in Pakistan's local parlance) to become active in the insurgency in Kashmir, which had been going on since 1989. By early May, the indications were clearer that the combatants operating across the LoC were better trained and equipped than those from militant groups, suggesting official Pakistani sponsorship. The conclusion that this was so apparently was formed by the US government about mid-May. Interviews with intelligence officials.

[9] Milam interview; Inderfurth interview.   [10] Talbott, *Engaging India*, 158.

that the resolution of the crisis depended on the removal of Pakistani infiltrators back across the LoC in Jammu and Kashmir.[11] Also at this juncture, the administration began to talk of the "sanctity" of the LoC for the first time.[12]

Although the new risk of nuclear confrontations in the subcontinent caused US alarm over Kargil, and the improving US–Indian relationship permitted an unprecedented degree of Washington–Delhi interaction throughout the crisis, neither of these factors was the reason the United States took India's side. That decision was driven solely by Washington's assessment that Pakistan had irresponsibly provoked a dangerous armed crisis, dashing the opportunities for constructive diplomacy that had been opened up by the Lahore Summit and ensuing negotiations.[13] Sympathy for India also was the typical reaction to administration briefings among many members of Congress, who saw Islamabad not only as having undercut the Lahore process but also as having attempted to take advantage of the Indian government's caretaker status in the run-up to new elections.[14] Shifts and inconsistencies in the Pakistani official line reinforced the inclination of US officials to take India's side in the conflict. In late May, as coverage of the fighting in the Kargil sector began to appear in the media, the Pakistan army's Director General of Military Intelligence (DGMI) convened foreign defense attachés in Islamabad and admitted that Pakistani regular troops were engaged.[15] A week later, however, a Foreign Ministry spokesman insisted to a group of ambassadors from many of the same countries that Pakistan had no control over those who

---

[11] State Department spokesman James Rubin attributed the crisis to "infiltrators from Pakistan on India's side of the line of control" at the State Department's daily press briefing on 4 June 1999, http://secretary.state.gov/www/briefings/9906/990604db.html. The same day, US ambassador to India Richard Celeste called for the withdrawal of Pakistani intruders as soon as possible. On 8 June, NSC senior director Bruce Riedel said at the Foreign Press Center in Washington, "We think ... the forces which have crossed the line, should withdraw to where they came from." www.fas.org/news/india/1999/990608-indopak-usia01.htm; see also chapter 5 in this volume.

[12] Walter Andersen comments.

[13] Inderfurth interview; interview with Hon. Robert Einhorn, former Assistant Secretary of State for Nonproliferation, 31 October 2002.

[14] Prime Minister Vajpayee's journey to Lahore in February 1999 and his interaction with Pakistan's prime minister Nawaz Sharif had led to widespread hopes of a permanent reconciliation between India and Pakistan. The Lahore process was welcomed by a large number of US legislators cutting across party lines. In mid-April 1999 Vajpayee's coalition government lost its narrow majority when a vote of confidence failed during a parliamentary debate. As a result, Vajpayee's government was reduced to a caretaker status – just before the Kargil conflict came into view. The Vajpayee government recovered its mandate through fresh parliamentary elections in September 1999. This is not to say that the Kargil operation was intended to take advantage of the Vajpayee government's precarious status, but it was seen that way on Capitol Hill.

[15] Milam interview.

were fighting in Kargil.[16] The cause of the inconsistency may have been a lack of internal coordination within the Pakistani government, but it created an impression of duplicity. In any case, the Pakistan army spokesman's assertion on 16 June that "the Americans are unaware of the ground situation ... we are within our own side of the border,"[17] did not square with the DGMI's earlier acknowledgment of the engagement of regular troops.

The backlash in Washington against Pakistan's "betrayal" of Lahore thus was exacerbated by what the US administration saw as Islamabad's prevarications about what was happening on the ground in Kargil. Over time, the negative attitudes generated during Kargil were reinforced by the Musharraf coup of October 1999, the sharpened American attitude toward Islamically motivated violence following the 9/11 terrorist attacks on the United States, and the terrorist attack on the Indian parliament soon after, in December 2001. This resulted, first in the Clinton administration and later under President Bush, in an increasing loss of sympathy for Pakistan and an erosion of its image as an ally of the United States. At the same time, US officials also saw Kargil as an opportunity to demonstrate to New Delhi that India could trust the United States as a strategic partner.[18]

The Kargil crisis also moved the US government to define and adopt as an objective the "sanctity" of the LoC in Kashmir.[19] The May 1998 nuclear tests and both sides' subsequent development of operational nuclear forces had already led the US government to take a very different view of the chronic low-intensity warfare that had characterized Indo-Pakistani interaction on the LoC off and on since the end of the 1971 war.

---

[16] *Ibid.*

[17] Brig. Rashid Qureshi, the spokesman, quoted by CNN in "Guerrillas Reject US Call to Pull Out of Kashmir," 16 June 1999, www.cnn.com/WORLD/asiapcf/9906/16/india.pakistan.02/.

[18] Milam interview.

[19] Einhorn interview; Camp interview. NSC drafting for the 4 July Blair House meeting with Nawaz Sharif contained the "sanctity" terminology from the start. Note that the LoC originated as a ceasefire line in 1948 and was modified with certain changes due to the 1965 and 1971 Indo-Pakistani wars; but, being part of an unresolved territorial dispute dating from the India–Pakistan partition, is not an international border. Military skirmishing across the LoC has been an endemic feature of India–Pakistan relations and has a different meaning and status in international law (or the UN Charter) than violation of a recognized international border. On the other hand, both sides agreed at Simla on 2 July 1972 to respect the LoC "without prejudice to the recognized position of either side," not to "seek to alter it unilaterally," and "to refrain from the threat or the use of force in violation of this Line." While both sides have repeatedly violated these pledges, India generally gives greater weight to the "sanctity" of the LoC and prefers to see it treated as tantamount to an international border. By inducing the United States to endorse the "sanctity" of the LoC as a principle of its South Asia policy, Pakistan's action in Kargil had the effect of undercutting international support for its own position on Kashmir.

Although the United States is still reluctant to play a pro-active role in resolving the status of Kashmir – the underlying issue that led to Kargil – it has been quicker since 1999 to try to tamp down crises and shore up respect for a norm of inviolability of the LoC. To some degree, this increased sensitivity to Indo-Pakistani confrontations may be a side effect of the global war on terrorism, which gives the United States a strong interest in keeping Pakistan engaged in fighting al Qaeda and not in fighting India. However, the experience of Kargil nevertheless informed the US understanding of the consequences of a military confrontation under the "nuclear shadow" that potentially could get out of control.

Lessons for nuclear stability and nonproliferation policy

Even before Kargil, the US government feared that a conventional India–Pakistan conflict could escalate to nuclear war. Indeed, for several years before the 1998 nuclear tests, an important element of US policy in the region had been to overcome what US officials saw as a lack of appreciation on both sides of the risks and complexities associated with the possession of nuclear weapons.[20] It was precisely this concern that led the United States to try to manage the crisis, despite other preoccupations, such as in the breakup of Yugoslavia, the attempted enforcement of UN resolutions in Iraq, and developments in the Arab–Israeli peace process. Deputy Secretary of State Strobe Talbott described Washington's rising alarm about the nuclear dangers, as it first tried to make sense of the Kargil fighting, in these graphic terms:

The American government followed the conflict with growing alarm. The biggest danger was that the Indians would launch an onslaught of their own across the Line of Control. It was conceivable that while mobilizing for all-out war, Pakistan might seek support from China and various Arab states, while India would perhaps turn to its old protector Russia and even to its newer partner Israel. The result could be an international free-for-all in which all the wrong outsiders would be looking for ways to score points against one another rather than concerting their energies to pull the combatants back from the brink of what could easily become a nuclear cataclysm.[21]

Indians and Pakistanis alike tend to view US concerns about the risks inherent in a nuclear-armed South Asia as an indictment of their ability to conduct themselves as mature, responsible countries. As a

---

[20] This extended even to special briefings to high-level Indian and Pakistani officials on the expense and effort required to maintain strategic stability between the United States and the Soviet Union.

[21] Talbott, *Engaging India*, 157.

consequence, they often react negatively to what they perceive as US condescension. In fact, US officials now acknowledge that both countries have demonstrated sobriety and responsibility in many aspects of their nuclear programs, taking seriously such questions as strategic doctrine, declaratory policy, command and control, and weapons security. On the whole, US officials accept that leaders in New Delhi and Islamabad recognize the gravity of any possible nuclear exchange,[22] and it is true that in the summer of 1999 both sides ultimately showed the necessary responsibility and restraint. Nevertheless, the experience of decades of US–Soviet nuclear crises – especially the Cuban missile crisis – combined with the incendiary rhetoric that often comes out of New Delhi and Islamabad in times of tension, continues to cause grave concern in Washington about the stability of the South Asian strategic situation. The lessons of Kargil as seen from an American perspective only reinforced those concerns.[23]

One of the most troublesome aspects of the Kargil crisis as seen from Washington was that neither India nor Pakistan seemed to have an accurate picture of what the other was doing or what it would do under various circumstances. Evidently, the Pakistani organizers of the Kargil operation believed that India would not view the incursions as particularly significant, because this intrusion was, so the Pakistanis now assert, within the established patterns of operations by both sides along the LoC.[24] Some US officials believed that Islamabad compounded this misapprehension by the way it managed the crisis after it had surfaced: Islamabad miscalculated that a caretaker government facing elections in a few months, as Vajpayee's government was at the time, was in a position of weakness and therefore less able to respond to a Pakistani *fait accompli*. Pakistanis did not anticipate the extent of modern media coverage and the nationwide welling up of public anger in India over the loss of lives as "martyred" soldiers were delivered in coffins to their homes for cremation, but the

---

[22] Inderfurth interview.   [23] Einhorn interview.

[24] Other chapters in this book examine Pakistan's Kargil motivations and India's response. We confine ourselves in this chapter to how these factors were viewed by US officials. Our interviews suggest that few in US official circles believed the Kargil operation was planned as a strategic move, but were then, and remain today, mystified by Pakistani motivations and rationales. In part, this is due to the obvious contradiction between the diplomatic openings of the Lahore process, and letting a military operation run that could cause those openings to clamp up. In part it is due to the loss of Pakistani image and leverage in the West, arguably a strategic loss for Pakistan. Why Islamabad failed to anticipate how this operation would appear internationally if it became a highly publicized confrontation with significant early loss of Indian lives but India exercised escalatory restraint – as it largely did – should be a major topic of any Pakistani assessment of lessons learned from the crisis.

stimulus this could impart to Indian anger and desire for retaliation was well understood by US intelligence analysts.[25]

At the same time, some US officials were concerned that India did not exhibit sufficient respect and understanding for the capabilities of the Pakistani missile program and might therefore be inclined to try preemption of the Pakistani nuclear capability in the expectation that Pakistan would be unable to retaliate decisively.[26]

Intelligence weaknesses were just as apparent at the operational level on both sides. New Delhi's official Kargil report highlighted these weaknesses on the Indian side.[27] Problems existed in all three phases of the intelligence cycle – collection, analysis, and distribution – with deficiencies in analysis being perhaps the most serious. Given "facts" of dubious reliability to begin with, each side tended (and still tends) to exaggerate the other's intentions, overestimate its quantitative capabilities, and underestimate its qualitative capabilities. The net result is a proclivity for overreacting to enemy moves and underestimating the potential negative consequences of one's own moves.

US officials believed that the United States consistently had better information than New Delhi and Islamabad had about each other's actions in the conflict. In fact, it is possible that the US government learned of Pakistani incursions across the LoC near Kargil before Indian forces in Kashmir did.[28] Nevertheless, it was still apparently a few weeks before the American intelligence community understood the scale of the operation and concluded that government troops were directly involved. Furthermore, President Clinton's disclosure to Nawaz Sharif that US intelligence believed the Pakistani armed forces were taking steps to prepare nuclear weapons for possible use has been the subject of considerable debate since Bruce Riedel, senior National Security Council official handling South Asian issues at the time, described it in his paper on the 4 July Blair House Summit.[29] In principle, this intelligence advantage should enable the United States to play a moderating role in future crises, offsetting at least the factual discrepancies in Indian and Pakistani intelligence assessments. A system of shared early warning for missile launches, for example, could prevent misperceptions and contribute to stability.

---

[25] Interview with a US intelligence official.   [26] *Ibid.*
[27] The executive summary of the Indian government's Kargil Committee Report was published in the *Times of India* on 25 February 2000 and is available at www.parliamentofindia.nic.in/rs/25indi1.htm#7.
[28] Interviews with US intelligence officials.   [29] Riedel, chapter 5 in this volume.

Two major obstacles, however, stand in the way. The first is the inevitable Indian and Pakistani distrust of Washington's motives that comes into play during any crisis. US credibility as a security partner may have been enhanced in India's eyes by its conduct during the Kargil crisis, but it was eroded in Pakistan's. The second is US intelligence-sharing policy. Assuming that one had in place the necessary modalities for sharing highly classified information, the fundamental principle under which the United States does not report "friend-on-friend" information would still stand in the way. For the United States to use its intelligence advantage to stabilize the South Asia confrontation therefore would require a significant rethinking of how the United States does business.

One of the post-Kargil concerns of some American observers was that Islamabad, in particular, might have learned the wrong lesson from the confrontation. The fear was that Pakistan may believe it not only holds escalation dominance, but also that its dominance is even more pronounced than it might have thought before Kargil. According to this assessment, Pakistan may believe that its own possession of nuclear weapons guarantees that India will not escalate vertically. Pakistan may also have interpreted India's disinclination to horizontal escalation – implied by the fact that Indian forces did not expand the fighting outside the stretch of the LoC where it began – as insurance that India will not attempt in the future to subject Pakistan to the kind of decisive conventional defeat that could force Pakistan to use its own nuclear weapons *in extremis*.[30]

If Pakistan has indeed reached such conclusions, some American officials fear it may misjudge Indian calculations in a future crisis. Their concern is underscored by the fact that certain Indian strategists reacted to the Kargil episode by advocating that India prepare itself for the conduct of limited conventional war under the nuclear umbrella. This could make the outcome of a future crisis highly unpredictable and dangerous for both sides.[31] American officials who led the US response to Kargil consider such Indian and Pakistani assessments to be rooted in a pre-nuclear strategic reality. Whereas in the past, a minor border clash could have escalated into a major confrontation, they reasoned that the process probably would have taken weeks as major conventional strike formations mobilized and deployed to the frontier. As neither side had the rapid power projection capability to deliver a quick knockout blow, there was every expectation that any major conventional conflict would in fairly

---

[30] Einhorn interview.
[31] Anthony Davis, "When Words Hurt: No Limits on Limited War," *Asiaweek*, 31 March 2000, www.asiaweek.com/asiaweek/magazine/2000/0331/nat.indiapak.war.htm.

short order settle into stalemate. That would buy the time for the international community to step in to mediate a truce and withdrawal.

With the continued development and fielding of nuclear weapons after 1998, however, the timelines have been shortened, both sides have destabilizing alternatives to such a war of attrition, and quick knockout blows are no longer inconceivable. Both sides now possess strategic assets – nuclear weapons – the loss of which would be considered a national disaster. The dynamic of the rivalry in an escalating crisis could lead either government to fear that it was being forced into a "use or lose" situation. Given the poor record each country has of accurately assessing the other's capabilities and intentions, American officials and observers agreed overwhelmingly that Kargil showed their earlier estimate of the fragility of strategic stability in South Asia to be correct, if not too optimistic.

Based on this thinking, President Clinton described South Asia less than a year after the Kargil crisis as "perhaps the most dangerous place in the world today because of tensions over Kashmir and the possession of nuclear weapons."[32] This view dovetailed with a significant shift in the US nuclear agenda for South Asia, in large part growing out of the Kargil experience. From the May 1998 tests until Kargil, US nonproliferation policy, in coordination with the policies of other members of the G-8, had five main components:

- discourage any further testing;
- gain Indian and Pakistani adherence to the Fissile Material Cutoff Treaty;
- achieve restraint in development and fielding of ballistic missiles;
- enhance Indian and Pakistani export controls to reduce the risks of further proliferation;
- promote dialogue on the underlying bilateral disputes, especially Kashmir.

After Kargil, promotion of dialogue became the centerpiece of US nuclear policy toward South Asia. Kargil led officials in Washington to conclude that avoiding conflict, lowering tensions, and building mutual trust and confidence had to take priority over the first four items, all of which were designed primarily to restrain the building and deployment of capabilities rather than shape intentions. The US administration still advocated a moratorium on testing, renunciation of further production of fissile material, restraint in missile delivery system deployment, and so on; but it now believed Kargil had demonstrated that it was possible for India

---

[32] Quoted by Terence Hunt, Associated Press, 19 March 2000, http://abcnews.go.com/sections/world/DailyNews/clinton_india000319.html.

and Pakistan to blunder from conventional into nuclear war. Preventing another Indo-Pakistani war of any kind was therefore increasingly seen as more important than securing an agreement to the classic nonproliferation agenda.[33] While this realization has not yet led to assertive US leadership toward solving the Kashmir dispute that underlay the Kargil war, it has nevertheless shaped the way Washington has approached the challenges presented by the reality of a nuclear South Asia since 1999.

The Kargil crisis also convinced most American officials dealing with South Asia that lingering hopes anyone may have harbored for rolling back nuclear capability in the subcontinent were unrealistic. Adjustments in US policy toward the region after Kargil implicitly acknowledged that both India and Pakistan had become *de facto* nuclear weapons states and were not going to renounce their capabilities. As a result, increased attention was given to ensuring that both countries functioned as responsible possessors of nuclear weapons, particularly to preventing leakage and other risks of onward proliferation. This was already part of the US agenda for the region, although restrictions imposed by treaty and law specifically prohibited US assistance in nuclear safety, security, and command and control.

US officials also realized that the legally mandated nonproliferation policy sanctions imposed on Pakistan in 1990 and on both countries in 1998 had outlived their usefulness. These sanctions, which were designed to dissuade or at least slow the acquisition of nuclear weapon capabilities, had become obstacles to generating positive political and military influence on the leaders of both countries. The administration found that it had few sticks or carrots readily available to influence the protagonists during the Kargil crisis. The sense that Kargil had brought India and Pakistan uncomfortably close to nuclear conflict, heightened awareness throughout the US government that the United States needed to rebuild its means of influencing the two governments. Proposals to modify sanctions therefore began to find new political traction. Unfortunately, just as progress was being made, the Musharraf military coup triggered another round of sanctions against Pakistan and undermined whatever momentum was building in Congress for relief, at least with respect to Islamabad. Nevertheless, the Clinton administration proceeded to remove some sanctions against India, and the attacks of 11 September ultimately provided the basis for more sweeping relief for both countries.

---

[33] Einhorn interview.

Lessons for future engagement

The United States actively sought to contain and resolve the Kargil crisis from its initial démarches to Islamabad and New Delhi on 24 May 1999 until the Pakistani force withdrawal in mid-July. This engagement took place at every level of the US administration from the president down to the assistant secretary of state, and involved daily communication by senior officials with both parties in the form of letters, telephone calls, and face-to-face meetings.[34]

According to Karl F. Inderfurth, then Assistant Secretary of State for South Asia, the administration concluded that the success of US diplomacy in managing the Kargil crisis rested on two factors. One was keeping the focus on Pakistan's responsibility for the confrontation, a point that was first expressed only in private, but eventually was stated publicly after quiet diplomatic discussion did not avail the desired result. Not only did Washington clearly place the blame for the crisis squarely on Pakistan; it also credited India throughout the crisis with exercising restraint, even when India resorted to decisive military force, including the use of air power to drive Pakistani units back across the LoC.[35]

The second factor was full transparency between the United States and India. Clinton administration officials believed that only by regularly reporting to New Delhi the results of their interactions with the Pakistanis could Washington offset India's historical suspicions of US motivations in South Asia. This policy of transparency took effect on 27 May, the same day that Under Secretary Thomas Pickering told Pakistani ambassador Riaz Khokhar that Pakistan should withdraw, and Assistant Secretary Inderfurth called Indian ambassador Naresh Chandra to relay to him what the US told the Pakistanis. Similarly, after the commander in chief of US Central Command, General Anthony Zinni, met with Pakistan's Chief of Army Staff, General Pervez Musharraf, and Prime Minister Sharif on 24–25 June, a senior State Department official

---

[34] In the response to the Kargil crisis the one US agency that had a lower profile than one might have expected was the Department of Defense, with the exception of General Anthony Zinni, Commander in Chief of US Central Command. Regional specialists in the Department of State and in the NSC staff seized the early initiative on Kargil, managed the crisis informally outside the normal Deputies and Principals Committee structure, and were able to count on an unusually high level of presidential involvement as the dimensions of the crisis were understood, obviating formal DoD participation in the process. In fact, the decision to dispatch Zinni as a presidential envoy seems to have been taken by the White House and State Department without prior consultation with the Pentagon. Telephone interview with Gen. Anthony C. Zinni, USMC (retd.), 2 April 2003.

[35] US officials believed India tried to keep its air assets and ground forces on its side of the LoC. Walter Andersen comments.

on Zinni's delegation was sent to New Delhi to brief the Indian government on the results of the consultations.[36] Even at Blair House on 4 July, President Clinton took advantage of a break in discussions with Sharif to telephone Indian prime minister Vajpayee and apprise him of progress.[37] The president's conversation with Vajpayee was backed up by parallel calls to their counterparts in India from the National Security Advisor Samuel (Sandy) Berger, and Acting Secretary of State Talbott.

In addition to the US reinforcement of its transparency by the high-level phone calls between US and Indian policymakers, India set up an informal back channel for confidence-building talks with the United States through a delegation to Washington led by Arun Nehru, reporting to then-Foreign Minister Jaswant Singh, and dealing with Deputy Secretary of State Strobe Talbott. This provided the Indian side an opportunity, coincidentally, to gauge the seriousness of US commitments by taking its own soundings with the administration, other Washington influentials, and the press, on the spot, in Washington, DC. Side meetings on Kargil incidental to these confidence-building talks probably played a critical role during the height of the Kargil crisis in overcoming Indian suspicion of long-term US strategic intentions in South Asia.[38]

Combined with the public focus on Pakistan's responsibility for the crisis, transparency was intended to ensure that India would work with the United States for a diplomatic solution rather than escalating the crisis militarily. However, US transparency may have had the unintended effect of reducing incentives for India to accept a de-escalatory settlement that the Pakistanis claim was developed in back-channel negotiations. This back-channel process, led by R. K. Mishra for the Indian side and Niaz Naik for the Pakistani side, had been underway for over a year as part of an effort to find ways out of the impasse on Kashmir. As the fighting intensified in June, Mishra and Naik reportedly took up the Kargil issue.[39] In the Pakistani version of events, Nawaz Sharif reportedly had Indian agreement to stop in New Delhi on his way home from Beijing on 28 June to nail down a deal. This meeting, negotiated by Mishra and Naik, would have provided an Indian commitment to restart the Lahore process in

---

[36] Inderfurth interview.
[37] Riedel, chapter 5 above; Talbott, *Engaging India*, 168.
[38] Walter Andersen comments.
[39] R. K. Mishra is a prominent Indian journalist and businessman with close ties to Brajesh Mishra, then-principal secretary to the prime minister, and through him to then-Prime Minister Vajpayee at the top of the Indian government. Niaz Naik, a retired Pakistani diplomat, had served as high commissioner to India and later as the senior career official in the foreign ministry. Naik had access to and the direct approval for his mission of Prime Minister Nawaz Sharif as well as then Chief of Army Staff General Pervez Musharraf.

exchange for Pakistan's withdrawal from the areas across the LoC in the vicinity of Kargil. However, he was told *en route* by the Indian government not to come.[40] Some Pakistani analysts conclude that the United States actively dissuaded India from moving ahead with the back-channel agreement as a way of punishing Pakistan.[41]

There are two problems with this interpretation. In the first place, the Indian side denies that any such deal was in the offing, and Mishra himself has refused to comment on the substance of his discussions with Naik. In any case, the idea that the United States would intentionally quash a process that might have led to a peaceful resolution of the Kargil conflict strains credulity given the very real concern in Washington that continued fighting could spin out of control. Indeed, the State Department said, in response to cryptic press reports apparently referring to these back-channel discussions, that any diplomatic breakthrough would be a welcome development.[42]

Inasmuch as the United States effectively sided with India and, as a matter of policy, back-briefed Vajpayee's government on US–Pakistani discussions,[43] it is possible that the Indians may have concluded that they could get what they wanted – Pakistani withdrawal – without acceding to a restart of the Lahore process.[44] But that reality had already been established on the battlefield. The Indian army had captured the important heights at Tololing by mid-June, and by 28 June was on its way to clearing Tiger Hill and the Batalik sector, clearly demonstrating that it would be able to prevail absent a major Pakistani escalation. It is therefore unlikely that US diplomacy was the decisive factor in India's decision not to move ahead with any back-channel agreement, assuming that one was in the works.[45]

Bruce Riedel and several other US officials who were involved in the crisis believed Kargil validated the importance of personal relationships between US and foreign officials at multiple levels of government in South Asia.[46] The State Department's ability to assure India that it was truly

---

[40] Milam interview.

[41] Roundtable with Pakistani analysts at Institute of Strategic Studies, Islamabad, 13 January 2003.

[42] Deputy Spokesman James Foley at State Department noon press briefing, 2 July 1999.

[43] Note that, as mentioned above, Deputy Assistant Secretary of State Gibson Lanpher broke off from the Zinni mission on 27 June to inform the Indians that Sharif and Musharraf had agreed to unilateral withdrawal.

[44] Milam interview.

[45] Our impression from interviews was that insofar as the policymakers in Washington had heard of the back channel, they did not put much stock in its prospects for success.

[46] This is an unremarkable point of view in diplomacy. Indeed, it may be thought of as a general expectation among top leaders. But in certain countries, India among them

being transparent in its approach to Kargil depended heavily on the positive personal relationship established between Deputy Secretary Talbott and Indian external affairs minister Jaswant Singh over the course of their nonproliferation negotiations following the 1998 nuclear tests.[47] More vitally, as noted by Riedel, President Clinton had met with Nawaz Sharif on several occasions prior to the Kargil crisis, felt comfortable dealing with him, and believed that he and the prime minister had a "genuine personal bond."[48] Clinton and Sharif also had conversed frequently by telephone following the 1998 Indian nuclear tests as Clinton tried to persuade Sharif not to follow suit. Although that effort did not succeed, the rapport that developed between the two leaders gave Clinton the entrée to communicate directly with Sharif on Kargil. This included at least three telephone conversations prior to the Blair House meeting. Moreover, the feeling that he knew the president personally was probably also a key element in Sharif's decision to seek political cover from Clinton when it became apparent that Pakistan would have to withdraw its troops.

Almost equally important was the personal connection between Generals Zinni and Musharraf. Because US policy restricted high-level military contacts with both governments in response to the May 1998 nuclear tests, Zinni was the only US officer above the rank of colonel who was permitted to have any regular interaction with the Pakistani military. Given the historically powerful role of the army within the Pakistan government as well as the importance of treating Kargil as both a military and a diplomatic problem, the Zinni–Musharraf channel was seen by the White House as an essential adjunct to the civilian political channels that had been established.

Zinni called Musharraf on 7 June, and again on 20 June, then finally met with him in person in Islamabad on 24 June. During that meeting, Zinni made clear that Pakistan's adventure in Kargil would not garner any US support for its position on Kashmir. The United States would not consider even talking about Kashmir issues – and President Clinton would certainly not consider meeting with Prime Minister Nawaz Sharif – unless Pakistani forces first withdrew from Kargil. Musharraf responded by asking Zinni what he could use as the rationale for a withdrawal. Zinni replied that what had begun as a tactical advance had spun into a strategic setback. He said that troop mobilizations on both sides

---

during the earlier decades, policies and strong personal friendships have tended to be kept in separate compartments, the latter seldom yielding real influence over the former. In the 1990s, this tradition may have begun to change.

[47] Inderfurth interview. By contrast, although Talbott had also interacted heavily with senior Pakistani officials, particularly Foreign Secretary Shamshad Ahmad, the relationship was much cooler and more contentious (Milam interview).

[48] Riedel, chapter 5 above, p. 135.

were already out of control and outlined the potential for the crisis to escalate unpredictably (including the risks of being placed in a "use-or-lose" situation with respect to the nuclear arsenal). Musharraf ultimately agreed that a withdrawal was the only choice.[49]

The next day, after a period of stalling by the civilian bureaucracy in Islamabad (apparently on the grounds that Zinni was of insufficient stature to meet with the prime minister), the two generals met jointly with Nawaz Sharif, who readily agreed to the withdrawal proposal.[50] While Sharif and his advisors evidently got cold feet after Zinni's departure, these military consultations obviously played an important role in setting the stage for the final withdrawal.

The broader question is just how decisive either Zinni's or Clinton's interventions really were. Riedel obviously believes the president's involvement was the key. He writes in his account of the "Kargil Summit" at Blair House that Clinton "successfully persuad[ed] Pakistani Prime Minister Nawaz Sharif to pull back Pakistani backed fighters from a confrontation with India that could threaten to escalate into a nuclear war."[51] Yet as Riedel and others note, President Clinton agreed to see Sharif only when it was clear that Sharif desperately needed the meeting – and even though there was as yet no clear evidence that Pakistani forces were withdrawing, as the Pakistani prime minister had promised. In fact, Riedel does not mention that Zinni already had such a promise,[52] a commitment that undoubtedly reflected Pakistan's fundamental recognition that it inevitably would lose the war on the ground. Any assessment of the success of US involvement must take into account this basic military reality.

Nevertheless, the roles played by Clinton and Zinni were far from insignificant. Throughout the week leading up to the Blair House meeting, the Pakistanis were trying to salvage some kind of advantage from the Kargil adventure. Even after promising Zinni that forces would be withdrawn, Sharif traveled to Beijing, evidently in search of Chinese backing for a negotiated compromise with India – backing that one former official in the Sharif government says was denied.[53] As already described, Sharif then tried but failed to strike a deal with New Delhi that would have restarted the Lahore process in exchange for Pakistani withdrawal. Once the Pakistanis got to Washington, they attempted to extract some kind of quid for withdrawal, finally settling for President Clinton's agreement to

---

[49] Zinni interview; Milam interview.   [50] Zinni interview; Milam interview.
[51] Riedel, chapter 5 above, p. 132.   [52] Milam interview.
[53] Roundtable with Pakistani analysts, Institute of Strategic Studies, Islamabad, 13 January 2003.

take a personal interest in the revival of the Lahore process and in the issue of Kashmir.[54]

All this activity suggests that Sharif – and probably Musharraf – realized how heavy the domestic political costs of unilateral withdrawal could be, especially considering the effort that had gone into selling Islamabad's version of the crisis to the Pakistani public.[55] At a minimum, therefore, the political cover provided by the Blair House Summit expedited Pakistan's withdrawal and thus saved scores if not hundreds of lives that might have been lost if Islamabad had delayed the inevitable.[56] At a maximum, there is always the possibility that Pakistani attempts to retrieve the situation could have led either side to take escalatory steps that might have spun out of control, and that the White House meeting prevented this. Odds are that the effect of the Washington meeting was at the lower end of this spectrum, but we may never know for sure.

Whatever the precise impact of the Clinton and Zinni interventions, all those involved on the US side came away believing that having a firsthand sense of the person on the other side of a negotiation was key to the successful exertion of influence. Indeed, having a chance to develop such firsthand knowledge of Pakistan's new leader, Pervez Musharraf, despite his having come to office in a military coup, was one of the principal factors in Clinton's decision to include a stop in Pakistan on his March 2000 trip to South Asia. Firmly convinced that South Asia was one of the most dangerous places on earth, and that firsthand experience with leaders on both sides had been essential to the success of the Blair House meeting, the president decided that the value of getting to know Musharraf in person outweighed whatever negative signals would be sent by appearing to countenance his ouster of Nawaz Sharif.

Until 11 September broke loose the policy restrictions on military interaction with Pakistan, however, the lesson of Zinni's role seems to have been less well learned. While Zinni's involvement highlighted the value of military-to-military contacts, the fact that no one below his level was in a position to interact with Pakistani officers underscored the

---

[54] Talbott describes the hard-nosed Blair House meeting strategy of the US side in considerable detail. The decision was to insist on Pakistani withdrawal of forces from Kargil without preconditions on either India or the United States. The Americans knew Sharif would plead for an immediate ceasefire, for instance, implying a negotiated withdrawal, and were clear in their position that no ceasefire would be accepted until and unless Pakistani troop withdrawal was complete. Nawaz Sharif would be praised if he went along, and could return home with a vague assurance from Clinton to help facilitate dialogue with India and to take an interest in Kashmir. If Sharif refused, the meeting would be a failure: he would return empty handed, with the focus on Pakistan as the perpetrator of the crisis. See Talbott, *Engaging India*, 161–169.

[55] Milam interview.   [56] Inderfurth interview.

damage that had been done over the years to US–Pakistani military relations. One lesson of Kargil should have been the extent to which US ability to shape Pakistani military officers' perspectives had been eroded by the decline in bilateral military-to-military ties, a decline that had begun in October 1990 when the first Bush administration found itself compelled by continued Pakistani nuclear developments to cut off US security assistance under the provisions of the Pressler Amendment.[57] The Kargil crisis led the Clinton administration to relax its policy on military contacts, but interaction remained tightly constrained in practice and was put back into the deep-freeze when the Pakistani army overthrew Nawaz Sharif's civilian government in October 1999, triggering a new set of legally mandated sanctions.

Department of Defense officials, along with the leadership of the State Department's South Asia Bureau, had maintained throughout the second Clinton administration that the Pakistan army's status as the dominant institution in Pakistan made it imperative that the United States develop influence among the Pakistani officer corps, and that the best way of doing that was through military-to-military contacts.[58] There was considerable concern, as time went on, that the United States essentially had "lost" an entire generation of Pakistani officers who had come of professional age in the decade since the imposition of the Pressler sanctions. There is, of course, always a risk that overreliance on the use of senior military channels unintentionally conveys to the Pakistani military that it does not need to listen to US civilian officials below the level of the president, that the US government is divided between a pro-Pakistan Pentagon and a pro-Indian State Department, and that the United States only gives lip service to its

---

[57] The 1985 Pressler Amendment to the Foreign Assistance Act of 1961 allowed the president to waive nuclear-proliferation-related prohibitions on most types of government-to-government assistance to Pakistan if he certified annually that Pakistan "did not possess a nuclear explosive device and that the proposed US assistance program will significantly reduce the risk that Pakistan will possess a nuclear explosive device." In October 1990, then-President George Bush declined to make this certification for fiscal year 1991, thus reinstating the proliferation sanctions that had been triggered by Pakistan's past nuclear technology acquisitions. The apparent reason for the president's decision not to certify under the Pressler Amendment was the conclusion that Pakistan had fabricated the critical components of a nuclear weapon device based on highly enriched uranium produced in its isotopic separation program. For details on the Pressler Amendment and other US nonproliferation legislation affecting Pakistan, see Rodney W. Jones and Mark G. McDonough, *Tracking Nuclear Proliferation: A Guide in Maps and Charts, 1998* (Washington, DC: Brookings Institution Press, 1998), 131–132.

[58] Inderfurth and Assistant Secretary of Defense Franklin D. Kramer attempted on several occasions to persuade Congressional leaders to permit the resumption of International Military Education and Training (IMET) funding for Pakistan, but without success.

commitment to Pakistani democracy.[59] Americans must keep in mind the possibility that they are conveying such an unintended message before they decide to dispatch a senior military interlocutor. Nevertheless, the Pakistani armed forces do play a dominant role in Islamabad's decision-making, even when a general is not actually occupying the presidency. The efficacy of bilateral military ties as a means of building US influence with present and future leaders of foreign armed forces is undeniable. In fact, on more than one occasion after the Musharraf coup, Washington took advantage of his personal relationship with Zinni to convey messages of the highest urgency.[60] The risk that overreliance on the military channel may have unintended consequences is reason for using it more judiciously, not for omitting it from the toolbox of US–Pakistan relations.

The problem of unintended consequences raises one final issue: whether US involvement in Kargil contributed to the downfall of Nawaz Sharif's government three months later. Ever since October 1999, when Pervez Musharraf drove Sharif into exile, it has been widely suspected that the embarrassment of having been forced out of Kargil by the United States was the ultimate cause of Sharif's downfall. If there is any connection at all, which is far from clear, this view certainly overstates the case. Given the direction of military events on the ground, the Pakistani government was going to be embarrassed one way or the other. If anything, the political cover Clinton gave Sharif created the opportunity for Pakistanis to blame the United States rather than their own leaders for the failure – an opportunity that Pakistani commentators eagerly seized. On the other hand, notwithstanding that the army chief Pervez Musharraf had signed up to the withdrawal, the episode and its aftermath did cause increased resentment of Nawaz Sharif within the army. Nawaz was blamed by the army for failing to get the United States to guarantee that India would not attack Pakistani forces as they withdrew. As it turned out, India did attack the withdrawing forces, and Pakistan says it suffered its heaviest losses during this extraction phase.[61]

It is true that once the Blair House Summit was over, Washington basically took a passive stance, apart from utilizing Zinni one more time to prod Musharraf to get on with issuing the withdrawal order. However, the *de facto* ceasefire arranged by the two armies' Directors General of Military Operations (DGMOs), under which the infiltrators were to retreat, was renounced by the Indian side only when it discovered that

---

[59] Milam interview. Several other senior Clinton administration officials involved in South Asia policy expressed the same view privately.
[60] Zinni interview.   [61] Milam interview.

the evacuation was not taking place as promised. The US administration might have been able to lean on New Delhi to show greater restraint, and thereby to avert some of the friction that was generated between Sharif and his generals as a result,[62] but the United States was neither party to nor guarantor of the DGMOs' withdrawal agreement. To hold Washington accountable for any Pakistani army retribution against Nawaz Sharif growing out of how the agreement was implemented is therefore unjustified.

In any case, it is exceedingly doubtful that restraining the Indians at this point could have had any pivotal bearing on the Pakistan army's instigating the October coup. Discontent with Nawaz Sharif was high long before Kargil, both inside and outside the military, as he moved against one Pakistani power structure after another. Finally, and most importantly, Sharif committed a series of serious political errors in the months after Kargil that probably would have led to his ouster even if Kargil had never happened. Sharif's agreement to Clinton's insistence on withdrawal from Kargil may have been a minor factor in the demise of his government. For one thing, he grew increasingly defensive vis-à-vis the military after Kargil, which may have accounted for some of his civil–military blunders. But if a factor in his downfall, it was not the decisive one.[63]

Conclusion

US policymakers and intelligence analysts were not surprised by Indian and Pakistani military skirmishing along the Kashmir LoC in May 1999. Such skirmishes have been a perennial problem over the years, and usually increased each spring after the melting of the snow at higher altitudes. Artillery exchanges by both sides were a well-known ritual. India jockeyed for advantage in pushing forces in 1983 onto the Siachen Glacier, near Kashmir's border with Tibet, where the LoC is not defined, touching off the world's highest-altitude warfare that continues to this day. Armed Pakistani militants have infiltrated into the Valley of Kashmir in significant numbers since the Kashmiri insurgency began in 1989.

What was surprising at first to Washington about the Pakistani incursion across the LoC near Kargil in 1999 was its preparation, scale, and initial tactical success in taking over high-altitude positions overlooking Kargil that had been vacated by Indian troops during the winter, the cost this imposed on Indian forces in their initial efforts to retake those

[62] *Ibid.* [63] Inderfurth interview; Milam interview.

positions, and the escalatory dangers the ensuing battles posed in light of the fact that India and Pakistan had tested and acquired nuclear weapons the year before. Those who accepted the conventional wisdom, that nuclear-armed rivals cannot afford to provoke conventional military engagements with each other, were surprised at the risk the Pakistani military boldly, albeit covertly, undertook.

Also surprising to US policymakers, once the government-sponsored basis of the operation had been ascertained, was Pakistan's evident failure to recognize its unsustainability, to anticipate the negative international repercussions it almost certainly would have on Pakistan's image, and to calculate the political damage it would do to Indian willingness to negotiate a settlement over Kashmir. The US administration and Congress were not only surprised but also exceptionally disturbed by the seemingly brazen contradiction between this action, which must have been organized months before, and the long-sought startup of a negotiating process at the Lahore Summit. The Vajpayee government of India, as well as the Clinton administration from the sidelines, both had invested significant political capital in this high-profile and hopeful breakthrough in India–Pakistan relations. At least in the short run, Kargil squandered Pakistan's gains from Lahore.

The danger of military escalation and the risk of nuclear weapons use were the driving factors in the US diplomatic intervention that culminated at Blair House on 4 July 1999. The new opportunity to cultivate a deeper, strategically significant, relationship with India, drawing on the previous efforts of the first Bush administration and the Clinton administration, was a fringe benefit. Washington's unequivocal assessment that Pakistan was responsible for the Kargil crisis and the transparency the US administration maintained with New Delhi by leaning on Pakistan to withdraw militarily as the crucial condition for defusing the Kargil confrontation had a profound effect on Indian attitudes. The way Washington approached Kargil also convinced many Indians for the first time that US professions of respect for Indian security interests were authentic. Pakistan's adventure in Kargil, whatever its operational or tactical motivations, reinforced the already apparent trend toward closer relations between the United States and India. From Pakistan's standpoint, this could only be viewed as a strategic setback.

US concerns about the nuclear risks in South Asia were sharpened by the Kargil crisis, and led to a significant shift in emphasis on the tools and future goals of nuclear-risk reduction. In part, this meant a cumulative shift away from reliance on the traditional sanctions in nuclear nonproliferation legislation. In part, it meant a reexamination of where leverage with the two South Asian states may have atrophied in the past, and a determination to rebuild influence in new forms. In Pakistan's case, given the central political influence of the military, this meant a renewed, albeit troubled, effort to reestablish US–Pakistani military-to-military relationships. In India's case, military cooperation was broadened significantly. But the central lesson US policymakers took from the Kargil affair was the vital importance of encouraging genuine dialogue and incremental steps between India and Pakistan to reduce the risks of military conflict across the board.

Kargil may have had unexpected and even undesirable consequences for the future. Some in Washington feared that influential strategic thinkers in India and Pakistan may have drawn mistaken lessons of their own about having sufficient space to pursue aggressive conventional military actions beneath the supposed threshold of nuclear escalation. That is, Indians and Pakistanis seemed to ignore the constraints against expanding military engagement across the international border or even within Kashmir. The retreat Pakistan was forced to accept by withdrawing its forces under pressure, though under the political cover provided Pakistan through President Clinton's meeting with Nawaz Sharif, undoubtedly contributed to further friction in Pakistan's civil–military relations and perhaps generated new impediments to an open political process.

US officials believe that Clinton's intervention was in no way directly responsible for the army coup that deposed Nawaz Sharif and brought General Musharraf to power. Those officials are much clearer in their own minds that the diplomatic outcomes at Blair House reduced the political costs to Pakistan of withdrawal and that the antecedents helped head off a deepening military confrontation between India and Pakistan. In this respect, US officials involved at the time believe US diplomacy over Kargil set positive precedents for rapid US determination of the causes and stakes in a regional military crisis, as well as for the pattern of high-level US engagement early on to contain escalation and defuse the crisis.

These precedents have since been borne out in succeeding Indo-Pakistani crises, particularly the ten-month-long military confrontation following the 13 December 2001 terrorist attack on the Indian parliament, a crisis which far outstripped Kargil in the number of troops deployed on both sides, if not in the number of lives that were lost. Once again, concern that things could easily spin out of control – this time with dire consequences for Pakistani cooperation in US operations against the Afghan Taliban and al Qaeda – rapidly led the United States to intervene diplomatically to tamp down the crisis. As in the case of Kargil, the intensive personal involvement of US officials at the highest level, combined with public musings by American officials about the possible destructiveness of a nuclear exchange, eventually led Pakistan to take the steps required by India to defuse the conflict.[64] Bilateral developments between India and Pakistan have been on an encouragingly positive track ever since, but it is still far too early to discount the possibility of rapid deterioration leading to renewed confrontation. Although even the most intensive American diplomatic intervention might not be able to prevent escalation, Washington's understanding of the enormous risks implicit in armed conflict between the two South Asian nuclear states – an understanding developed largely in the context of the Kargil conflict – guarantees that no American administration will stand aside should another crisis arise in the future.

[64] John H. Gill, "Dissuasion and Confrontation: US Policy in India–Pakistan Crises," *Strategic Insights* 3, no. 10 (October 2004), www.ccc.nps.navy.mil/si/2004/oct/gillOct04.asp.

15 Kargil, deterrence and international relations theory

Robert Jervis

Introduction

The challenger faces a much stronger adversary and is frustrated by its inability to protect itself and change the status quo. Blocked from advancing its cause and enraged by the adversary's hostile if not aggressive actions, it hits upon a clever if desperate move. The adversary's superiority makes it overconfident and the challenger proceeds in secret, disguises its actions, and does what is believed to be unlikely, thus enabling it to put its forces in position without being discovered. By taking actions that bear some resemblance to what the adversary has done, the challenger gives itself added legitimacy. Nevertheless, when the adversary discovers what is happening it reacts very strongly, and the rest of the world sides with it. After an exchange of nuclear threats and conventional maneuvering, the challenger is forced to withdraw, humiliated and with little to show for it. One result is that the challenger's leader is overthrown. The world has come uncomfortably close to a nuclear exchange, but years later we still debate the motives on each side, the nature of the interaction, the relative importance of conventional and nuclear arms, the actions of third parties, the role of intelligence, and whether a better diplomacy could have diffused the crisis.

This awkwardly abstract description applies to both the 1999 Kargil conflict and the 1962 Cuban missile crisis. Although it would go too far to argue that we could simply transfer what we know about the latter to the former (and vice versa), the parallels do reveal that even if international politics lacks invariant laws, situations and behavior do recur. Furthermore, parallels continue. "India was prepared for nuclear war, but we were confidant our neighbor would not resort to such madness," Prime Minister Vajpayee said. Pakistan's president replied: "Our capability was being doubted and it was being said with arrogance that Pakistan's nuclear bluff had been called. We were compelled to show then, in May 1998, that we were not bluffing and in May 2002, we were compelled to show that we do not bluff."[1] These statements were made in the context of a much more serious Indo-Pak military crisis triggered by a terrorist attack on the Indian parliament on 13 December 2001, but they reveal that it was a priority for each country to demonstrate that it had a robust capability for military escalation, should either the 1999 or 2002 crisis escalate, and that it was prepared to employ this capability if need be.

The orienting questions of this chapter are what does Kargil tell us about theories of how states behave in nuclear crises and how do these theories help explain this incident? Put another way, much of our knowledge of crises in general and nuclear crises in particular is derived from the Soviet–American experience, supplemented by analysis of the crises that preceded World War I. This makes it hard to separate what we think are general strategic imperatives from the particularities of national styles and cultures, interacting pairs, and historical periods.

This is not to say that Kargil or any other case can unambiguously speak to the question of the extent to which the structure of the situation determines behavior in the face of differences in context, cultures, and personalities. To start with, our general theories are quite loose and vague. They can accommodate a wide range of behavior and outcomes. Furthermore, we have not one theory but many variants of deterrence theory with alternative views of when threats will be employed and how they are likely to work, as well as competing theories that argue that threats are likely to backfire for reasons both rational and psychological.[2] The other side of this coin is that it is a rare case that permits only one explanation. Seen one way, Kargil easily fits our standard theories, but seen in other ways it does not. Indeed, the reason that I think that Kargil is explicable with standard deterrence models may be that they provide the intellectual tools that guide my interpretation of the case.

---

[1] Both quoted in Celia W. Dugger, "The Kashmir Brink," *New York Times*, 20 June 2002. Musharraf uttered these words in an address to the Pakistani scientific community on 17 June 2002, in which he highlighted the ballistic missile tests conducted on 28 May 2002 at the peak of the crisis with India. This remark acknowledges that Pakistan deliberately timed the flight tests as a means of signaling deterrence. Conversely, Pakistan denies having done any nuclear preparation or signaling during the Kargil crisis. Feroz Hassan Khan, "Nuclear Signaling, Missiles, and Escalation Control in South Asia," in *Escalation Control and Nuclear Option in South Asia*, ed. Michael Krepon, Rodney Jones, and Ziad Haider (Washington, DC: Henry L. Stimson Center, 2004), 75–100. Musharraf denied any nuclear preparations during the 1999 crisis. See Pervez Musharraf, *In the Line of Fire: A Memoir* (New York: Free Press, 2006), 97–98.

[2] For reviews of the literature, see Paul Stern, Robert Axelrod, Robert Jervis, and Rog Radner, eds., *Perspectives on Deterrence* (Oxford University Press, 1989); and Patrick Morgan, *Deterrence Now* (Cambridge University Press, 2003). Also see Robert Jervis, "Security Studies: Ideas, Policy, and Politics," in *The Evolution of Political Knowledge: Democracy, Autonomy, and Conflict in Comparative and International Politics*, ed. Edward Mansfield and Richard Sisson (Columbus: Ohio State University Press, 2004).

Even if India and Pakistan behaved roughly like the United States and the Soviet Union, we cannot readily determine if the reason is the compelling nature of the situation or that the later participants learned from the earlier experiences. If we had full records we could look for references to Soviet–American interactions, but we could not determine whether their presence was mere window-dressing or their absence indicated lack of impact. In principle, one could try to see whether behavior matched idiosyncratic aspects of Soviet or American behavior, which would indicate learning or emulation, or whether on the contrary behavior differed from the Western experience but conformed to what was expected from some form of deterrence theory. But these kinds of inferences are hard to draw and the evidence available would not permit matching them against actual behavior. Nevertheless, it is worth noting that although India scorned Western approaches to deterrence and said that its stance was quite different, not only did its behavior resemble that of the United States, but so did some of the striking rhetoric. During and after the Kargil crisis India talked about responding to a proxy war "with prompt retaliation, in a manner, time, and place of India's choosing," an eerie echo of the words of John Foster Dulles, whom most Indians considered the epitome of a dangerous and short-sighted Cold warrior: "The way to deter aggression is for the free community to be willing and able to respond vigorously at places and with means of its own choosing."[3]

For many purposes, it would be useful to compare Kargil both with several Soviet–American crises and with other confrontations between India and Pakistan. But the range of available cases is not large, many of them remain obscure, and the details of the comparisons need to be derived from the questions we are asking and the theories we are seeking to probe. So in most of this chapter the comparisons are only hinted at.

Nature of the puzzle

Kargil, like any crisis, almost automatically seems puzzling, but the nature of the puzzle depends on how we think the actors see the situation. By definition a crisis is unexpected and dangerous.[4] One if not both sides

---

[3] Kargil Review Committee, *From Surprise to Reckoning: The Kargil Review Committee Report* (New Delhi: Sage, 2000), 264, also 221; John Foster Dulles, "The Evolution of Foreign Policy," *Department of State Bulletin*, vol. 30, 25 January 1962. More generally, in chapter 6 of this book, Hoyt concludes, "India is following a path similar to those of the superpowers during the 1950s."

[4] The literature on crises is large, but one of the first studies is still well worth consulting: Charles Hermann, ed., *International Crises: Insights from Behavioral Research* (New York: Free Press, 1972).

presumably miscalculated; both would have benefited by reaching the same outcome through a less costly and risky route.[5] The actors themselves are surprised and if they have basically the same information and beliefs about the world that theorists do, then the latter must be surprised as well.[6] The fact that crises violate actors' expectations creates problems for them and us. Since they have to base their behavior on estimates of how their adversaries will respond, the fact that their prevailing views have already been disconfirmed makes rational policymaking difficult. This also complicates the job of subsequent explanation. Game theory, whether formal or informal, is the obvious tool to use, but it assumes that actors have stable and reliable expectations about how others will behave, something that is called into question by the crisis itself.[7] It is then not surprising that at the start of a crisis one often finds thoughtful decision-makers puzzling about why the other side behaved in such a strange way. In the first meeting of the Cuban missile crisis, President Kennedy kept coming back to this question, although his less perceptive advisors did not seem to realize the relevance of this question to how they should behave.

For later analysts as well, one fundamental puzzle is why the state that did not fare well in the crisis (which often is the state that initiated it, for reasons discussed below) acted in what appears to be such a self-defeating way. Here exploration can follow one of two quite different paths depending on whether the state blundered into the crisis or acted as it did with good – if not necessarily full – knowledge of the risks and costs involved. Explanations for the American decisions to fight in Vietnam bring this out quite clearly. At first, the dominant arguments assumed that the decision-makers believed that the war could be won relatively easily. If this was so, the central question was to explain this error. Did the United States fail to grasp the nature of guerrilla warfare? Did it think that the South Vietnamese regime was stronger than it proved to be? Did the United States greatly underestimate the skill and resolve of the rebels in the South and the leaders in the North? But when the relevant records became public, it became clear that the costs and risks were in fact seen as high, even if not as high as they turned out to be. This pushed candidate explanations down quite a different path, inquiring as to what motives could have been strong enough to impel the Americans to embark on a

---

[5] This is the Hicks paradox explored by economists and developed for international politics in James Fearon, "A Rationalist Explanation of War," *International Organization* 49, no. 3 (Summer 1995), 379–414.

[6] Erik Gartzke, "War is in the Error Term," *International Organization* 53, no. 3 (Summer 1999), 567–587.

[7] David Krebs, *Game Theory and Economic Modeling* (Oxford University Press, 1990).

course that they knew would be perilous. Were presidents driven by the fear of electoral punishment for withdrawal? Was Johnson's advisory system and personal insecurity to blame? How much of the answer lies in the prevailing belief in the domino theory, which foresaw drastic international consequences from failure (a belief that itself calls for explanation, especially since most analysts believe it was wrong and did not rest on an unbiased assessment of the evidence)? Of course, in any particular case elements from these two branches can intertwine; indeed in Vietnam and perhaps in Kargil the strong motivation to reach an objective may have led to the belief that the costs and risks were manageable.

Routes to Kargil

One of the fundamental questions about the Kargil crisis is what Pakistan intended. Note that we pose the question this way because the crisis ended in a Pakistani defeat, and behavior that comes to an unhappy end is not self-explanatory. Similarly, in the immediate aftermath of the Cuban missile crisis people asked what Khrushchev thought he could accomplish by the adventure because it appeared that he got nothing significant out of the attempt. Now that we know that the US pledge not to invade Cuba was of some value and was supplemented by a promise that the United States would soon withdraw its missiles from Turkey, Soviet behavior seems at least slightly less reckless (although the missiles probably would have come out only slightly later without the crisis and the promise arrived in Moscow only after Khrushchev had decided to withdraw). Of course this form of reasoning is dangerous because it assumes that what happened could have been foreseen; we usually see the results as strongly determined and so see outcomes that fail as predictably doomed to failure. Thus most of us have a hard time imagining how Pakistan's maneuver could have yielded much, although it is less clear whether this reflects the actual situation or a failure of our imagination.

Nevertheless, in Kargil as in Cuba the deck does seem stacked against the challenger. Like the United States in Cuba, India had conventional and possibly nuclear superiority and a strong motivation to prevail. As Zafar Iqbal Cheema notes in chapter 2 of this book, it is impossible to reconstruct Pakistani calculations because of the paucity of documents, inside accounts, and only a few memoirs.[8] But I think, as Feroz Hassan

---

[8] This situation is slowly changing. The two army chiefs at the time of Kargil have written their respective accounts. For the Indian perspective, see General V. P. Malik, *Kargil: From Surprise to Victory* (New York: HarperCollins, 2006). For the Pakistan perspective, see Pervez Musharraf, *In the Line of Fire: A Memoir* (New York: Free Press, 2006).

Khan, Peter R. Lavoy, and Christopher Clary point out in chapter 3, the components are now known, fit well with our general theories, and track Soviet motives in Cuba.

Most fundamentally, Pakistan like the Soviet Union followed a bad course of action because no good one was available. Pakistan's strategic situation was weak: it had ambitious objectives and few resources. Pakistan seeks to change the status quo, which is difficult enough even under propitious circumstances.[9] Although the logic is not quite as clear as it would seem from common sense, preserving the status quo is generally easier than changing it, and deterrence is generally easier than compellence.[10]

States rarely yield territory without a fight and Kashmir is particularly valuable to India for showing that it is not a purely Hindu state.[11] The second element of Pakistan's dilemma is equally obvious. It is much smaller and weaker than India. The obvious way to change the status quo is to use or threaten massive force, but this Pakistan cannot do. Indeed, the military and economic imbalance is even greater than it was in the Soviet–American case. Pakistan then had – and still has – few tools with which to accomplish a forbidding task.

Seen in this light, the fundamental question may be why Pakistan persists, especially after the bifurcation of the country in 1971, which produced the independent country of Bangladesh in the territory that had been East Pakistan. Pakistan cannot achieve what it wants and so should have no choice but to adjust, a response consistent with Realism. Although critics sometimes equate Realism with bellicosity, in fact Realist statesmen and analysts argue that states not only should muster the resources needed to protect their interests, but also have to trim their interests to fit their resources. When E. H. Carr argued for appeasement in the first edition of *The Twenty Years' Crisis*, he was being a true representative of Realist thought.[12] It is easy to see why Pakistan dislikes what John Kenneth Galbraith called "the North American

---

[9]   I grant that this statement might be tautological because if the status quo were easy to change, the dissatisfied party would have already changed it.

[10]   Thomas Schelling, *Arms and Influence* (New Haven, Conn.: Yale University Press, 1960), 69–78, 100–105; Robert Jervis, *The Meaning of the Nuclear Revolution* (Ithaca, NY: Cornell University Press, 1989), 29–35.

[11]   This concern is stronger in secular segments of Indian society and so logically one might expect the BJP to care less about Kashmir. But logic can be overridden, especially by nationalism. It was Prime Minister Vajpayee who explained that "Kashmir is not a piece of land for us, it is a test of our secular credentials" ("India's Leader Says Pakistan Still Backs Kashmiri Militants," *New York Times*, 16 August 2002).

[12]   E. H. Carr, *The Twenty Years' Crisis: An Introduction to the Study of International Relations* (1939; reprint, NY: Harper Perennial, 1964).

solution" – the sacrifice of Kashmir and acceptance of a subsidiary if not subordinate role in South Asia – but it is less easy to see why this stance has been maintained in the face of such little encouragement. In fact, students of international politics rarely raise the question of when and how states adjust to an unacceptable situation, and this is a yawning gap in our knowledge.

Given a refusal to adjust, Pakistan has a number of alternatives, but none of them are promising. Furthermore, while some complement others, there also are tensions among them. One is to seek allies. These can be countries that have reason to bolster Pakistan (or weaken India), China being the prime example. In the best of all worlds, such assistance could be a great equalizer, counterbalancing or even outweighing India's bilateral advantages. But such an extreme case is unlikely: few allies will adopt the client's cause whole-heartedly, and any such alliance is likely to increase the chance that India will gain foreign support as well, which happened in the form of the Soviet Union during the Cold War and then Russia. Outsiders can play a somewhat different role in this conflict, however. As I discuss more below, one of Pakistan's continuing hopes is that the dispute will become internationalized, as outsiders become moved by the justice of Pakistan's cause or, more likely, the dangers of leaving the conflict to the two parties. In fact, a leading Pakistani official could claim Kargil as a success because it established the Kashmir dispute "as being a dangerous nuclear flashpoint ... The world now had a vested interest in ensuring that India takes the negotiations for the resolution of the dispute seriously."[13]

The second Pakistani strategy is to increase the costs and risks to India of maintaining the political status quo in Kashmir, something that also serves to increase the chances of drawing outsiders in. We often think of crises as highly dangerous situations that are the byproduct of actions taken to produce desired outcomes. This was true of the Cuban missile crisis, for example. Khrushchev wanted to put missiles into Cuba and would have been happy if he could have done so without calling up a strong American response. But although Pakistani leaders did not foresee the Indian and world responses to their incursion in Kargil, they may well have expected and wanted a great increase in attention. As long as the status quo seems safe, why should India agree to change it? The ability and willingness to create a crisis is then part of Pakistan's strategic arsenal.

[13] See chapter 13 of this book by Hasan-Askari Rizvi. Musharraf subsequently declared that "diplomatically [Kargil] highlighted Kashmir. It has been in focus ever since." Quoted in Isabel Hilton, "Letter from Pakistan: The General in His Labyrinth," *New Yorker*, 12 August 2002, 54.

Nuclear weapons play a central role: without them Pakistan would lack the ability to trigger a crisis that could menace India. Incursions like Kargil would be little more than a major nuisance in a nonnuclear world, because India could either safely repel the attack or threaten to respond elsewhere (what is known as "horizontal escalation"). Because carrying out these actions would be safe and relatively cheap, India not only could undertake them if need be, but the threat to do so would be credible enough to make it unlikely that Pakistan would launch the adventure. With nuclear weapons, however, India has to worry about the possibility, even if small, that a confrontation could have devastating consequences.

A third way to bring pressure to bear on India is to slowly bleed it by increasing the costs of occupying Kashmir. This can be done through sponsoring violent opposition in the province itself or through terrorism in the rest of India. This tactic is both linked to and inhibited by the danger of escalation. The hope is that India will have to make concessions out of the fear that these incidents could set off an action–reaction spiral that could lead to nuclear confrontation, but the danger of such an outcome, or of Indian raids against the terrorists' camps in Pakistan, puts limits on what Pakistan can do. Thus as Tellis, Fair, and Medby note, "this strategy requires Islamabad to inflict high enough costs on New Delhi *without* provoking it into unleashing punitive reprisals. Whether Islamabad can 'calibrate' the insurgency so successfully remains an open question."[14] Furthermore, even if such calibration is possible it leaves open the question of why it should be India rather than Pakistan that prefers making concessions to the continuing risk of escalation. Nuclear weapons are a two-edged sword here, as they were in Soviet–American relations. Their existence allows a state to put pressure on its adversary because no one can guarantee that a crisis will remain under control, but this danger also inhibits the state from triggering a crisis or continuing it.

Although the Kargil incursion was not designed to support the armed resistance inside Kashmir, it exacted costs on India in other ways. Perhaps most importantly, it showed that despite the many handicaps Pakistan was laboring under, it was not willing to accept the status quo. Indeed, for this purpose the very likelihood of its failure made the operation efficacious as a demonstration that Pakistan would act in the face of very long odds. Even if India and others did not infer that a country that was willing to be so reckless might continue to escalate in the face of danger, they might conclude that short-run defeats would not solve the underlying problem,

---

[14] Ashley J. Tellis, C. Christine Fair, and Jamison Jo Medby, *Limited Conflicts under the Nuclear Umbrella: Indian and Pakistani Lessons from the Kargil Crisis* (Santa Monica, Calif.: RAND, 2001), 63.

that Pakistan would continue to seek ways of putting pressure on India, and that diplomatic flexibility was in order.

The probable motives and objectives of the Kargil planners, as brought out in chapter 3 by Khan, Lavoy, and Clary, were at least in part a response to India's 1984 military occupation at the Siachen Glacier, which Pakistan had claimed as lying within its territorial juris- diction. Had Pakistan been able to consolidate its position in the Kargil- Dras sector of the Line of Control (LoC), it could have freely shelled Indian Highway 1A, the road leading to the Indian positions in Siachen, and perhaps compelled a withdrawal. Although this would not have changed the fundamental situation in Kashmir, it would have been an important symbolic victory that could have shaken Indian confidence and led India to at least contemplate political concessions. Here again are parallels to the Cuban missile crisis. Just as one of Khrushchev's motivations was his sense of humiliation in seeing American missiles across the Black Sea in Turkey and his concomitant belief that there was no reason why he should not similarly place missiles close to the United States, so Pakistani leaders may have been indignant at what they felt was the Indian violation of the Simla Agreement and thought that it would be a ratification of their inferior position not to respond.

If Pakistan's leaders believed that the incursion would bring great benefits, however, they should have realized that it would have been a great defeat for India. This, of course, was to be desired, but the problem is that the very fact that India would pay a high price for letting the incursion succeed meant that it would feel strong pressures not to permit this outcome. That this was in some ways a zero-sum game meant that there was no clever way by which Pakistan could make a gain without engaging in a major conflict, and one in which it would be at a significant disadvantage due to the basic structural problems discussed earlier. There was no ready escape from the fundamental disproportion between Pakistan's goals and the resources it could deploy to reach them.[15]

Logically there was an inverse relationship between what Pakistan could have expected to gain and the likelihood of success. But if Pakistani leaders were like many others, they may have perceived a positive relation- ship. The work on "motivated biases" in psychology tells us that when people feel great pressures to act in a certain way, they are prone to make

---

[15] It is possible that Pakistani authorities originally planned a smaller incursion with fewer potential gains, and that the operation grew through momentum. See chapter 3 of this book by Khan, Lavoy, and Clary and Cheema's chapter 2, explaining Pakistan's motivations.

themselves believe that their actions can succeed.[16] Thus if Pakistanis were desperate because there was no good way to loosen India's hold on Kashmir, they may have come to the unwarranted conclusion that Kargil would succeed. Although hindsight always makes an outcome seem inevitable, I think it is fair to say that even before the fact most disinterested observers would have doubted that the incursion could have overcome the obstacles described above. But the situation may have looked different to Pakistanis not because they had better or even different information, different theories of international politics, or believed that India was a paper tiger, but rather because a more accurate assessment would have left them with the psychologically intolerable choice between accepting the status quo and taking a dangerous action that was likely to fail. Most people – political and military leaders included – avoid painful value trade-offs like this.[17] The same psychological dynamics help explain Khrushchev's blunder in putting missiles in Cuba: the strong pressures he felt to take this action led him to be excessively optimistic about the prospects for success.[18]

A significant consequence of the crisis similarly parallels the Cuban missile crisis and also does not fit with modern utility maximization theories. Both Sharif and Khrushchev were removed from office in part because of their role in the misadventures. This is significant theoretically because while traditional Realists said that leaders should be prepared to sacrifice their own well-being for that of the nation, more recent theorists argue that the main goal of leaders is to gain and maintain power even at the expense of the broader national interest. Thus it could be argued that the expected costs of losing in Vietnam that drove Johnson to fight were more domestic than foreign. Cuba and Kargil are then puzzles because

---

[16] Irving Janis and Leon Mann, *Decision Making: A Psychological Analysis of Conflict, Choice, and Commitment* (New York: Free Press, 1977); Richard Ned Lebow, *Between Peace and War: The Nature of International Crisis* (Baltimore, Md.: Johns Hopkins University Press, 1981); Jack Snyder, *The Ideology of the Offensive: Military Decision-Making and the Disasters of 1914* (Ithaca: Cornell University Press, 1984); Robert Jervis, Richard Ned Lebow, and Janice Gross Stein, *Psychology and Deterrence* (Baltimore, Md.: Johns Hopkins University Press, 1985).

[17] Robert Jervis, *Perception and Misperception in International Politics* (Princeton University Press, 1976), 128–142; Robert Jervis, "Understanding Beliefs," *Political Psychology* 27 (October 2006), 641–663.

[18] One methodological problem should be noted with this argument. The generalization is built upon the numerous cases in which states act in apparent disregard for the long odds they face, and the psychological explanation for the distorting perceptions fits nicely with the behavior. But actors are not likely to challenge the status quo when they think they will be rudely rebuffed, and because judging the likelihood of success is very difficult, random errors are also likely. Since crises will occur only when a challenge is made, it is possible that we are witnessing, not motivated bias, but rather the outcome of essentially random errors. There may be lots of cases when the value trade-off is made and people judge that the action is too risky to take, in which case we will not have any dramatic event to study.

they resulted in the leader losing power, a danger that was not entirely unforeseeable at the start. Unless they thought that they would have been overthrown in the absence of a dramatic foreign policy victory, they should have behaved more cautiously.

A final irony about Kargil points to an analogy not to Cuba but to the Arab–Israeli conflict. Although the Pakistani demand for a referendum in Kashmir is never likely to bear fruit, it is supported by a UN resolution and most standards of justice and fairness. But since most of the world has no stake in this dispute, Pakistan must draw attention to it and show that the status quo is not only morally unacceptable, but dangerous. In principle, one might imagine some ways to call attention to the issue that would build on, and even increase, world sympathy, such as an effective public relations campaign focusing on India's repressive occupation or the use of nonviolent resistance. Whether such campaigns are feasible is unclear, but Pakistan has chosen military raids and the Kargil incursion. These tactics, while calling the world's attention to the region, shifted the focus from the underlying grievance to Pakistan's unacceptable behavior. The issue then becomes not the status of Kashmir, but Pakistani aggression or support for terrorism. In much the same way, while there is international backing for a Palestinian state, attacking Israeli civilians makes this the issue, and it is one that evokes vehement opposition from the most important actors the Palestinians need to influence – the United States and moderate Israelis.

Surprise

The surprise experienced by India in this case, so well discussed by the Kargil Review Committee and by James Wirtz and Surinder Rana in chapter 8 of this book, is unique in its particulars but familiar in its general outline.[19] The Kargil planners knew that their only chance of success lay in taking India by surprise. By definition, this meant doing something that India did not expect. As was the common practice along the LoC, the Indians did not man the forward outposts during winter, patrolled the valleys but not the heights, and conducted only limited aerial surveillance. This gave Pakistan the opportunity to do what was unexpected, in only the latest in a long series of cases in which a state is able to take advantage of its adversary's belief that some operations are so unlikely that few safeguards against them are needed. Indeed, those heights can only be taken by surprise and stealth, as was the case of India's surprise occupation of Siachen in 1984. The Indians detected some evidence that in retrospect

[19] See, for example, Richard Betts, *Surprise Attack* (Washington, DC: Brookings Institution, 1982).

indicated a major incursion. But, as in all other cases, they filtered this information through the prism of their expectations, thereby maintaining their preexisting views.[20]

India did not expect the incursion not only because it was so difficult to undertake, but also because it seemed to have little point. Like many other cases such as the Cuban missile crisis, Kargil was a double surprise. If India was surprised at the incursion, Pakistan was surprised that it was so readily rebuffed. Thus it fit a familiar pattern of being a tactical success but a strategic failure. Indeed, much of the reason why it was a tactical success was that the defender believed that it would prove to be a failure. States rarely expect their adversaries to behave foolishly.[21] The Pakistani incursion simply did not make sense; it was therefore sensible of India not to expect it. When a high Central Intelligence Agency (CIA) official was taxed with having failed to predict that the Soviets would put missiles into Cuba, he is said to have replied, "I didn't make an error, Khrushchev did." To put it slightly differently, in this case India made an error because Pakistan did.

Nuclear weapons, nuclear wars

Toward the end of the Cold War, an American analyst said to his Soviet counterpart how glad he was that their two countries had been able to avoid a nuclear war. "To the contrary," the Soviet replied, "all the wars during the Cold War were nuclear." He was quite right in that the crises and limited wars of this period were strongly influenced by the existence of nuclear weapons.[22] This was true in the subcontinent as well. "Although none of the Indo-Pak crises involved deployed nuclear weapons, they were *about* nuclear weapons: the threat to use them, the threat to prevent their construction, and the threat of future use."[23] The effects were varied in the Cold War and in the conflict in South Asia, being sometimes inconsistent and interacting with other variables. They emboldened and

---

[20] For the specifics of the Kargil case, see Kargil Review Committee, *From Surprise to Reckoning*, 152–157, 228–229; for the general processes involved, see Jervis, *Perception and Misperception*, 143–202.

[21] An interesting exception is the British obsession that Mussolini might undertake a "mad dog" act in the 1930s.

[22] Whether the details of the nuclear balance mattered is a more debatable question: see, for example, Richard Betts, *Nuclear Blackmail and Nuclear Balance* (Washington, DC: Brookings Institution, 1987); Jervis, *Meaning of the Nuclear Revolution*.

[23] Waheguru Pal Singh Sidhu, "India's Nuclear Use Doctrine," in *Planning the Unthinkable: How New Powers Will Use Nuclear, Biological, and Chemical Weapons*, ed. Peter Lavoy, Scott Sagan, and James Wirtz (Ithaca: Cornell University Press, 2000), 132.

inhibited by turns, in addition to sometimes being the very focus of the dispute, as was true in Cuba.

We will never know how close India and Pakistan came to nuclear war in the spring and summer of 1999 or at any other time, and indeed even the notion of "closeness" to war is vague and difficult. But it is worth pausing to consider how such a war might start. One obvious possibility is through accidents, weaknesses in the command and control systems, and decisions made at various levels of the military, as Scott Sagan has stressed (and Kenneth Waltz has denied).[24] Since I cannot add to what these scholars have said, I will focus on the incentives facing the top leaders.

Because it has conventional superiority, only prevention or preemption would give India a reason to use nuclear weapons first. But India has pledged not to use nuclear weapons first and apparently has not developed the intelligence or military planning that would permit a disarming strike. India also undoubtedly realizes that such a strike – or any nuclear war – would use most of India's stockpile, thus leaving little retaliatory capability against China. So any nuclear war would be likely to result from Pakistan's initiative. But for that country to use nuclear weapons first would be pointless. Even if it were able to wipe out India's nuclear force, India would surely conquer and dismember Pakistan shortly thereafter. As long as Pakistan has no reason to believe that such an all-out Indian attack is imminent, a disarming strike makes no sense.

This does not mean that nuclear war could not occur, however. The most obvious path to it is continued terrorism in Kashmir or, even more, the rest of India, which could lead to a large-scale Indian incursion to destroy the terrorist training camps and/or punish Pakistan. If conventional defense failed, Pakistan might resort to using nuclear weapons against Indian troops either in Pakistan or massed at the border. Such a response would be especially likely if Pakistan feared that India's objectives were unlimited and that the target was the Islamabad regime, not the training camps. India's response, of course, cannot be predicted, but an all-out nuclear war could not be excluded.

This scenario implicitly invokes Schelling's "threat that leaves something to chance," which I believe was very important during the Cold War.[25] In any crisis, unexpected sequences occur for a variety of reasons. Almost by definition, the path to war cannot be fully delineated ahead of time. But there are innumerable ways in which war can result even though

---

[24] Scott Sagan and Kenneth Waltz, *The Spread of Nuclear Weapons: A Debate Renewed*, 2nd edn (New York: Norton, 2002).

[25] Thomas Schelling, *The Strategy of Conflict* (Cambridge, Mass.: Harvard University Press, 1960), chapter 8; Jervis, *Meaning of the Nuclear Revolution*, chapters 1, 3, and 5.

neither side wants it. Interestingly enough, at the Vienna Summit meeting Khrushchev ridiculed Kennedy when he talked about the danger of inadvertent war, but once the Cuban missile crisis erupted his letters to Kennedy explained the dangers quite eloquently: "we and you ought not now to pull on the ends of the rope in which we have tied the knot of war, because the more the two of us pull, the tighter that knot will be tied. And a moment may come when that knot will be tied so tight that even he who tied it will not have the strength to untie it, and then it will be necessary to cut that knot, and what that would mean is not for me to explain to you, because you yourself understand perfectly well of what terrible forces our countries dispose."[26] I doubt whether the fact that the leaders on the subcontinent know that this and other crises remained in control gives them great confidence that they would have nothing to worry about.[27]

For this and other reasons, it is impossible to determine with certainty the influence of nuclear weapons on the occurrence and course of confrontations, although I do not think it is an accident that Soviet–American crises essentially ceased after the Soviets gained secure second-strike capability.[28] To project an image of high resolve and preserve their bargaining power for future confrontations, states have an interest in minimizing the extent to which others believe that they were influenced by their adversary's threats, especially threats to use nuclear weapons. Indeed, the dangerous Brasstacks exercise of 1987 may have been motivated at least in part by the Indian desire to disabuse Pakistani leaders of the notion that India would be cowed by nuclear weapons.[29] India has tried to judge as well as influence how nuclear weapons might affect Pakistani behavior, and the Kargil Review Committee revealed that "assessments made by the JIC [Joint Intelligence Committee] since 1991 have emphasized how Pakistan might use its nuclear capability to advance its

---

[26] US Department of State, *Foreign Relations of the United States, 1961–1963*, vol. V, *Soviet Union* (Washington, DC: Government Printing Office, 1998), 177–178, 183–184; *Foreign Relations of the United States, 1961–1963*, vol. VI, *Kennedy–Khrushchev Exchanges* (Washington, DC: Government Printing Office, 1996), 177.

[27] A complicating factor is that because nuclear crises represent "competition in risk taking," leaders often have an interest in downplaying their fear, thus making it hard for later analysts to judge their level of concern. A particularly acute example of this occurred in June 2002, when US Secretary of Defense Donald Rumsfeld provided Indian and Pakistani leaders with detailed US estimates of the likely consequences of an Indo-Pak nuclear war, which would result in 9 to 12 million deaths. According to reports from Rumsfeld's assistants, neither the Indian nor the Pakistani leadership displayed much interest in these calculations. See CNN, "US Warns of Doomsday Scenario," 1 June 2002, http://edition.cnn.com/2002/WORLD/asiapcf/south/05/31/kashmir.attack.toll/index.html.

[28] Jervis, *Meaning of the Nuclear Revolution*, 35–42.

[29] Sidhu, "India's Nuclear Use Doctrine," 137.

objectives in Kashmir."[30] At Kargil, nuclear weapons were figuratively if not literally in the front lines, with each side issuing something like half-a-dozen public nuclear threats.[31]

But given the strong incentives against using them, what could nuclear weapons do? Most obviously, the immense destruction of nuclear war not only means that the risk of use is very low, but that even a slight risk can exert significant influence. The danger can also bring in third parties, especially the United States. These states care little about how the conflict is settled, but care a great deal that it is settled without the use of nuclear weapons. They might worry that a nuclear war could spread, most obviously by involving China. They also could be concerned about the precedent and believe that a war between these two countries would lead other countries to develop nuclear weapons or fight a nuclear war. But one could just as easily make the opposite argument that a nuclear war on the subcontinent would be a terrible negative example and make the rest of the world less rather than more violent. So I think the main reason for concern is altruism – the desire to save the lives of millions of innocent civilians. While some American lives and property would be lost in the war, I doubt if narrow national self-interest can account for the level of American concern.

External involvement, especially by the United States, is not likely to be neutral in its effects. A major Pakistani goal was to use any crisis to internationalize the Kashmir dispute, thereby gaining more weight for the role of justice and compensating for Pakistan's material weakness. Third parties were of course involved in previous wars and crises, but it is questionable whether Clinton would have played as active a role as he did if nuclear weapons were not in the picture. After Pakistan's and India's nuclear tests, Indian intelligence inferred that "Pakistani expectations have been that with the heightened non-proliferation concerns, the international community, particularly the [permanent members of the Security Council] would have a vested interest in involving itself with the resolution of the single 'core issue' of Jammu and Kashmir and adopt a much more interventionist role than in the past."[32]

This does not mean that third parties will necessarily support Pakistan, and none did at Kargil, partly because that country was so clearly the aggressor.[33] But even though Sharif largely used his 4 July trip to

---

[30] *From Surprise to Reckoning*, 197, which also provides an interesting set of examples.
[31] See chapter 6 of this book by Timothy Hoyt.
[32] Quoted in Kargil Review Committee, *From Surprise to Reckoning*, 198.
[33] This was one of Pakistan's many errors: Tellis, Fair, and Medby report that "Pakistani informants and public opinion shapers expressed varying degrees of surprise at the

Washington to provide some cover for his inevitable retreat, the very fact of American involvement, even more than Clinton's statement that the United States would remain concerned with the issue, may have had the perhaps unintended consequence of positioning the United States more prominently for a role in future negotiations.[34] Indeed, most observers agree that the hope for such an outcome probably was a prime motive for the incursion.

Nuclear weapons have had an even greater effect on the bilateral relations between India and Pakistan, although it is difficult to determine exactly what the impact is. What is perhaps most striking from a broad perspective, however, is how slow both sides were to develop these weapons, something we tend to lose sight of because this is an undramatic "nonevent." Whether each was deterred by the fear that going nuclear would lead the adversary to do likewise and the belief that it was better off if neither of them had such weapons than if both did is not clear.[35] Having a large conventional advantage, it is hard to see how India would gain a great deal even from a nuclear monopoly on the subcontinent. Concern for status and self-image and the desire to balance against China were understandable, but there is little plausibility to Home Minister Advani's claim that "India's decisive step to become a nuclear weapons state has brought about a qualitative new stage in Indo-Pak relations, especially in finding a lasting solution to the Kashmir problem."[36]

Pakistan's motives were both offensive and defensive in ways that are intertwined beyond the possibility of separation. It does not want to be forced to accept India's dominance in general or the status quo along the LoC in particular. A nuclear weapons program, and, even more, one that was overt, presumably was seen as a deterrent against India's nuclear weapons and its superior conventional military capability. But, as noted, India does not need nuclear weapons to threaten or coerce Pakistan, so neutralizing them would not be a valuable achievement. The hope and perhaps expectation probably were a good deal more that nuclear weapons were a "great equalizer" that nullified the other side's conventional

international response to Kargil and the nearly unanimous conviction that Pakistan was culpable" (*Limited Conflicts under the Nuclear Umbrella*, 8). Ironically, the necessity for secrecy made it impossible for Pakistan to either cultivate world opinion ahead of time or gauge what it would likely be when the crisis broke out, as Hasan-Askari Rizvi points out in chapter 13 of this book. Again, there is some parallel to Khrushchev's dilemma in Cuba.

[34] See Hoyt, chapter 6. Rodney Jones and Joseph McMillan develop this point more fully in chapter 14.

[35] The most complete analysis of India's program is George Perkovich, *India's Nuclear Bomb: The Impact on Global Proliferation*, 2nd edn (Berkeley: University of California Press, 2001).

[36] Rajesh Basrur provides a more careful assessment of how India gained from its nuclear weapons status in chapter 12 of this book.

advantage. This after all was much of the rationale for American nuclear weapons, which were seen as providing "extended deterrence" against a Soviet attack on close allies. But in the subcontinent as in Soviet–American relations, the unanswerable question is exactly what nuclear weapons can deter. Do they simply neutralize each other or cast a long shadow over all conflicts between the parties? In 1983 Robert McNamara famously argued that the "sole purpose [of strategic nuclear weapons], at present, is to deter the other side's first use of its strategic force."[37] In this view, Pakistan's weapons would deter little more than Indian first use. This represents an application of what Glenn Snyder called the "stability–instability paradox."[38] Strategic stability permits if not creates instability by making lower levels of violence relatively safe because escalation up the nuclear ladder is too dangerous.

The Kargil war is a demonstration of this paradox because it was the second case of a direct clash between nuclear-armed states (the first being the Sino-Soviet border clashes of 1969). This did not prove that escalation was impossible, but at least showed that it was not inevitable, and that, concomitantly, nuclear weapons did not prevent all forms of war between parties. Indian defence minister George Fernandes recognized this in speeches delivered in January 2000 when he confirmed that India's nuclear weapons were for "retaliation only" and that therefore "war remains a possibility ... below the nuclear threshold" and that India therefore needed to maintain large conventional forces.[39] Five years earlier, Indian intelligence had argued that "in Pakistan's perception a nuclear capability would enable them to deter India from escalating the [low-intensity conflict] in Kashmir to a full scale war [and would allow

[37] Robert McNamara, "The Military Role of Nuclear Weapons," *Foreign Affairs* 62 (Fall 1983), 68. Whether he believed this when he was Secretary of Defense is not entirely clear. For his explanation of how he reached this conclusion, see his interview in Michael Charlton, *From Deterrence to Defense* (Cambridge, Mass.: Harvard University Press, 1987), 18.

[38] Glenn Snyder, "The Balance of Power and the Balance of Terror," in *The Balance of Power*, ed. Paul Seabury (San Francisco: Chandler, 1964), 184–201; also see Jervis, *Meaning of the Nuclear Revolution*, 19–23; for an application to the subcontinent, see Peter Lavoy, "South Asia's Nuclear Revolution: Has It Occurred Yet?" in *The Nuclear Non-Proliferation Regime: Prospects for the 21st Century*, ed. Raju G. C. Thomas (New York: St. Martin's Press, 1998), 260–271. I am assuming that each side has sufficient nuclear weapons so that an all-out war would be mutually disastrous and worse than whatever concessions would have been required to have avoided it. Of course the situation is not symmetric because India is a very large country and Pakistan's force is relatively small. Nevertheless, we saw in the Cuban missile crisis that the possibility of losing even one or two American cities was a very potent deterrent and Indian leaders, unlike Mao Tse-Tung, have never denied that a nuclear war would do their country irreparable damage.

[39] Quoted in Sidhu, "India's Nuclear Use Doctrine," 128.

Pakistan to] continue its support to insurgency knowing India would be constrained from retaliating."[40]

Even before Kargil, everyone seems to have agreed that nuclear weapons would not prevent all violence. The stability–instability paradox then clearly was present. But how far did it extend? Did it prevent all forms of force short of the first use of nuclear weapons? Much of American defense policy revolved around this question, with Eisenhower and Khrushchev justifying large cuts in conventional forces on the grounds that a large-scale war in Europe would inevitably involve the use of nuclear weapons, and their opponents vigorously disagreeing and calling for robust conventional capabilities and flexible nuclear options. Agreeing with Eisenhower and Khrushchev, Musharraf said that nuclear weapons ruled out a major conventional war.[41] But this still leaves open how large is large. If we take the stability–instability paradox to its logical conclusion, only conventional violence that threatens the existence of the state should be ruled out by nuclear weapons.

This view was central to much American nuclear strategy in the post-Eisenhower era, but I believe it is deeply flawed because it neglects threats that leave something to chance. Leaders of both countries of the subcontinent seem to have understood this and concluded that nuclear weapons would indeed cast a significant shadow over any clash that occurred even if – or rather because – there was no way to be sure what levels and kinds of force would lead to uncontrolled escalation. This explains Musharraf's statement referred to in the previous paragraph. At first glance it is puzzling that he would argue that nuclear weapons made a large conventional war impossible because this removes a weapon from Pakistan's arsenal. It was a weapon that could hardly be used because of India's conventional superiority, however, and what the Pakistani leader was doing was explaining that thanks to nuclear weapons India would be unable to launch a massive conventional response to lower levels of Pakistani violence.

Pakistan might have expected a lot from its nuclear weapons capabilities. Not only countering what slight advantages India might have gained by the sole possession of them and inhibiting India from launching a large and unprovoked conventional attack, but also providing a shield behind which Pakistan could engage in provocations serious enough to change Indian policy in Kashmir. Pakistan then needed to deter India from moving even part way up the escalation ladder to defend its interests. This was a much more demanding requirement than the United States faced in its project of extended deterrence. In that case, the danger of

---

[40] Quoted in Kargil Review Committee, *From Surprise to Reckoning*, 198; also see 242.
[41] *Ibid.* 242.

escalation was seen as preventing the USSR from using its conventional superiority *offensively*. But Pakistan needed to stop India from responding *defensively* to its own attempts to change the status quo. This meant that it had to stretch the stability–instability paradox in an unprecedented way: the situation had to be stable enough to permit Pakistan to stage a menacing incursion, but not so stable as to permit India to make an effective response.

The expectation that this was possible is part of the explanation for Pakistan's decision to stage the Kargil incursion and arguably as confirmed by India's restraint during the crisis. The Kargil Review Committee report included that without this "it is inconceivable that it could sustain its war against India, inflicting thousands of casualties, without being unduly concerned about India's 'conventional superiority.'"[42] But it remains unclear exactly what Indian actions Pakistan thought its nuclear forces could deter, and, in the event, what they did deter. It is probable that the Pakistanis believed that India would not dare respond with a major invasion across the international border, or even across the LoC. But it is hard to see how they could have believed that India would be deterred from using its conventional superiority to retake the heights, which is what happened. Pakistan's deterrent position was particularly weak because in order to assuage world opinion and perhaps reduce the Indian reaction, it claimed that the soldiers were insurgents, not members of the Pakistani armed forces, thus reducing any deterrent umbrella that Pakistan might have been able to extend over them.

There are lots of distinctions in what could be expected from nuclear weapons. For example, did the Pakistanis think that India would not escalate by using its air power? Did they expect India to refrain from menacing conventional mobilizations? But the basic problem Pakistan faced was that India could respond effectively without particularly dangerous escalation. Even someone like myself who thinks that the possibility that events will get out of control exerts a powerful inhibiting effect would not expect this fear to discourage India from physically regaining the territory.

This does not mean that Pakistan's nuclear posture was entirely inefficacious. India suffered significant casualties in the assaults, being forced to fight on unfavorable terrain. It almost surely would have been cheaper and perhaps quicker for India to force Pakistan to withdraw by engaging in horizontal escalation and threatening or using force elsewhere along the LoC. There is then reason to believe that the fears of nuclear war did moderate Indian behavior. Of course there were other factors that also

[42] *Ibid.* 241.

could have been involved: world (and especially American) opinion, the desire not to trigger closer ties between Pakistan and China, and the fear of escalation that would have been present even without nuclear weapons. It would be useful to systematically compare India's behavior at Kargil with what it did in previous confrontations, but my suspicion is that the results would be ambiguous due to the difficulties in holding all factors other than nuclear weapons constant, the fact that in some of the pre-Kargil clashes India had to fear Pakistani nuclear weapons even though that country had not tested them, and the difficulties in comparing military operations across crises. But while the pre-nuclear wars had remained limited, it does seem as though India was particularly restrained in this case, even though it used military aircraft in combat for the first time since the 1971 war.

Conclusion

One difficulty with our standard social science approach of comparing events and expecting the past patterns to hold in the future is that, unlike historians, we tend to neglect the way things change through time. As the chapters on "lessons learned" indicate, the future is not likely to be the same as the past because the actors do not remain static. How each side – and third actors – understands the change that each has undergone is important but quite elusive. It would be difficult but interesting to try to determine how Kargil influenced the crisis in 2002, and to see if behavior was more or less dangerous because of it.

At Kargil and subsequently, the American role is also important. Both India and Pakistan of course want American support, but the latter faces a particular dilemma. On the one hand, the United States is likely to become involved only if it thinks it can solve the underlying conflict (and this is unlikely) or if the situation becomes dangerous, as it did at Kargil. But unless India behaves particularly foolishly and starts a crisis, the only way that the level of danger can rise significantly is for Pakistan to provoke it, which will lead the United States to side with India, as it did at Kargil.

The United States faces a situation of dual or pivotal deterrence, which was rare during the Cold War but more frequent previously and subsequently. That is, the United States seeks to deter both sides from engaging in aggressive or provocative behavior.[43] The problem is that the more the

---

[43] For a general discussion, see Jervis, "What Do We Want to Deter and How Do We Deter it?" in *Turning Point: The Gulf War and US Military Strategy*, ed. L. Benjamin Ederington and Michael Mazaar (Boulder, Colo.: Westview, 1994), 122–124; Timothy Crawford, *Pivotal Deterrence: Third-Party Statecraft and the Pursuit of Peace* (Ithaca: Cornell University Press, 2003).

United States overtly deters one side, the more it is likely to inadvertently embolden the other. If India feels that it has whole-hearted American support, then it is free to be completely unyielding with Pakistan and repressive in Kashmir; if Pakistan believes that the United States will protect it against a major Indian attack, then it will have a shield behind which it can launch small raids. In principle, the United States can make its threats and promises conditional by telling each side that it will support it if and only if that country is reasonable. But reasonableness is notoriously difficult to judge, and different countries are likely to judge it quite differently.

Any effective policy requires the United States not only to understand each of the countries, but also to understand how each understands the other. The former exercise is difficult enough; the latter is rarely tried. The United States routinely produces National Intelligence Estimates (NIEs) on most countries in the world. But it also needs NIEs that try to replicate India's NIE of Pakistan and vice versa. Although states often realize that they need to see the world through their adversary's eyes, it remains hard for them to grasp that others live in very different perceptual worlds.[44] Here the requirement of seeing how each of two other parties sees each other is even more obscure, and it remains to be seen whether the United States is up to the challenge.

---

[44] We often think that such efforts are in the service of developing a more cooperative relationship, but they also can be part of an effort to take advantage of and defeat the other, as Hitler did for a number of years. In *Strange Victory* (New York: Hill and Wang, 2000), Ernest May showed that the Germans' victory in May 1940 was partly due to their having understood the French not only better than the French understood the Germans, but also better than the French understood themselves.

Index

relations with India, 129, 131, 132, 141,
142–143, 236, 354–359
relations with Pakistan, 129, 134, 135,
143, 204, 253–256, 354–359
strategic behavior, 144
summit meeting at Blair House,
130–131
transparency between the United States
and India, 365, 366
Uttar Pradesh, 265, 268–269

Vajpayee, Atal Behari, 18, 157,
263–264, 276
initiation of the Lahore process, 26, 86,
133, 213, 234, 300, 321

and Nawaz Sharif, 193, 194
restraint in not crossing the LoC, 12

Waltz, Kenneth, 31, 176
Washington Declaration, 22, 203, 296, 300
Wirsing, Robert, 44, 195, 301
Wohlstetter, Roberta, 214

Yadav, Yogendra, 263

Zia ul-Haq, Mohammed, 55, 75,
77, 151
Zinni, Anthony, 134, 196–197, 201, 365,
368–369, 370
Zins, Max-Jean, 262